ASP.NET 2 and Tips

ASP.NET 2.0 MVP Hacks and Tips

David Yack, Joe Mayo, Scott Hanselman, Fredrik Normén, Dan Wahlin,
J. Ambrose Little, Jonathan D. Goodyear

Wiley Publishing, Inc.

ASP.NET 2.0 MVP Hacks and Tips

Published by
Wiley Publishing, Inc.
10475 Crosspoint Boulevard
Indianapolis, IN 46256
www.wiley.com

Copyright © 2006 by Wiley Publishing, Inc., Indianapolis, Indiana

Published simultaneously in Canada

ISBN-13: 978-0-7645-9766-4
ISBN-10: 0-7645-9766-3

Manufactured in the United States of America

10 9 8 7 6 5 4 3 2 1

1MA/RR/QV/QW/IN

About the Authors

David Yack is the president of Colorado Technology Consultants, a Microsoft Gold Certified Partner based in Colorado. He is a Microsoft Regional Director and a Microsoft MVP for ASP.NET. As a senior hands-on technology and business consultant with over 18 years of industry experience, David enjoys developing applications for both the Windows and Unix platforms, specializing in large system architecture and design. David embraced .NET during the final beta days of version 1.0 and has been helping clients migrate and build new applications on the technology, as well as helping to mentor and train their staffs. David is a frequent speaker at user group and industry events and is on the author teams of two NET 2.0–related books. David also founded and is on the leadership team for the South Colorado .NET User Group. He lives in Colorado Springs with his wife and two children. You can always track David down via his blog at http:/blog.davidyack.com where he writes about his .NET adventures.

Joe Mayo runs his own company, Mayo Software, and is an author, consultant, and instructor specializing in .NET technologies. He operates the C# Station website (www.csharp-station.com) and is a Microsoft Most Valuable Professional (MVP). Joe's previous books include *C# Unleashed* (Sams) and *C# Builder Kick Start* (Sams). For more information about Joe, please visit mayosoftware.com.

Scott Hanselman is currently the chief architect at the Corillian Corporation (NASDAQ: CORI), an eFinance enabler. He has over 13 years experience developing software in C, C++, VB, COM, and certainly in VB.NET and C#. Scott is proud to be both a Microsoft RD as well as an MVP for both ASP.NET and Solutions Architecture. Scott has spoken at dozens of conferences worldwide, including three TechEds and the North African DevCon. He is a primary contributor to "newtelligence DasBlog Community Edition 1.8," the most popular open-source ASP.NET blogging software hosted on SourceForge. This is the fourth book Scott has worked on for Wrox. His thoughts on the Zen of .NET, programming, and Web Services can be found on his blog at www.computerzen.com. He welcomes e-mail at mailto:scott@hanselman.com.

Fredrik Normén is a consultant who works for Callista Knowledgebase AB. He works mostly as a mentor, solution developer, architect, and instructor. He has worked with the .NET framework since the first bit of .NET 1.0 was released in 2000. He has over 10 years of experience building web applications, started with Perl and moving on to ASP and ASP.NET. You can find Fredrik's blog at http://fredrik.nsquared2.com.

Dan Wahlin (Microsoft MVP for ASP.NET and XML Web Services) is the president of Wahlin Consulting LLC, which provides enterprise consulting and training services as well as ASP.NET server controls. He also founded the XML for ASP.NET Developers website (www.XMLforASP.net), which focuses on using XML, ADO.NET and Web Services in Microsoft's .NET platform. Dan is a regular speaker at different .NET conferences and is a member of the INETA Speaker's Bureau, which enables him to interact with .NET user groups around the United States. He has also authored/co-authored five books on various .NET technologies and writes for several technical magazines.

J. Ambrose Little is an ASP Insider and Microsoft MVP who works as a senior software engineer for a Tampa-based commercial software company and as the content director for ASPAlliance.com. He's an author of numerous articles, co-author of *Professional ADO.NET 2* and *ASP.NET 2.0 MVP Hacks and Tips*, and has spoken at various .NET user groups and events in Florida.

Jonathan D. Goodyear is the president of ASPSOFT, Inc, a software consulting company based out of Orlando, Florida. He is a contributing editor for both *Visual Studio Magazine* and *asp.netPRO Magazine,* and frequently speaks at major technology conferences such as VSLive and ASP.NET Connections. Jonathan was a featured speaker at the Visual Studio 2005 Launch Event in Orlando, Florida, and speaks at numerous .NET user groups through the International .NET Association (INETA). He wrote one of the first books about .NET development, *Debugging ASP.NET* (New Riders Publishing), and appeared in a video, *Visual Studio .NET: An Introduction,* by WatchIT.com. He is the founder and editor of the online magazine *angryCoder.com,* and is a Microsoft Most Valuable Professional (MVP) for ASP.NET, an ASP Insider, and the Microsoft regional director (RD) for Florida.

Credits

Acquisitions Editor
Jim Minatel

Development Editor
Sydney Jones

Technical Editors
Andrew Watt
Cody Reichenau
Phred Menyhert
Alexei Gorkov

Production Editor
William A. Barton

Copy Editor
Luann Rouff

Editorial Manager
Mary Beth Wakefield

Vice President & Executive Group Publisher
Richard Swadley

Vice President and Publisher
Joseph B. Wikert

Project Coordinator
Michael Kruzil

Graphics and Production Specialists
Lauren Goddard
Joyce Haughey
Barbara Moore
Alicia B. South
Ron Terry

Quality Control Technician
Brian Walls

Media Development Specialists
Angela Denny
Kit Malone
Travis Silvers

Proofreading and Indexing
Techbooks

To my wonderful wife, Julie, who not only supported me in doing this but jumped in when times got busy and I needed help keeping things moving. To my two great kids, Drew and Jacqueline, who I'm sure had no idea how much time they where giving up when they said I could do this, but just kept on supporting me one hug at a time. — David Yack

To Barbara and Richard Bickerstaff — Joe Mayo

Non nobis Domine non nobis sed nomini Tuo da gloriam. — J. Ambrose Little

For Joy, CJ, Rylee, Ginger and Cherie, because they put up with me every day. For my mother and father, because they believed in me. — Jonathan D. Goodyear

Contents

Contents

Contents

Contents

Acknowledgments

It's always interesting to look back in time at the history of how an idea came to life. In this case, we go back to the end of 2004 as Jim Minatel approached me with the concept of a MVP Hack book. I was speaking in Las Vegas at DevConnections, and between sessions we sat and started to hash out the details of the book. One by one authors joined the team and things started to come together. During 2005 and early 2006, the writing was completed. All during this period, the team managed to use the betas and adapt to the minor changes each brought along. A few topics never made it to print simply because they turned out to be fixed in the released version of the product! Of all the people I worked with at Wrox, Jim's professionalism and support are unparalleled.

Earlier, when I did work on *Wrox Professional ADO.NET* with Wallace McClure, who was the lead author on that title, I got to watch and learn from a distance. Thanks, Wally, for all the work you did on that title (I had no idea!), and for answering all my questions and providing feedback as I wondered my way through this one.

Without my wife, Julie, and Jim Minatel, I think sanity would not have been possible. With their support, I can avoid getting gray hair until my kids fully become teenagers! Their continued encouragement to keep focused on the big picture enabled this book to get to print. For all the MVPs involved in this book, balancing the demands during the launch of .NET 2.0 and trying to complete this book took a lot of focus from everyone. To that end I thank the author team for this project, which was nothing short of fun to work with.

I know that each of the authors relied on the help from the Microsoft product team to help with answers to the difficult questions. From my midnight e-mails from Scott Guthrie, who heads the ASP.NET/IIS team to answers from other members, such as Bradley Bartz, Omar Khan, Nikhil Kothari, and Bradley Millington, a big thanks! Each MVP has a Microsoft MVP lead assigned; mine is Ben Miller. For the last few years Ben has been my answer man when I didn't know to whom to turn to at Microsoft. Even when Ben didn't have all the answers, he had all the connections. Thanks, Ben, for all your support in getting us to the right people inside Microsoft.

Countless people behind the scenes influenced this book in one way or another. Some even endured the torture of early review of chapters as they were still under development. I'd like to thank Julie Yack, Chris Sutton, Rob Hope, and David Milner for their constructive feedback early on.

The seven MVP authors of this book are part of the larger group of MVPs who all work together to support the ecosystem of the Microsoft .NET community. When the MVP program started, contributions were limited to just online activities such as newsgroup postings. Today, MVPs participate in a broad set of community activities that are both online and offline. Often their contribution also involves helping one another out.

Here's a list of some of the MVPs who in some way had an influence on this book, including links to their blogs. Each offers his unique insight into the .NET world. For their support, we say thanks!

Acknowledgments

Paul Wilson — http://weblogs.asp.net/pwilson/

Wallace McClure ("Wally") — http://weblogs.asp.net/wallym/

Christian Wenz — www.hauser-wenz.de/s9y/

Mitch Denny — http://notgartner.com/

Paul Glavich — http://weblogs.asp.net/pglavich

—*David Yack*

Thanks to all the people at Wiley/Wrox who made this book possible. I particularly appreciated the attention to detail, patience, and grace of Sydney Jones, our development editor. She is well organized, persistent, and offered good advice. Thanks to Andrew Watt, technical editor, for his insight and perspective, which helped me see things I hadn't considered. I'd also like to thank Jim Minatel for seeing the value of this book, and providing support and leadership.

Thanks to the other authors of this book for participating. I've admired all their work and am thrilled to have the opportunity to co-author with them. Most of all, I would like to let David Yack know how much I appreciate his role in the book. He is an amazing person who shepherded this idea from the beginning and put together a concept I truly believe in. Dave gave me a lot of ideas for hacks. In one case, parameterizing the SQL IN expression, he actually gave me the code. Thanks a bunch, Dave, for inviting me to be a part of this book and for all the time and care you put into it. —*Joe Mayo*

I want to thank my wife, Ntombenhle ("Mo"), for her infinite patience and understanding as I pecked away on the computer into the wee hours when I should have been hanging with her. Much love to my new son, Zenzo, who will one day be old enough to read this. Thanks to Scott Guthrie and the ASP.NET 2.0 team for making a rocking sweet development platform. I thank all the folks at Corillian, including my CTO, Chris Brooks, for his constant mentoring, and especially Patrick Cauldwell, for his friendship and technical wisdom over the years. Thanks to Jim and everyone at Wiley/Wrox for all their hard work, and to the folks who read my blog and allow me to bounce code and thoughts off them. Finally, I want to thank David Yack for leading the charge. —*Scott Hanselman*

Thanks to my wife, Christiane, for her loving support and to my whole family for their patience and understanding. —*J. Ambrose Little*

Introduction

Whether you picked up this book from the bookstore, ordered it from an online site, or just got lucky and got a free copy, you had some notion of what you expected to be inside of it from the moment you first laid eyes on it. We discussed the concept with the publisher and others and it was interesting to hear the various perceptions that people had. The actual intent of this book is not to teach you how to "hack" ASP.NET applications from a security perspective, nor is it a guide about how to hack together a poorly written application. Its intent is to give you insight into techniques that you can use to build and deliver real-life applications using ASP.NET.

Now that we have clarified the book's simple purpose, we should probably explain more about what it is and why it should be one of the few books you buy and recommend to everyone you know. Each of the authors of this book is a seasoned professional and is experienced with the .NET platform. All of us are Microsoft MVPs (Most Valuable Professionals) and have answered thousands of ASP.NET developer questions in various online and offline communities. In this book we share our insights into solutions for many questions we answer all the time. You can benefit from the cumulative experience we have gained in building real-life applications. Additionally, with the release of ASP.NET 2.0, we discuss a whole set of new issues in print for the first time.

This is not an introductory book on ASP.NET, as you can find several on the market already that provide an excellent overview and introduction to ASP.NET application development. Further, this is not intended to be a reference guide that explains every feature and option in ASP.NET. Again, between the numerous books that focus on providing a reference source and the ever-improving MSDN documentation, the sources of rich reference information are numerous.

What Is a Hack?

We are using the term *hacks* to refer to little-known solutions, undocumented features, and tips and tricks. Some people call them *hacks*; others call them *creative solutions*. You might have your own name for them, but they are all basically the same thing. Every application of any significance pushes the capabilities of ASP.NET and uses some form of a hack as part of the overall solution.

Some of the past hacks that you might recognize are page templates, multiple forms, URL rewriting, and SQL cache dependencies. These popular hacks have found their way into countless production applications. For each of these there are hundreds of other hacks that simply did not become as widely accepted, and therefore the community (meaning ASP.NET developers) suffered from the lack of opportunity. This book exposes several little-known, but useful hacks that you, as developers, can employ in production environments.

Why Use a Hack?

First of all, we should address the notion that all applications should be perfect, or, for that matter, that they should be well architected and implement every aspect of the chosen methodology and philosophy during development. In doing so, they must also come in under budget, and, of course, on time. Then, once in production, the application should be maintenance free. Further, you will hear the drum beating that you should never use undocumented capabilities, and should avoid tips, tricks, and techniques that are not mainstream. Not all of us live in such a fairytale world; the reality is that we are called upon to deliver tangible business value by building robust ASP.NET applications.

In a perfect world, the ASP.NET Framework would fulfill the needs of all applications, and development would be a code-generation activity with no exceptions. However, MVPs are constantly dealing with real-life application issues that arise within the community, and they try to deliver solutions with ASP.NET

We firmly believe that no such perfection exists, and no application in existence is "perfect." In addition, you could almost be assured that at least one of the items in this book is utilized in most major ASP.NET applications in existence.

Having unlimited time to wait for a feature to be supported in the base product or spending unlimited time researching and trying various approaches to conquer a problem is not always feasible. Finding creative solutions to challenges while considering the pros, cons, and potential pitfalls leads to the delivery of real applications in a timely fashion.

Hacks Ultimately Improve the Product

"They've got a bad name, but hacks are an important part of creating the next wave of developer tools."
—*Jonathan Goodyear*, Microsoft MVP, *asp.netPRO,* November 2003

The real measure of an application's success is the business value it provides and its ability to leverage technology to reach a sustained competitive advantage.

Chapter 1, "Hacks Revisited," discusses some of the past hacks that are now included in ASP.NET 2.0. This chapter will walk you through many of the improvements in ASP.NET 2.0 that used to be hacks but are now part of the base product. This is an important chapter to read through, and it will act as an excellent introduction to many of the new features of ASP.NET 2.0 if you are just starting out.

As a hack evolves and is ultimately implemented in the product, it is important to learn and leverage the built-in approach where possible.

If you are saying ASP.NET 2 sounds great but I'm stuck using ASP.NET 1.x, this book can still help you. First of all, many of the discussions in the book will apply either as is or with slight modifications to ASP.NET 1.x applications. Additionally, Chapter 1 is an excellent place to begin looking for 1.x solutions and planning for your move to 2.x.

Somewhere around beta 2 of a product's release, most of the product feedback suggestions that are submitted end up being marked as "Future." The reason for this is simple: If they kept allowing additions to the product it would never ship.

Clearly, as ASP and .NET continue to mature, you will see fewer major hack inventions, but the creative juices of the community will continue offering innovative ways to get things done and deliver your application faster.

Hacks Help You Learn

Even if you don't find one of the hacks applicable to your particular problem, the insight into how it works can be invaluable. The in-depth discussions of the solutions we present can be a great way to learn more about the inner workings of ASP.NET. For example, Microsoft MVP Paul Wilson, who has published techniques to allow multiple forms on a page in ASP.NET 1.x, explained a lot about the life of a page request. This provided great insight that was not only applicable to his hack but could also be used to gain greater understanding of the page life cycle. This knowledge can ultimately help you when you apply it to specific problems in your application.

How to Use This Book

There is no one specific way that you should use this book. While this book is not intended to be an introduction to ASP.NET, it would be a great help to you as you learn ASP.NET. It is intended to be an invaluable project survival guide to help you as you build your ASP.NET applications. We believe every team should have one as part of their team library.

Making a Hack Work for You

This book and the hacks inside are intended to give you ideas and provoke deep thoughts about how you can solve real application problems. In no way is this intended to be prescriptive advice, because everyone's application is different. One of the most important things you need to do as you use the book is determine how to adapt an item to your application and business environment. Not all solutions will be a good fit for all applications.

For example, while looking at a code snippet, you may suddenly realize what a great idea it would be to make one for something you do all the time or that is specific to your application.

Who This Book Is For

MVP hacks are not for MVPs — quite the opposite. The hacks here are for developers that want to learn these tips and tricks to not only build a better application, but to build their own professional bag of tricks as well.

What This Book Covers

- ❑ **Chapter 1** looks back at hacks in prior versions of ASP.NET. It describes how they influenced today's technology and improved the technology and tools developers use today. Some hacks are good enough to stand the test of time, which you'll see via an ASP.NET v1.1 URL rewriting hack. This is a great place to read about something you might be using and how it is now provided as part of the ASP.NET Framework. For example, Template Pages are now in the product as Master Pages.

- ❑ **Chapter 2** will get you started. Organization, planning, and getting your projects off on a solid foundation are vital and are covered here in detail. This chapter contains many resources, most of which are best utilized when starting a new project.

- ❑ **Chapter 3** covers providers. You will be able to extend the built-in providers as well as build your own. You will also find hints for using providers, even if you are stuck in ASP .NET 1.1!

❑ **Chapter 4** presents the smart client (yes, smart(er) client). From client callbacks to AJAX with a dose of ATLAS, you will see how smart client really can apply to ASP .NET 2.0.

❑ **Chapter 5** describes some new and powerful ways to make debugging your applications easier. It demonstrates techniques for viewing the contents of complex objects, ways to reduce the clutter of the debug window, as well as methods to make your business objects self-validating.

❑ **Chapter 6** explains how you create hacks via custom controls. While creating an RSS control, you'll learn how to solve some difficult problems with a few control hacks. You'll also learn how to implement some of the new ASP.NET 2.0 control features, such as action lists.

❑ **Chapter 7** covers dynamic row expansion, updating all rows, and the pager template for the GridView control. This chapter will give you the knowledge to create and define your own templates for GridView.

❑ **Chapter 8** explores ways that you can extend the various controls that are used with data binding. This chapter focuses on methods to increase the reuse and reduce the redundant code that is required. Examples are provided for extending the DataSource, Parameters, and BoundFields.

❑ **Chapter 9** demystifies the ordinarily opaque ViewState, giving you the tools to crack it and the hacks to manipulate it to your heart's desire.

❑ **Chapter 10** covers a strongly typed, object-oriented way to handle application caching and Web form refreshes. The pros and cons compared to traditional ASP.NET caching are discussed. In addition, the chapter covers an ASP.NET cache viewer and manager drag-and-drop add-in that you can add to any of your ASP.NET applications.

❑ **Chapter 11** shows you how to operate the ASP.NET 2.0 Conversion Wizard. The chapter builds a code example with features you could see in an ASP.NET v1.1 site. You'll see what the conversion process does to this code, and maybe a few things that will delight or surprise you.

❑ **Chapter 12** explores ways to deploy all these new items you have learned to create, define, and manipulate. This includes content on the new Web Deployment Project and how to customize it for your own projects.

❑ **Chapter 13** discusses the Visual Studio 2005 IDE and its plethora of new features. Implementing productivity boosters, such as snippets, item templates, and project templates, have a lot to do with hacks and making you and other developers much more productive.

❑ **Chapter 14** describes security hacks to help you harden your sites. What would a .NET book be without discussing security? This chapter discusses SQL Injection and hacks to help avoid related attacks while minimizing your pain, such as the ability to parameterize a SQL IN clause. You'll also see how to customize a Login control for better input validation.

❑ **Chapter 15** is where you learn more about how to create your own hacks. You'll learn several different ways to package your hacks to share them and make your own contribution to the community. Who knows? Maybe your hack will become part of a future version of .NET, Visual Studio, or another tool that millions of developers around the world will use every day.

❑ **Chapter 16** provides details about different ways Master Pages can be used in ASP.NET 2.0 applications. Some of the topics covered in this chapter include dynamically changing Master

Pages, sharing Master Pages across IIS applications, and programmatically manipulating Master Page controls.

❑ **Chapter 17** delves into the ASP.NET HttpHandler and HttpModule architecture, including boilerplate templates and uses for handlers and modules you may not have thought of.

What You Need to Use This Book

Most of the authors used Visual Studio 2005 Standard or higher during the course of writing this book. Most of the examples should run on all versions of Visual Studio 2005. If you encounter an error, before banging your head on the wall too many times, check the errata to see whether an updated example is available.

Conventions

To help you get the most from the text and keep track of what's happening, we've used a number of conventions throughout the book.

> **Boxes like this one hold important, not-to-be forgotten information that is directly relevant to the surrounding text.**

Tips, hints, tricks, and asides to the current discussion are offset and placed in italics like this.

As for styles in the text:

❑ We *highlight* new terms and important words when we introduce them.

❑ We show keyboard strokes like this: Ctrl+A.

❑ We show filenames, URLs, and code within the text like so: `persistence.properties`.

❑ We present code in two different ways:

```
In code examples we highlight new and important code with a gray background.
```

```
The gray highlighting is not used for code that's less important in the present
context, or has been shown before.
```

Source Code

As you work through the examples in this book, you may choose either to type in all the code manually or to use the source code files that accompany the book. All of the source code used in this book is available for download at www.wrox.com. Once at the site, simply locate the book's title (either by using the Search box or by using one of the title lists) and click the Download Code link on the book's detail page to obtain all the source code for the book.

Because many books have similar titles, you may find it easiest to search by ISBN; this book's ISBN is 0-7645-9766-3 (changing to 978-0-7645-9766-4 as the new industry-wide 13-digit ISBN numbering system is phased in by January 2007).

Once you download the code, just decompress it with your favorite compression tool. Alternately, you can go to the main Wrox code download page at www.wrox.com/dynamic/books/download.aspx to see the code available for this book and all other Wrox books.

Errata

We make every effort to ensure that there are no errors in the text or in the code. However, no one is perfect, and mistakes do occur. If you find an error in one of our books, such as a spelling mistake or a faulty piece of code, we would be very grateful for your feedback. By sending in errata you may save another reader hours of frustration, and at the same time you will be helping us provide even higher quality information.

To find the errata page for this book, go to www.wrox.com and locate the title using the Search box or one of the title lists. Then, on the book details page, click the Book Errata link. On this page you can view all errata that has been submitted for this book and posted by Wrox editors. A complete book list, including links to each book's errata, is also available at www.wrox.com/misc-pages/booklist.shtml.

If you don't spot "your" error on the Book Errata page, go to www.wrox.com/contact/techsupport .shtml and complete the form there to send us the error you have found. We'll check the information and, if appropriate, post a message to the book's errata page and fix the problem in subsequent editions of the book.

p2p.wrox.com

For author and peer discussion, join the P2P forums at p2p.wrox.com. The forums are a Web-based system for you to post messages relating to Wrox books and related technologies and interact with other readers and technology users. The forums offer a subscription feature to e-mail you topics of interest of your choosing when new posts are made to the forums. Wrox authors, editors, other industry experts, and your fellow readers are present on these forums.

At http://p2p.wrox.com you will find a number of different forums that will help you not only as you read this book, but also as you develop your own applications. To join the forums, just follow these steps:

1. Go to p2p.wrox.com and click the Register link.
2. Read the terms of use and click Agree.
3. Complete the required information to join as well as any optional information you wish to provide and click Submit.
4. You will receive an e-mail with information describing how to verify your account and complete the joining process.

You can read messages in the forums without joining P2P but in order to post your own messages, you must join.

Once you join, you can post new messages and respond to messages other users post. You can read messages at any time on the Web. If you would like to have new messages from a particular forum e-mailed to you, click the Subscribe to this Forum icon by the forum name in the forum listing.

For more information about how to use the Wrox P2P, be sure to read the P2P FAQs for answers to questions about how the forum software works as well as many common questions specific to P2P and Wrox books. To read the FAQs, click the FAQ link on any P2P page.

1

Hacks Revisited

Hacks exist in an ever-changing world. One day they are the cutting-edge, clever inventions of a developer with a need. Another day in the future, they can become mainstream code or practices that are integrated into a product or process. The mark of a successful hack is that one day it will become the norm.

This chapter is all about hacks that have become successful. We revisit ASP.NET v1.1 to look at a group of hacks that received much attention. They became so useful that Microsoft felt compelled to add support for them in ASP.NET v2.0. Rather than redo hacks that have already been invented, this chapter highlights the pioneers and their work that influenced Microsoft to add support in ASP.NET v2.0. For those of you making the move to ASP.NET 2.0, you'll learn how these hacks have been integrated into the .NET Framework and related Visual Studio 2005 support. Seeing how previous hacks have positively influenced the current version of ASP.NET can give you and others a greater appreciation for hacks, and provide motivation for new hacks that will have a positive influence on future versions of ASP.NET.

Wizards Hacks Replaced by ASP.NET 2.0

Wizards are user interface tools for gently guiding users through a process. This discussion refers to wizards that you add to your applications. Developers have used them for many years, from installation programs to simplifying complex activities through a series of steps. They've traditionally been a normal part of client desktop applications, but have surfaced as hacks in Web applications.

ASP.NET Wizard Pioneers

An early ASP.NET v1.1, a wizard hack by John Peterson was published as a sample on ASP101.com (asp101.com/samples/wizard_aspx.asp) titled "ASP.NET version of Wizard (Multi-Page Form)." This was an update from a previous implementation for classic ASP 3.0. After support for ASP.NET 2.0 wizards was announced, Tom Blanchard wrote the article "CodeSnip: Simulating the ASP.NET 2.0 Wizard Control with ASP.NET 1.x." at 123aspx.com/redir.aspx?res=32798. Another pre-existing solution that some people used was the Wizard Navigator in the User Interface Process (UIP) Application Block, created by the Microsoft Patterns and Practices Group at `http://msdn.microsoft.com/library/default.asp?url=/library/en-us/dnpag2/html/cabctp.asp`.

Microsoft's online links break a lot, but you should still be able to find the UI Application Block with a search of the MSDN Architecture Center's Patterns and Practices resource pages.

Wizards in ASP.NET v2.0

Wizards are no longer a hack in ASP.NET 2.0. They are easy to use and well supported by Visual Studio 2005. The next section shows how to implement a wizard.

Implementing an ASP.NET 2.0 Wizard

ASP.NET 2.0 wizards are implemented as controls. To use them, simply add a new wizard control to the Visual Designer and start setting properties. This section describes how to implement ASP.NET 2.0 wizards through a sample menu selection application. There are various choices to be made along the way, and the wizard will manage navigation based on input preferences. The following steps explain how to create our sample application:

1. Create a new Web project. To do this, select File⇨New⇨Web Site, select the ASP.NET Web Site template, and change the directory location to WizardDemo as shown in Figure 1-1.

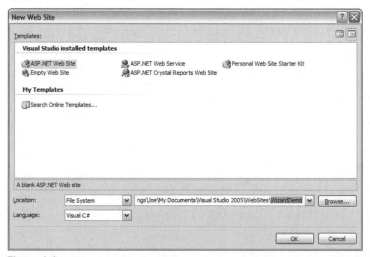

Figure 1-1

2. Click the OK button and Visual Studio 2005 will create a new project, as shown in Figure 1-2.

3. If you are in HTML view, as shown in Figure 1-2, click the Design link at the bottom left of the editor to enter Design view.

4. In Design view, locate the Toolbox, which is on the left side of the IDE. You can open it by hovering over the tab labeled Toolbox. Click on the Standard area of the Toolbox and select the Wizard control. Drag and drop a Wizard control onto the form as shown in Figure 1-3.

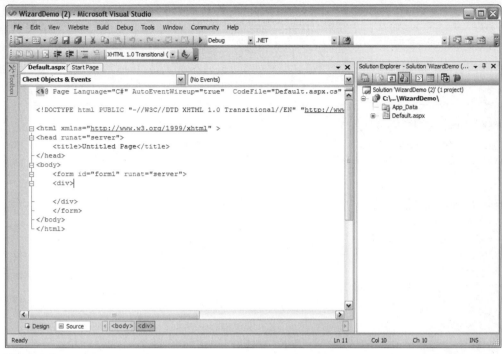

Figure 1-2

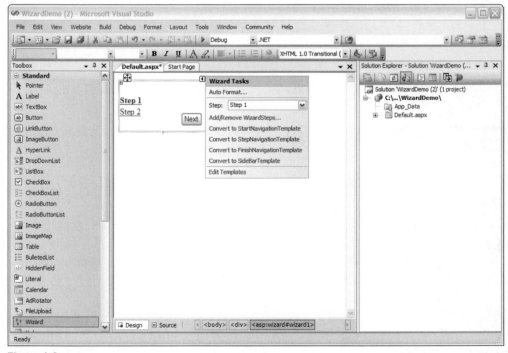

Figure 1-3

5. Select View⇨Properties Window to show the Properties window. In the Properties window, set the `HeaderText` property to **Menu Selector**.

6. Enlarge the Wizard control to approximately 400 × 200.

7. The Wizard control shows a couple of links labeled Step 1 and Step 2 the first time it is added to a Web form. Select Step 1 in the Wizard control.

8. Select the edit area in the Wizard control and type **What is your Eating Preference?**

9. Drag and drop a RadioButtonList control from the Toolbox to the Wizard control edit area, select Edit Items on the Action List, and add **Meat Eater** and **Vegetarian** items to the `Text` properties of two new items in the ListItemCollection Editor. Figure 1-4 shows the results of steps 5 through 9 of these instructions.

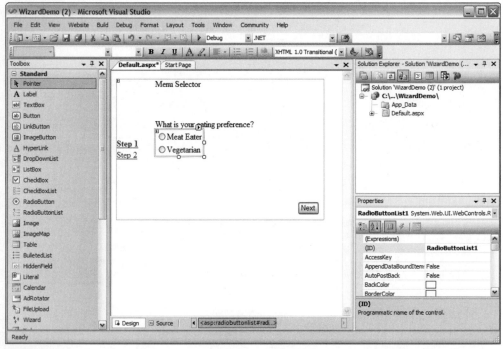

Figure 1-4

10. Select Step 2 in the Wizard control.

11. Type **Please Select Main Course:** in the edit area.

12. Drag and drop a RadioButtonList control from the Toolbox to the Wizard control edit area, select Edit Items in the Action List, and add **Chicken**, **Fish**, and **Steak** items to the `Text` properties of three new items in the ListItemCollection Editor. Figure 1-5 shows the results of steps 10 through 12 of these instructions.

13. Click Add/Remove WizardSteps from the Wizard Tasks list and add Step 3 to the Wizard control.

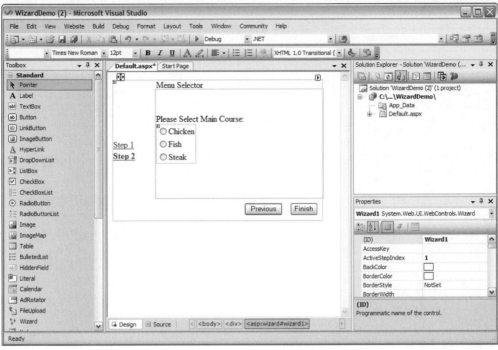

Figure 1-5

14. Select the new Step 3 link that you just added to the Wizard control.

15. Type **Please Select Main Course:** in the edit area.

16. Drag and drop a RadioButtonList control from the Toolbox to the Wizard control edit area. Select Edit Items in the Action List and add **Bread**, **Salad**, and **Veggie Tray** items to the Text properties of three new items in the ListItemCollection Editor. Figure 1-6 shows the results of steps 13 through 16 of these instructions.

17. Click Add/Remove WizardSteps from the Wizard Tasks list and add a new Step 4 to the Wizard control.

18. Select the Step 4 link that you just added to the Wizard control.

19. Type **Please Select Beverage:** in the edit area.

20. Drag and drop a RadioButtonList control from the Toolbox to the Wizard control edit area, select Edit Items in the Action List, and add Coffee, Water, and Wine items to the Text properties of three new items in the ListItemCollection Editor. Figure 1-7 shows the results of steps 17 through 20 of these instructions.

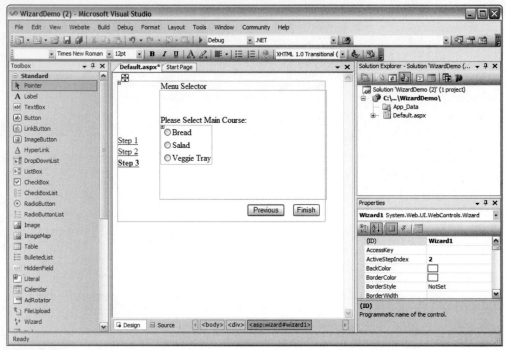

Figure 1-6

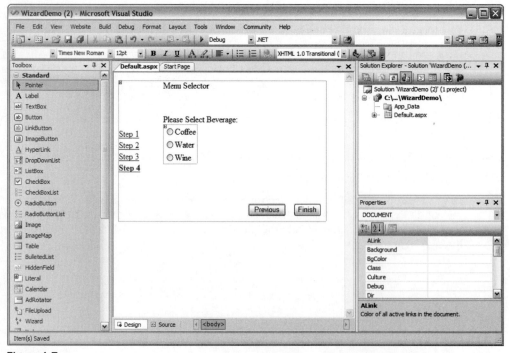

Figure 1-7

This creates HTML with a Wizard that contains multiple steps. Listing 1-1 shows the HTML of this page with modifications made in the later parts of this section. The HTML you see in Listing 1-1 was automatically generated by Visual Studio 2005 as you performed steps 1 through 20. Select the HTML tab at the bottom of the Visual Studio 2005 editor to switch from Design view to HTML view. When you do this, you will see code similar to Listing 1-1.

Listing 1-1: The ASP.NET v2.0 Wizard control with multiple steps

```
<%@ Page Language="C#" AutoEventWireup="true" CodeFile="Default.aspx.cs"
Inherits="_Default" %>

<!DOCTYPE html PUBLIC "-//W3C//DTD XHTML 1.0 Transitional//EN"
"http://www.w3.org/TR/xhtml1/DTD/xhtml1-transitional.dtd">

<html xmlns="http://www.w3.org/1999/xhtml" >
<head runat="server">
    <title>Wizard Demo</title>
</head>
<body>
    <form id="form1" runat="server">
    <div>
        <asp:Wizard ID="Wizard1" runat="server"
                    ActiveStepIndex="0" HeaderText="Menu Selector"
                    Height="200px" Width="400px"
                    OnFinishButtonClick="Wizard1_FinishButtonClick"
                    OnNextButtonClick="Wizard1_NextButtonClick">
            <WizardSteps>
                <asp:WizardStep runat="server" Title="Step 1">
                    What is your eating preference?<br />
                    <br />
                    <asp:RadioButtonList ID="RadioButtonList1" runat="server">
                        <asp:ListItem>Meat Eater</asp:ListItem>
                        <asp:ListItem>Vegetarian</asp:ListItem>
                    </asp:RadioButtonList>
                </asp:WizardStep>
                <asp:WizardStep runat="server" Title="Step 2">
                    Please select main course:<br />
                    <br />
                    <asp:RadioButtonList ID="RadioButtonList2" runat="server">
                        <asp:ListItem>Chicken</asp:ListItem>
                        <asp:ListItem>Fish</asp:ListItem>
                        <asp:ListItem>Steak</asp:ListItem>
                    </asp:RadioButtonList>
                </asp:WizardStep>
                <asp:WizardStep runat="server" Title="Step 3">
                    Please select main course:<br />
                    <br />
                    <asp:RadioButtonList ID="RadioButtonList3" runat="server">
                        <asp:ListItem>Bread</asp:ListItem>
                        <asp:ListItem>Salad</asp:ListItem>
                        <asp:ListItem>Veggie Tray</asp:ListItem>
                    </asp:RadioButtonList>
                </asp:WizardStep>
                <asp:WizardStep runat="server" Title="Step 4">
```

(continued)

7

Listing 1-1 *(continued)*

```
                Please select beverage:<br />
                <br />
                <asp:RadioButtonList ID="RadioButtonList4" runat="server">
                    <asp:ListItem>Coffee</asp:ListItem>
                    <asp:ListItem>Water</asp:ListItem>
                    <asp:ListItem>Wine</asp:ListItem>
                </asp:RadioButtonList>
            </asp:WizardStep>
          </WizardSteps>
        </asp:Wizard>
    </div>
    </form>
</body>
</html>
```

As you can see from the steps of Listing 1-1 and Figure 1-8, the user is either a Meat Eater or a Vegetarian. They should see only the menu items corresponding to their selection.

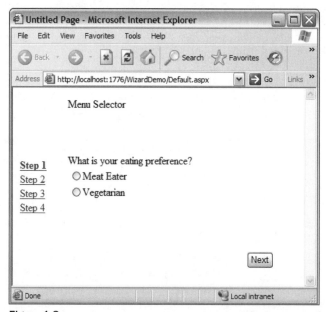

Figure 1-8

To specify different menus, the Wizard control will have to navigate to a different step, depending on what was selected in Step 1. ASP.NET Wizard controls support events, and that is what we'll use to ensure that the proper step appears, depending on eating preference. Listing 1-2 shows how to navigate properly when the user clicks the Next button. Click the lightning bolt icon on the Properties window and double-click the NextButtonClick event to produce an event handler shell, which will have a default name of Wizard1_NextButtonClick. Type in the algorithm for the Wizard1_NextButtonClick event handler as shown in Listing 1-2.

Listing 1-2: Altering the sequential progress of a wizard

```
protected void Wizard1_NextButtonClick(
    object sender, WizardNavigationEventArgs e)
{
    if (Wizard1.ActiveStepIndex == 0)
    {
        if (RadioButtonList1.SelectedValue == "Vegetarian")
        {
            Wizard1.ActiveStepIndex = 2;
        }
    }

    if (Wizard1.ActiveStepIndex == 1)
    {
        Wizard1.ActiveStepIndex = 3;
    }
}
```

By capturing the NextButtonClick event, as shown in Listing 1-2, you can control the navigation sequence of the Wizard. This event is called in the context of the current page when the Next button is clicked. Therefore, check the ActiveStepIndex first to determine the current page, which is indicated by a zero-based integer. All step controls are accessible during the postback, so we can get to their values easily. In this case, the code sets the ActiveStepIndex to the Step 3 page, at index 2, if the eating preference is Vegetarian.

When the eating preference is Meat Eater, the Wizard will naturally navigate to Step 2, at index 1. In this case, clicking the Next button should bring the user to Step 4, at index 3, to select a beverage. The Vegetarian who navigated to Step 3 will naturally move to Step 4 after clicking the Next button.

When the Wizard reaches the end, the Next button will be replaced with a Finish button. You can capture an event from the Finish button to take action when it is clicked, as shown in Listing 1-3.

Listing 1-3: Handling the Finish button event

```
protected void Wizard1_FinishButtonClick(
    object sender, WizardNavigationEventArgs e)
{
    if (RadioButtonList1.SelectedValue == "Vegetarian")
    {
        Response.Write(
            "Your meal will be " +
            RadioButtonList3.SelectedValue +
            " and " +
            RadioButtonList4.SelectedValue);
    }
    else
    {
        Response.Write(
            "Your meal will be " +
            RadioButtonList2.SelectedValue +
            " and " +
            RadioButtonList4.SelectedValue);
    }
}
```

In Listing 1-3, we're primarily interested in whether the eating preference was Meat Eater or Vegetarian so we can extract values from the proper controls. The code emits, via Response.Write, the selected menu items, depending on whether the user selected Meat Eater or Vegetarian when running the Wizard.

Going through the process of adding steps, handling events, and altering properties, you can see how sophisticated the ASP.NET v2.0 Wizard control is. It's an example of an extremely useful hack being transformed into a full product feature.

Master Pages: Then and Now

Master Pages enable you to develop a visual template for a common look and feel across multiple pages of a website. In ASP.NET v1.1, developers used a few different techniques to accomplish similar goals, including user controls, inheriting from a common base page class, and a form of Master Pages that used templates. This section refers you to resources showing how Master Page template hacks were implemented in ASP.NET v1.1, and then describes how they are implemented as a major feature of ASP.NET v2.0.

Master Page Templates in ASP.NET v1.1

The closest thing to ASP.NET v2.0 Master Pages in ASP.NET v1.1 was one of the template management techniques. Paul Wilson, `wilsondotnet.com`, has written several articles on the subject of page templates. In October 2003, he wrote "Page Templates: Introduction" (`http://authors.aspalliance.com/PaulWilson/Articles/?id=14`) for ASP Alliance, which describes the user controls and page inheritance techniques. However, more interesting is his article "MasterPages: Introduction" (`http://authors.aspalliance.com/PaulWilson/Articles/?id=13`) for ASP Alliance. For many developers, this was essentially a first look at what was to come by way of Master Pages in ASP.NET v2.0. Paul Wilson's article shows how to accomplish the same thing with ASP.NET v1.1.

There are other credible ways to accomplish templating in ASP.NET v1.1. In his Code Project article "MasterPages Reinvented: A Component-Based Template Engine for ASP.NET" (`codeproject.com/aspnet/sumitemplatecontrols.asp`), Philipp Sumi shows another method of using Master Page templates in ASP.NET v1.x. There are other examples available, but the articles by Paul Wilson and Philipp Sumi are credible references you can use in ASP.NET v1.1.

Master Pages in ASP.NET v2.0

In ASP.NET v2.0, Master Pages have grown from a great hack to a major feature. They're built into ASP.NET with new page directives, placeholders, and controls that enable you to create a common look and feel across your application or website. Additionally, they are well supported in Visual Studio 2005.

Implementing Master Pages

In ASP.NET v2.0, Master Pages are implemented as a Web page with a default look and feel that content pages can use. Multiple content pages can use this Master Page's common look and feel, and all they need to do is provide content markup, which is merged with the Master Page. The example in this section walks through creating a Master Page and simple content page with VS 2005.

To get started, create a new Web project and delete the `Default.aspx` page that is automatically created. We'll re-create `Default.aspx` later as a content page that uses a Master Page we're about to create.

1. To create a Master Page, right-click on the Web project in Solution Explorer, select Add New Item, select Master Page, give it the name **Company.master**, and click the OK button. This creates a new Master Page.

2. If the Master Page is in HTML view, change it to Design view by clicking the Design button at the bottom left corner of the editor. Add a new table to Company.master by selecting Layout➪Insert Table.

3. On the Insert Table dialog, choose Template and then pick Header, footer, and side from the drop-down list, as shown in Figure 1-9.

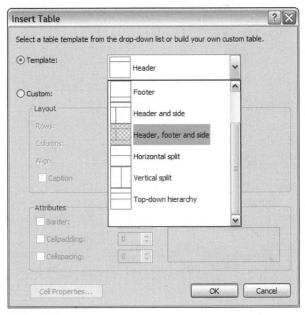

Figure 1-9

4. Once the table has been added to the page, select the cell in the top table row and type **My Company Header**, select the first cell in the second table row and type **Menu Goes Here**, and select the cell in the third (last) row and type **Copyright (C) 2006 My Company, All Rights Reserved**.

5. When a Master Page is first created, it has a ContentPlaceHolder control added to it automatically. Company.master has this also. Drag and drop the ContentPlaceHolder control to the second cell of the second row in the table that you just inserted into the Company.master Master Page. The results should look similar to Figure 1-10.

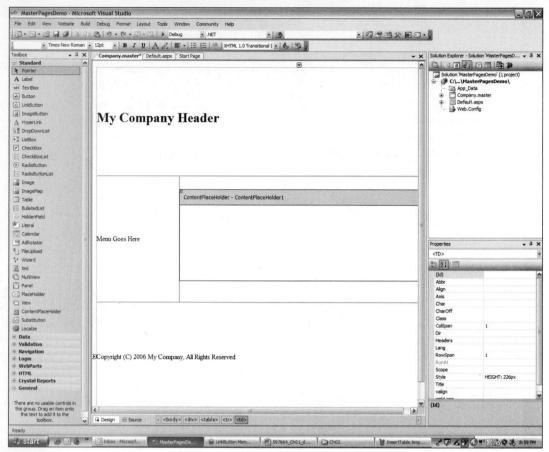

Figure 1-10

After creating and modifying the Company.master Master Page, you can view the automatically generated HTML code by clicking the HTML button at the bottom-left corner of the editor. Listing 1-4 shows what the HTML for the Company.master Master Page looks like after making the modifications described in the previous paragraph.

Listing 1-4: A Master Page with formatting for custom page elements: Company.master

```
<%@ Master Language="C#" AutoEventWireup="true" CodeFile="Company.master.cs"
Inherits="Company" %>

<!DOCTYPE html PUBLIC "-//W3C//DTD XHTML 1.0 Transitional//EN"
"http://www.w3.org/TR/xhtml1/DTD/xhtml1-transitional.dtd">

<html xmlns="http://www.w3.org/1999/xhtml" >
<head runat="server">
    <title>My Company</title>
</head>
<body>
```

```
<form id="form1" runat="server">
<div>
    <table border="0" cellpadding="0" cellspacing="0"
            style="width: 100%; height: 100%">
        <tr>
            <td colspan="2" style="height: 200px">
                <h1>My Company Header</h1>
            </td>
        </tr>
        <tr>
            <td style="width: 200px">
                Menu Goes Here</td>
            <td>
        <asp:contentplaceholder id="ContentPlaceHolder1" runat="server">
        </asp:contentplaceholder>
            </td>
        </tr>
        <tr>
            <td colspan="2" style="height: 200px">
                Copyright (C) 2006 My Company, All Rights Reserved
            </td>
        </tr>
    </table>
</div>
</form>
</body>
</html>
```

The first thing you should notice about Listing 1-4 is that it contains a Master directive at the top of the page. As implied by the codefile and inherits attributes, you can add a code file to the Master Page. Most of the page is primarily HTML formatting markup.

The other pertinent part of this page is the contentplaceholder element. You can place default content in here, but content pages will use the id to specify where their content will appear, which will override any default content.

You can now use this Master Page with any content pages. The process of creating a content page is very similar to the process required to create any other Web Form. Right-click on the Web project in Solution Explorer, select Add New Item, select Web Form, accept the suggested name of Default.aspx, check the Select Master Page option, and click the OK button. Listing 1-5 shows the new content page, after I modified it.

Listing 1-5: Content page that uses a Master Page: Default.aspx

```
<%@ Page
    Language="C#"
    MasterPageFile="~/Company.master"
    AutoEventWireup="true"
    CodeFile="Default.aspx.cs"
    Inherits="_Default"
    Title="Content Page" %>

<asp:Content ID="Content1"
```

(continued)

Listing 1-5 *(continued)*

```
                    ContentPlaceHolderID="ContentPlaceHolder1"
                    Runat="Server">
        <h2>This is my content.</h2>
    </asp:Content>
```

The two interesting parts of Listing 1-5 are the MasterPageFile attribute and the Content element. The Page directive contains a new attribute named MasterPageFile, specifying the filename of the Master Page to use.

It is evident from Listing 1-5 that content pages don't have HTML markup as normal Web Forms do. Instead, add a Content element that identifies where to place content markup within the Master Page by specifying the id of the contentplaceholder (in the Master Page) to use with the ContentPlaceHolderID attribute. Only the markup in the Content element appears in the Master Page.

Because you don't have normal HTML markup, such as a Head, set the Title attribute of the Page directive with what you would have normally put into the Head title element.

This shows how elegant and simple it is to use Master Pages in ASP.NET v2.0. Supported by VS 2005, it is a much easier solution than ASP.NET v1.1 hacks.

URL Rewriting

URL rewriting is the practice of accepting URLs with meaningful naming conventions and translating them into real query strings. A couple of reasons why you would want meaningful naming conventions include the capability to organize information into a logical hierarchy or to mask query string parameters. In this section I'll show you how URL rewriting can improve your user interface, describe the old and new ways to accomplish URL rewriting, and give you some code that demonstrates the concept.

> I also add some extra code in this section to demonstrate best practices in n-tier architecture and data handling, rather than cheat with a simpler datasource control.

Why URL Rewriting?

An example of hierarchical organization could be described by looking at how a blog is organized by time. From the user's perspective, the following query string could be considered very cryptic:

```
http://www.someblogsite.com/username/?y=2005&m=01&d=31
```

The preceding query string returns blog entries for January 1, 2005, which isn't easy to determine. You could modify code so that the parameters were more meaningful, such as this:

```
http://www.someblogsite.com/username/?year=2005&month=01&day=31
```

No matter how query string parameters are presented, average users will have a hard time understanding. Instead, it would be much clearer to write the query string with a nice hierarchical representation, like this:

```
http://www.someblogsite.com/username/2005/January/31
```

For a typical visitor of a site, the preceding URL is not too hard to figure out. For example, if users were to remove the day, they would see all of the entries for the entire month of January.

Even when you don't have a natural hierarchy or just a single parameter, a URL with a meaningful name, rather than a query parameter, is still easier for a consumer to understand.

The ASP.NET v1.1 Hack

One of the best resources available for performing URL rewriting in ASP.NET v1.x is Scott Mitchell's MSDN article titled "URL Rewriting in ASP.NET" at `msdn.microsoft.com/library/default.asp?url=/library/en-us/dnaspp/html/urlrewriting.asp`. In this article, Scott describes how to perform URL rewriting with both HTTP Modules and HTTP Handlers, and explains when each is best to use. He also builds a reusable URL rewriting engine that uses regular expressions via a configuration file.

The ASP.NET v2.0 Replacement

Rewriting URLs is supported, somewhat, in ASP.NET v2.0 with the `urlMappings` configuration element. Add a new entry to `web.config`, similar to this for mapping a URL:

```
<urlMappings enabled="true">
   <add url="~/Articles/AspDotNet/UrlRewriting"
mappedUrl="~/Articles.aspx?cat=1&id=16" />
</urlMappings>
```

The `url` attribute is what the user sees and the `mappedUrl` attribute describes the actual requested page. In the preceding `urlMappings` element, imagine that there is an articles page that dynamically returns articles based on category and article identifier. The `url` shows the preferred user interface, but the `mappedUrl` attribute shows the actual page and parameters that will be requested.

Implementing the URL Mapping Capability

I've written an example application to show how to use this capability. It is a variation of the article viewing concept shown previously, but based on year and month. For example, the articles application will allow you to select the year and then the month. Each page is displayed with readable URLs that you can use to navigate the application by simply modifying the page address. Listing 1-6 shows the initial page of the articles application.

Listing 1-6: Main page that uses readable URLs for identifying years: Default.aspx

```
<%@ Page Language="C#" AutoEventWireup="true" CodeFile="Default.aspx.cs"
Inherits="_Default" %>

<!DOCTYPE html PUBLIC "-//W3C//DTD XHTML 1.0 Transitional//EN"
"http://www.w3.org/TR/xhtml1/DTD/xhtml1-transitional.dtd">

<html xmlns="http://www.w3.org/1999/xhtml" >
```

(continued)

Listing 1-6 *(continued)*

```
<head runat="server">
    <title>.NET Article Archive</title>
</head>
<body>
    <form id="form1" runat="server">
        <h1>.NET Article Archive</h1>
        <p>
            Pick a Year:
        </p>
        <p>
            <asp:HyperLink ID="HyperLink1" runat="server"
                NavigateUrl="~/2006">2006</asp:HyperLink><br />
            <asp:HyperLink ID="HyperLink2" runat="server"
                NavigateUrl="~/2005">2005</asp:HyperLink>
        </p>
    </form>
</body>
</html>
```

The NavigateUrl attribute of the HyperLink elements contain readable URLs that will be rewritten as query string parameters. Similarly, after users select a year, they will see the year page shown in Listing 1-7.

Listing 1-7: Year page with readable URLs: YearView.aspx

```
<%@ Page Language="C#" AutoEventWireup="true" CodeFile="YearView.aspx.cs"
Inherits="YearView" %>

<!DOCTYPE html PUBLIC "-//W3C//DTD XHTML 1.0 Transitional//EN"
"http://www.w3.org/TR/xhtml1/DTD/xhtml1-transitional.dtd">

<html xmlns="http://www.w3.org/1999/xhtml" >
<head runat="server">
    <title>Articles for the Year</title>
</head>
<body>
    <form id="form1" runat="server">
        <h1>
            <asp:Label ID="lblTitle"
                        runat="server"
                        Text="Articles for the Year #">
            </asp:Label>
        </h1>
        <p>
            <asp:Panel ID="pnlMonths" runat="server" Height="50px" Width="125px">
                <asp:HyperLink ID="hypJanuary"   runat="server"
                    NavigateUrl="~/YEAR/01">January</asp:HyperLink><br />
                <asp:HyperLink ID="hypFebruary"  runat="server"
                    NavigateUrl="~/YEAR/02">February</asp:HyperLink><br />
                <asp:HyperLink ID="hypMarch"     runat="server"
                    NavigateUrl="~/YEAR/03">March</asp:HyperLink><br />
                <asp:HyperLink ID="hypApril"     runat="server"
                    NavigateUrl="~/YEAR/04">April</asp:HyperLink><br />
```

```
                        <asp:HyperLink ID="hypMay"        runat="server"
                            NavigateUrl="~/YEAR/05">May</asp:HyperLink><br />
                        <asp:HyperLink ID="hypJune"       runat="server"
                            NavigateUrl="~/YEAR/06">June</asp:HyperLink><br />
                        <asp:HyperLink ID="hypJuly"       runat="server"
                            NavigateUrl="~/YEAR/07">July</asp:HyperLink><br />
                        <asp:HyperLink ID="hypAugust"     runat="server"
                            NavigateUrl="~/YEAR/08">August</asp:HyperLink><br />
                        <asp:HyperLink ID="hypSeptember" runat="server"
                            NavigateUrl="~/YEAR/09">September</asp:HyperLink><br />
                        <asp:HyperLink ID="hypOctober"    runat="server"
                            NavigateUrl="~/YEAR/10">October</asp:HyperLink><br />
                        <asp:HyperLink ID="hypNovember"   runat="server"
                            NavigateUrl="~/YEAR/11">November</asp:HyperLink><br />
                        <asp:HyperLink ID="hypDecember"   runat="server"
                            NavigateUrl="~/YEAR/12">December</asp:HyperLink>
                </asp:Panel>
            </p>
        </form>
    </body>
    </html>
```

Listing 1-7 shows HyperLink elements with NavigateUrl attributes set to readable URLs. They include a level for each month of the year, where the number corresponds to the order of the month. To process these URLs properly, edit the code file for the YearView Web form as shown in Listing 1-8.

Listing 1-8: Reading the query string parameter of a page called with a parameterized URL: YearView.aspx.cs

```csharp
using System;
using System.Data;
using System.Configuration;
using System.Collections;
using System.Web;
using System.Web.Security;
using System.Web.UI;
using System.Web.UI.WebControls;
using System.Web.UI.WebControls.WebParts;
using System.Web.UI.HtmlControls;

public partial class YearView : System.Web.UI.Page
{
    string year;  // passed in query string

    protected void Page_Load(object sender, EventArgs e)
    {
        // we'll use this in multiple methods
        year = Request.QueryString["year"];

        // set page title
        SetTitle();

        // configure months to refer to proper page
```

(continued)

Listing 1-8 *(continued)*

```csharp
        SetMonths();
    }

    /// <summary>
    /// configure months to refer to proper page
    /// </summary>
    private void SetMonths()
    {
        foreach (Control ctrl in pnlMonths.Controls)
        {
            HyperLink monthLink = ctrl as HyperLink;

            if (monthLink != null)
            {
                monthLink.NavigateUrl =
                    monthLink.NavigateUrl.Replace("YEAR", year);
            }
        }
    }

    /// <summary>
    /// set page title
    /// </summary>
    private void SetTitle()
    {
        lblTitle.Text = "Articles for the Year " + year;
    }
}
```

The Page_Load method of Listing 1-8 extracts the year parameter out of the query string so it can be used in subsequent methods. The SetTitle method uses this value to rewrite the title on the page with the correct year.

Also, notice the NavigateUrl properties for the HyperLink controls in Listing 1-8, where they all contain the text "YEAR" in the year's position of the URL. This makes the code more dynamic because, depending on the year, these NavigateUrl properties must be rewritten. That's what the SetMonths method of Listing 1-8 is for. The code in Listing 1-8 deliberately places each HyperLink control into a Panel so we can get to its Controls collection in code. Therefore, in the code file, the SetMonths method can simply iterate through the Controls collection and set the year with a simple string.Replace method call. To get this built-in URL rewriting functionality to work for this application, there is a web.config file with a urlMapping element, as shown in Listing 1-9.

Listing 1-9: The urlMapping element in a web.config file enables URL rewriting in ASP.NET v2.0

```xml
<?xml version="1.0"?>
<configuration>
  <system.web>
    <urlMappings>
      <add url="~/2006"
           mappedUrl="~/YearView.aspx?year=2006"/>
```

```
        <add url="~/2006/01"
            mappedUrl="~/MonthView.aspx?year=2006&amp;month=01"/>
        <add url="~/2006/02"
            mappedUrl="~/MonthView.aspx?year=2006&amp;month=02"/>
        <add url="~/2005"
            mappedUrl="~/YearView.aspx?year=2005"/>
        <add url="~/2005/01"
            mappedUrl="~/MonthView.aspx?year=2005&amp;month=01"/>
        <add url="~/2005/02"
            mappedUrl="~/MonthView.aspx?year=2005&amp;month=02"/>
    </urlMappings>
    <compilation debug="true"/>
  </system.web>
</configuration>
```

In each one of the `add` elements of Listing 1-9, the hackable URL translates into a `mappedUrl`, which is the actual address and query string sent to the page. The tilde (~) symbol represents the application directory that each page is relative to. You must use `&amp;` in place of just the & symbol to separate parameters. We've left out entries for some months to shorten the listing.

To see the list of articles, users select the month they are interested in. Listing 1-10 shows how `MonthView.aspx` is implemented. I used the GridView control in Listing 1-10 because I needed to format the output nicely for multiple data rows and I wanted to bind it to the ObjectDataSource control. The GridView control is a new control added to ASP.NET in v2.0 that replaces the DataGrid control.

Listing 1-10: Using the GridView to read query parameters: MonthView.aspx

```
<%@ Page Language="C#" AutoEventWireup="true" CodeFile="MonthView.aspx.cs"
Inherits="MonthView" %>

<!DOCTYPE html PUBLIC "-//W3C//DTD XHTML 1.0 Transitional//EN"
"http://www.w3.org/TR/xhtml1/DTD/xhtml1-transitional.dtd">

<html xmlns="http://www.w3.org/1999/xhtml" >
<head runat="server">
    <title>Articles for the Month</title>
</head>
<body>
    <form id="form1" runat="server">
        <h1>
            Requested Articles:</h1>
        <br />
        <asp:GridView ID="GridView1" runat="server"
            AutoGenerateColumns="False" DataSourceID="ArticlesODS">
            <Columns>
                <asp:BoundField DataField="Year"
                    HeaderText="Year" SortExpression="Year" />
                <asp:BoundField DataField="Month"
                    HeaderText="Month" SortExpression="Month" />
                <asp:BoundField DataField="Title"
                    HeaderText="Title" SortExpression="Title" />
                <asp:BoundField DataField="Content"
                    HeaderText="Content" SortExpression="Content" />
```

(continued)

Listing 1-10 *(continued)*

```
            </Columns>
        </asp:GridView>
        <asp:ObjectDataSource ID="ArticlesODS" runat="server"
            SelectMethod="GetArticles" TypeName="Articles">
            <SelectParameters>
                <asp:QueryStringParameter DefaultValue="2006"
                    Name="year" QueryStringField="year"
                    Type="String" />
                <asp:QueryStringParameter DefaultValue="01"
                    Name="month" QueryStringField="month"
                    Type="String" />
            </SelectParameters>
        </asp:ObjectDataSource>
    </form>
</body>
</html>
```

Being an advocate of well-designed n-tier architectures, I decided to implement article management with business objects and a formal data access layer. This is why you see the ObjectDataSource control in the MonthView.aspx page. It was handy to map query string parameters directly to the GetArticles method of the Articles class, as shown in Listing 1-11.

Listing 1-11: The Articles class contains a list of article objects: articles.cs

```
using System;
using System.Collections.Generic;

/// <summary>
/// List of Articles
/// </summary>
public class Articles : List<Article>
{
    public List<Article> GetArticles(string year, string month)
    {
        ArticleData dal = new ArticleData();
        dal.GetArticles(this, year, month);
        return this;
    }
}
```

The Articles class in Listing 1-11 takes advantage of the new *generics* feature of the C# programming language to create a strongly typed collection of Article objects. By inheriting List<Article> we get the benefits of generics with the capability to name our type something a bit more understandable. Listing 1-12 shows the data access layer, represented by the ArticleData class.

Listing 1-12: The ArticleData class populates the current list with new articles from the data source: ArticleData.cs

```
using System;
using System.Collections;
using System.Collections.Generic;
```

```
using System.Data;
using System.Web;

/// <summary>
/// Summary description for ArticleData
/// </summary>
public class ArticleData
{
    public void GetArticles(List<Article> articles, string year, string month)
    {
        DataSet dsArticles = new DataSet();
        dsArticles.ReadXml(HttpContext.Current.Server.MapPath("Articles.xml"));
        DataView dvArticles = new DataView(dsArticles.Tables["article"]);
        dvArticles.RowFilter =
            "year = '" + year + "' " +
            "and month = '" + month + "'";

        Article currArticle = null;

        IEnumerator articleRows = dvArticles.GetEnumerator();

        while (articleRows.MoveNext())
        {
            DataRowView articleRow = (DataRowView)articleRows.Current;
            currArticle = new Article(
                (string)articleRow["year"],
                (string)articleRow["month"],
                (string)articleRow["title"],
                (string)articleRow["content"]);

            articles.Add(currArticle);
        }
    }
}
```

This class loads an XML file (see Listing 1-13) into a DataSet. It uses a DataView to filter the results based on the year and month parameters that were passed in. The Article class is the business object that will eventually be bound in the UI layer to a GridView. Of course, the UI layer doesn't need to know that the data came from an XML file or was processed via ADO.NET components. It can be easily changed later to facilitate new requirements. Fortunately, the GridView is able to display business objects in a Generic collection, which is why we pass the data back as List<Article> through the articles parameter.

Listing 1-13: Article data is represented via an XML file: Articles.xml

```
<?xml version="1.0" encoding="utf-8" ?>
<articles>
  <article>
    <year>2005</year>
    <month>01</month>
    <title>Title1</title>
    <content>This is the text of Title1.</content>
  </article>
  <article>
```

(continued)

Listing 1-13 *(continued)*

```xml
      <year>2005</year>
      <month>02</month>
      <title>Title2</title>
      <content>This is the text of Title2.</content>
    </article>
    <article>
      <year>2005</year>
      <month>02</month>
      <title>Title3</title>
      <content>This is the text of Title3.</content>
    </article>
    <article>
      <year>2006</year>
      <month>01</month>
      <title>Title4</title>
      <content>This is the text of Title4.</content>
    </article>
    <article>
      <year>2006</year>
      <month>01</month>
      <title>Title5</title>
      <content>This is the text of Title5.</content>
    </article>
    <article>
      <year>2006</year>
      <month>02</month>
      <title>Title6</title>
      <content>This is the text of Title6.</content>
    </article>
</articles>
```

The code in Listing 1-12 uses an XML file (see Listing 1-13) as the datasource for a very simple implementation. The ArticlesData class uses the data to populate Article objects, as shown in Listing 1-14.

Listing 1-14: The Article class is a business object that will be bound to a GridView in the UI layer: Article.cs

```csharp
using System;
using System.Data;
using System.Configuration;
using System.Web;
using System.Web.Security;
using System.Web.UI;
using System.Web.UI.WebControls;
using System.Web.UI.WebControls.WebParts;
using System.Web.UI.HtmlControls;

/// <summary>
/// Represents an Article
/// </summary>
public class Article
{
```

```
        private string m_year;

        public string Year
        {
            get { return m_year; }
            set { m_year = value; }
        }

        private string m_month;

        public string Month
        {
            get { return m_month; }
            set { m_month = value; }
        }


        private string m_title;

        public string Title
        {
            get { return m_title; }
            set { m_title = value; }
        }

        private string m_content;

        public string Content
        {
            get { return m_content; }
            set { m_content = value; }
        }

    public Article(string year, string month, string title, string content)
    {
            Year = year;
            Month = month;
            Title = title;
            Content = content;
    }
}
```

Data in the Articles class is exposed through properties as its public interface, providing encapsulation. This gives you the ability to change the underlying implementation as necessary, including adding business rules and validation logic.

If I had used a datasource control other than the OjectDataSource control in my code, adding business rules would not have been an option. I chose not to for the purpose of simplifying the code in this example, but I still have a choice. Using the Object DataSource control properly, you can design applications so they are flexible and maintainable.

Using the ASP.NET v2.0 URL Mapping feature appears to be a great capability, but there is one catch: You can't use regular expressions. The articles example in this section could have been better written using regular expressions. Notice that the urlMappings elements contain very similar code that only differs by year or month. This could have been implemented better with a single regular expression that mapped the year and month with parameter placement. If you used Scott Mitchell's URL rewriting engine, the configuration would look like this:

```
<RewriterConfig>
   <Rules>
      <!-- Rules for Blog Content Displayer -->
      <RewriterRule>
         <LookFor>~/(\d{4})/(\d{2})/Default\.aspx</LookFor>
         <SendTo><![CDATA[~/YearView.aspx?year=$1&month=$2]]></SendTo>
      </RewriterRule>
      <RewriterRule>
         <LookFor>~/(\d{4})/Default\.aspx</LookFor>
         <SendTo>~/YearView.aspx?year=$1</SendTo>
      </RewriterRule>
   </Rules>
</RewriterConfig>
```

This is a simple, one-time configuration. However, with the Visual Studio 2005 implementation, demonstrated by the urlMapping elements of the configuration file in Listing 1-9, you must continually update the file for every year and every month of every year. This is not practical because the file will continually grow and it requires manual intervention. For serious URL rewriting capabilities with regular expressions, I recommend you use the hack in Scott Mitchell's article. Use the URL mapping feature of ASP.NET v2.0 in only the simplest cases.

Wrapping Up

This chapter introduced a few hacks that were invented by pioneers of ASP.NET v1.1. These people and others had such a great influence that Microsoft turned their hacks into major product features in ASP.NET v2.0. Wizard hacks became the Wizard control. Template, inheritance, and user control Master Page hacks became Master Pages in ASP.NET v2.0. URL rewriting hacks influenced URL mapping in ASP.NET v2.0, and are still so good that the URL rewriting hacks will continue to be a preferred method of implementing URL rewriting when regular expressions are desired.

2

Getting Started

Whether you are migrating an existing ASP.NET 1.1 application or beginning a brand-new ASP.NET 2.0 application from scratch, it is best to have a strategy that helps you get started. This chapter will help you develop a strategy by exploring some of the different techniques that can be used when starting new projects. The strategy you adopt should be used consistently on your projects and evolve over time to implement the best practices you adopt. Having consistency in your projects not only enables you to move from project to project easier, but also helps when training new people on your team. This chapter offers some ideas for getting started that you could adopt as your own best practices.

When setting up a new application, you'll need to consider the organization of your solution. For example, putting all the code in a single website and not preparing for later sharing with other projects might not be the best choice. There is no better time to consider how you will share code or custom controls with other projects than when you are starting a new project. If you've built any common server controls or utility routines that you use in every project, you'll want to set up the necessary references.

One of the concepts we will discuss in this chapter is using a `BaseUIPage` class on every Web form, instead of having the Web form inherit from `System.Web.UI.Page`, which is the default when adding new Web forms to your project. Because that requires a change to every Web form, doing that from the start makes much more sense than adopting it later in the project. If the concept of using base classes to inherit from is new to you, don't worry; we will be exploring how they fit in later in the chapter. Master Pages is another important example because it affects each Web form, but it's not a requirement to think about that up front. If you later decide to implement Master Pages, you would have to modify any of your existing pages to take advantage of the new Master Page model.

This chapter complements Chapter 11, which discusses migrating from 1.x to 2.0 in greater detail. You might decide to implement some changes discussed in this chapter during the conversion process. For example, as part of the conversion you may adopt Master Pages or extract some common code to a class library for broader reuse. As you read this chapter, you might consider whether there are any techniques you want to apply during your migrations.

Many of the concepts discussed in this chapter are best implemented when starting a new project. While it is not impossible to implement the techniques described here later in a project life, typically it would take more effort when they are not implemented from the beginning. Many of these techniques can also be packaged up and applied as you build your site by leveraging the export template capabilities in Visual Studio 2005. Using the templates will save many hours of repetitive work by taking the best practices you adopt and allowing them to be reused page after page. This chapter describes how that can be applied during project startup, and in Chapter 13 the template concept is discussed in greater detail.

It would be unrealistic to assume that all of the suggestions and discussions in this chapter make sense in all projects. Like most of the topics in this book, you do not need to adopt 100 percent of the recommendations — find what works for your organization and the specific application being developed.

Organizing Projects and Solutions

One of the first decisions that should be made when starting development on a new application is how to organize your project. While it is possible and sometimes easier for smaller applications to have just a single ASP.NET Web folder, often it is better to have a multi-project structure. This is definitely the case if in the future you think your application might consist of multiple websites that share a single database structure or if you might provide a Windows Form, Windows Service, or another type of non-Web application that could share some of the common project items.

For example, one of the most common forms of sharing between projects is the utility code that your company has developed over the years that is not specific to a single application. If you were to place code like that in your Web project, there is no easy way to reference that from other Web applications that you might build. What happens is that the code is copied, and instead of having a single version you end up with several copies, all slightly different. Then, when a bug is encountered, it is fixed in only one of the copies, and instead of having one fire drill when something breaks in production you have three or four.

Of course, if you already have utility or common code in your Web project, nothing says you can't move that into a common class library at any point. However, in the end this results in more work because you must change your current application to reference the new library. Because specific application namespaces are not used by default for ASP.NET 2.0, you might have to add namespace references to each of your classes that use the utility or common code. If you start with a multi-project approach and the determination to share code across your applications, you avoid this extra work.

There is no one right way to organize projects in an application. The ideas presented here are not intended to be a one-size-fits-all solution, but rather to offer ideas so you can get started on the right path. Unless the application you're building is very small, starting out by creating a blank solution is probably the best approach.

Solutions exist to enable you to have multiple projects loaded, and by using Solution Explorer you can navigate from one to the next. In addition to acting as a container for multiple projects, when you reference one project from another project in the same solution, the reference information is stored inside the solution file.

All projects have a solution file even if it is not visible. With VB.NET and Visual Web Developer project settings, the solution doesn't appear in Solution Explorer until you add a second project by selecting

File⇨Add⇨New Project. With Visual C# settings, the solution appears in Solution Explorer all the time. Regardless of where you put your website, Visual Studio will create a solution file in the Default Projects Location directory. In both VB.NET and Visual C#, you can set this location by selecting Tools⇨Options⇨ Environment⇨General. Visual Web Developer doesn't expose properties for you to change this directory. However, you can go to My Documents⇨Visual Studio 2005⇨Settings, select CurrentSettings.vssettings, and change the location. In that file, if you did a find on the following string 'name="ProjectsAndSolution"' and then looked for the following element in the XML configuration file, you would locate the string that needs to be modified. Modify this string to point to your location of choice.

```
<PropertyValue
 name="ProjectsLocation">%vsspv_visualstudio_dir%\Projects</PropertyValue>
```

The following is an XPath expression that would get you to the same location in the file:

```
/UserSettings/ToolsOptions/ToolsOptionsCategory[@name=Environment]/ToolsOptionsSub
Category[@name=ProjectsAndSolution]/PropertyValue[@name=ProjectsLocation]
```

Creating the Solution

There are three basic ways to create a solution:

❑ As described in the preceding discussion, you can create a new website, and a solution will be created for you in the Default Project Locations directory. Depending on your settings, you may or may not see this in Solution Explorer until you have multiple projects active.

❑ When you create a project such as a class library, if an existing project is open, you have the option to add this new project to an existing solution or create a new solution. If you select Add to Existing, no new solution is created and the project is simply added to the currently active solution. Otherwise, you have to decide whether you create a new directory for the solution. If you don't select Create a New Directory, then the solution will be named the same as the project you are adding and will be placed in the same directory. This is not an ideal setup for solutions projects that contain multiple projects.

If you choose to create a new directory you will be prompted for the name of the directory — that name will also be used to name the solution file. When the wizard completes, a directory for the solution will be created under the path specified in the location input and the project will be created as a directory under that. For example, if the project name were Common, the path were c:\, and solution were MySolution, you would see the following directory structure:

```
C:\MySolution
C:\MySolution\MySolution.sln
c:\MySolution\Common\
c:\MySolution\Common\Common.csproj
```

Using this approach, as long as you create a new directory, it is not bad and can accomplish two steps in one by creating your common project at the same time as your overall solution file.

❑ The final common way to create a solution is by selecting File⇨ New Project. Then, in the New Project Wizard, you should expand the Other Project Types option. You will find the Blank Solution item, as shown in Figure 2-1.

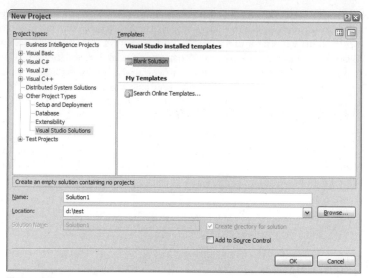

Figure 2-1

> If you are using Source Safe, all projects included in a solution must be bound to the
> same Source Safe database or you receive an error and Visual Studio 2005 will load
> the projects from only one of the databases. If you are not able to accomplish this
> because of projects residing in different locations, then you might want to use the
> bin file referencing techniques discussed later in this chapter.

Creating the Web Project

In Visual Studio 2005, the way you create an ASP.NET project has changed. You no longer select File⇨
New⇨Project, and then select the ASP.NET Web Application Wizard. Instead, select File⇨New Web Site
and it will run the wizard automatically. The wizard provides three options: File, FTP, or HTTP. The
HTTP project requires IIS and is similar to what you are accustomed to with ASP.NET v1.1. It is a
common scenario to use a file-based approach during development and then use IIS for deployment.

The FTP option enables you to maintain files on a server and access them via FTP. This is a possible configuration for a shared environment where you want multiple people to be able to work on the project at
the same time. In addition, you could use the FTP setting to edit files remotely, where the remote server
IIS had a virtual directory mapped to where your FTP files resided. The biggest drawback to the FTP
option is that you lose the capability to use source control and risk multiple people in a team making
conflicting changes.

A file project is based on the physical directory in which you are working. Any file or folder created in or
copied into that directory and all subdirectories become a part of your project.

If you are using the File option and you launch the website from within Visual Studio, you will be using
the built-in Web server that comes with Visual Studio. You will quickly notice that you no longer have a
project file. Your Web project is made up of files that are in the folder identified as your Web project. IIS
is no longer required and it will not create a new IIS virtual application by default.

You may also notice that you don't have a web.config or a global.asax file created for you. While this depends on the template you chose, the goal in ASP.NET 2.0 is to create as few extra files as possible, enabling you to add them as you go along. For example, the first time you run the debugger or perform certain other actions, such as using the Web Administration application, the web.config file is created for you. The global.asax file will not be created unless you explicitly add it.

Excluding Files from Web Folders

One of the side effects that occurred in ASP.NET 2.0 as a result of not having a project file is the loss of the simple capability to exclude a file. To address this concern, the ASP.NET team added the capability to exclude a file from Visual Studio using the Exclude from Project or Include in Project menu option on the context menu for each Web folder item.

When an item is excluded from a Web folder, Visual Studio renames the item and appends .exclude, as shown in the following table:

Before exclude	After exclude
Default.aspx	Default.aspx.exclude
Default.aspx.cs	Default.aspx.cs.exclude

Although the item is excluded from the build process of the Web folder, it is not excluded from being managed by the source control provider. When a source-controlled item is excluded, you will be prompted whether the rename of the files should be reflected in the source control repository.

A Hack from the ASP.NET Team

This section could also be called "Late-Breaking Project News" because as we were completing our final review, the ASP.NET team, after a few months of work, unveiled an add-in that will create a new project model for Web applications. The reason for the new model is to address early feedback on the projectless model that was released with Visual Studio 2005. The biggest complaint with the new model introduced in the released version wasn't related to building new applications but migrating existing Visual Studio 2003 websites. A lot of the pain can be focused on the new compilation model that results in multiple assemblies. This caused more work than desired when migrating applications that were not expecting that level of isolation.

The new project model that will be released will not replace the one that shipped with Visual Studio 2005; it will be an additional option. The new model will behave very similarly to what people were used to in Visual Studio 2003:

❑   All code will be compiled into a single assembly in the \bin folder during each compile.

❑   All files will be defined in a project file; they will not be compiled if they just exist inside the folder.

❑ Unlike the new Web project model introduced when Visual Studio 2005 shipped, which required class files to reside only inside the `app_code` folder, you will be able to put standalone class files anywhere.

❑ Standard MSBuild compilation will be used and can be extended using the standard MSBuild extensibility.

Because the compilation model of this will be closer to the Visual Studio 2003 model, the converting and using of this model is expected to require fewer changes for existing applications. For new applications, you will have a choice, depending on the workflow and your style of development.

One area in which we expect this type of project will be used more often is to support the sharing of Web common user controls and Master Pages across projects. This is because the single assembly compilation model makes it ideal for easy referencing using the standard Visual Studio referencing.

At the time of publication, this option existed only in a preview release that Scott Guthrie, the head of the ASP.NET team, was hosting. You can read more about the preview on his site at `http://webproject .scottgu.com`.

Creating a Common Class Library Project

One of the more important decisions to make is whether you put all your code inside your website or put common code in a separate class library. Nothing stops you from putting standalone classes, utility classes, custom server controls, and data classes all inside the `App_Code` folder on your website.

The problem with putting everything inside a single Web project is apparent when you later have another project that needs to reference that same code. At that point, you have two options: You can either copy it, making the code redundant, or you can expend the effort to move the code to a common class library and update all references to it in your existing application. If you decided to duplicate the code, any fixes you made in one project would not show up in the other. You could move it to a shared library, but because you didn't set up a good namespace hierarchy you may have to change a lot of code to be able to use the new shared copy.

A better approach is to decide up front which code might be worth sharing across projects and then create a common library with as much code as possible in it. This new common library could be referenced not only by your current application but also by future applications.

To add a new class library to your solution, make sure you select the Solution Level in Solution Explorer; then select File⇨Add⇨New Project. If this is the first project you've added to your solution, beyond the website, the Solution Explorer will show the projects as branches under the solution.

Strategies vary regarding how many of these class libraries to create. Most of this depends on the size of both your project and your development team. The type of code you are sharing can also affect the decision as well. For example, if you are sharing database code and use two different database vendors, then you might want to put that code in two different libraries that are referenced using a provider model. Refer to Chapter 3 for more information about providers.

You should also keep dependencies in mind as you are creating the library, but the biggest thing you want to avoid is a circular reference. For example, it would be bad to create the following:

❏   Lib A depends on Lib B

❏   Lib B depends on Lib C

❏   Lib C depends on Lib A

Not only does this create complexity, if not errors, in the build process, it doesn't represent a strong architecture. Without getting into an in-depth discussion of architecture, one of the simpler ways to keep that from happening is by using the concept of layers, as shown in Figure 2-2. In the layer concept, all references are done downward, meaning that a library would never reference an item in a layer above it.

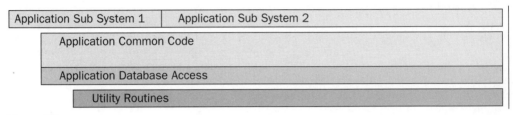

Figure 2-2

To put this example in more specific terms, a class in the Utility Routines would never access code in any of the other layers above it. A class in the Application Common Code, however, could access classes in the Application Database Access and Utility Routines libraries.

You can create any number of class libraries that you can include in your solution. For example, in this book we are going to create one that we call Common. Keep in mind that creating too many class libraries does increase the management of them, so find the balance between too few and too many. Often, using folders inside a class library can suffice, eliminating the need for separate libraries.

> **All projects that are part of a solution do not have to be written in the same language. Starting with Visual Studio 2005, you can now mix different language files within the same project.**

Selecting Namespaces

You should consider what namespaces you will use for your projects. One possibility is to select a namespace for a Web application similar to `CompanyName.ApplicationName`, as in `Wiley.MVPHacks`. You can also give reusable libraries a similar namespace, but make sure it is generic, rather than containing a specific application name. For example, if I had a library for handing accounting tasks, it could be named `Wiley.Accounting`.

Another common practice is to extend the namespace so that each folder within a project appends the folder name to the project-level namespace. This extends the intuitive nature of the folder structure for use in referencing the class from other projects.

Project files contain default namespace settings. Web projects don't have a project file, which means that you can't set a default namespace. However, if you add a class library to your solution, you will be able to set the default namespace for the class library. You can select Properties from the Class Library project node in Solution Explorer, select Application, and then set the Default Namespace field.

While setting the namespace on a class library, you might want to also consider the name given to the assembly. Naming your project Common might make sense because it is code common to the application, but that will cause the assembly name to be `common.dll`. A good practice is to have your assembly name match the project root namespace. For example, `Wiley.MVPHacks.Common` would have an assembly name of `Wiley.MVPHacks.Common.dll`. This reduces the chance that the name you choose will collide with third-party or other projects in your organization.

As we mentioned earlier, websites, by default, do not have a namespace specified when they are created new to Visual Studio 2005. If you are converting an existing site, all existing pages will retain the namespace that was in use, but new pages added will not have one added by default. Of course, nothing prevents you from manually adding one to the file. In addition, if you elect to use `app_Code` to store some classes, it is recommended that you still consider putting some form of a namespace on those classes if you think you might ever move them to a separate class library. This will prevent you from having to make extensive changes if you later make that decision.

Using Database Projects

Database projects are designed to hold SQL scripts, queries, and stored procedures. The Database Project is often one of the features of Visual Studio that developers don't know about unless they have been told about it by another developer. Make sure you don't confuse the Database Project, which is for SQL scripts, with a SQL Server Project (discussed in the next section of this chapter), which is used to store CLR Managed code that runs inside Microsoft SQL Server.

If you are not using a Database Project currently to store your scripts and stored procedures, you are probably just storing them in files and then applying them to SQL Server. If you are really living dangerously, you might just store your original copy inside SQL Server.

One of the great benefits of using a Database Project for storing stored procedures and other SQL scripts is the fact that the project can be included in a Visual Studio solution. This means that you can easily switch between your main project file and the Database project to access stored procedures. Additionally, when you do searches, your project can easily be included in the search results. Finally, an additional benefit is the capability to integrate with source control supported by Visual Studio and have version control on your stored procedures and SQL scripts.

Adding a Database Project to the solution you created previously in this chapter is easy. Using File➪New Project, expand the Other Project Types section. Then select the Database category. You will see the Database Project template shown in the template list, as shown in Figure 2-3.

If the default template is used it will create a few initial folders for you as part of the project setup. These folders are very generic and have names like "Queries," "Create Scripts," etc. These are just initial names and there is no requirement to use them. In fact, using names that are meaningful to your application will make the project more usable and maintainable.

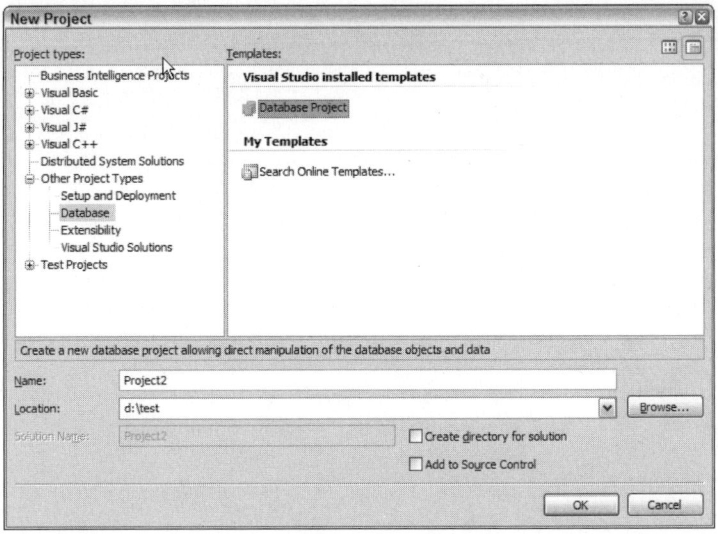

Figure 2-3

When using stored procedures, one approach that you could take is to partition your stored procedures into folders that are related to your database domain objects. For example, if you had several address-related stored procedures, you could create an `Address` folder and store them in there. It's important to note that while the project provides a folder hierarchy that you can use to partition your scripts, once they are run and applied to a database you lose the partitioning. Despite the fact that during development the procedures are in a nice meaningful folder hierarchy, SQL Server does not have a concept of folders, so after adding something to SQL Server you will see one big list.

While we are talking about what to put in which folder, another important question to think about is whether you have non-stored procedure scripts that you are also storing in the project — for example, the create/drop table script or one that refreshes data in the table. If you decide to store those also in the Database Project and store them in the same folder with stored procedures, it's possible you might end up running them when you don't intend to do so. This is a great way to test your backup from the night before! How can this happen? One of the features of the database project is the capability it offers you to select the items in the folder and click "run" or "run on" and have it run the script on the target database. If you have drop/create scripts mixed in the folders, then the unsuspecting team member selects all items and runs on the database thinking all they are doing is adding the stored procedures to the database. Surprise — time to find the backup!

Adding a Database Reference

When the database project is added to your solution, the wizard launches the Add Database Reference dialog box shown in Figure 2-4 to prompt selection of a database reference. The reference will be used when you perform actions on an item in your database project. A reference is not required to use a database project; you can decide to cancel this dialog and not select a reference at this time. The reference can also be added or removed at any point in the future. You are also able to have multiple references and select which one is the active one used for actions on the items in the project.

Figure 2-4

If you are adding a new reference, you will be promoted for the obvious information such as the server name. Additionally, you choose the type of authentication and whether you want to store the user and password. If possible, Windows Authentication provides the least intrusive way when working in a team environment. If you choose to use a user and password and do not allow that to be stored, each time you open the project you will be prompted.

Adding Existing Scripts

Existing scripts can easily be added into the database project by right-clicking a folder and selecting Add Existing. If the scripts are in a different location, a copy of them will be placed in the target folder.

If the existing scripts are not in files, you can take advantage of the Generate Script capabilities of the SQL Server administration tools. Make sure you select the option to put each object in a separate file. Many of the benefits provided by a database project are diminished if all objects are generated to a single file. Make sure you generate the files as Windows text, not ANSI; otherwise, you end up with some interesting characters in your scripts.

Using a SQL Server Project

One of the new features added in Microsoft SQL Server 2005 is the capability to create database objects such as stored procedures, user-defined functions, and user-defined types using managed code. Database objects implemented in managed code need to be added to a SQL Server Project. You might be tempted to just put classes that run in SQL Server as managed code as part of one of the application class libraries recommended previously in this chapter, but there are special references and characteristics of the SQL Server Project that make that type of project the only place you will want to put this type of code.

While a complete discussion of building managed database objects is beyond the scope of this book, it is mentioned here because this type of project might apply to the application you are building. While database objects written in managed code can provide great benefits and access to more complex language capabilities, they are not a requirement or a good fit for all applications. Careful thought should be given to the types of data access and manipulation your application does before venturing down this path.

Merely converting a Transact-SQL (T-SQL) stored procedure that runs a simple query would not be a good use of the managed database object capability. Conversely, using it where you are doing intense mathematical functions on every row in your result or in order to qualify your result set might be a better fit. Using managed database objects will provide you access to much richer language syntax and in many cases can result in more maintainable code than if you were to develop the equivalent database object using T-SQL

Deploying managed code database objects increases the complexity of an application when compared to deployment of Transact-SQL database objects. If you are using user-defined types and return them as part of the queries done in your application, pay special attention to versioning strategies and deployment to the database server and the calling application installation to ensure version compatibility.

Using Web Setup and Deploy Projects

In Chapter 12 you will look at the various options for deployment of your website. During setup, you might want to consider creation of either a Web Setup project or a Web Deployment project. By establishing your deployment model early on, you can put in place good practices up front, rather than wait until the week before deployment.

Creating Project References

Now that the solution has been set up and the initial projects have been added, it is time to create references so the Web project can see and utilize classes in the common library. If multiple libraries were added companywide or third-party libraries are being used, now is a good time to establish those references as well.

The following table describes the four types of references you can establish:

Type	Description
Project to Project	Used when a solution contains multiple projects and one project needs to reference another one from the same solution. This type of reference is updated automatically when you perform a build on your solution. This type of reference is recommended when the project is included in your solution. Visual Studio tracks this type of reference by adding the entry to the `ProjectReferences` tag inside your solution file. This means that if you were to also use this project in another solution and it had project-to-project references, they would have to be re-established.
Bin	This indicates that you are referencing a shared component located outside the application's `bin` directory and not registered with the GAC (Global Assembly Cache). These items are copied at the time of reference into the `bin` directory and only updated by default during a build. If you look in the folder in addition to the assembly, a `<assemblyname>.dll.refresh` file is created. If you were to look inside it would contain the reference to the location to pull a fresh copy. If this file is deleted, then a fresh copy will not be pulled during the build.

Table continued on following page

Type	Description
GAC	Items that are registered with the Global Assembly Cache (GAC) won't be copied into your project's bin folder. In the compilation section of your web.config file, a new entry is added to track the reference to the GAC component. Because this is not a copied file it is automatically updated to pick up the current version installed into the GAC.
Web Reference	This type of reference is used to track registration of a Web service. When a new Web reference is added, a new app_WebReferences folder is created, which contains the client proxy files that are generated. These types of references are updated only by selecting Update Web References in the folder inside the app_WebReferences folder in Visual Studio Solution Explorer.

Visual Studio 2005 changed the way to view and modify references on Web projects. In prior versions you were able to add and view references using the References tree node in Solution Explorer. This capability has been moved to the project Property Pages on the Web project. Figure 2-5 shows the new page that has been added to Property Pages, which enables you to view and modify your references. To get to the Property Pages, right-click on the website in Solution Explorer and select Properties.

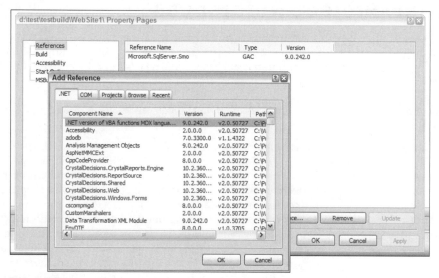

Figure 2-5

One of the things that might confuse you is why some assemblies such as System.Web do not need to be manually referenced but other System.* assemblies do. By default, in the system web.config file located in your framework installation directory, the following are part of the assemblies added as references by default:

```
<compilation defaultLanguage="c#" debug="true">
    <assemblies>
        <add assembly="System.Data.OracleClient, Version=2.0.0.0,
                Culture=neutral, PublicKeyToken=B77A5C561934E089"/>
    <add assembly="System.Design, Version=2.0.0.0, Culture=neutral,
                PublicKeyToken=B03F5F7F11D50A3A"/>
    </assemblies>
</compilation>
```

Think about how your class libraries will be used in deployment. If they are deployed with only a single application, using them as private assemblies is what you would normally do. In shared hosting or other environments where you don't have any control over the deployed machine, you'll have to deploy class libraries as private assemblies.

If your class library is being deployed to a machine on which many applications will use it, then you can use the Global Assembly Cache (GAC). This approach registers the assembly and the specific version of the assembly so applications can reference a common version. The advantage of this is that all applications reference the same copy; and if you update it (and maintain the same version number), they all get the updates at the same time. Oftentimes, though, the negatives of this approach outweigh the benefit achieved by the reduced duplication. For example, in production you often want to quickly patch a single application, rather than all applications that are using the module. Using the GAC you do not have this capability unless you version the control and create a new distinct version that only the application you want to patch references. This versioning can lead to complexity in referencing that assembly for other and future deployments. If the GAC is the chosen approach, the assembly must have a strong name applied to be registered in the GAC. Careful consideration should be given to ensure that the GAC is the appropriate place for your shared assemblies.

Using Source Control

Although there are several benefits to using some form of source control with your projects, the greatest benefit is the ability to work better as a team. Those who use source control can tell you about the countless times they have looked at the history of a file to see when or who made a change that caused a problem. It also provides a good way to recreate a specific version using labeling or similar capabilities to ensure that you can get all files that made up a specific version at any point in the future.

Right after you finish setup of a new project is usually the best time to think about using source control. After you have gone through setting up all the initial projects you use, consider putting your solution and associated projects under source control.

You have several source control providers to choose from and we will not attempt to discuss all of them in this book. The most common provider in the past was Visual Source Safe, which shipped with Visual Studio and products before that. New with Visual Studio 2005 is Team System, which provides a new source control capability that is intended for teams of five or more people. You can also find a number of third-party vendor solutions as well as open-source solutions.

A complete discussion of source control is beyond the scope of this book, but it is always recommended that, even on the small projects, you use some concept of source control to ensure the safety of your project source.

Using a Base Page Class

By default, all Web form pages in an ASP.NET application inherit from System.Web.UI.Page. This class implements the necessary functionality to act as an HttpHandler and is invoked by the ASP.NET runtime when it detects a request to invoke the specific page. Simplified, HttpHandlers are end points for processing the request. The Page class is a specific implementation of an HttpHandler designed to process and present Web forms. Chapter 17 shows examples of other ways you can implement HttpHandlers to accomplish other tasks.

When establishing the architecture patterns for building applications, finding ways to reduce redundancy and build in flexibility is always a high priority. One pattern that can be leveraged is the concept of defining a base page class that all your pages inherit from instead of System.Web.UI.Page. That way, even if you don't use it initially, you establish the plumbing that will allow adding properties and functionality that will be visible to all of your pages. This new base class will inherit from System.Web.UI.Page so that you don't have to re-invent the wheel and implement all the functionality in your new base page. By doing this, your new base page class will build on the capabilities of the System.Web.UI.Page class. Additionally, this will allow the new base class to have access to all protected properties, methods, and events of the system class.

The following example shows a minimal implementation of a BaseUIPage class:

```
/// <summary>
/// Base UI Page
/// </summary>
public class BaseUIPage : System.Web.UI.Page
{
 public BaseUIPage()
 {

 }
}
```

Even if this is all that is added to the class at this time, you will have established an extensibility point for your application. Once you have this in use, you can add a property, method, or event handler to the base page in the future and have it take effect across all the pages that use this base class.

The next step is adding a Web form to your application to modify the code-file for the Web form to inherit from your new BaseUIPage class. The following example shows a code-behind before changing to use the new BaseUIPage class:

```
'VB.Net example

Partial Class _Default
    Inherits System.Web.UI.Page

End Class

//C# Example
public partial class Default2 : System.Web.UI.Page
{
    protected void Page_Load(object sender, EventArgs e)
```

```
        {

        }
    }
```

The following is what the code will look like after you modify the code to use the new `BaseUIPage` class:

```
'VB.Net example

Partial Class _Default
    Inherits BaseUIPage

End Class

//C# Example
public partial class Default2 : BaseUIPage
{
    protected void Page_Load(object sender, EventArgs e)
    {

    }
}
```

At this point you are probably thinking that this sounds great but seems like extra work. Later in the chapter, you will see how you can use the export template capablity in Visual Studio 2005 to create a page template that you can use repeatedly to avoid the redundant changes. Specifically, the redundant change that can be avoided is having to change inheritance from `System.Web.UI.Page` to `BaseUIPage`.

Depending on the size and complexity of the application you are building, you may decide to implement more than one layer of base pages. For example, the lowest-level base page might be part of a utility class library that is non-application-specific. Inheriting from that might be one that is specific to the application being built. It can expose properties and methods that are more useful in the context of the application, such as exposing the `ActiveProductID`. Finally, if you have a set of pages that all do similar tasks, such as DataInput or SearchResults, then you could inherit from your application-specific base page to create one that is relevant for that set of pages. Each of these layers provides extensability points and can help you reduce redundancy across your pages.

Using Master Pages

Master Pages is one of the new features in ASP.NET 2.0 that is a great example of a "hack" that has been turned into a product feature. The goal of Master Pages is to define a layout template that will be used by your pages. Not all pages in an application have to use the Master Page, and it is possible and sometimes desirable to have the application use multiple Master Pages on different pages. A Master Page can define one or more `ContentPlaceHolder` regions so that a content page can either use the default content provided in the Master Page, or override and provide its own content. Web form pages become content pages when using the Master Page feature. Content pages only provide content to fill in the `ContentPlaceHolders` defined in the Master Page. Figure 2-6 shows an example of a Master Page that defines three content areas.

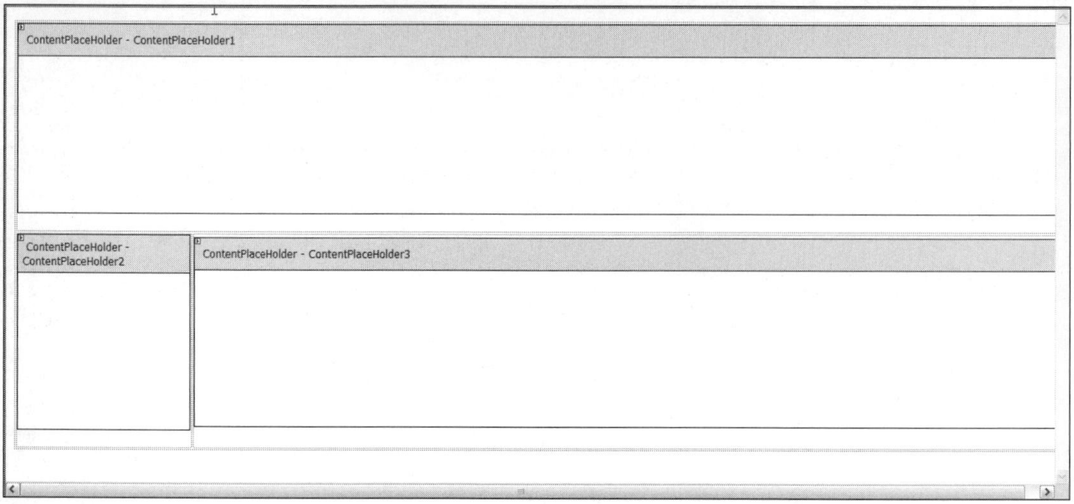

Figure 2-6

When you are setting up a new application it is important to decide whether you are going to use the Master Page concept. If you decide later in your development cycle, you will have to make modifications to each page to change it to a content page.

Creating a Master Page should be a joint effort with whoever handles the look and feel aspects of your applications. Because you will be defining ContentPlaceHolders that will affect the flexibility of your layout, some good thought should be given to the possible configurations your site might use.

If you were to look at the HTML markup for the example shown in Figure 2-6, you would notice that three PlaceHolder controls are used with standard HTML tables to organize them on the page. Figure 2-6 shows the HTML markup for the previous sample. Notice that the names of the content placeholders are ContentPlaceHolder1, 2, and 3. While there is nothing inherently wrong with just using the default names, we recommend picking names that better describe the use of the content region. This enables the developer who is looking at a content page to have a better idea of how that region was intended to be used. For example, the top region could have been called ContentTopNav to provide more clarity when used.

```
<form id="form1" runat="server">
    <div>
        <table width="100%">
            <tr>
                <td colspan="2">
                    <asp:ContentPlaceHolder ID="ContentPlaceHolder1" runat="server" />
                </td>
            </tr>
            <tr>
                <td width="200px">
                    <asp:ContentPlaceHolder ID="ContentPlaceHolder2" runat="server" />
                </td>
                <td>
                    <asp:ContentPlaceHolder ID="ContentPlaceHolder3" runat="server" />
```

```
            </td>
        </tr>
    </table>
    </div>
</form>
```

It is also possible to allow the Master Page, and therefore the layout of your site, to be modified dynamically at runtime. We discuss this in more detail in Chapter 17.

When using Master Pages, your page does not inherit from the Master Page; rather, it is merged with the Master Page to produce a composite output page. In fact, from your page class you can access the active Master Page using the `Page.Master` property. By default, that property is of type `System.Web.UI.MasterPage`.

You can add custom properties, methods, and events to your Master Page. Using the following page directive, you can modify the type of the property. The following example modifies the `Page.Master` property to `MVPHacks.BaseClasses.BaseMasterPage`:

```
<%@ MasterType TypeName="MVPHacks.BaseClasses.BaseMasterPage" %>

Or
<%@ MasterType VirtualPath="~/Masters/SiteMaster.master" %>
```

If the actual type of your Master Page is not of the type specified on the `MasterType` directive, you receive an error. For example, if you had exposed a property named `ActiveProductID` from your Master Page, then you could then access it using the strongly typed name, as shown in the following example:

```
this.Master.ActiveProductID=50;
```

Setting Up Your First Content Page

Now that you have set up the `BasePage` class and defined a Master Page that will define the layout of your content pages, it is time to use them. Content pages, unlike a typical Web form, will not have their own form element or other markup such as the `<head />` or `<body />`; they will simply have Content controls that reference the `ContentPlaceHolder` controls in your Master Page. The following example shows the HTML markup for a page using the Master Page defined in Figure 2-6:

```
<%@ Page Language="C#" MasterPageFile="~/MasterPage.master" AutoEventWireup="true"
CodeFile="Default2.aspx.cs" Inherits="Default2" Title="Untitled Page" %>
<asp:Content ID="Content1" ContentPlaceHolderID="ContentPlaceHolder1"
Runat="Server" >
</asp:Content>
<asp:Content ID="Content2" ContentPlaceHolderID="ContentPlaceHolder2"
Runat="Server" >
</asp:Content>
<asp:Content ID="Content3" ContentPlaceHolderID="ContentPlaceHolder3"
Runat="Server" >
</asp:Content>
```

As you can see, not much is actually defined in a content page. In the previous example, and by default, Visual Studio creates a Content control for each of the ContentPlaceHolders that are in your Master Page. If you did not intend to provide custom content, and you want to inherit or use the default content provided by the Master Page, then simply remove the Content control from the content page and it will automatically pick up the default content.

As mentioned earlier regarding the names for the ContentPlaceHolder controls, the ID value that is used will show in the designer to enable developers to know which region they are modifying. Accepting the default names will give you Content1, Content2, and Content3. Of course, that is pretty useless, and it is recommended that you change those to something more meaningful, such as TopNav, LeftNav, and MainContent. These values are a little more flexible regarding when you can change them; if you don't change the values of your ContentPlaceHolder names in the Master Page before you start creating content pages, you will have to update all your content pages. The ID values can be modified at any time without affecting the Master Page or other content pages.

There are basically four ways that you can get a content page. First, you can add a new Web form; and when the Add New Webform dialog box appears, it will ask you whether the page uses a Master Page. If Master Page is checked, the next dialog shown will allow you to pick which Master Page you want to reference, and it will add it to your page by referencing it in the MasterPageFile attribute on the Page tag, as shown in the preceding example code. Second, in the Page OnPreInit event handler, you can set the Master Page in your code. You will see this used later in Chapter 16, when we describe how to dynamically swap out Master Pages at runtime. Third, you can establish the Master Page in your web.config file, but the downside of this is that it will force all pages in your project to be content pages. Finally, there is always the hard way to do everything, which means converting an exsting page into a content page.

Now that you have completed setup of your first content page, you have a great model for applying the same changes to each page you add to the application. If you prefer a more automated approach, read the sections that discuss exporting templates later in this chapter.

Setting Up Themes

The look and feel of an application is often as important as its functionality. Master Pages addressed the layout of your pages; themes exist to provide flexibility with the look and feel. Simply stated, they provide a way to remove the style aspects from your page and your control definitions on the pages.

Using a theme you can define everything — from how a GridView should render to how a Logon Control should look. A theme consists of one or more style sheets, skin files, and any associated images. The concept of using one or more CSS style sheets still exists with themes, but now you can also define control style properties using the skin files.

Skins are files that enable you to put a control definition in them, minus the functional/behavior properties such as ProductID=5. This control definition acts like a template and when you use that control on a page that references the theme, the skin is applied to the control.

Themes are local to a project and stored in a special ASP.NET folder named App_Themes or they can be stored in the global theme directory. In the App_Themes folder you can have one or more themes folders defined. The theme can be set on the Page tag using the Theme attribute, via the Page OnPreInit event handler or in the web.config file.

You certainly are not required to use themes, but they make it easier for you to apply styles to each page; and they certainly are better than including style inline in the page. In ASP.NET 1.1, it was quite common to use a CSS file that you had to then include a reference to in each page. Even if you do nothing else but still use CSS and do it via the theme infrastructure, the include of that CSS file will be done automatically for you.

Skins or CSS?

You might be wondering when you should use CSS and when you should use a skin file. There is no single right answer to that question but there are some advantages that the skin files bring to the table. When you use CSS, you are limited to customizing the style based on the rendered version of the control. The CSS constructs have no concept of understanding the custom properties some controls have. Skin files work by taking the attributes specified on the tag in the skin file, and at page render time those properties are set on the corresponding control on the page. That accomplishes two things: First, it makes it easier to modify all GridView controls without having to add a specific class name on it everywhere you use one. By default, unless you use SkinIDs to specify particular skins, a GridView skin specification will apply to all GridViews on pages that are theme enabled (the default). Second, if you use skins, it is clearer what properties are being set on the control, so it is easier to know what you will get on output.

Building Your Skin Files

One of the tricks to start building your skin files is to leverage the Auto Format capability that is built into Visual Studio 2005. On many of the controls, right-clicking and selecting Auto Format will allow you to pick from several styles and then set those properties on the control. You can then copy that into a skin file, remove any properties that are more behavior related, and you have a great starting point for your skin file.

Naming the Skin File

Nothing says that you can't just create a skin file called `myskins.skin` or whatever you want. One useful technique for quickly locating a skin would be to name the skin file with a similar name to the control that is being skinned. For example, the GridView skin file would be `GridView.skin`.

Themes offer a powerful way to further allow customization of the look and feel of the site. When combined with Master Pages, and if you take the time to allow users to choose both and modify them on-the-fly, you offer users a level of customization they are not typically accustomed to.

Tips for Converting from 1.x to 2.0

Visual Web Developer 2005 has an automated wizard to convert your legacy ASP.NET 1.1 applications to ASP.NET 2.0. For the simplest scenarios, this works great. However, there are several things you need to know to avoid trouble. ASP.NET 2.0 has specially named directories, files are moved, and other transformations occur during the process. To keep things organized, see Chapter 12 for more information about the specifics of the conversion process and differences between versions.

Web Config and Your Team

One of the areas that can cause conflict when doing team development is the settings in your `web.config` file. Many of the items are generic and all team members would use them—for example, things such as registering controls, or the providers that are being used, or even the `HttpHandlers` or `HttpModules`. While not impossible to imagine times where different team members would have their own `web.config` settings, it is much more common that the application settings or connection strings are specific to a team member.

The Sledgehammer Approach

The `appSettings` and `connectionStrings` sections typically cause the most contention between team members. The most simplistic sledgehammer method for avoiding this problem is for the `web.config` that is checked into source control to have the settings that would be appropriate for most team members. The team member who needs specific settings would then create a local writable copy of the file and modify the settings. Probably the biggest drawback of this method is that the first time the user gets the latest set of files from source control, he or she will be prompted each time to replace the file. One accidental click and all their customization is gone.

External File Approach

Another common option is to store these settings in an external file that the user keeps local. These files are included using appropriate references in the `web.config`, which we will discuss shortly. Prior to Visual Studio 2005, these files could be stored in the website folder. If you do this in Visual Studio 2005, though, the file will be checked into source control, defeating the purpose of enabling team members to have their own settings. To work around this change, the files can be stored in the parent directory. It's often a good idea to keep a sample of the files in the project that is the master, which team members can copy. This is especially useful when you are setting up a new team member or redoing your environment.

The `appSettings` section is handled slightly differently than the `connectionStrings` section with respect to how the file is referenced for including. The following example shows how to specify that you are including from a file named `localhost.config` that is in the parent directory:

```
<appSettings file="..\localhost.config">
```

If you were to look at the `localhost.config` file contents, it would pretty much mimic what you would expect the `appSettings` section to look like, as shown in the following example:

```
<appSettings>
 <add key="DefaultDaysLate" value="7" />
</appSettings>
```

While we chose `localhost.config` for the name of the file, what to call it is completely up to you.

Including the `connectionStrings` section is only slightly different. Instead of using the `file` attribute to specify the filename, the `configSource` attribute is used, as shown in the following example:

```
<connectionStrings configSource="..\localhostConnectionStrings.config"/>
```

Again, if we were to look at the contents of `localhostConnectionStrings.config`, it would look like the following example:

```
<connectionStrings >
 <add    name="MyDB"
    connectionString="server=myServer;uid=myuser;password=***;database=MyDB" />
</connectionStrings>
```

These are just a couple of approaches, and clearly there are many options for managing project settings. Each of these approaches has pros and cons. For example, having all team members share the same checked-in files, which is the default, ensures that all members get the latest settings. That said, it is also common for someone to be surprised by another person making modifications to the settings and not telling them. That same problem can also happen in the reverse: When each member has their own local copy, they might not be informed of a critical setting change that another team member made. Like many things in life, you just have to decide what works best for your project and go with it.

Exporting a Template

New in Visual Studio 2005 is the capability to export a template for use later when you are creating new projects or new items in an existing project. Using this wizard you can create templates that are either whole projects or project items such as a new page or a new class.

Some of the modifications in this chapter are an excellent example of where this type of automation would help. For example, with the `BaseUIPage` and Master Pages, we could create an example Web form that inherits from `BaseUIPage` and also references our `Site.Master` file. Then, using the File⇨Export Template menu option in Visual Studio 2005, we could create a reusable template that all members of our team could use to create new Web form pages that looked just like our example. Using this technique we could save several hours and ensure that our pages are more consistent. Chapter 13 delves more deeply into how templates work and how you can leverage them.

Wrapping Up

One chance, and then it becomes more work!

At the beginning of each new project, you get only one chance to get started with a solid foundation. The purpose of this chapter is to illustrate some techniques that could be adopted as best practices for setting up a new project.

Ideally, as you and your development team find what works for your projects, you will create your own set of best practices, modified to work within your environment.

3

The Power of Providers

One of the new features that is prevalent throughout ASP.NET 2.0, and which provides an increased level of extensibility, is the *provider model*. The concept of a provider model really isn't new, but for the first time it has been packaged up as part of the base .NET Framework.

In the past, for all the various services of ASP.NET, such as session or cache management, when you wanted to customize it, very few extensibility points existed to which you could plug in your own solution. A key focus of the ASP.NET team in release 2.0 was to provide more extensibility points to enable developers to provide custom implementation of core functionality and features of ASP.NET.

For example, take the session management capability (which has been there since ASP.NET 1.0 and provided support for storing in process, State Server, as well as in a SQL Server database, but provided no capability to customize it beyond that without extraordinary measures). In ASP.NET 2.0, the session management capability can be replaced in its entirety, and you can provide your own custom storage of the data in whatever store you want.

Those capabilities are not limited to just the session store; several new providers are introduced in ASP.NET 2.0 for services such as Membership, Roles, Profile, and Personalization. Each of these use the concept of a provider model as well and are completely extensible.

Additionally, you can use the provider model concept to build your own plug-and-play services for your application. This is a great technique to use when you have different implementations — for example, one that uses XML files and another that uses SQL Server. This is a great technique for independent software vendors (ISVs) and others who build applications that will be used by other companies. By using the provider concept, ISVs enable their customers to have similar extensibility points.

In this chapter, we will explore some of the fundamental extensibility points that exist. We will also discuss how you can use the provider model to create your own provider-based solution that would enable end users of your application or other development teams to ultimately plug in their own implementation of your provider model–based service.

What Is the Provider Model?

Simply put, the goal of the provider model is to provide a way to allow applications to define a set of methods with which it can interact allowing for multiple implementations. It is also used to hide from the application knowledge of the implementation that is used. The application should be unaware that through configuration file options that a SQL Server implementation is in use instead of a simple XML file.

At this point you are probably wondering why you couldn't just use an interface for that. Technically, using an interface could accomplish providing a contract for the methods that will be available and for multiple implementations. Using interfaces, though, you end up with a more rigid structure because the interface is intended to be an irrevocable contract of methods and properties that will be provided. The provider model concept is built around the concept of class inheritance from `ProviderBase`, which is now part of the `System.Configuration.Provider` namespace in the `System.Configuration` assembly. `ProviderBase` is an abstract class intended to be inherited from, inherited by implementers of providers. This class is very simple and provides only a few methods and properties that would be useful in most providers. The following table describes the key methods and properties of the `ProviderBase` class.

Property	Description
Name	Intended to return the name of the provider. Will be pulled from the configuration entry for the provider `<add name="MyProviderName" />`
Description	Provides a fuller text description of the provider. Useful if a list of providers is given for a selection.

Method	Description
Initialize	Called to initialize the provider, and passed the name of the provider and a NameValueCollection to allow access to the provider-specific attributes specified on the configuration

Providers That Come with ASP.NET 2.0

Out of the box, ASP.NET 2.0 comes with several features that implement and leverage the provider model concept. Most of these implement capabilities that result in retrieval and storage of data from a data store. For example, the `MembershipProvider` class establishes the contract that is used to manage users. Like several of the other providers, ASP.NET 2.0 comes with controls that are designed to work with the `MembershipProvider` that is configured in the application. These controls work because they can depend on the configured provider to implement a consistent set of methods that are defined on `MembershipProvider`.

Like `ProviderBase`, the `MembershipProvider` class is also an abstract class and provides the contract or method/property definition only for membership management. To make it usable out of the box, the ASP.NET team provides `SqlMembershipProvider`, which inherits from `MembershipProvider` and provides a concrete implementation of the `MembershipProvider` contract. In the following example, ASP.NET learns which `MembershipProvider` is active by using configuration information in `web.config` or `machine.config` to identify and load the appropriate provider. If you were to look in the `machine.config` file and search on membership, you would find the default configuration for the `MembershipProvider`. The following example is the default from the `machine.config` file for the `MemberShipProvider`:

```
<system.web>
 <membership>
  <providers>
      <add name="AspNetSqlMembershipProvider"
type="System.Web.Security.SqlMembershipProvider, System.Web, Version=2.0.0.0,
Culture=neutral, PublicKeyToken=b03f5f7f11d50a3a"
connectionStringName="LocalSqlServer" enablePasswordRetrieval="false"
enablePasswordReset="true" requiresQuestionAndAnswer="true" applicationName="/"
requiresUniqueEmail="false" passwordFormat="Hashed" maxInvalidPasswordAttempts="5"
minRequiredPasswordLength="7" minRequiredNonalphanumericCharacters="1"
passwordAttemptWindow="10" passwordStrengthRegularExpression="" />
  </providers>
 </membership>
</system.web>
```

This configuration entry tells ASP.NET about the `SqlMembershipProvider` class and passes various settings to the provider to control the provider's behaviors. The purpose of this example is not to dissect each of the parameters passed to the provider but to demystify how the membership provider works with the default installation. Each of these parameters can be modified in your application's local `web.config` file, and the MSDN documentation provides detailed information on each of their possible settings. Later in the chapter you will see how you can access those settings if you were building your own provider.

You will find similar configuration entries in the `machine.config` file for other built-in provider model–supported features within ASP.NET.

The following table describes ASP.NET's built-in provider model features and their implementations.

Provider Type	Description
Membership	Manages users and comes with two providers in the `System.Web.Security` namespace: `SqlMembershipProvider` and `ActiveDirectoryMembershipProvider`.
Role	Manages roles associated with users and has three built-in providers in the `System.Web.Security` namespace: `AuthorizationStoreRoleProvider`, `SqlRoleProvider`, and `WindowsTokenRoleProvider`.
Site Map	Used to feed site map controls and comes with only a single built-in provider: `System.Web.XmlSiteMapProvider`.

Table continued on following page

Provider Type	Description
`Session State`	Allows for managing session state for a site user — providers match and expose capabilities that are similar to those found in ASP.NET 1.1. However, now users can extend or replace with their own session state provider. Session state providers can be found in the `System.Web.SessionState` namespace. `InProcSession StateStore`, `OutOfProcSessionStateStore`, and `SqlSessionStateStore` implement the session state providers.
`Profile`	`System.Web.Profile.SqlProfileProvider` provides a SQL Server implementation to store user profile entries. Look for a future one to become available that will allow you to map normal database tables to profile entries.
`Web Event`	Web Event providers allow for externalization or publishing of Web events. Found in `System.Web.Management`. The following are built-in providers: `EventLogWebEventProvider`, `SimpleMailWebEvent Provider`, `TemplateMailWebEventProvider`, `Sql WebEventProvider`,`TraceWebEventProvider`, and `WmiWebEventProvider`.
`Web Part Personalization`	Handles saving locations and other personalization options for Web parts, which are found in the `System.Web.UI.WebControls.WebParts` namespace. `SqlPersonalizationProvider` is the only built-in provider.
`Protected Configuration`	Provides for protection of configuration sections in the application configuration files. Two providers are built in: `DPAPIProtectedConfigurationProvider` and `RSAProtectedConfigurationProvider`.

Before we start discussing how you can build your own providers and extend the built-in providers, let's cover one of the more common questions that come up, which is "How do I get my application to use something other than the local SQLExpress instance?" In the preceding example of the `Membership Provider` configuration, there is an entry for the connection string `LocalSqlServer`. A quick look into `machine.config` would also reveal its definition, as shown in the following markup:

```
<connectionStrings>
    <add name="LocalSqlServer" connectionString="data
source=.\SQLEXPRESS;Integrated
        Security=SSPI;AttachDBFilename=|DataDirectory|aspnetdb.mdf;User
Instance=true"
        providerName="System.Data.SqlClient" />
</connectionStrings>
```

Note that this affects all the SQL Server implementations of the providers that come with ASP.NET, so changing it would result in changing it for any of the providers that use the SQL Server versions unless you had changed their configuration sections to have a different connectionStringName specified.

If you want to point to a different SQL Server instance, you can simply clear out the existing connection or remove it and add your own, as you can see in the following example:

```
<connectionStrings>
   <clear/>
   <add name="LocalSqlServer" connectionString="Data Source=ctcdev2;Initial
Catalog=MyDB;Integrated Security=True" providerName="System.Data.SqlClient" />
 </connectionStrings>
```

The other thing that you might want to do is use the built-in providers with your existing database. In the .NET Framework 2.0 installation directory is a utility, aspnet_regsql.exe, that will set up the necessary database tables and stored procedures that support the built-in SQL version of all the providers.

Extending a Built-in Provider

One of the simplest ways to extend the providers is to inherit from one of the built-in implementations such as SqlMembershipProvider. While there are several reasons why you might want to do this, the reason we are going to demonstrate limits the hours during which a user can log in. To do this, we are going to inherit from the built-in provider and then override the ValidateUser method to implement our hour limits.

Inheriting from SqlMembershipProvider

The first step to accomplish this is to create a class and inherit it from the existing SqlMembership Provider. The following code example shows how this is done:

```
namespace MVPHacks.Security
{
    /// <summary>
    /// Summary description for MVPHacksSQLMembershipProvider
    /// </summary>
    public class MVPHacksSQLMembershipProvider :
System.Web.Security.SqlMembershipProvider
    {
        public MVPHacksSQLMembershipProvider()
        {

        }
    }
}
```

Configuring Your New Provider

Once this is accomplished you can modify your web.config file to enable your application to use your newly built provider. Because it will act just like the built-in one at this point, you can go ahead and edit the web.config file as shown here:

```
<membership defaultProvider="MVPHacksMembershipProvider" >
    <providers>
        <add name="MVPHacksMembershipProvider"
             connectionStringName="LocalSqlServer"
             type="MVPHacks.Security.MVPHacksSqlMembershipProvider"/>
    </providers>
</membership>
```

If you happen to put your custom class in the app_code folder, you may need to use the following syntax for the assembly name when you reference it:

```
<membership defaultProvider="MVPHacksMembershipProvider" >
    <providers>
        <add name="MVPHacksMembershipProvider"
type="MVPHacks.Security.MVPHacksSqlMembershipProvider, app_code"/>
    </providers>
</membership>
```

Notice that app_code was added after the fully qualified class name. This allows the type to be instanced by the provider from the app_code assembly that is built on-the-fly when you run your website. If you had placed the class in a common assembly, it would add that assembly name instead, e.g., namespace.classname,mycommoncode.

Checking Your Provider Configuration

Now you should be able to run a quick test on the application to make sure you haven't broken anything. Also, if you bring up the Web Site Administration. Tool (by selecting the Visual Studio 2005 WebSite menu and then the ASP.NET Configuration option) and go to the Provider tab, you would see that your provider is now selectable as a membership provider (see Figure 3-1).

Figure 3-1

Overriding ValidateUser

When a user attempts to log in, the `ValidateUser` method is called by the Login control. You need to implement a check to determine whether the login is between business hours and only allow login if that is the case:

```
public override bool ValidateUser(string username, string password)
{

    if ((DateTime.Now.Hour > 18) || (DateTime.Now.Hour < 6))
        return false;

    return base.ValidateUser(username, password);
}
```

In the preceding example, while we accomplish the goal of limiting the hours during which the user can log in, we provide very little flexibility for controlling the hours. While we could simply use `appSettings`, another available option with the provider is overriding the `Initialize` method. The `Initialize` method is called and passed as a `NameValueCollection` to all the attributes in the membership provider's `add` statement. The following example includes the Start and End hours that we will intercept in our provider:

```
<membership defaultProvider="MVPHacksMembershipProvider">   <providers>
    <add connectionStringName="LocalSqlServer" name="MVPHacksMembershipProvider"
        NoLoginStartHour="2" NoLoginEndHour="10"
         type="MVPHacks.Security.MVPHacksSqlMembershipProvider,MVPHacksCommon"/>
    </providers>
</membership>
```

The next step is to override the `Initialize` methods and look for the values for the Start and End hours:

```
private int m_StartHour = 24;
private int m_EndHour = 24;

public override void Initialize(string name, NameValueCollection config)
{
    if (config["NoLoginStartHour"] != null)
    {
        m_StartHour = int.Parse(config["NoLoginStartHour"].ToString());
        config.Remove("NoLoginStartHour");
    }

    if (config["NoLoginEndHour"] != null)
    {
        m_EndHour = int.Parse(config["NoLoginEndHour"].ToString());
        config.Remove("NoLoginEndHour");
    }

    base.Initialize(name, config);
}
```

It's important to note that in the preceding example, you remove the parameter prior to calling the `base.Initialize` method because the built-in providers will throw an exception if they are passed attributes they are not familiar with. Removing them prior to calling the `base.Initialize` method enables you to leverage the configuration properties without extensive customization. Furthermore, because you inherit from the existing SQL provider, you don't have to re-implement any of the other logic.

The following example shows our revised method, which uses the values that we obtained from the configuration entry:

```
public override bool ValidateUser(string username, string password)
        {

                if ((DateTime.Now.Hour >= m_StartHour) && (DateTime.Now.Hour <=
m_EndHour))
                    return false;

                return base.ValidateUser(username, password);
        }
```

While this is a rather simplistic example, it does show how easy it is to leverage the built-in providers to add additional business requirements needed by your application but without having to re-implement the full capabilities that have been provided.

Building Your Own Membership Provider

One of the options that you have with the built-in providers is to implement a custom class that implements the contract of the provider. A common reason for doing that would be so that you could control the storage of the provider data. For example, by default the `Membership` provider is an interface to ASP.NET's membership service, which stores data in proprietary ASP.NET tables in a data store. Many existing applications already have the concept of membership tables, and replacing them to leverage some of the built-in controls that work with the membership provider would be a lot of work for little reward. However, by creating a class that implements key methods of the `MembershipProvider` class, you can have the custom class perform the membership operations against your existing data store. This type of customization is not just limited to working against a database; you could also call third-party vendor APIs from the custom class.

In our last example, we started by inheriting from `SqlMembershipProvider` and overriding the `ValidateUser` method to inject some of our own logic. We used the existing features of storing in a SQL Server database. In this next example, we are going to start from scratch and just use the contract provided by the `MembershipProvider` class. Therefore, we will inherit from `MembershipProvider` instead of from `SqlMembershipProvider`:

```
namespace MVPHacks.Security
{
    /// <summary>
    /// Summary description for MVPHacksCustomMembershipProvider
    /// </summary>
    public class MVPHacksCustomMembershipProvider :
System.Web.Security.MembershipProvider
```

```
        {
            public MVPHacksCustomMembershipProvider()
            {

            }
        }
    }
```

> **Watch out if you are creating your classes inside a common class library; by default, when the class is added to the project, "public" is not specified on the class declaration. It is therefore a private class and won't be accessible outside that class library. This can cause you grief when you try to reference or use that class in the Web project or web config and it claims it can't find the class that you know you just created!**

One of the nice features of Visual Studio 2005 is its ability to easily allow you to create a skeleton implementation of an abstract class or interface. As shown in Figure 3-2, simply clicking the little line under the first letter in the class or namespace being inherited presents a drop-down list of options from which you can select to have Visual Studio 2005 create a skeleton implementation for you.

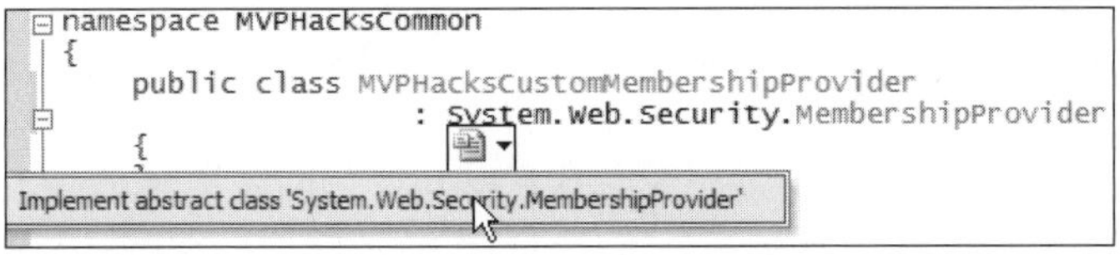

```
namespace MVPHacksCommon
{
    public class MVPHacksCustomMembershipProvider
                    : System.Web.Security.MembershipProvider
    {

        Implement abstract class 'System.Web.Security.MembershipProvider'
```

Figure 3-2

Once you do this for the membership provider, each of the properties or methods that are `abstract` (C#) or `MustInherit` (VB.NET) on the class will be stubbed out for you in the file and will contain one line that will throw an exception stating "The method or operation is not implemented." This is a great help because it saves you time looking at the documentation and trying to figure out what methods you must implement or have defined in your class. In addition, with providers, it is OK not to implement all the methods; it may simply throw a `NotSupportedException` to indicate to the caller that the active provider does not support that property or method.

The following is partial output of what Visual Studio 2005 would generate when you select the implement option:

```
public class MVPHacksCustomMembershipProvider
    : System.Web.Security.MembershipProvider
{
        public override string ApplicationName
        {
            get{throw new Exception("The method or operation is not
                    implemented.");}
            set{throw new Exception("The method or operation is not
                    implemented.");}
        }
        public override bool ChangePassword(string username,
                    string oldPassword, string newPassword)
```

```
        {
            throw new Exception("The method or operation is not implemented.");
        }

    }
```

You can try this in your own sample to see all of the methods and properties—again, we have shortened it here for clarity. One of the things you probably want to do is change any of the methods you won't implement from throwing a generic exception to throwing `NotSupportedException`. That way, someone using the implementation has a consistent and clean way of detecting at runtime whether you implemented a particular method.

Before:

```
public override bool ChangePassword(string username,
                    string oldPassword, string newPassword)
    {
        throw new Exception("The method or operation is not implemented.");
    }
```

After:

```
public override bool ChangePassword(string username,
                    string oldPassword, string newPassword)
    {
        throw new NotSupportedException();
    }
```

The easiest way to accomplish this is doing a Quick Replace on the `Exception("The method or operation is not implemented.");` string with `NotSupported();` This change makes the non-implemented methods more consistent with the provider concept of allowing the user to be notified with a consistent exception for unsupported methods.

Next let's look at a very simple class that will simulate your existing authentication manager. Remember that the purpose here is to demonstrate the concept, not to provide a full-blown custom provider. In fact, this demonstrates a great way to simply add login behavior to an ASP.NET application for which you have existing security but want to use the built-in login control. In this example, with only a few lines of code and some configuration, we can have a login capability to the site talking to our existing security manager:

```
Namespace MVPHacks.CustomAuthentication
{
    public class ExistingAuthManager
    {
        public bool ValidateUser(string username, string password)
        {
            if (string.Compare(username, "mvphacks", true) != 0)
                return false;
            if (string.Compare(password, "mvphacks", true) != 0)
                return false;

            return true;
```

```
            }
        }
    }
```

The next step is to modify our custom `MembershipProvider` class to call that when the `ValidateUser` method is called. The following is all the code required to accomplish that:

```
public override bool ValidateUser(string username, string password)
    {
        ExistingAuthManager authMgr = new ExistingAuthManager();
        return authMgr.ValidateUser(username, password);
    }
```

You might have noticed that our namespace for the `ExistingAuthManager` is different from our custom `MembershipProvider` class. Because that is the case, we need to add a `using` (C#) statement or `imports` (VB.NET) statement for that namespace to our custom `MembershipProvider` class. Did you know that there's an easy way to do that in Visual Studio 2005? As you can see in Figure 3-3, clicking on the line under the last character in the class name will bring up the automation that will add the `using` statement for you.

Figure 3-3

Keep your eye out for other quick automation features like the one shown in Figure 3-3 that were added to Visual Studio 2005 — many of them are very simple in their implementation like this and can easily be passed over.

Now that we have implemented the single method in the class to call `ExistingAuthManager`, which is simulating an existing security manager in an application, we can now proceed to configure the provider in the `web.config`. As you can see, this is very similar to what we did when we extended the `SqlMembershipProvider`:

```
<membership defaultProvider="MVPHacksMembershipProvider">
    <providers>
        <add connectionStringName="LocalSqlServer" name="MVPHacksMembershipProvider"
            type="MVPHacks.Security.MVPHacksCustomMembershipProvider,MVPHacksCommon"/>
    </providers>
</membership>
```

The other `web.config` change we will make to get this to work is configuration of the authentication and authorization sections, as shown here:

```
<authentication mode="Forms">
    <forms loginUrl="/user/login.aspx"></forms>
</authentication>
```

```
<authorization>
      <deny users="?"/>
</authorization>
```

The preceding example requires all unauthenticated users to be transferred to the `loginUrl` page specified. As a side note, `loginUrl` is not required for this example, but people often assume that when using forms authentication you have to put the login page in the root of the site.

Building the login page is now a simple drag and drop process. After adding the `login.aspx` form to our user folder we can simply drag the Login control from the Login section on the Toolbox onto our page, as shown in Figure 3-4. While there are a number of properties that could be configured, they are beyond the scope of this chapter. You would want to configure the `DestinationPage` property to point to `default.aspx` or some other landing page after login is completed.

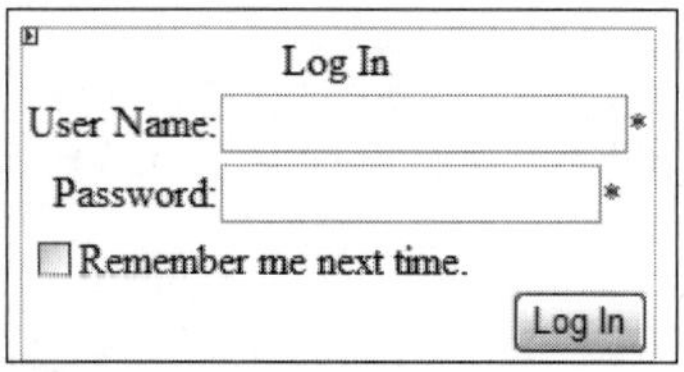

Figure 3-4

One of the nice things now is that you can also take advantage of the LoginStatus, LoginName, and LoginView controls as well without doing any additional work.

You could also implement the methods to create a user and perform other membership operations, and continue to take advantage of the other built-in controls such as the Create User Wizard.

If you want to dive deeper into some more examples of providers that are based on the built-in Membership, Role Manager, Profile, and Web Part Personalization providers, you should visit the Microsoft ASP.NET Developer Center and download the Sample Access Provider Start Kit (`http://msdn.microsoft .com/asp.net/downloads/providers/`). This kit is a C# class library project that has implemented each of those providers to work with Microsoft Access as the storage medium. While an Access-based provider probably isn't the support you are looking for, it provides a specific example of how to implement a more complete replacement of a provider based on an existing built-in model.

Also available are detailed whitepapers that discuss each of the built-in providers and various details of their implementations.

Building Your Own Role Provider

The role provider is another provider that can also be easily replaced to facilitate your custom store. In fact, in many applications the role of a user is dynamic and inferred based on current state or attributes, and is not persisted. In that type of usage, the built-in role providers would not be adequate. Additionally, like the membership provider, you may already have your own concept of roles in your application, and having a way to expose them to various controls such as the LoginView would enable you to leverage them without writing extensive custom code.

In our example for this section, we are going to build a read-only role provider. Its sole purpose is to allow us to use existing user/role associations in our applications. Specifically, we want to be able to use the LoginView control and specify a view for specific roles a user might have.

As we did earlier when we implemented a custom membership provider, we are going to inherit our custom role provider from the built-in RoleProvider class, as shown in the following example:

```
using System;
using System.Collections.Generic;
using System.Text;
namespace MVPHacks.Security
{
    public class MVPHacksCustomRoleProvider: System.Web.Security.RoleProvider
    {


        public override string[] GetRolesForUser(string username)
        {
            string[] noRoles = { };
            string[] adminRoles = { "admin" };

            if (username == "mvphacks")
                return adminRoles;

            return noRoles;

        }

        public override string[] GetUsersInRole(string roleName)
        {
            throw new NotSupportedException();
        }
        Other non implemented methods removed to conserve space...
    }
}
```

In the preceding example we also had Visual Studio 2005 implement stubs for each method and property, as you saw in Figure 3-2. Next, we changed all of the generic exceptions to the NotSupported Exception, and finally we implemented the GetRolesForUser method. This is the one method that LoginView uses to determine which template it should use to display content on a page. You will see how to identify roles to the LoginView later in the chapter.

In order for our new custom role provider to be used, we must configure it in the web.config file, as shown in the following example:

```
<roleManager defaultProvider="MVPHacksRoleProvider" enabled="true">
    <providers>
        <add name="MVPHacksRoleProvider"
            type="MVPHacks.Security.MVPHacksCustomRoleProvider,MVPHacksCommon"/>
    </providers>
</roleManager>
```

> Make sure you include the `enabled="true"`; otherwise, it will appear as though your role provider is not working.

Now, with the configuration in place, we can modify a page to have a LoginView control that uses the roles of the user to determine what to show.

The LoginView control is designed to enable you to have different templates that show content to users based on their status as either a logged in or an anonymous user. The following example shows what the LoginView control markup would look like with those two templates:

```
<asp:LoginView ID="LoginView1" runat="server">
        <LoggedInTemplate>
            Logged In Users See This Content
        </LoggedInTemplate>
        <AnonymousTemplate>
            Anonymous Users See This Content
        </AnonymousTemplate>
</asp:LoginView>
```

When combined with roles, the LoginView control becomes even more powerful. What if we wanted to display different content to users based on the roles they have? LoginView allows us to do that by adding a `RoleGroups` section to the preceding markup. Inside the `RoleGroups` section, you identify one or more `RoleGroup` elements that identify the roles and the content template that should be used. The following is an example defining an Admin RoleGroup:

```
<asp:LoginView ID="LoginView1" runat="server">
        <LoggedInTemplate>
            Logged In Users See This Content
        </LoggedInTemplate>
        <AnonymousTemplate>
            Anonymous Users See This Content
        </AnonymousTemplate>
        <RoleGroups>
            <asp:RoleGroup Roles="Admin">
                <ContentTemplate>
                    This is the admin view
                </ContentTemplate>
            </asp:RoleGroup>
        </RoleGroups>
</asp:LoginView>
```

Because the LoginView depends on the RoleProvider contract definition, it doesn't care whether it's getting the role information from the built-in providers, e.g., `SqlRoleProvider`, or from the custom role provider we built in this chapter.

Building a Role Provider Proxy

The capability to extend the existing role providers or to build your own provides a lot of flexibility. One limitation that you might encounter is when your application depends on roles from multiple sources.

For example, maybe you have some roles that you wish to pull from the `SqlMembershipRoleProvider` but you also have a concept of your own roles. Your own roles might be static roles assigned to a user and stored inside an existing business database. You could simply inherit from `SqlMembershipRoleProvider` and add your own roles, but that would limit you to only working with the `SqlMembershipRoleProvider`, and what happens when you want to use a great third-party role provider for a portion of your role management?

The concept we will discuss now is a *role provider proxy*. The role provider proxy will act as the go-between of all the configured providers. Using this concept you could implement various role providers and use them all together in your applications for things such as LoginViews or other controls that leverage roles.

One up-front limitation of this approach is that when you are using the `RoleProviderProxy`, you need to either specify a default provider to use for add and update requests or reference a specific provider in your code. Otherwise, the `RoleProviderProxy` won't know which provider to interact with.

In the following example, we are going to leverage the simple role provider that we built earlier in the chapter. In fact, since we need two role providers to proxy, we will clone that one for simplicity as `MVPHacksCustomRoleProvider2`. One of the nice things about the proxy concept is it requires no code changes to users of the roles because they see the proxy as simply another role provider.

Implementing the Role Proxy Provider

Just as we did with the custom role provider we extended from `RoleProvider` and for which we implemented certain methods, we will do the same with `MVPHacksRoleProxyProvider`. The following example performs this implementation:

```
namespace MVPHacks.Secuirty
{

    /// <summary>
    /// Summary description for MVPHacksRoleProxyProvider
    /// </summary>
    public class MVPHacksRoleProxyProvider : System.Web.Security.RoleProvider
    {
        private List<string> m_ProviderList = new List<string>();

        public MVPHacksRoleProxyProvider()
        {

        }

        public override void Initialize(string name,
    System.Collections.Specialized.NameValueCollection config)
        {
            if (config["ProviderList"] != null)
            {
                char[] cSplitchars = { ',' };
                string[] providers =
    config["ProviderList"].ToString().Split(cSplitchars);
                foreach (string providerName in providers)
                    m_ProviderList.Add(providerName);
                config.Remove("ProviderList");
```

```
            }

        base.Initialize(name, config);
    }

    public override string[] GetRolesForUser(string username)
    {
        List<string> userRoles = new List<string>();

        foreach (string providerName in m_ProviderList)
        {
            RoleProvider rp = Roles.Providers[providerName];
            string[] roles = rp.GetRolesForUser(username);
            foreach (string role in roles)
            {
                if (!userRoles.Contains(role))
                    userRoles.Add(role);
            }

        }

        return userRoles.ToArray();

    }
    // - other code removed for simplicity
}
}
```

In the preceding example we have implemented the absolute minimum methods — `Intialize` and `GetRolesForUser` — that will allow our proxy to function. What is not shown are the other methods that currently just return `NotSupportedException`. For most read-only methods you would implement them similarly to the `GetRolesForUser` method, which calls each of the providers configured on the Provider List.

We override the `Initialize` method because we want to get control to grab the `ProviderList` attribute, which will provide a comma-separated list of the provider names that the proxy will combine to a single view of the user's roles.

In the `GetRolesForUser` method to acquire our list, we will look at the names in the `ProviderList` attribute and call the `GetRolesForUser` method on each of those providers. Not shown in the example is handling behavior if the requested provider is not configured or if other common configuration errors occur. Once the lists are retrieved from each of the configured providers, the array of roles is returned to the caller just as if a single provider were invoked.

Web.Config Changes for Role Proxy Provider

The key to the role proxy concept is simplicity; it does not require a complex implementation or complex configuration to allow a single view of roles across multiple providers. The following example shows the `web.config` entry to configure the role proxy and two custom role providers:

```
<roleManager defaultProvider="MVPHacksRoleProxyProvider" enabled="true">
    <providers>
```

```
        <add name="MVPHacksRoleProxyProvider"
 type="MVPHacks.Secuirty.MVPHacksRoleProxyProvider,MVPHacksCommon"
        ProviderList="MVPHacksRoleProvider,MVPHacksRoleProvider2"/>
        <add name="MVPHacksRoleProvider"
 type="MVPHacks.Secuirty.MVPHacksCustomRoleProvider,MVPHacksCommon"/>
        <add name="MVPHacksRoleProvider2"
 type="MVPHacks.Secuirty.MVPHacksCustomRoleProvider2,MVPHacksCommon"/>
     </providers>
    </roleManager>
```

As you can see, three providers have been configured: the two custom providers plus our role proxy provider. The proxy provider is set as the `defaultProvider` so that all requests automatically go through our proxy. The `ProviderList` attribute is specified to configure the providers for which a proxy should be used. You might be wondering why you can't just enumerate all the providers configured. That certainly could be an alternate implementation, but we chose to use an explicit list. The separate lists allows for additional providers to be configured and used by direct specification of the provider name while allowing them to be excluded from the proxy aggregation of roles.

The concept of the proxy getting between the caller and one or more providers could be applied to other areas beyond roles. For example, with the `MemberShipProvider` you might find yourself in between two membership databases or you might want to support multiple active providers for authentication without requiring the application to know.

Building a Custom Provider

So far the providers that have been discussed in this chapter have all started with one of the existing provider definitions, and we simply extended or tweaked it to do what we want. While this is a great way to leverage all the hard work that has already been done, and often this will provide all that is needed, there are times where starting from scratch and building your own custom provider makes sense.

As you start thinking about building a custom provider it is important to think about the interface up front. You should consider building a custom provider when you have a portion of your application that lends itself to multiple implementations or extensibility. While creatively you could use a provider to help render UI elements, they are typically better suited for implementations that are storage based or will have more than one algorithm implementation.

When we talk about different storage providers, this is an example where you might want an implementation that stores the data in a database while another might be network ready and communicate via Web services to the data store, and yet another one might simply store it in XML files. The value of building custom providers is allowing the application to call a defined interface without having to know the details of its implementation.

Example of Custom Providers

As of this writing we are just starting to see some providers being built in the developer community. For example, CommerceStartKit.Org has implemented a start kit to help build PayPal-enabled commerce sites. To ensure flexibility and to easily enable users to download the starter kit and adopt it for their use, they have used the provider design pattern to build their major subsystems. For example, the following are subsystems they support out of the box with the provider design pattern:

- ❏ Catalog provider
- ❏ Orders provider
- ❏ Payment provider
- ❏ Shipping provider
- ❏ Shopping Cart provider
- ❏ Tax provider

For each of these, the Community Start Kit provides the abstract class that defines the contract/interface for the provider and then provides a SQL Server–based concrete class (implementation of an abstract class). A user who downloads and uses the starter kit could easily build an Oracle- or XML-based version of these providers and the application would not be affected.

Not only does having the providers make the concept extendable for what you built, it also establishes an architecture that promotes others to add their customizations with a similar style and concept. An example of this is David Hayden (www.davidhayden.com). He built an `InventoryProvider` that works with the commerce starter kit. David saw the need for a more functional and feature-rich inventory management system and built his provider. By using similar concepts, others could adopt his provider. By plugging it into their start kit implementation, they would already be familiar with the high-level architecture of how it works. Expect to see many other examples like this where you can leverage fragments of code and plug them in as providers.

The Tax provider is a good example of how you can use the provider model with algorithms. By abstracting key algorithms in your application, you leave the flexibility to plug in different implementations over time. This also makes it extremely easy to test new versions of the algorithms; simply plug the new version into the application configuration without any required code changes. Another example of this might be to plug in a scoring type algorithm.

There is no question that creating providers for your components will take longer up front due to more robust interface design time and setting up the necessary code infrastructure to support the component being configurable, but you will see savings in the future if you leverage the capabilities. More design time is required because you should carefully think through your public interface. Once published, ideally it should not be altered, as that would affect existing users.

Leveraging off-the-shelf components can save hundreds of hours, and building provider interfaces around them and providing an easy point of replacement when someone publishes a better version is an attractive option.

The Basics of a Custom Provider

When building a custom provider, you must complete a number of steps. The rest of this section steps through building a very basic custom provider with only the minimum required parts.

The custom provider we build here works with the Virtual Earth Map control. Imagine that you have written a Virtual Earth Custom Server control to put on your ASP.NET page. The control will show points of interest on the map that is displayed. You could hard-code knowledge of how to get the points of interest for our one application into the control and simply have it make calls to our database to load the points, but that would prevent us from working with other data sources in the future without major rework.

To better position our control for reuse, we have decided we are going to build a `MVPHacksMapData Provider` that will expose a `GetPoints` method to get the points of interest. Our control will pass the current latitude/longitude to that method so the data provider can determine the points to return.

In the following steps we are going to define the basic parts that would be necessary to set up the infrastructure for this to work.

Configuring the Custom Provider

The first step is dealing with the configuration capabilities of the custom providers. Being able to specify the provider(s) via the configuration file is a key part of the provider design pattern. This allows them to be easily configured without changes to code. To accomplish this we want to be able to have a custom configuration section that is defined and paired up with our provider. This section will list the providers that are available and the options that are specific to each provider, such as connection strings. The following example shows what our map data provider configuration section might look like:

```
<configuration>
<MVPHacksMapDataProvider defaultProvider="SamplePointDataProvider">
    <providers>
      <add name="SamplePointDataProvider"
                type="MVPHacks.SamplePointDataProvider,app_code" />
    </providers>
</MVPHacksMapDataProvider>
</configuration>
```

The preceding example shows the minimum code that would be needed to identify a provider using the provider design pattern. In the example, one provider is defined and the `defaultProvider` identifies it as the preferred provider.

You will notice that the preceding example is a custom configuration section. In order for this not to cause an error, the section must be defined; and the custom class that supports the custom section must be identified. In step 2 we will complete this action.

Setting Up the Custom Configuration Section

As mentioned in the preceding section, because a custom configuration section is used it must be defined prior to use, and the type/class that provides support for the custom section must be identified. The following code shows the entry necessary in the configuration file to accomplish that:

```
<configSections>
    <section name="CTCVEMapDataProvider"
          type="MVPHacks.Common.MVPHacksMapDataProviderConfigSection,
          mvphacks.common"  />
</configSections>
```

`MVPHacksMapDataProviderConfigSection` is the class that will be the section handler when the section is accessed. This class will implement type-safe access to the entries in that configuration section. In the next step we will begin to build that class.

Implementing a Custom Section

Compared to NET 1.1, .NET 2.0 makes it easier to build custom configuration sections without having to do as much of the heavy lifting (coding). The code in the following example shows what is necessary to build a custom configuration section that matches our section shown in step 1. This will provide for a custom section named MVPHacksMapDataProvider, a child element of <provider> that will contain one or more provider definitions. Additionally, it will support the defaultProvider attribute to identify the provider to use if one is not requested explicitly:

```
using System;
using System.Configuration;

namespace MVPHacksCommon.CustomData
{
    public class MVPHacksMapDataProviderConfigSection : ConfigurationSection
    {
        [ConfigurationProperty("providers")]
        public ProviderSettingsCollection Providers
        {
            get
            {
                return (ProviderSettingsCollection)base["providers"];
            }
        }
        [ConfigurationProperty("defaultProvider",
                DefaultValue="MVPHacksNullMapDataProvider")]
        [StringValidator(MinLength = 1)]
        public string DefaultProvider
        {
            get
            {
                return (string)base["defaultProvider"];
            }
            set
            {
                base["defaultProvider"] = value;
            }
        }
    }
}
```

As you can see from the preceding example, a minimal amount of code is required to implement a custom section. Note a couple of key things and then we will move along to building the rest of a simple custom provider. First, notice that the class inherits from ConfigurationSection. The Configuration Section class is new to .NET 2.0. This used to be done by implementing the IConfigurationSection Handler interface, which is now deprecated in .NET 2.0.

Custom section handlers can now be implemented in either a programmatic or a declarative implementation. The preceding example uses the declarative approach, allowing the framework — along with the attributes specified — to do much of the work for us. For example, where we placed a Configuration Property attribute and specified a name such as defaultProvider, the implementation takes care of binding the defaultProvider data in the configuration file to our class property without any additional code. Second, it's also important to note the capability to specify validators using attributes as well. Again, this helps reduce the amount of custom code but still preserves the ability to do validation in a robust manner.

A complete discussion of custom configuration sections is beyond the scope of the book, but it is important to note the changes that happened in .NET 2.0. These changes make it easier to build custom configuration sections.

Creating the MVPHacksMapDataProvider Abstract Class

The next step is to create a class that inherits from `System.Configuration.Provider.ProviderBase` and define the contract that the custom provider will expose.

The following are the key points to recognize here:

- ❑ **The provider inherits from** `ProviderBase` — This provides the lowest level of consistency across various providers.

- ❑ **The class is defined as abstract** — This is not an actual implementation of the provider but simply the contract. That said, nothing says you can't put some helper-type methods inside this class that the inheritors could use.

- ❑ **The class defines any abstract methods for the contract it is going to expose** — This is cleanest on a new provider. It is possible that as the provider evolves, you specify methods with a default version to ensure compatibility with older providers.

- ❑ **An abstract class is used instead of an interface** — Certainly a contract could be defined with an interface, but over time the interface would make the provider more rigid. This is because when you modify an interface, all inheritors or implementers of that interface must add the new method or property. An abstract class can shield implementers to a certain extent.

The following listing sets up the class that inherits from ProviderBase:

```
using System;
using System.Collections.Generic;
using System.Text;
using System.Configuration.Provider;

namespace MVPHacksCommon.CustomData
{
    public abstract class MVPHacksMapDataProvider : ProviderBase
    {
        public abstract List<MVPHacksMapDataLocation>
                    GetDataForRegion(double lattitude,
                                        double longitude,double miles2show);

    }
}
```

> `ProviderBase` **is part of the** `System.Configuration.Provider` **namespace located in the** `System.Configuration` **assembly. You will need to add a reference to that manually because one is not automatically created as part of a class library project.**

One way you might get yourself in the right mindset to keep this from including implementation specifics is to look at some of the built-in providers as patterns. Notice how they kept away from the implementation issues.

If you're building the providers only for use in your internal application, it is possible to interpret that more literally than it would make sense. But if you're an ISV building an interface that will be exposed to third parties, it would be more appropriate to interpret it more literally.

Implementing the MVPHacksMapData Static Class

The next class we are going to implement is a static class that acts as a façade for the actual provider. Simply put, this class is designed to make using the provider specified as the `DefaultProvider` in the configuration entry easy to use. The user of the provider would simply reference the static methods exposed on this class. This class manages looking into the configuration section and uses the information to create a singleton instance (one copy) of the provider specified as the `DefaultProvider`:

```csharp
using System;
using System.Collections.Generic;
using System.Text;
using System.Configuration;
using System.Web.Configuration;

namespace MVPHacksCommon.CustomData
{
    public static class MVPHacksMapData
    {
        static MVPHacksMapData()
        {
            SetupDefaultProvider();
        }

        private static string _initLockString = "MapDataProviderLock";
        private static MVPHacksMapDataProvider _provider = null;

        private static void SetupDefaultProvider()
        {
            lock (_initLockString)
            {
                if (_provider != null)
                    return;

                MVPHacksMapDataProviderConfigSection providerConfig =
                    ConfigurationManager.GetSection("MapDataProvider")
                        as MVPHacksMapDataProviderConfigSection;

                if (providerConfig == null)
                    return ;

                ProviderSettings settings =
providerConfig.Providers[providerConfig.DefaultProvider];

                _provider = ProvidersHelper.InstantiateProvider(settings,
                    typeof(MVPHacksMapDataProvider)) as
MVPHacksMapDataProvider;

            }
        }

        public static List<MVPHacksMapDataLocation>
```

```
                        GetDataForRegion(double lattitude,
                                    double longitude, double miles2show)
        {
            return _provider.GetDataForRegion(lattitude, longitude, miles2show);
        }
    }
}
```

> Notice that we are using the `ProviderHelper` to get the instance of our provider. This is from the `System.Web.Configuration` namespace. In the `Instantiate Provider` method, it takes care of creating an instance of the provider using the type specified in the configuration file and calling the initialization method.

Completing the Concrete Implementation of MVPHacksMapDataProvider

The final step is to create a concrete implementation of our provider. To do that we will create a class that inherits from `MVPHacksMapDataProvider`. In this class we provide our implementation of how to retrieve the map data points. In our sample, this is simple; we are just hard-coding them to a couple of specific locations. A more realistic example might be a version that pulled the points from a remote Web service in addition to a version that read from a local file or SQL Server:

```csharp
using System;
using System.Collections.Generic;
using System.Text;

namespace MVPHacksCommon.CustomData
{
    public class HardCodedMapDataProvider : MVPHacksMapDataProvider
    {
        public override List<MVPHacksMapDataLocation> GetDataForRegion(double
lattitude, double longitude, double miles2show)
        {
            List<MVPHacksMapDataLocation> list = new
List<MVPHacksMapDataLocation>();

            MVPHacksMapDataLocation loc1 = new MVPHacksMapDataLocation();
            loc1.Latitude = 33.35860433839252;
            loc1.Longitude = -93.43521000572602;
            loc1.Caption = "Somewhere in Lafayette";
            list.Add(loc1);

            return list;

        }
    }
}
```

Now we have completed the basic components to build a custom provider from scratch. Clearly this is a very simplistic example, but that is by design. The important point is that building your own providers is not an overly complex endeavor.

The best time to be thinking about providers is during the design stage of your application. That doesn't mean, however, that if you have an existing application then you can't introduce custom providers into its architecture. In fact, one creative way to use providers is to help during transition of capability to a new version. For example, suppose you have an application that performs sales tax calculations. In this example, the application knows how to calculate tax only within your local county. Your company decides that it wants to start selling statewide, and must therefore calculate tax using a more complex algorithm depending on a number of factors. What you could do as a first step is define a provider that would expose a `CalculateTax` method and refactor your current logic into a `LocalTaxCalcProvider` class. Next, you could build a `StateWideTaxCalcProvider` class using the same interface. The application could then be easily switched between the two providers to support testing. At the time of deployment, the new tax calculation would consist simply of a configuration change to specify the `StateWideTaxCalcProvider`.

The few examples demonstrated here only highlight how you can find opportunities in your own applications to increase the flexibility available by using extensibility approaches similar to the ones used by the ASP.NET team. Because of their broad use, these approaches will be familiar to users of your custom providers.

But I'm Using ASP.NET 1.1

At its heart, the provider is just a design pattern. While the majority of uses of the provider model are ASP.NET 2–oriented, nothing says you can't leverage it with your 1.1 application. That said, you won't have the benefit of the great built-in providers as a starting place, but you can still start using the design pattern. If you closely follow the building blocks we described but build a few helper classes in your 1.1 application, you can easily set up to build provider-based applications that you can move forward. In fact, if you built your membership modeled after the ASP.NET 2.0 membership, you could probably just throw away a bunch of code when you move to 2.0. I know, you're wondering why not move to ASP.NET 2.0 now? In a perfect world that would happen, but we all know that not everyone will have that option and some will migrate at a slower pace. By starting to get familiar with the provider concept while still using 1.1, you can jump-start your 2.0 thinking even though you can't start using the other cool features.

Rob Howard has written an interesting article on using providers with ASP.NET 1.1 that you can find on the Microsoft Developer Center link found at the end of this chapter.

Wrapping Up

In this chapter we looked briefly at the providers that come out of the box with ASP.NET 2.0. We explored how you can save time by simply extending those to add missing capabilities that your application needs. Then we looked at providing our own implementations from the abstract class and not relying on any of the built-in implementations.

In our custom provider section you learned how you could start from scratch and build services for your application using the provider design pattern.

If nothing else, if you step back and look at the extensibility and clarity on the interfaces that the provider model has implemented in ASP.NET 2.0, you can't help but be impressed. At the same time, as with anything, it is easy to say how they could have done it with a different approach. At the end of the day, the important thing is to adopt an approach and use it consistently.

If you choose to leverage the provider design pattern for your own application, it can be a key part of your extensibility story as well. Often, in the rush to get a product to market, vendors forget that having an extensibility story is important until after it is too late in the product design. Remember to consider the provider model and other architecture patterns for promoting extensibility and reuse early in your application development life cycle to ensure you don't fall into that trap!

Internal applications can also benefit from this capability, as it makes it easier to leverage code for other projects or business units to rapidly build new business applications or adjust to evolving business models.

Other Providers Resources

Microsoft ASP.NET Developer Center — Provider Toolkit:`http://msdn.microsft.com/asp.net/downloads/providers/`

4

The Smarter Web Client

No, you didn't pick up the wrong book. You are reading *ASP.NET 2.0 MVP Hacks and Tips*. I'm sure you didn't buy this book on ASP.NET to read about what one would traditionally think of as a *smart client*.

Smart client today has become the buzzword for a Windows Forms application that is deployed to the user's desktop, typically involving some smarts in terms of how it interacts with a back-end application and with capabilities to auto update and perform other actions that differentiate it from what in the past had been referred to as the *fat client*.

At the same time that the marketing buzz is swirling around about smart clients, a renewed focus on making the Web-browsing experience even better for the user has come about. This follows several previous approaches that have been attempted to provide a richer client experience, ranging from simple techniques using JavaScript sent to the client browser with the HTML to technologies such as Flash or Java. Most of these faded into the sunset among the browser wars and the complexity associated with providing that richer client experience. The lack of tools and vendor support at the most fundamental level, such as the browser and development tools, also ensured that this did not prosper.

Today, armed with a series of new buzzwords such as AJAX and Atlas, the revolution of the smarter Web client has begun. In this chapter you will explore how this refocused effort is attempting to make the user's Web experience livelier, hiding from the user much of the traditional Web request/Web response model that is typical of today's Web applications.

Despite the hype surrounding smart clients (Windows Forms) and the doubling of efforts to make websites more interactive, it is clear that both have their place in the overall architecture of applications today. While the path to the future may result in the *real smart client* that is adaptive to the needs of the user, today it is up to the application architects to deploy the technique that is best suited to the needs of the users, and works the way they do.

On the Road to a Smarter Web Client

Like all evolutions in technology, the path to a smarter Web client is not an overnight transition. Leading the charge are the high-end business sites such as MSN HotMail, Google, and Virtual Earth. Driven by the fierce competition, these sites are pushing the rest of us back down the road of moving some our Web application's functionality toward the client. Because of those sites, users tolerate fewer delays and reject the clunky nature of waiting for the screen to refresh simply because you choose your state from a drop-down list.

Even as this book was published, the story of the smarter Web client was still being told. That means that depending on your application requirements, you may be faced with difficult decisions about the leveraging techniques you use to accommodate features that are no longer just cool, but are becoming necessary if you want a competitive Web presence.

The AJAX Experience

Many might think of AJAX as the product sold in stores to clean their bathtub, but today AJAX refers to asynchronous JavaScript and XML. More specifically, it uses client-side JavaScript to make asynchronous calls back to the application Web server application using XML without the user's intervention. For example, suppose a user selects a country from a drop-down list. Without causing a refresh of the user's browser screen, the client-side script would call back to the Web server and obtain and populate the state drop-down list. This trick gives users the impression that the client is "smart" enough to prepare the list based on the country.

At the heart of the AJAX concept is the use of JavaScript on the client and the use of XmlHTTP to make the request to the Web server. XmlHTTP is a protocol supported by most major recent browsers to package and send an XML request to the Web server. Using the results from an XmlHTTP interaction, the browser's current view is updated with the results using JavaScript.

It is important to note that this is a client technique and in its purest form is independent from the server-side capabilities of the Web server application and the platform on which the server resides.

Using these capabilities a developer can create the richer application experience users have come to expect. Because these are core building blocks, they don't offer the rich development experience that is typical of server-side Web applications or Windows Forms–type applications. JavaScript is not an object-oriented language; it lacks strong typing and many other qualities that we appreciate when building a full-scale enterprise application. Regardless, they are the founding corner posts of the capabilities we will continue to explore in the rest of the chapter and then build on toward the goal of the smarter Web client.

And Then There Was ASP.NET 2.0

Client Callbacks is a new technology that ships with ASP.NET 2.0 to call server-side methods from client-side code. Different kinds of technologies have been available in the past few years for calling server-side code from client-side code. One technology that you have probably used is *remote scripting*. With remote scripting, you were able to make client-side calls from a page to server-side code located in an Active Server Page (ASP) without having to submit the page. The remote scripting technology uses

Java applets to make the communications to the server. The Java applet communicates with the server using the HTTP protocol and wraps the data in XML. To use remote scripting, you needed two files: one that handles the client-side request (rs.htm) and one for firing the code on the server side (rs.asp). With remote scripting, you can perform server-side code that will query a database or perform other server-side operations without reloading the page. Because remote scripting runs on the server while the client page is still active, your scripts are greatly simplified and the application can present a richer interface to the user. Another simple technique that can be used to call a server-side code without doing a postback (submitting the page) of the main page is to add an IFRAME to the page and make it hidden. The client-side code will post data to the hidden IFRAME, which will process a page that has the server-side code that should be executed. The value returned from the response of the page within the IFRAME will be the value that the client-side script will use. This solution is very common — for example, when a Tree on a page will get data from a datasource and add nodes dynamically without doing a postback.

With ASP.NET 2.0 there is a new technology for making remote calls possible from the client side. This new technology is called Client Callbacks, and it is easier to use and set up than, for example, remote scripting.

With the Client Callbacks feature you can make client-side script call server-side code without causing a postback. This will be a perfect solution for situations such as executing server-side code without refreshing the page, preloading of data from a datasource, performing validations, etc. This new callbacks technology is very similar to remote scripting, but instead of using a Java applet, Client Callbacks uses XmlHTTP to communicate with the server, and instead of the rs.htm and rs.asp files, ASP.Net 2.0 uses the script library named CallBackManager.

> To use Client callbacks, XmlHTTP must be supported by the browsers. A new property, SupportsCallBack, added to the HttpBrowserCapabilities class can be used to determine whether the browser supports Client callbacks. You'll find out more about this later in this chapter.

How Client Callbacks Work

The client makes the call of a client-side method that will use the CallBackManager. The CallBackManager creates the request to an .aspx page on the server. The server processes the page and all its events up to the Pre_Render event, and makes the call of the sever-side method. The CallBackManager then parses the server response and issues a callback method that is a client-side method. Figure 4-1 illustrates client callbacks.

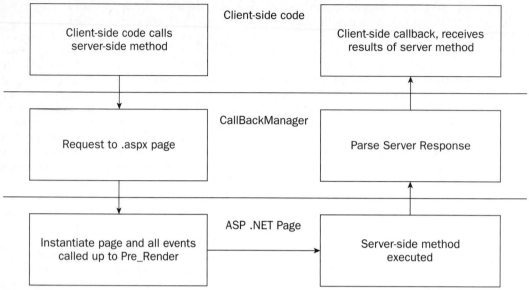

Figure 4-1

The `CallBackManager` must know the name of the client-side callback method in order to determine which method it should call on the client side when the server-side method is called and its response is parsed by `CallBackManager`. To specify which client-side method should be called after the server-side method is processed, you can use the `GetCallBackEventReference` method of the `Page` class. The `GetCallBackEventReference` method can be found in the `ClientSideScriptManger` class and can be accessed from the `Page` class's `ClientScript` property:

```
Page.ClientScript.GetCallbackEventReference(...)
```

With the `GetCallBackEventReference`, you can also specify which method the `CallBackManager` should call if the server throws an exception. You will learn more about the `GetCallBackEvent Reference` method later in this chapter.

There is one limitation with the Client Callback feature: You can't specify which method on the server should be executed. The Client Callback will execute the `RaiseCallbackEvent` method on the server, which is defined in the `ICallbackEventHandler` interface. Therefore, when you use the Client Callback to execute a server-side method, you must implement the `RaiseCallbackEvent` method and add your server-side logic to that method. Because you can't specify which server-side method you will call, only one server-side code can execute and return the result to the client. If you want to specify which method to call, you can, for example, pass an argument to the `RaiseCallbackEvent` that specifies which method to call, and handle that in the `RaiseCallbackEvent`. The following example illustrates that:

```
public string RaiseCallbackEvent(string eventArgs)
{
    if (eventArgs == "Method1")
        //call method 1
```

```
        else if (eventArgs == "Method2")
            //call method 2
    ...
}
```

Another solution for calling different server-side methods based on a control is to implement the use of the Client Callback feature with a custom control. By doing that you can have different `Raise CallbackEvent` methods, which will be executed based on which control you use on the page.

Let's see how client callbacks can be implemented and used by a Web form. The following example will use the Client Callback to do a validation on the server without doing a postback. The server-side method will validate that the user has entered a number between 1 and 1,000 in a text box. If the value of the text box is not a number, or if the number is not between 1 and 1,000, then a message box will be displayed with an error message (when an exception occurs on the server-side, the specified client-side error callback method will be executed on the client):

```
<%@ page language="C#" %>
<%@ implements interface="System.Web.UI.ICallbackEventHandler" %>

<script runat="server">

    private string _returnFromServer;

    public void RaiseCallbackEvent(string eventArgs)
    {
        try
        {
            int value = Int16.Parse(eventArgs);

            if( value >= 1 && value <= 1000 )
                this._returnFromServer = "You entered the number: " + eventArgs;
            else
                this._returnFromServer = "Please enter a number between 1 and
1000";
        }
        catch
        {
            throw new ApplicationException("You must enter a number.");
        }
    }


    public string GetCallbackResult()
    {
        return this._returnFromServer;
    }


    public void Page_Load(object sender, EventArgs e)
    {

        if (!Request.Browser.SupportsCallback)
```

```
        throw new ApplicationException("This browser doesn't support Client callbacks.");

        string src = Page.ClientScript.GetCallbackEventReference(
                                this,
                                "arg",
                                "ClientCallback",
                                "ctx",
                                "ClientErrorCallback",
                                false);

        string mainSrc = @"function ValidateNumber(arg, ctx)
                        { " + src + "; }";

        Page.ClientScript.RegisterClientScriptBlock(
                                this.GetType(),
                                "ValidateNumber",
                                mainSrc,
                                true);
    }

</script>

<html>
<head runat="server">
    <title>Client Callback</title>

    <script language="javascript">

        function Validate()
        {
            var n = document.forms[0].txtNumber.value;

            //Call the server-side method to validate the number
            ValidateNumber(n, "txtNumber");
        }

         //ClientCallback will be executed after the server-side method
         //is executed and the server response is parsed.
  function ClientCallback( result, context )
        {
            alert(result);
        }

        //If the server-side method throws an exception, the ClientErrorCallback
        //will be executed to show the exception.
        function ClientErrorCallback( error, context )
        {
            alert("The validation failed. " + error);
        }

    </script>

</head>
<body>
    <form runat="server">
      Please enter a number between 1 and 1000:<br />
```

```
        <input id="txtNumber" name="txtNumber" type="text"/>
        <button id="butValidate" OnClick="Validate()">Validate</button>
    </form>
</body>
</html>
```

Let's break the important part of the code into pieces and look at them individually:

```
<%@ page language="C#" %>
<%@ implements interface="System.Web.UI.ICallbackEventHandler" %>
```

The `System.Web.UI.ICallbackEventHandler` must be implemented to ensure that the callback events will be processed during a postback when the Client Callback is used. The `ICallbackEvent Handler` interface can also be implemented by controls, such as Buttons, TextBoxes, and so on. You will look at an example later in this chapter in which a control uses the `ICallbackEventHandler`. To specify which interface a Web form should implement, you use the `implements` directive, which has the attribute `interface`, enabling you to specify the name of the interface you want to implement.

The `ICallbackEventHandler` has two methods that must be implemented for making callback work—`RaiseCallbackEvent` and `GetCallbackResult`. The `RaiseCallbackEvent` method takes one argument that will contain the data from the client-side method, and the `GetCallbackResult method` returns a string to the client that represents the output of the server-side method. The return value will be passed as an argument to the client-side callback method. In the preceding example, the `Raise CallbackEvent` will check whether the argument (`eventArgs`) is a numeric value or between 1 and 1,000. If not, an exception will be thrown and a message box will be displayed on the client side telling the user to enter a value between 1 and 1,000. If the argument contains a permitted value, the value will be returned:

```
public void RaiseCallbackEvent(string eventArgs)
public string GetCallbackResult()
```

When you want to use Client Callback it's important that you check whether the user's browser supports the Client Callback feature. This can be done by using the `SupportsCallback` property of the `Page` class `Browser` property. The following code will check whether the client supports Client Callbacks. If not, an exception will be thrown:

```
if (!Request.Browser.SupportsCallback )
throw new ApplicationException("This browser doesn't support Client callbacks.");
```

The next important part of the example is to get a callback event reference. The reference represents a client-side method that will be generated and used to make the call to the server-side code. When you get a callback event reference, you need to specify a callback method. This is required so the Client Callback knows which client-side method should be called after the server-side method is processed. To add a reference, the `GetCallbackEventReference` method of the `Page` class will be used. `Get CallbackEventReference` has three overloaded methods:

```
public string GetCallbackEventReference(
Control control,
            string argument,
            string clientCallback,
            string context)
```

```
public string GetCallbackEventReference(
        Control control,
          string argument,
                  string clientCallback,
                  string context,
string clientErrorCallback)

public string GetCallbackEventReference(
string target,
string argument,
string clientCallback,
string context,
string clientErrorCallback)
```

The following table describes the arguments of the GetCallbackEventReference.

Argument	Description
control	The control that implements IcallbackEventHandler.
target	If no control is specified, this would be the ID of a control that implements the ICallbackEventHandler.
argument	The value that will be sent to the RaiseCallbackEvent.
clientCallback	The name of the client-side callback method.
context	A value that will be passed back from the client-side event to the client-side callback method.
clientErrorCallback	The name of the client-side error callback method. This method will be executed if the server throws an exception.

The following code uses the GetCallbackEventReference to specify the client-side callback methods and the control that implements ICallbackEventHandler:

```
public void Page_Load(object sender, EventArgs e)
{
    string src = Page.GetCallbackEventReference(
                          this,
                          "arg",
                          "ClientCallback",
                          "ctx",
                          "ClientErrorCallback");

    string mainSrc = @"function ValidateNumber(arg, ctx)
                       { " + src + "; }";
```

In the preceding example, the current page has implemented the ICallbackEventHandler, so the current page object is passed as a value to the control argument of the GetCallbackEventReference method. When the server-side method has been executed and the CallBackManager has parsed the server response of the server-side call, the ClientCallback method on the client side will be executed. The returned value from the server-side method will be passed as an argument to the client's Callback method. If the servers throw an exception, the client-side ClientErrorCallback method will be executed. The `arg` and `ctx` values passed to the `GetCallbackEventReference` are names of the arguments of the client-side event that calls the server-side method. The arguments and the callback event reference are created as a string and added to the `mainSrc` variable in the code snippet—`Validate Number`. The `mainSrc` will contain the following string:

```
function ValidateNumber(arg, ctx)
{   WebForm_DoCallback('__Page',arg,ClientCallback,ctx,ClientErrorCallback,false); }
```

The method `WebForm.DoCallback` and its arguments are generated by the `GetCallbackEvent Reference` method. The `ValidateNumber` event must be added to the client as a client-side script, so it can be called by client-side methods or via an HTML control's event (such as a button's `OnClick` event, etc.). In ASP.NET 1.x, client-side scripts can be added to a page with the `RegisterClientScriptBlock` and `RegisterStartupScript` methods, which are accessible through the `Page` object and will still work in ASP.NET 2.0 for backward compatibility, but this example will use the new ASP.NET 2.0 `Register ClientScriptBlock` method to add the client-side script to the client. The new method is accessible through the current `Page` class' new `ClientScript` property (`ClientScriptManager`). The `Register ClientScriptBlock` in ASP.NET 1.x version takes two arguments: a unique key to identify the script block and a script string with the client-side script. The new method can take two more arguments, `type` and `addScriptTags`. The new `RegisterClientScriptBlock` has two overloaded methods:

```
Public void RegisterClientScriptBlock(
                    Type type,
                    string key,
                    string script)

Public void RegisterClientScriptBlock(
                    Type type,
                    string key,
                    string script,
                    bool addScriptTags)
```

The following table describes the arguments of `RegisterClientScriptBlock`.

Argument	Description
Type	A type, so the same key could be used twice
Key	A unique key to identify the script block
Script	The script block to be added to the client
addScriptTags	Allows the method to insert the `<script>` tag

The client-side method that will call the server is registered with the new `RegisterClientScript Block` method:

```
Page.ClientScript.RegisterClientScriptBlock(
                    this.GetType(),
                    "ValidateNumber",
                    mainSrc,
                    true);
```

The preceding `RegisterClientScriptBlock` will generate and add the following code to the client:

```
<script type="text/javascript">
<!--
function ValidateNumber(arg, ctx)
{ WebForm_DoCallback('__Page',arg,ClientCallback,ctx,ClientErrorCallback,false);
}// -->
</script>
```

The `WebForm_DoCallback` method takes five arguments: the current page, the argument value that will be sent into the `RaiseCallbackMethod` on the server-side, the client-side callback method, the context value that will be sent to the client-side callback method, and the client-side method that will be triggered if the server throws an exception.

The `WebForm_DoCallback` method can be directly executed through a client-side function or directly from a client-side control event, such as the `onClick` event of a button. In this example, `WebForm_Do Callback` will be executed through the `ValidateNumber` method.

Let's take a look the client-side callback methods. The `Validate` method will be executed by the button control `OnClick` event. This method will get the value entered in the txtNumber TextBox control and pass it as an argument through the `arg` argument of the `ValidateNumber` method that was previously described. The `Validate` method will also pass the id of the TextBox control through the `context` argument of the `ValidateNumber` method (the value of the context argument will be sent to the client-side callback method). `ClientCallback` will take two arguments: the result returned from the `RaiseEvent Callback` method and the context passed through the `ValidateNumber` method. The `RaiseEvent Callback` will be executed when the server has completed its request and displayed the returned value in a message box. If the server throws an exception, the `ClientCallErrorCallback` method on the client side will be executed and the error message returned from the `RaiseErroEventCallback` will be displayed in a message box:

```
function Validate()
{
    var n = document.forms[0].txtNumber.value;
    ValidateNumber(n, "txtNumber");
}

function ClientCallback( result, context )
{
    alert(result);
}

function ClientErrorCallback( error, context )
{
    alert("The validation failed. " + error);
}
```

The `Validate` method is hooked up to a button's `onClick` event, so when the button is clicked the `Validate` method is triggered and the server-side code will be executed:

```
<form runat="server">
        Please enter a number between 1 and 1000:<br />
        <input id="txtNumber" name="txtNumber" type="text"/>
        <button id="butVaidate" OnClick="Validate()">Validate</button>
</form>
```

Let's take a look at the example in action. When this example is running, a page with a text box and a button will be displayed, and the page will prompt us to enter a number between 1 and 1,000.

When the Validate button is clicked, the client callback will be performed. The code on the server side will determine whether a correct number is entered. A non-numeric value on the server-side method will throw an exception, displaying an error message that requests a number between 1 and 1,000. The `Client ErrorCallback` will be called on the client side if the exception is thrown. The client-side method will show the error returned from the server in a message box.

If the validation succeeds, the `ClientCallback` method is executed and displays the number entered into the textbox in a message box.

As you can see in the example, you don't need to do a postback to execute a server-side method from client-side code. That is the main benefit of using Client Callback. Client Callback can also be implemented into a control, as described in the following section.

Implementing Client Callback into a Custom Control

It's not only a Web form that can implement and use the Client Callback feature; you can also implement the use of Client Callback for a custom control. For example, if you build a Tree control and have a large hierarchy of nodes, you probably want to get the child nodes from a datasource when you expand a node to save resources, and so on, but not by doing a postback, and dynamically add the nodes. There can be only one `RaiseCallbackEvent` on a page, so by implementing Client Callback for custom controls, you can ensure that different server-side methods will be executed on the same page for different controls. The following example is a simple HtmlButton that implements the Client Callback feature:

```
using System;
using System.Web.UI;
using System.Web.UI.HtmlControls;

namespace CallbackTest
{

    public class CallbackButton : HtmlButton, ICallbackEventHandler
    {
        private string _value;

        public string MyCallBackArgument
        {
            get
            {
                string s = (string)ViewState["MyCallBackArgument"];

                if (s == null)
                    return String.Empty;

                return s;
            }
            set
            {
                ViewState["MyCallBackArgument"] = value;
```

```
                }
            }

            protected override void RenderAttributes(HtmlTextWriter writer)
            {
                base.RenderAttributes(writer);
                writer.WriteAttribute("onClick",
                                        Page.ClientScript.GetCallbackEventReference(
                                            this,
                                            this.MyCallBackArgument,
                                            "ButtonCallback",
                                            base.UniqueID,
                                            "ButtonErrorCallback",
                                            false) + "; return false;");
            }




    public string RaiseCallbackEvent(string eventArgument)
        {
            this._value = eventArgument;
        }

        public string GetCallbackResult()
        {
            return this._value;
        }
    }
}
```

The preceding code is a custom control that inherits the HtmlButton control and implements the
ICallBackEventHandler interface:

```
public class CallbackButton : HtmlButton, ICallbackEventHandler
```

The RenderAttributes method of the HtmlButton is overridden to add the onClick attribute and give
it the value of the client-side reference to the callback event:

```
writer.WriteAttribute("onClick",
                        Page.ClientScript.GetCallbackEventReference(
                            this,
                            this.MyCallBackArgument,
                            "ButtonCallback",
                            base.UniqueID,
                            "ButtonErrorCallback",
                            false) + "; return false;");
```

The GetCallbackEventReference takes six arguments: the value from the MyCallBackArgument
property, the name of the callback method located on the client-side ButtonCallback, the unique id of
the control, the context, the error callback, and whether the callback should be an asynchronous call. The
preceding code will generate something similar to the following code on the client side:

```
onClick="WebForm_DoCallback('CallbackButton1',TextBox1.value,ButtonCallback,
CallbackButton1,ButtonErrorCallback,false); return false;"
```

As you can see in the generated code, the _DoCallback method will be executed when the onClick event of the control is executed. _WebForm_DoCallback will pass the value from a TextBox as an argument to the RaiseCallBackEvent method (the TextBox1.Value is the value from the custom control's MyCallBackArgument property used in the preceding example). The RaiseCallBackEvent method in this example will store the value of the TextBox into a private field. The value will be returned by the GetCallbackResult method:

```
public void RaiseCallbackEvent(string eventArgument)
{
    this._value = eventArgument;
}

public string GetCallbackResult()
{
    return this._value;
}
```

The following example uses two custom controls (the control is rendered as a button because it inherits the HtmlButton class), whereby each of them will get the value from a TextBox and display the value in a message box when the custom control is clicked.

> **This example demonstrates only how you can implement Client Callback within a custom control. In real life, this example could be used instead of using Client Callback; it uses a simple client-side script to display the value entered into the text box without doing the postback.**

```
<%@ Page Language="C#" %>
<%@ Register tagprefix="nsquared2" namespace="CallbackTest"%>

<html>
<head>
    <title>Implementing Client callback into a custom control</title>

    <script>

        function ButtonCallback(result, context)
        {
            alert('The arguments are ' + result);
        }

        function ButtonErrorCallback(result, context)
        {
            alert('Invalid input!' + result);
        }

    </script>

</head>
```

```
<body>
    <form id="form1" runat="server">
    <div>
        <asp:TextBox id="TextBox1" runat="server" Text="My value"></asp:TextBox>
        <asp:TextBox id="TextBox2" runat="server" Text="My value2"></asp:TextBox>
        <nsquared2:CallbackButton id="CallbackButton1" runat="server"
MyCallBackArgument="TextBox1.value">Run</nsquared2:CallbackButton>
        <nsquared2:CallbackButton id="CallbackButton2" runat="server"
MyCallBackArgument="TextBox2.value">Run</nsquared2:CallbackButton>
    </div>
    </form>
</body>
</html>
```

The preceding example has two client-side scripts: `ButtonCallback`, which will be executed after the server-side code is processed during a Client Callback, and `ButtonErrorCallback`, which is executed if the server-side code during a Client Callback throws an exception:

```
function ButtonCallback(result, context)
{
    alert('The arguments are ' + result);
}


function ButtonErrorCallback(result, context)
{
    alert('Invalid input!' + result);
}
```

`ButtonCallback` will display a message box with the results from the server-side code, where the result is the value entered into a text box. `ButtonErrorCallback` will display a message box with information about the exception.

The preceding code example uses two custom controls on the page, where the `MyCallBackArgument` attribute of the controls is set to the name of a TextBox and its `Value` property:

```
<asp:TextBox id="TextBox1" runat="server" Text="My value"></asp:TextBox>
<asp:TextBox id="TextBox2" runat="server" Text="My value2"></asp:TextBox>

<nsquared2:CallbackButton id="CallbackButton1" runat="server"
MyCallBackArgument="TextBox1.value">Run</nsquared2:CallbackButton>

<nsquared2:CallbackButton id="CallbackButton2" runat="server"
MyCallBackArgument="TextBox2.value">Run</nsquared2:CallbackButton>
```

When the CallbackButton control is clicked, the value from the property specified for the `MyCall BackArgument` will be passed as an argument to the custom control's `RaiseCallBackEvent` method, and the value will be returned to the `ButtonCallback` method on the client side from the `GetCallbackResult` method.

When you run the example you will see two TextBoxes and two buttons. When you click on the left button, the value from the left TextBox's (TextBox1) `Text` property will be passed to the server and a Client Callback will be executed. After processing the server method, the client-side callback will display a message box with the value from TextBox1's `Text` property. If you click the right button, the value from the right TextBox's (TextBox2) `Text` property will be passed to the server. Implementing the use of Client Callback on a custom control makes it possible for you to execute several different pieces of server-side code on one page. You can also reuse the code by adding the control to other pages, and so on.

With Client Callbacks and the use of DHTML (if you use IE 4.0 or later), you can create a rich client. You can make server-side code execution from the client much easier. You don't need to add a Java applet or use an IFRAME; instead, implement the `ICallBackEventHandler` and generate and register the Client Callbacks client-side method with the `GetCallBackEventReference` and `RegisterClientScript` block. With the Client Callbacks, you can get, save, delete, insert, and update data against a database with server-side code without reloading the page. You can also execute server-side validations, and so on.

Along Comes Atlas

It's not that developers don't like the AJAX concept; it's just downright complex to build applications and get them to market in a timely manner. Over the last year, though, with the support of the community and various community projects, more and more options have been developed to make using AJAX in applications easier and more common.

Microsoft, recognizing the shift toward a smarter Web client and feeling the competitive pressure from the community projects and other competitive vendors, launched project Atlas. Atlas is Microsoft's solution for making it easier to build rich, interactive Web-based applications.

A Hack from the ASP.NET Team

Atlas is not part of the official ASP.NET product at this time, but an initiative that was launched publicly at Microsoft's Professional Developers Conference (PDC) 2005. It is intended to be used with Visual Studio 2005/ASP.NET 2.0 and future releases. As of the publication of this book, the Atlas project is still in beta testing, so some of the discussion presented here is subject to change as the feature set is finalized.

Not Just a Client-Side Script Library

Atlas is much more than just a simple JavaScript library to use on the client and perform client-side operations. Atlas takes a more holistic approach, providing support both on the server and on the client.

JavaScript on Steroids

Thinking back to the first look I had at some of the Atlas, I thought I was looking under the covers of some of the Virtual Earth., In reviewing some of the JavaScript, you could see fresh thinking in how to organize and use JavaScript in a manner closer to how C# and VB.NET is done in a full application. Atlas formalized that thinking by focusing on how to make JavaScript development easier. Part of this focus is supported by allowing support for namespaces, inheritance, and interfaces.

Namespaces allow for the partitioning, or grouping, of common functionality. In fact, oftentimes JavaScript, packaged up using these techniques, can resemble a typical class you would expect to see in a more OO-capable language. Typically, JavaScript you will run across has no structure or organization and is just running amok inside the page.

At the heart of Atlas JavaScript enhancements is the ScriptManager control. This control is put on the page as a nonvisual ASP.NET server control. When the page renders, this control emits the necessary scripts to the client to enable the JavaScript extensions. The following is what the markup would look like for ScriptManager:

```
<atlas:ScriptManager ID="ScriptManager1" runat="server" />
```

Namespaces are registered using the `Type.registerNamespace` method that is exposed by Atlas. Registering a namespace is a great way to group and partition your code so that not only is it more readable, it is also less likely to collide as smaller components are aggregated together on a page from various sources. The following is an example of registering a namespace:

```
Type.registerNamespace("MVPHacks");
```

Like namespaces, classes can be registered, as shown in the following example:

```
MVPHacks.MapLocation = function(lattitude, longitude, caption)
{
    var _lattitude = lattitude;
    var _longitude = longitude;
    var _caption = caption;

    this.GetLatitude = function()
    {
        return _lattitude;
    }
    this.SetLatitude = function(value)
    {
        _lattitude = value;
    }

    this.GetLongitude = function()
    {
        return _longitude;
    }
    this.SetLongitude = function(value)
    {
        _longitude = value;
    }

    this.GetCaption = function()
    {
        return _caption;
    }
    this.SetCaption = function(value)
    {
        _caption = value;
    }
    this.dispose = function()
    {

    }

}
Type.registerClass('MVPHacks.MapLocation', null, Web.IDisposable);
```

That takes care of registering the class but it does not create an instance of it for use. Clearly, this provides a lot more structure around client-side scripting than has previously been used. This type of definition might be put in a `MapLocation.js` file so it could be easily reused in multiple pages or applications.

To get you to start thinking about other interesting uses, there is also a `registerAbstractClass` and `registerSealedClass` method.

The following shows how an instance of this class would be created and used:

```
var loc1 = new MVPHacks.MapLocation( 32.70233321087224,
                                     -117.13402484219676, 'Point #1');
    alert(loc1.GetLatitude() + " , " +
                             loc1.GetLongitude() + "  " + loc1.GetCaption() );
```

It gets even better because you can also inherit from a previously registered type. In the following example, I inherit `DBMapLocation` from my `MapLocation` class and add a `DbID` property:

```
MVPHacks.DBMapLocation = function(dbid,lattitude, longitude, caption) {
    MVPHacks.DBMapLocation.initializeBase(this, [lattitude, longitude, caption]);
        var _dbid = dbid;
    this.GetDbID = function()
        {
        return _dbid;
        }
    this.SetDbID = function(value)
        {
        _dbid = value;
        }
}
Type.registerClass('MVPHacks.DBMapLocation', MVPHacks.MapLocation);
```

Notice that in the call to `registerClass` I pass `MVPHacks.MapLocation` to indicate I want to inherit from that class. The rest is taken care of by the Atlas type framework. In the following example I create an instance of the `DBMapLocation`, passing `12345` as the `DbID`:

```
var dbloc1 = new MVPHacks.DBMapLocation(12345, 32.70233321087224,
                                        -117.13402484219676, 'Point #2');
    alert(dbloc1.GetDbID() + " - " + dbloc1.GetLatitude() + " , " +
          dbloc1.GetLongitude() + "  " + dbloc1.GetCaption() );
```

Note in the preceding example that no special code is required to access the inherited properties other than simply calling the Atlas Type framework `registerClass` method.

These examples offer a glimpse into the capabilities of the Atlas type framework. It's easy to see how these can promote increased structure and reuse in JavaScript client-side scripting.

Using Services from the Browser

Earlier in the chapter we talked about using XmlHTTP to make asynchronous requests back to the server to retrieve data. As powerful as that is, it is still a pretty rough interaction with the server. Another area that Atlas focuses on is making interaction with Web services on the server easier. Additionally, it extends server-side capabilities such as Membership Authentication and Profile to the Atlas-enabled browser application. I would expect that over time the list of server-side services will be enhanced to give the browser access to other rich capabilities of ASP.NET 2.0.

Exposing a Web service from the page is probably the simplest to accomplish. In your page, by simply decorating a method with the [WebMethod] attribute, a proxy will be built for it, which can be referenced as part of the PageMethods namespace on the client. The following is an example of a method definition in our page:

```
[WebMethod]
 public string FormatLocation(double lat,double lon,string cap)
 {
     return cap + " Lat=" + lat + " Long=" + lon;
 }
```

Now, from the client, and as long as we have referenced ScriptManager, we can use the PageMethods namespace to call the method. The following code shows an example of calling the page method:

```
PageMethods.FormatLocation(loc1.GetLatitude(),
            loc1.GetLongitude(),loc1.GetCaption(),onComplete);
```

While it seems like magic, what is really happening is that as part of page rendering, the following is put on the page that registers the PageMethods:

```
<script type="text/javascript">
var PageMethods = new function() {
var cm=Web.Net.PageMethodRequest.createProxyMethod;
cm(this,"FormatLocation","lat","lon","cap");
}
</script>
```

The other way is to reference it from the service.asmx file. To do that, the first step is to specify a reference to the Web service on the ServiceManager tag, as shown in the following example:

```
<atlas:ScriptManager ID="ScriptManager1" runat="server">
    <Services>
        <atlas:ServiceReference Path="MapLocFormatter.asmx" />
    </Services>
</atlas:ScriptManager>
```

Before we get ahead of ourselves, we should build the Web service that we are going to call. In this example we are going to pass an instance of our MapLocation object and have it return a formatted string. The following listing shows the Web service that we will create to support this:

```
using System;
using System.Web;
using System.Collections;
using System.Web.Services;
using System.Web.Services.Protocols;
namespace MVPHacksHost.HostWS
{
    public class MapLocation
    {
```

```
        private double _Lattitude;
        public double Lattitude
        {

            get { return _Lattitude; }
            set { _Lattitude = value; }
        }
        private double _Longitude;
        public double Longitude
        {
            get { return _Longitude; }
            set { _Longitude = value; }
        }
        private string _Caption;
        public string Caption
        {
            get { return _Caption; }
            set { _Caption = value; }
        }
    }
    [WebService(Namespace = "http://mvphacks.com/")]
    [WebServiceBinding(ConformsTo = WsiProfiles.BasicProfile1_1)]
    public class MapLocFormatter : System.Web.Services.WebService
    {

        public MapLocFormatter()
        {
        }
        [WebMethod]
        public string FormatLocation(MapLocation loc)
        {
            return loc.Caption + " Lat=" + loc.Lattitude + " Long=" +
loc.Longitude;
        }
    }
}
```

What happens under the covers is that when the service reference renders, it invokes the Web service filename and passes a /js to generate a proxy. The following is generated and registers the service on the browser:

```
Type.registerNamespace('MVPHacksHost.HostWS');
MVPHacksHost.HostWS.MapLocFormatter = new function()
{
this.path = "http://localhost:11164/atlasexample/MapLocFormatter.asmx";
var cm=Web.Net.ServiceMethodRequest.createProxyMethod;
cm(this,"FormatLocation","loc");
}
var gtc = Web.Net.MethodRequest.generateTypedConstructor;
MVPHacksHost.HostWS.MapLocation = gtc("MVPHacksHost.HostWS.MapLocation");
```

In addition to being able to define and call your own Web methods, Atlas exposes — via a service bridge — access to Membership Authentication and the users profile. You access those via the methods in the Web .Services namespace. For example, the authentication is Web.Services.AuthenticationService and the profile is Web.Profile.

As you can see, accessing and using services is really easy. The capability to have the Atlas framework build the necessary proxy calls and manage requests makes life much easier.

The challenge now is to ensure that all this is done in a security responsible manner and that via the Web methods we don't expose too much that could compromise any private data.

Getting the Data

Another part of Atlas is the capability to expose a DataSource. A DataSource is exposed using a construct very similar to a regular Web service, but instead of inheriting from WebService, you inherit from the DataService class that is a part of the Microsoft.Web.Services namespace that comes with Atlas. The following illustrates a very simple DataSource that exposes a DataTable:

```
using System;
using System.ComponentModel;
using System.Data;
using System.Data.SqlClient;
using System.Web.Services;
using System.Web.Services.Protocols;
using Microsoft.Web.Services;

/// <summary>
/// Summary description for MapDS1
/// </summary>
[WebService(Namespace = "http://MVPHacks.com/")]
[WebServiceBinding(ConformsTo = WsiProfiles.BasicProfile1_1)]
public class MapDS1 : DataService  {

    public MapDS1 () {


    }

    [DataObjectMethod(DataObjectMethodType.Select)]
    public DataTable GetMapPoints()
    {
        DataTable dt = new DataTable();
        dt.Columns.Add("cap");
        dt.Columns.Add("lat",typeof(double));
        dt.Columns.Add("lon",typeof(double));
        for(int i =1;i< 100;i++)
            AddRow(dt, 1+i, 2 + i, "test " + i.ToString());
        return dt;
    }

    private void AddRow(DataTable dt, double lat, double lon, string cap)
    {
        DataRow row = dt.NewRow();
        row["lat"] = lat;
        row["lon"] = lon;
        row["cap"] = cap;
        dt.Rows.Add(row);
    }

}
```

When this is invoked by the Atlas-enabled browser page and the `select` method is invoked, the following is returned to the page:

```
HTTP/1.1 200 OK
Server: ASP.NET Development Server/8.0.0.0
Date: Sun, 26 Feb 2006 10:04:22 GMT
X-AspNet-Version: 2.0.50727
Cache-Control: private, max-age=0
Content-Type: text/html; charset=utf-8
Content-Length: 291
Connection: Close
new Web.Data.DataTable([{"cap":"test 1","lat":2,"lon":3},{"cap":"test
 2","lat":3,"lon":4},{"cap":"test 3","lat":4,"lon":5},{"cap":"test
 4","lat":5,"lon":6}],[new Web.Data.DataColumn("cap",String,null),new
 Web.Data.DataColumn("lat",Number,null),new
 Web.Data.DataColumn("lon",Number,null)],[])
```

This output from the DataService was captured using Fiddler. Notice we sent back only five rows to make it readable.

Now that you have seen how we will get the data and how it comes back to the browser, let's take a look at what causes this DataService to be invoked and how we can use the Atlas framework to show the data on the browser.

The first thing we are going to do is define a template that acts as a placeholder to hold our data. The following defines a table with three columns:

```
<div id="resultsTemplate">
    <table border="1" cellspacing="0">
        <thead>
            <tr>
                <td>Latitude</td>
                <td>Longitude</td>
                <td>Caption</td>
            </tr>
        </thead>
        <tbody id="resultsTemplateParent">
            <tr id="resultsItemTemplate">
                <td id="resultsItemLatLabel"></td>
                <td id="resultsItemLonLabel"></td>
                <td id="resultsItemCapLabel"></td>
            </tr>
        </tbody>
    </table>
</div>
```

Now, to bring that to life, we will take a brief look at another innovation that comes with Atlas: Atlas XML Script. Atlas XML Script is a declarative script format that enables the separation of the user interface from the behaviors of your application. When the following script is parsed, it is able to define a datasource `myDS` and knows its location via the `serviceURL`. The item template binds the data to the layout we defined in our previous example. Finally, in the application/load tags, we define that we want to invoke the `select` method on the datasource:

```
<script type="text/xml-script">
        <page xmlns:script="http://schemas.microsoft.com/xml-script/2005">
            <components>
                <dataSource id="myDS" serviceURL="MapDS1.asmx"
propertyChanged="onChange"/>

                <listView targetElement="results"
                    itemTemplateParentElementId="resultsTemplateParent"
propertyChanged="onChange">
                    <bindings>
                        <binding dataContext="myDS" dataPath="data"
property="data"/>
                    </bindings>
                    <layoutTemplate>
                        <template layoutElement="resultsTemplate"/>
                    </layoutTemplate>
                    <itemTemplate>
                        <template layoutElement="resultsItemTemplate">
                            <label targetElement="resultsItemLatLabel">
                                <bindings>
                                    <binding dataPath="lat" property="text"/>
                                </bindings>
                            </label>
                            <label targetElement="resultsItemLonLabel">
                                <bindings>
                                    <binding dataPath="lon" property="text"/>
                                </bindings>
                            </label>
                            <label targetElement="resultsItemCapLabel">
                                <bindings>
                                    <binding dataPath="cap" property="text"/>
                                </bindings>
                            </label>
                        </template>
                    </itemTemplate>
                </listView>

                <application>
                    <load>
                        <invokeMethod target="myDS" method="select"/>
                    </load>
                </application>
            </components>
        </page>
    </script>
```

This example only looked at how a `select` method could be identified. The DataService can also identify `Update`, `Insert`, and `Delete` methods. Also, in addition to the ListView, which is intended to work in a tabular fashion, there is a ItemView, which is designed to provide a one-row view.

AutoComplete Made Easy!

One of the first third-party controls created for ASP.NET were the smart drop-downs, which made finding things in the program much easier. These controls use callbacks to the server page to load up the data, providing users with an improved lookup experience. You had to go to a third party for those, as nothing for this basic capability came out of the box with ASP.NET. This changes with Atlas, which includes Auto Complete capabilities that are tied in with the capability to pull data from a Web service.

AutoComplete is implemented using the `atlas:AutoCompleteExtender` control. This control is an add-in to a control such as Textbox to add to or extend the functionality of that control to include auto complete. The following is an example of the markup to tie an `AutoCompleteExtender` to a Textbox control:

```
<asp:TextBox runat="server" ID="stateTextBox" />
<atlas:AutoCompleteExtender runat="server" ID="auto1">
        <atlas:AutoCompleteProperties TargetControlID="stateTextBox"
                Enabled="true" ServicePath="StateListWS.asmx"
                ServiceMethod="GetMatchingStates" />
</atlas:AutoCompleteExtender>
```

In the preceding example we associate the `AutoCompleteExtender` to the Textbox via the `TargetControlID` property. `AutoCompleteExtender` will call a Web service we identify via the `ServicePath` and `ServiceMethod` to retrieve the data. The following illustrates what that method looks like on the Web service:

```
[WebMethod]
  public string[] GetMatchingStates(string prefixText,int count)
  {
    StateDataTable dt = new StateDataTable("US");
    dt.DefaultView.RowFilter = "StateProvName like '" + prefixText + "%'";
      List<string> stateList = new List<string>();
      foreach (DataRowView row in dt.DefaultView)
          if (stateList.Count < count)
              stateList.Add(row["StateProvName"].ToString());

      return stateList.ToArray();
  }
```

The key thing to note here is the prototype for the function. It takes `prefixText` and `count`. In the current release, those are not controlled by the caller but are part of the `AutoCompleteExtender` function. I'm hopeful that more control over that will be provided so that, for example, you could pass other filter type criteria along. In this example I happened to grab a helper DataTable that simply has one row for each state and is organized by country. The contents were excluded because they weren't important for the example. What is important is that this returns an array of strings that will be used by the `AutoCompleteExtender` to show a list of options. Figure 4-2 shows what would be displayed to users if they typed "new" into the text box.

Figure 4-2

`AutoCompleteExtender` is part of a new set of extender-enabled controls that inherit from `Extender Control`. The concept behind extender controls is simple: They are designed to work alongside other controls, adding specific feature sets. In our example it adds the auto complete capability. One could argue that you could just keep adding on more capabilities to a custom text box that inherits from the built-in Textbox, but you can quickly end up with a one-size-never-fits-all custom control. Extenders, on the other hand, can add on a specific capability and attach themselves to the target control. You could also attach multiple extenders to simply add the needed features. Best of all, you can inherit from `ExtenderControl` and build your own extenders.

The UpdatePanel

As you start playing around with your choice of AJAX-related capabilities, you will find that doing more interactive work with a single control is pretty easy; but when you start trying to coordinate that across multiple controls, the task gets more challenging. Additionally, there are times when as a result of a change in selections or the data you want to update, only a region of a page is presented on the browser. In ASP.NET 2.0 this is accomplished by doing a postback, and the browser page will be re-rendered. The flash of the page in the browser can be disruptive to users and takes their focus away from the task they are performing.

To help improve this problem, the Atlas framework includes an UpdatePanel control. Using this control a developer can define updatable regions on a page that can do partial rendering. The Atlas framework both on the client and on the server takes care of most of the housekeeping to make this happen.

The first step in using an UpdatePanel control is to configure the `ScriptManager` instance on the page to allow partial rendering. This is done by setting the `EnablePartialRendering` property to `true`, as you can see in the following example:

```
<atlas:ScriptManager runat="server" ID="scm"  EnablePartialRendering="true" />
```

The UpdatePanel control is similar to other Panel-type controls in that its content is what is managed and rendered by the control. The UpdatePanel specifies this content inside the `ContentTemplate` element, as shown in the following example:

```
<div>
           Page Time: <%# DateTime.Now.ToString() %>
           <atlas:UpdatePanel runat="server" ID="up1" Mode="conditional">
               <ContentTemplate>
                   Update Panel Time:    <%# DateTime.Now.ToString() %>
               </ContentTemplate>
               <Triggers>
                   <atlas:ControlEventTrigger ControlID="button1"
EventName="Click" />
               </Triggers>
           </atlas:UpdatePanel>
           <asp:Button runat="server" ID="button1" Text="Update Panel" />
</div>
```

In the preceding very simple example, a `DateTime` shows outside the UpdatePanel, and one is contained inside the `ContentTemplate` of the `UpdatePanel`. On a complete page refresh, both are kept in sync and will have the same value. To make this useful, we leverage another key component of the `UpdatePanel`, the ability to trigger refreshing the contents based on events that happen on the page. In this case we will drive a refresh of the region when the button is pressed. When this trigger occurs, the Atlas framework will refresh only the `UpdatePanel` region and the two times will no longer be in sync.

This will be accomplished with minimal indication to the user — in other words, the page will not refresh completely.

Refresh with a Timer

One of the other controls that comes with the Atlas framework is the TimerControl. The TimerControl is a great time-saver when you need something to occur every so often on the page. In the following example we combine the timer concept with our update panel to produce a panel that updates every 10 seconds:

```
<atlas:TimerControl runat="server" Interval="10000" ID="myTimer" />

          <atlas:UpdatePanel runat="server" ID="UpdatePanel1"
Mode="conditional">
              <ContentTemplate>
                  Auto Update Panel Time:    <%# DateTime.Now.ToString() %>
              </ContentTemplate>
              <Triggers>
                  <atlas:ControlEventTrigger ControlID="myTimer" EventName="Tick"
/>
              </Triggers>
          </atlas:UpdatePanel>
```

In the preceding code for this example, we simply call the DataBind() method during the page load to force it to update the date/time information. The following code shows the page load that would be invoked.

```
protected void Page_Load(object sender, EventArgs e)
{
        this.DataBind();
}
```

This type of auto update concept would be great for monitoring type applications for which you want to refresh portions of the page at certain intervals.

We just finished a whirlwind look at some of the new capabilities that will be available when the Atlas framework is released. It is hoped that from a few of the examples you were able to glean the power that is available with the Atlas framework. The fact that it is much more than a simple client-side scripting helper library is important. Atlas provides integration of the server and client request to help enable you to build more interactive applications.

Connecting with Project Atlas

More information on Microsoft's Atlas initiative can be found at atlas.asp.net. The ASP.NET team has been frequently releasing updated releases of the Atlas framework in order for the community to provide feedback. It is anticipated that later in 2006 a version that includes a go-live license will be made available.

Help! What Do I Do Now?

A challenge that you will face with the current support for the AJAX concept is determining what you use to build your application with today. Unless your intent is to build your own framework to support the AJAX concept, you should probably look to support from the community, third-party control vendors, and finally from Microsoft, as they provide support for AJAX in the form of the Atlas project.

Community Projects

A variety of community projects exist in support of AJAX. Some are simply focused on singleton controls such as a drop-down list or other UI widgets that can be leveraged. Others offer a full suite of controls that are designed to work together to make building AJAX applications easier.

The following is a sample of some of the AJAX-oriented frameworks:

❑ **Engine for Web Applications** (`immmotion.com/projects/engine/`) — Started in 2002.

❑ **BitKraft** (`tiggrbitz.com/`) — BitKraft extends the ASP.NET architecture to provide JavaScript callbacks using XmlHttp. BitKraft is not a client-only framework; it combines client with server support to translate CLR types using JSON (JavaScript Object Notation) to materialize the objects on the client side as well.

❑ **Prototype** (`http://prototype.conio.net/`) — JavaScript framework designed to make building dynamic Web applications easier. Heavily driven by the Ruby on Rails framework, it can be used on any environment. It's very lacking in documentation, but is used as a building block for other community projects such as script.aculo.us, Ruby on Rails, and others.

❑ **Script.aculo.us** (`http://script.aculo.us/`) — Builds on top of prototype, adding features such as drag and drop, Auto complete, and more.

❑ **Rico** (`http://openrico.org/`) — Grew out of work within Sabre Airline Solutions.

❑ **AJAX.NET Professional** (`schwarz-interactive.de/`) — Michael Schwarz's creation, AJAX.NET is one of the more well-known frameworks in the ASP.NET community.

Third-Party Controls

A variety of community projects exist in support of AJAX. Similar to the Community Projects, some third-party controls are simply focused on singleton controls such as a drop-down list or other UI widgets that can be leveraged.

The following is a sample of some of the commercial support for AJAX. This is not a recommended list of vendors, but a sample to get you more familiar with what exists:

❑ **Tibco General Interface** (`http://developer.tibco.com/`) — Client-side framework that strives to help you build *Rich Internet Applications (RIAs)* using AJAX. Their framework tries to provide a simple interface to register AJAX request handlers and other related objects to help manage the interaction. Drag and drop, cinematic effects, and various other behaviors are also supported.

❑ **Web.UI 3.0** (`componentart.com`) — AJAX-enabled Web user interface control suite by ComponentArt. It includes controls such as Grid, TreeView, Calendar, and more.

Kicking the Tires

If you don't do anything else, download a couple of the frameworks listed in this chapter and take a look at how the samples work. By getting familiar with the different techniques used by the frameworks you might learn innovative ways that you can build custom controls as needed for your specific project.

Each of the approaches brings to the table innovation in how they are attempting to build these applications easier.

By getting involved early and if you are not pushed by your company to use the AJAX concept, you have the opportunity to watch as the evolution of the smart Web client occurs. You don't have to sit idle and do nothing, though. One of the best moves to consider is what steps you can take now to make building more interactive applications easier. By doing things like moving common features to either user controls or custom server controls, you create components that can later be upgraded to be more AJAX-like. The conversion can happen over time as the benefits can be achieved by your application.

One thing is certain: Almost all the vendors involved are providing aggressive development cycles that result in several releases per year of updated controls As you pick a technique, make sure that it's one that will be there for the long haul and not just a fun sideline project that will end up leaving your mission-critical application broken when the vendor chooses not to support the framework in the future.

Wrapping Up

Will the real smart client please stand up . . . . Nothing short of a train wreck occurs when you combine technology innovations and the marketing spin masters, and words like "Smart," "Fat," "Lite," and "Rich" are used to describe the emerging techniques and capabilities. We all know it's a necessary evil, but at the end of the day you have to ask yourself whether we have really seen the real smart client yet.

Simply put, using the AJAX concept along with community and vendor innovations will make it easier to build Web applications that are more interactive. Some of the capabilities discussed in this chapter and those that are planned to be provided by Microsoft under the umbrella of the Atlas initiative take the AJAX concept a step further by providing integrated host capabilities, and in many cases extending host capabilities to the client. If you build Web applications, its not a matter of if you will use some form of AJAX, but when.

Recognizng the need for tools that make such tasks as debugging easier is an important step in ensuring the successful broad-scale use of this emerging set of techniques. The great ideas in the community combined with the support of the vendors help increase the speed with which the prototype of a concept becomes reality in a released supported product.

Another important area that is not widely talked about at the same time as the concept of AJAX or re-emergence of client-side activities is security. By pushing more logic to the client, applications must also keep up from a security and integrity standpoint to ensure that the rogue client can't hack or take advantage of the server-side application. For example, we must ensure that we don't solely rely on the client to validate and pass an approved price, because for all we know that price may have been tampered with on a rogue client. In the excitement of making smarter Web clients, we can't forget about the need for security, and to be even more vigilant as we move logic from the server to the extended client platform.

All said, AJAX and the other related concepts are just another step in the progression to the real smart client as we will know it in the future. The techniques and capabilities described in this chapter certainly make taking this step easier.

As you sit back and think about what to do in your own application, use this chapter as your starting point to explore the capabilities that are out there. Implement AJAX-oriented techniques and capabilities as needed to support the business needs of your application, but at the same time balance the evolution of the AJAX concept. As the tools and support mature, so will the ease of building the applications that provide a richer and more interactive experience for the user.

5

Debugging
What You Created

All of the whiz-bang functionality in your application won't mean a thing if your code has bugs. The debugging capabilities in Visual Studio get better with each new version of the tool, and Visual Studio 2005 does not disappoint. Several key new features have been added to help you debug your code faster and more effectively. In this chapter, you'll learn how to dynamically view the contents of complex objects while debugging, reduce the clutter of the debug window, and add custom messages to the debug window. It won't take you long to realize just how powerful these features are and what they can do to make your life easier.

One-Stop Visualization

While you are stepping through your code in Visual Studio 2005, it is important to be able to determine the values contained in the variables and parameters that your code is using. If you are working with a simple data type such as an integer or string, you can get its value easily by either hovering your mouse over the variable or adding it to the Watch window. Simple business objects can be handled in a similar manner because you can expand the object out in the Watch window to see the values of its members. The new DataTips feature in Visual Studio 2005 enables you to drill down into an object directly from the ToolTip that appears when you hover your mouse over it in your code.

Some objects, however, are not so easily represented in a textual grid format. Some examples include complex business objects, GDI images, streams, and large blocks of text. *Visualizers* can be used to tackle this problem.

What Is a Visualizer?

A visualizer is a plug-in to Visual Studio 2005 that enables you to represent the contents of an object in a way that is most suitable to its particular data type. A few visualizers ship with Visual Studio 2005 out of the box. Some of these include XML, HTML, and Multi-Line textbox visualizers for the string data type, and a grid visualizer to show the contents of a `DataSet` or a `DataTable` object. More than one visualizer can be associated with a particular data type, and they are accessed by clicking the magnifying glass that appears next to the object in either the Watch window or the DataTips window (shown later in this chapter in Figure 5-5).

Building a Visualizer

To demonstrate how to build your own visualizer, imagine a scenario in which you are going to use GDI+ to manipulate images in a project. As you might imagine, it would be much easier to check on the progress of your image edits if you could see what the image currently looks like in memory after you apply each change. The standard debug window isn't much help in that regard, so let's build a visualizer that enables us to display the contents of an `Image` object. By actually displaying the `Image` object's contents on a form, you will be able to see right away whether your GDI+ code has gone awry.

> Note that there are security implications when using visualizers created by third parties. Visualizers must run under Full Trust, so it is possible that the visualizer could execute malicious code on behalf of an executable that is running under Partial Trust. You can learn more about this at the following URL: `http://msdn2 .microsoft.com/en-us/library/ms242209.aspx`.

Creating the Visualizer Project

Visualizers are implemented as standard class library projects, so to start off you should add one to a blank solution in Visual Studio 2005. Delete the default `Class1.cs` (or `Class1.vb`) file that is created for you. Then, right-click the project in the Solution Explorer and select the option to add a new item to the project. Select Debugger Visualizer from the list of Visual Studio installed templates, name it ImageVisualizer, and click the Add button (see Figure 5-1).

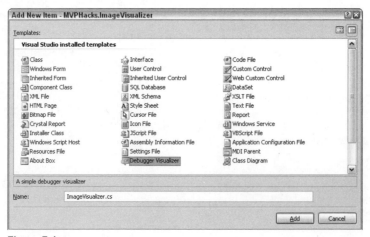

Figure 5-1

As you can see in the following example, most of the plumbing code to build your visualizer is already in place for you. All you need to do is make a few modifications based on the data type that you want to visualize (in this case, the `Image` data type), and then add the implementation of the visualizer form itself. We'll cover that in a moment.

```csharp
using System;
using System.Collections.Generic;
using System.Diagnostics;
using System.Windows.Forms;
using Microsoft.VisualStudio.DebuggerVisualizers;

namespace MVPHacks.ImageVisualizer
{
    // TODO: Add the following to SomeType's definition to see this visualizer when
    debugging instances of SomeType:
    //
    // [DebuggerVisualizer(typeof(ImageVisualizer))]
    // [Serializable]
    // public class SomeType
    // {
    //   ...
    // }
    //
    /// <summary>
    /// A Visualizer for SomeType.
    /// </summary>
    public class ImageVisualizer : DialogDebuggerVisualizer
    {
        protected override void Show(IDialogVisualizerService windowService,
IVisualizerObjectProvider objectProvider)
        {
            // TODO: Get the object to display a visualizer for.
            //       Cast the result of objectProvider.GetObject()
            //       to the type of the object being visualized.
            object data = (object)objectProvider.GetObject();

            // TODO: Display your view of the object.
            //       Replace displayForm with your own custom Form or Control.
            using (Form displayForm = new Form())
            {
                displayForm.Text = data.ToString();
                windowService.ShowDialog(displayForm);
            }
        }

        // TODO: Add the following to your testing code to test the visualizer:
        //
        //     ImageVisualizer.TestShowVisualizer(new SomeType());
        //
        /// <summary>
        /// Tests the visualizer by hosting it outside of the debugger.
        /// </summary>
```

```
        /// <param name="objectToVisualize">The object to display in the
visualizer.</param>
        public static void TestShowVisualizer(object objectToVisualize)
        {
           VisualizerDevelopmentHost visualizerHost = new
VisualizerDevelopmentHost(objectToVisualize, typeof(ImageVisualizer));
           visualizerHost.ShowVisualizer();
        }
    }
}
```

Adding the Visualizer Implementation

The ImageVisualizer class that you added to your project has two methods, Show and TestShow Visualizer. The TestShowVisualizer method is used (as its name implies) for testing your visualizer. We'll worry about that in a bit. For now, turn your attention to the Show method, which accepts two parameters, windowService and objectProvider. The windowService parameter is an instance of the IDialogVisualizerService interface, which enables your visualizer to display forms, dialog boxes, and controls. You'll be using it to show the form that will contain the contents of the image that you want to visualize. The objectProvider parameter is an instance of the IVisualizerObject Provider interface, and is the broker that transfers the object data that you are going to visualize from the debuggee process (the application you are debugging) to the debugger (in this case, Visual Studio 2005's debugger process).

> It is also possible to transfer data from the visualizer in the debugger process back to the debuggee process using the ReplaceData, ReplaceObject, TransferData, or TransferObject methods. This topic is not covered here, as it is not needed for the Image visualizer that we are building.

Because we'll be working with the GDI+ Image object, add a reference to the System.Drawing namespace. Next, in order to properly visualize your data, you need to extract it from the objectProvider parameter using its GetObject method and cast it to the proper type. Change the generic code that exists in the template to the following:

```
Image data = (Image)objectProvider.GetObject();
```

We could easily use the generic Form displayForm = new Form() code to display the image data, but to make the implementation cleaner, add a Windows Form to the project, name it **ImageForm**, and set its Text property to **Image Visualizer**. After that, add a PictureBox control to the design surface of ImageForm. You can leave its default name as pictureBox1. ImageForm should now look something like what is shown in Figure 5-2.

Figure 5-2

The PictureBox control is private to ImageForm, so in order to make it available to ImageVisualizer, add the following public property code to the code for ImageForm:

```
public PictureBox ImageToView
{
get { return pictureBox1; }
}
```

Now that ImageForm is complete, swing back over to the Show method in the ImageVisualizer class. There is a sample visualizer implementation there that merely displays the ToString method of the object that you passed in as the caption of a generic form. Delete all of that code and replace it with this code:

```
using (ImageForm displayForm = new ImageForm())
{
//set image position on form
      displayForm.ImageToView.Left = 0;
      displayForm.ImageToView.Top = 0;

      //set image data on form
displayForm.ImageToView.Image  = data;

//set image size on form
      displayForm.ImageToView.Width = data.Width;
      displayForm.ImageToView.Height = data.Height;

      //set form size in relation to image size on form
      displayForm.ClientSize = new Size(displayForm.ImageToView.Width,
displayForm.ImageToView.Height);

//display the form
      windowService.ShowDialog(displayForm);
}
```

The first thing that the implementation code does is make sure that the PictureBox control (exposed via the ImageToView property of ImageForm) is positioned in the top-left corner of ImageForm. Next, it sets the Image property of the PictureBox control to the image data that was passed into the visualizer. The PictureBox control must be set to the proper width and height, which is taken care of by the next couple of lines of code. The visualizer will look cleaner if ImageForm is only as big as the image that it will be displaying, so the next couple of lines of code set its ClientSize property to the width and height of the PictureBox control using a Size object. Finally, the ShowDialog method of the windowService parameter is used to actually display the visualizer to the user.

The last item to take care of when building a visualizer is to add a DebuggerVisualizer attribute to the assembly. You can do this by adding the following code just above the namespace declaration in your ImageVisualizer class file:

```
[assembly: System.Diagnostics.DebuggerVisualizer(
typeof(MVPHacks.ImageVisualizer.ImageVisualizer),
      Target = typeof(Image),
  Description = "Image Visualizer")]
```

So what does all of that mean? The DebuggerVisualizer attribute lets the .NET runtime know that this assembly is a visualizer. The first parameter passed in is the fully qualified class name of the visualizer. The Target parameter is the data type of the class that this visualizer is designed to visualize. Although this visualizer is designed for one of the built-in classes of the .NET Framework, it doesn't have to be used for that. You can build visualizers for your custom business objects as well. The only requirement is that the visualizer project must contain a reference to the project that contains the class definition of your business object (exactly as you added a reference to the System.Drawing namespace in order to visualize the Image class). Last, the Description parameter is the textual description that will appear in the visualizer drop-down list (indicated by a magnifying glass) when you view an instance of the class defined by the Target parameter in the debug window.

Here is what your completed ImageVisualizer class should look like:

```csharp
using System;
using System.Collections.Generic;
using System.Diagnostics;
using System.Windows.Forms;
using Microsoft.VisualStudio.DebuggerVisualizers;
using System.Drawing;

[assembly: System.Diagnostics.DebuggerVisualizer(
 typeof(MVPHacks.ImageVisualizer.ImageVisualizer),
        Target = typeof(Image),
        Description = "Image Visualizer")]

namespace MVPHacks.ImageVisualizer
{
    /// <summary>
    /// A Visualizer for System.Drawing.Image
    /// </summary>
    public class ImageVisualizer : DialogDebuggerVisualizer
    {
        protected override void Show(IDialogVisualizerService windowService,
         IVisualizerObjectProvider objectProvider)
        {
            // TODO: Get the object to display a visualizer for.
            //       Cast the result of objectProvider.GetObject()
            //       to the type of the object being visualized.
            Image data = (Image)objectProvider.GetObject();

            // TODO: Display your view of the object.
            //       Replace displayForm with your own custom Form or Control.
            using (Form displayForm = new Form())
            {
                displayForm.Text = data.ToString();
                windowService.ShowDialog(displayForm);
            }
        }

        /// <summary>
        /// Tests the visualizer by hosting it outside of the debugger.
        /// </summary>
        /// <param name="objectToVisualize">The object to visualize.</param>
        public static void TestShowVisualizer(object objectToVisualize)
```

```
    {
        VisualizerDevelopmentHost visualizerHost = new
    VisualizerDevelopmentHost(objectToVisualize,
    typeof(ImageVisualizer));
        visualizerHost.ShowVisualizer();
    }
  }
}
```

Testing the Visualizer

You just built your first visualizer! Of course, you're going to want to test it out before you deploy it. Remember the TestShowVisualizer method mentioned earlier? This is where that method comes into play. The great part is that the template code that was provided does not need to be modified in order to make it work. You can optionally change the data type of the objectToVisualize parameter to the type that you will be visualizing, but it is not necessary because it will be cast back to Object when it is passed from the debuggee process to the debugger process.

While the visualizer that you just created can be used from any client platform (including ASP.NET), for simplicity, let's keep our test simple and straightforward. Add a console application project to your solution in Visual Studio 2005. Name it **MVPHacks.TestImageVisualizer**. Because you are testing the MVPHacks.ImageVisualizer project, add a project reference to it. In addition, you'll need to add a reference to the System.Drawing and Microsoft.VisualStudio.DebuggerVisualizers assemblies because you will be using classes contained in both of these libraries. Add a using statement for the System.Drawing namespace at the top of the code in the Program.cs file that is created with your console application.

In the Main method of the Program class of the console application, add the following code:

```
static void Main(string[] args)
{
    Image img = Image.FromFile(@"c:\data\UserGroup\angryCoderLogo.gif");

    MVPHacks.ImageVisualizer.ImageVisualizer.TestShowVisualizer(img);

    img.RotateFlip(RotateFlipType.RotateNoneFlipY);

    MVPHacks.ImageVisualizer.ImageVisualizer.TestShowVisualizer(img);
}
```

The first thing that the code does is load an image from disk into an Image variable. Next, it calls the static TestShowVisualizer method of the ImageVisualizer class that you just created. This displays the visualizer, just as if you had deployed it and executed it using the visualizer magnifying glass in the debug window (see Figure 5-3).

Figure 5-3

> Note that the visualizer may appear as an item in your task bar only when in debug mode, forcing you to click on the item to view it. Once you compile and deploy your visualizer, it will appear normally when you access it via the magnifying glass in the debug window.

Next, the code uses the `RotateFlip` method to flip the image along its *y* axis. The `TestShow Visualizer` method is then called again so that you can see the results of the change to the image (see Figure 5-4).

Figure 5-4

Deploying the Visualizer

Now that you are done building and testing the ImageVisualizer visualizer, you will want to deploy it, so that you can use it to visually inspect the contents of `Image` objects in any of your projects that use GDI+. Luckily, deploying visualizers is easy. The first thing that you need to do is compile the ImageVisualizer project in Release mode (which can be selected from a drop-down list in the standard toolbar in Visual Studio 2005). Once you have done that, locate the compiled `MVPHacks.ImageVisualizer.dll` assembly. It will be in the `/bin/Release/` sub-directory under your `MVPHacks.ImageVisualizer` project directory. There may be an `MVPHacks.ImageVisualizer.pdb` file alongside it. You don't need this file because it merely contains the debug symbols for the `.dll` assembly.

If you would like your visualizer to be available only to you, then copy the assembly into your `\MyDocuments\Visual Studio 2005\Visualizers` directory. If you would like to make your visualizer available to anyone who is using your computer, then copy the assembly into the `\ProgramFiles\Microsoft Visual Studio 8\Common7\Packages\Debugger\Visualizers\` directory. One of the neat parts about the deployment process is that there is no need to close and re-open Visual Studio 2005. The next time you start a debugging session, your new visualizer will be available to you.

In order to see the ImageVisualizer working in a real project, first make sure that you are back in Debug mode. Comment out the two lines of code that call the `TestShowVisualizer` method and put a breakpoint on the line of code that calls the `RotateFlip` method of the `img` variable. To truly demonstrate that you are running the visualizer with no strings attached, you can remove the references to the `MVPHacks.ImageVisualizer` project and the `Microsoft.VisualStudio.DebuggerVisualizers` assembly. You'll need to keep the reference to `System.Drawing`, though.

Go ahead and run the `TestImageVisualizer` project again. When the breakpoint that you set is hit, hover your mouse over the `img` variable. When the DataTip appears, it will contain a magnifying glass, indicating that this data type has one or more visualizers associated with it. If you click on the magnifying glass, then the default visualizer associated with the data type (e.g., the last one that you used) will execute. You can also click the arrow next to the magnifying glass to display a drop-down list of available visualizers (see Figure 5-5).

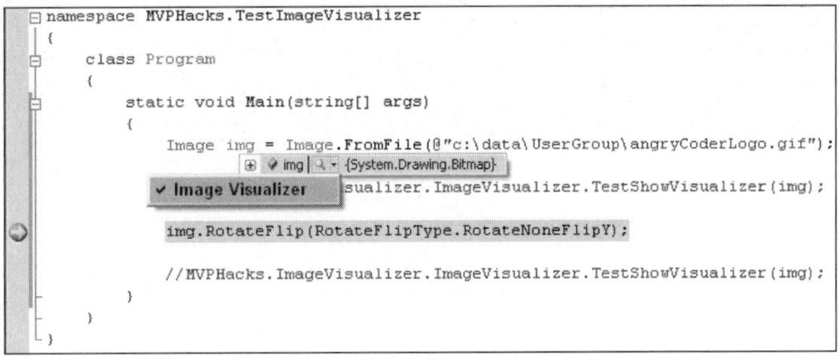

Figure 5-5

So there you have it. Visualizers are a powerful tool because they enable you to see the contents of complex objects and make better decisions when debugging your applications

Tuning Objects for Debugging

Sometimes, you don't quite need the power of a visualizer, but you still want to make it faster and easier to view and interpret your business objects in the debug window. The `System.Diagnostics` namespace implements a few different attributes that you can use to decorate your classes and their members to tune up your objects for debugging. In essence, you can reduce the clutter of the debug window and take control of what is displayed about your custom business objects.

Setting Object Member Visibility

The `DebuggerBrowsable` attribute enables you to decorate object members such as properties with instructions regarding their visibility in the debug window. It accepts the `DebuggerBrowsableState` enumeration as a parameter, which has one of three values: `Collapsed`, `Never`, or `RootHidden`. Their definitions are outlined in the following table.

Member Name	Description
Collapsed	Show the element as collapsed. This is the default behavior.
Never	Never show the element in the debug window.
RootHidden	Do not display the root element; display the child elements if the element is a collection or an array of items.

To illustrate how these attributes work, consider the `Person` class implemented in the following example:

```
class Person
{
    private string _lastName = string.Empty;
    private string _firstName = string.Empty;
    private int _age = 0;
    private List<Person> _children = new List<Person>();
    private List<string> _pets = new List<string>();
```

```
    private List<string> _cars = new List<string>();

    public string LastName
    {
        get { return _lastName; }
        set { _lastName = value; }
    }

    public string FirstName
    {
        get { return _firstName; }
        set { _firstName = value; }
    }

    public int Age
    {
        get { return _age; }
        set { _age = value; }
    }

    [DebuggerBrowsable(DebuggerBrowsableState.Collapsed)]
    public List<Person> Children
    {
        get{return _children;}
    }

    [DebuggerBrowsable(DebuggerBrowsableState.Never)]
    public List<string> Pets
    {
        get { return _pets; }
    }

    [DebuggerBrowsable(DebuggerBrowsableState.RootHidden)]
    public List<string> Cars
    {
        get { return _cars; }
    }

    public Person()
    {
    }

    public Person(string lastName, string firstName, int age)
    {
        _lastName = lastName;
        _firstName = firstName;
        _age = age;
    }
}
```

Three of the properties of the Person class (Children, Pets, and Cars) are decorated with one of the DebuggerBrowsable attribute options. When viewed in the Watch window, it looks similar to Figure 5-6.

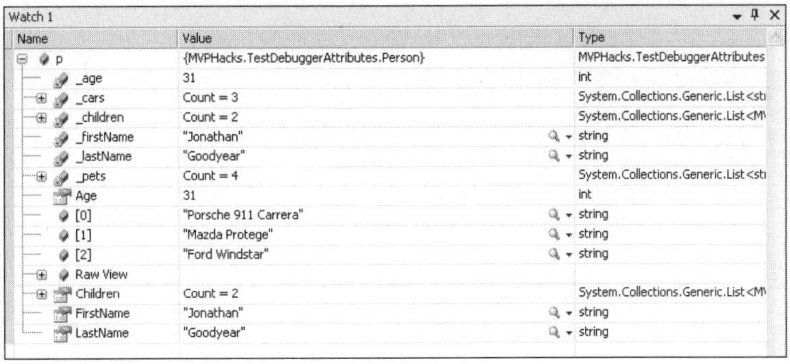

Figure 5-6

As you can see, the `Children` property that was decorated with `DebuggerBrowsableState` `.Collapsed` shows up as collapsed in the Watch window. You can expand it by clicking on the plus sign next to the property name in order to see the `Person` objects that it contains. The `Pets` property doesn't show up at all in the Watch window because it was decorated with `DebuggerBrowsableState.Never`. Don't confuse this with the `_pets` internal field that appears in the Watch window. In the next section, you'll see how to look at the `Person` class in the Watch window without the clutter of internal fields. Finally, the `Cars` property doesn't appear directly, but its contents do, as indicated by the `[0]`, `[1]` and `[2]` items in the Watch window. This is the behavior that results from decorating it with `DebuggerBrowsableState.RootHidden`.

Simplifying the Object View with a Type Proxy

Have you ever noticed how cluttered the debug window gets when you're analyzing a complex business object like the one described earlier? A large part of the confusion is created because the debug window uses reflection to show you the values of internal fields that aren't directly accessible via the object's interface. It also doesn't help that objects often implement properties that are sometimes used by the program but aren't needed very often for debugging. Wouldn't it be great if you could get a view of just the information about the object that's important to you? Well, you can. *Type proxy* functionality was created for just this purpose.

A type proxy is implemented as an internal class within your business object. Its purpose is to define only the elements that you want displayed in the debug window. By design, internal fields are never shown in the debug window. Let's go ahead and add a type proxy to the `Person` class:

```
internal class PersonProxy
{
    private Person _person;

    public PersonProxy(Person person)
    {
        _person = person;
    }

    public string Children
    {
```

```
        get
        {
            string[] children = new string[_person.Children.Count];

            for(int i = 0; i<_person.Children.Count;i++)
            {
                children[i] = _person.Children[i].FirstName;
            }

            return string.Join(", ",children);
        }
    }

    public string Pets
    {
        get { return string.Join(", ", _person.Pets.ToArray()); }
    }

    public string Cars
    {
        get { return string.Join(", ", _person.Cars.ToArray()); }
    }

    public string Person
    {
        get
        {
            return "Name = " + _person.FirstName + " " + _person.LastName +
                ", Age = " + _person.Age;
        }
    }
}
```

A type proxy class must implement a constructor that accepts an instance of the class for which it is going to be a proxy, so that is what the preceding proxy contains first. Next, you can add as many properties as you would like to represent the data contained in the class that the proxy represents. They can be formatted in any way (although typically they are represented as strings), and they can even have names that differ from their corresponding properties in the underlying class.

In order to wire up the PersonProxy class to act as a type proxy for the Person class, you need to decorate the class declaration with the DebuggerTypeProxy attribute:

```
[DebuggerTypeProxy(typeof(PersonProxy))]
class Person
{
  //implementation removed for clarity
}
```

> The DebuggerTypeProxy attribute can also be used at the assembly level using the Target parameter to specify the class that the type proxy will represent. For clarity, however, it is usually best to decorate the class itself with the DebuggerTypeProxy attribute.

Once that has been done, if you view an instance of the `Person` class in the Watch window, it will look something like what is shown in Figure 5-7.

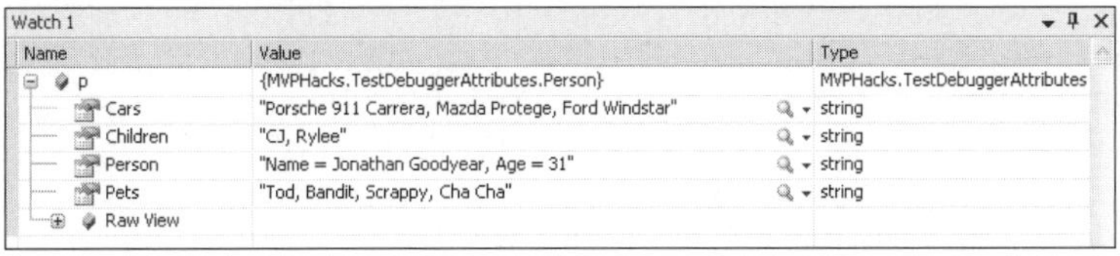

Watch 1			▼ ⊣ X
Name	Value		Type
⊟ ● p	{MVPHacks.TestDebuggerAttributes.Person}		MVPHacks.TestDebuggerAttributes
🔎 Cars	"Porsche 911 Carrera, Mazda Protege, Ford Windstar"	🔍 ▾	string
🔎 Children	"CJ, Rylee"	🔍 ▾	string
🔎 Person	"Name = Jonathan Goodyear, Age = 31"	🔍 ▾	string
🔎 Pets	"Tod, Bandit, Scrappy, Cha Cha"	🔍 ▾	string
⊞ ● Raw View			

Figure 5-7

The `PersonProxy` class combines the basic name and age demographic information into a single `Person` property. In addition, the `Cars`, `Children`, and `Pets` properties are represented as comma-separated lists, instead of lists of items implemented via generics. Notice also that even though the `Pets` property of the underlying `Person` class is decorated as `DebuggerBrowsableState.Never`, the proxy class still has access to its information in order to show it in the Watch window. Of course, if a case arises for which you need to get at all of the underlying data associated with the `Person` class, you can expand the Raw View node in the Watch window. This will expose the same view that you saw in Figure 5-6 where a type proxy was not used.

> Avoid putting any logic that is expensive to process in the constructor for your type proxy class because that logic will automatically be executed each time an instance of the underlying class is displayed in the debug window. A nice feature of type proxies, though, is that the logic in their properties is not executed until they are visible in the debug window.

Adding Debugging Logic to Your Business Objects

Type proxies are great for creating an easy-to-interpret view of your business objects, but you can also add some business logic into the mix by implementing the `DebuggerDisplay` attribute. You can decorate properties on either the properties of your underlying class or on your type proxy class. Note that the logic and output that is interpreted by the `DebuggerDisplay` attribute replaces anything that your underlying class or type proxy would normally display in the debug window.

As an example, you could add some logic to your `PersonProxy` class to quickly determine whether the person represented by the `Person` object is old enough to drink alcohol (in the United States) using the following:

```
[DebuggerDisplay("{_person.Age >= 21 ? \"Old Enough\" : \"Too Young\"}",
  Type = "Alcohol Age Check")]
public string AlcoholAgeCheck
{
  get { return string.Empty; }
}
```

In the preceding code, the `DebuggerDisplay` attribute is attached to a new read-only property named `AlcoholAgeCheck`. The first parameter that it accepts is a string, which denotes the text that you want displayed in the `Value` field of the debug window. Any text that is included inside curly braces is executed as actual code, which is how the ternary operation is able to access the fields of the private _person instance. The backslash can be used as an escape character for quotes, curly braces, backslashes, or any other reserved character that you may need to include in the output. The Type parameter is optional, and allows you to override the contents of the Type field in the debug window. Incidentally, the property getter returns an empty string because it is going to be overridden by the DebuggerDisplay attribute anyway.

When the preceding code is executed for someone who is older than or equal to 21 years old, the debug window would look like the one shown in Figure 5-8.

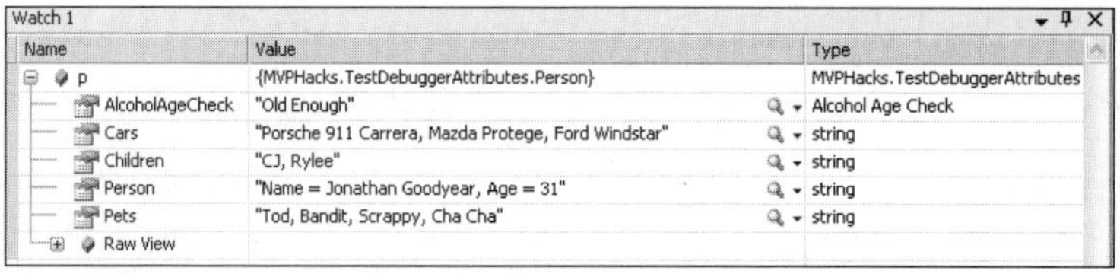

Name	Value	Type
⊟ ● p	{MVPHacks.TestDebuggerAttributes.Person}	MVPHacks.TestDebuggerAttributes
AlcoholAgeCheck	"Old Enough"	🔍 ▾ Alcohol Age Check
Cars	"Porsche 911 Carrera, Mazda Protege, Ford Windstar"	🔍 ▾ string
Children	"CJ, Rylee"	🔍 ▾ string
Person	"Name = Jonathan Goodyear, Age = 31"	🔍 ▾ string
Pets	"Tod, Bandit, Scrappy, Cha Cha"	🔍 ▾ string
⊞ ● Raw View		

Figure 5-8

If working with ternary operators to interpret business rules isn't your thing, then you can separate the logic out into a private function that returns a string, and then call that from your DebuggerDisplay attribute. The following code implements a generic BusinessRulesViolations property that will contain messages for any business rules that the current Person instance violates:

```
private string ValidateObject()
{
    List<string> violations = new List<string>();

    //make sure that a first name has been specified
    if (0 == _person.FirstName.Length)
    {
        violations.Add("FirstName is empty");
    }

    //make sure that a last name has been specified
    if (0 == _person.LastName.Length)
    {
        violations.Add("LastName is empty");
    }

    //make sure that age is greater than 0
    if (0 > _person.Age)
    {
        violations.Add("Age is less than 0");
    }

    //put additional validations here

    //return results to DebuggerDisplay attribute
    return string.Join(", ", violations.ToArray());
}

[DebuggerDisplay("{ValidateObject()}")]
```

```
public string BusinessRulesViolations
{
    get { return string.Empty; }
}
```

If I ran the preceding code using a person with no last name and an age of -1, then the debug window would look like the one shown in Figure 5-9.

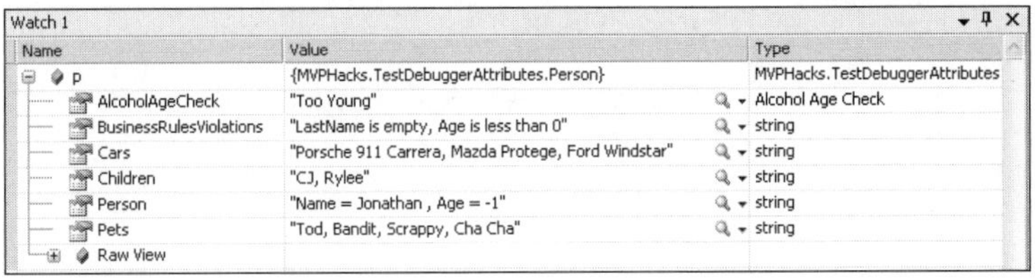

Name	Value	Type
⊟ ◉ p	{MVPHacks.TestDebuggerAttributes.Person}	MVPHacks.TestDebuggerAttributes
AlcoholAgeCheck	"Too Young"	Alcohol Age Check
BusinessRulesViolations	"LastName is empty, Age is less than 0"	string
Cars	"Porsche 911 Carrera, Mazda Protege, Ford Windstar"	string
Children	"CJ, Rylee"	string
Person	"Name = Jonathan , Age = -1"	string
Pets	"Tod, Bandit, Scrappy, Cha Cha"	string
⊞ ◉ Raw View		

Figure 5-9

A possible expansion of this example would be to recursively iterate the `Person` objects of the `Children` property to make sure that none of them were violating any business rules, so that you would know just by looking at the parent object whether any object in the hierarchy was invalid. Using the approach described here makes sense when you want a quick snapshot of anything that is wrong with your business object in the debug window. You'll then know immediately whether you need to investigate further.

Recap

To close out this section, here is what the `Person` class code looks like now:

```
using System;
using System.Collections.Generic;
using System.Text;
using System.Diagnostics;
using MVPHacks.TestDebuggerAttributes;

namespace MVPHacks.TestDebuggerAttributes
{
    [DebuggerTypeProxy(typeof(PersonProxy))]
    class Person
    {
        private string _lastName = string.Empty;
        private string _firstName = string.Empty;
        private int _age = 0;
        private List<Person> _children = new List<Person>();
        private List<string> _pets = new List<string>();
        private List<string> _cars = new List<string>();

        public string LastName
        {
            get { return _lastName; }
            set { _lastName = value; }
        }

        public string FirstName
```

```
{
    get { return _firstName; }
    set { _firstName = value; }
}

public int Age
{
    get { return _age; }
    set { _age = value; }
}

[DebuggerBrowsable(DebuggerBrowsableState.Collapsed)]
public List<Person> Children
{
    get{return _children;}
}

[DebuggerBrowsable(DebuggerBrowsableState.Never)]
public List<string> Pets
{
    get { return _pets; }
}

[DebuggerBrowsable(DebuggerBrowsableState.RootHidden)]
public List<string> Cars
{
    get { return _cars; }
}

public Person()
{
}

public Person(string lastName, string firstName, int age)
{
    _lastName = lastName;
    _firstName = firstName;
    _age = age;
}

//type proxy used to filter the data that appears in the debug window
internal class PersonProxy
{
    private Person _person;

    public PersonProxy(Person person)
    {
        _person = person;
    }

    public string Children
    {
        get
        {
```

```
            string[] children = new string[_person.Children.Count];

            for(int i = 0; i<_person.Children.Count;i++)
            {
                children[i] = _person.Children[i].FirstName;
            }

            return string.Join(", ",children);
        }
    }

    public string Pets
    {
        get { return string.Join(", ", _person.Pets.ToArray()); }
    }

    public string Cars
    {
        get { return string.Join(", ", _person.Cars.ToArray()); }
    }

    [DebuggerDisplay("{_person.Age >= 21 ? \"Old Enough\"" +
    " : \"Too Young\"}", Type = "Alcohol Age Check")]
    public string AlcoholAgeCheck
    {
        get { return string.Empty; }
    }

    private string ValidateObject()
    {
        List<string> violations = new List<string>();

        //make sure that a first name has been specified
        if (0 == _person.FirstName.Length)
        {
            violations.Add("FirstName is empty");
        }

        //make sure that a last name has been specified
        if (0 == _person.LastName.Length)
        {
            violations.Add("LastName is empty");
        }

        //make sure that age is greater than 0
        if (0 > _person.Age)
        {
            violations.Add("Age is less than 0");
        }

        //put additional validations here

        //return results to DebuggerDisplay attribute
        return string.Join(", ", violations.ToArray());
```

```
            }

            [DebuggerDisplay("{ValidateObject()}")]
            public string BusinessRulesViolations
            {
                get { return string.Empty; }
            }

            public string Person
            {
                get
                {
                    return "Name = " + _person.FirstName + " " + _person.LastName +
                        ", Age = " + _person.Age;
                }
            }
        }
    }
}
```

Wrapping Up

This chapter demonstrated how you can reduce the amount of time it takes to debug your code by taking advantage of some of the new Visual Studio 2005 debugging features. Visualizers enable you to create a custom user interface to easily view the contents of complex objects. You can use the Debugger Browsable attribute to control the circumstances surrounding when certain properties of your custom business object appear in the debug window. Type proxies enable you to clear the clutter of the debug window by creating an object that provides a concise overview of the important aspects of your custom business object, while still enabling you to drill into the complete details if desired. Lastly, you can use the DebuggerDisplay attribute to display messages in the debug window based upon the current state of your custom business object. All of these new and useful debugging features will help you take your code debugging to the next level.

6

Control Hacks

A great way to package and distribute hacks is via controls. Hacks should be as reusable as possible, and the marriage with controls is quite natural. The code examples in this chapter are dedicated to building a control for publishing RSS feeds. This control is supported by material on type converters, type editors, and designers. While discussing, controls, I'll introduce some of the new design-time features offered in Visual Studio 2005.

Besides being a hack itself, the RSS control is made up of a few smaller mini-hacks. Because the time required to obtain data over the network has a significant performance effect, you'll learn how to make the control perform better by using data caching. You've probably noticed the action lists that pop up for working with controls in Visual Studio 2005. You'll learn how to add those to your controls, too. In addition, you'll learn how to obtain design-time project file paths by tapping into the Visual Studio 2005 automation object model.

Publishing RSS with the XML Control

The RSS control hack is a control that combines other controls and techniques so you can publish an RSS feed on a Web form. It uses the ASP.NET XML control, which takes the RSS feed as its input and runs it through an XSLT style sheet. One tremendous benefit is that you can achieve content management with zero effort. While learning how this control was built, you'll also be exposed to several mini-hacks you can reuse in other development endeavors.

> The RSS control was tested on different feeds, including RSS v1.0 and RSS v2.0 feeds. The version really doesn't matter because the XML is being translated via the XSLT style sheet. If you have a need to support another RSS version, you can do so by modifying the XSLT style sheet.

Content Management with Zero Effort

In addition to being able to publish one or more feeds, the RSS control enables you to perform content management with zero effort. For example, you can set up a blog for the sole purpose of publishing content on a Web page. Because blogs publish via an XML RSS feed, anyone can read content from that RSS feed. By configuring the RSS control to publish a specific feed, you can update the blog using the blog software, and the update will automatically appear on the Web form where the RSS control resides. Your content is published immediately without any extra effort on your part.

Defining the Control

When creating a control, you need to pick a type of control to build: user control, composite custom control, or rendered custom control. User controls are easy for control caching and are very quick to build and use. The problem with user controls is that they are not reusable across projects. Copy and paste is *not* my idea of reuse! This leaves you with one of the custom control types. Rendered custom controls are nice if you need to design the entire control from scratch. Perhaps existing server controls have bulk that you don't want or you need to manage HTML rendering in detail. The drawback to rendered custom controls is that they require more work with tasks such as manually implementing your own post-back data and post-back event code. For the RSS control, we could easily reuse existing controls and combine a couple of controls to get the effect we need. At the same time, we need reuse across multiple projects. This is precisely what a composite custom control is good for.

ASP.NET v2.0 includes a new type for composite custom controls, named `CompositeControl`. You no longer need to inherit `WebControl` or implement the `INamingContainer` interface. Additionally, `CompositeControl` is decorated with a default designer class that automatically provides design-time rendering. Listing 6-1 shows the definition of the `RssControl` class.

Listing 6-1: Implementing a composite custom control: RssControl.cs

```
[assembly: TagPrefix("Hacks.Controls", "hacks")]

namespace Hacks.Controls
{
    [DefaultProperty("URL")]
    [ToolboxData("<{0}:RssControl runat=server></{0}:RssControl>")]
    [Designer(typeof(RssControlDesigner))]
    public class RssControl : CompositeControl
    {
        // code removed for clarity
    }
}
```

The `RssControl` in Listing 6-1 inherits `CompositeControl`. Other interesting features of Listing 6-1 include several attributes. `TagPrefix` ensures that controls from the `Hacks.Controls` namespace have a prefix of `"hacks"` in the Web form HTML. A related attribute, `ToolboxData`, describes the HTML for the `RssControl`. Combined with the prefix, a new `RssControl` dropped onto the designer will produce the following HTML:

```
<hacks:RssControl runat="server"></hacks:RssControl>
```

The `DefaultProperty` attribute identifies which property is highlighted when you first visit the Property Grid. This control uses an action list to enhance the developer's design experience. To accomplish this we need a designer class, which is the purpose of the `Designer` attribute. The section later in this chapter titled "Building Custom Action Lists and Designers" discusses in greater detail how to do this.

Pulling Content

The first task is figuring out how to pull content from the RSS feed. If you could point the ASP.NET XML control at an RSS feed to get the XML back with a simple property that would be great. The problem with getting the XML data into the XML control is that the XML control has only `Document`, `DocumentSource`, and `XPathNavigator` properties, which take an `XmlDocument`, filename string, or `XPathNavigator`, respectively, as input.

The `DocumentSource` property isn't a good choice because you need the XML file to be physically located on the local file system. The additional effort to retrieve the feed and save it to the file doesn't offer the best performance because of the additional file I/O.

There are pros and cons to using the `Document` property. It's a better choice than `DocumentSource` because it accepts an `XmlDocument` object. The problems to overcome with using `XmlDocument` are that neither its `Load` nor its `LoadXml` methods are suitable for addressing the URL of an RSS feed. Another alternative is to use one of the built-in XML types to retrieve the RSS feed. A good type to use in this case is the `XmlTextReader`. Fortunately, because `XmlDocument.Load` has an overload for a `TextReader` parameter and `XmlTextReader` inherits `TextReader`, we now have a way to load the `XmlDocument`, which allows us to load the XML control. The downside of using the `Document` property is that it is deprecated in .NET v2.0.

The `XPathNavigator` property is the best choice of all because it accepts an `XPathNavigator` object. The benefit of using `XPathNavigator` is that it is a read-only object and is much faster than `XmlDocument`. Also, in ASP.NET v2.0, the XML control's `Document` property is obsolete.

You can get an `XPathNavigator` by instantiating an `XPathDocument` object with a parameter identifying the URL of the RSS feed. Calling `CreateNavigator` retrieves an `XPathNavigator` object to load into the XML control. Listing 6-2 shows how this works.

Listing 6-2: Loading an XML control with an RSS feed

```
// identify RSS feed
XPathDocument doc = new XPathDocument(m_url);
XPathNavigator nav = doc.CreateNavigator();

// load the RSS feed and style sheet
// into the Xml control
Xml xmlCtrl = new Xml();
xmlCtrl.XPathNavigator = nav;
```

In Listing 6-2, the variable `m_url` is a string containing the Web address of the RSS feed. `XPath1Document` and `XPathNavigator` are members of the `System.Xml.XPath` namespace and the code not shown for this listing has the appropriate using declaration. This code is part of the `CreateChildControls` method of the custom RSS control.

Caching for Performance

If this control were deployed on a small website with occasional hits, its performance would be just fine. However, you should consider the impact on performance for a busy website and the load being put on the source site of the RSS feed. The solution to getting better performance in this case is *data caching*.

In many cases, RSS feeds are ideal for caching. If the RSS feed originates from a blog, consider how often the blog is updated. In most cases, it isn't very frequent. You could possibly cache once a day (your choice), giving the best performance for a long period of time.

Another consideration is that caching data for a long time isn't always what you want to do. Before developing a caching strategy, consider the currency of the information. If there is no problem waiting for updates until a certain time each day, then there is no problem. However, what if you want to know about changes within a specified period of time? In that case, set the cache for the period of time you are willing to wait for an update, e.g., five minutes, 30 minutes, or one hour. Even caching data for a few seconds can yield much better performance than no cache at all. Listing 6-3 shows the caching policy in place for the RSS control.

Listing 6-3: Caching RSS feed data

```
HttpContext ctx = HttpContext.Current;
XPathDocument doc = null;

// get RSS feed
if (ctx.Cache[XPathDoc] == null)
{
    ctx.Cache.Insert(
        XPathDoc,                       // key
        new XPathDocument(m_url),       // RSS feed
        null,                           // no dependency
        DateTime.Now.AddHours(1),       // keep for an hour
        Cache.NoSlidingExpiration,      // no slide
        CacheItemPriority.Normal,       // evict normally
        null);                          // no callback
}

doc = (XPathDocument)ctx.Cache[XPathDoc];
```

With custom Web controls, you don't have direct access to intrinsic `Page` objects such as `Cache`. To get around this limitation, you use the `HttpContext` type and read its `Current` property, as shown in Listing 6-3, to get an instance of the current context, which does contain a property you can use to access the cache.

Another trick I use to avoid errors is to use a constant string field as the `Cache` key. Being a type `string`, the `Cache` key is not strongly typed, and spelling errors could lead to a hard-to-find bug. In Listing 6-3, `XPathDoc` is the constant string. I do this with the other intrinsic objects, such as `Session` and `ViewState`, for the same reasons.

Managing the XSLT Source

Instead of exposing properties for visual appearance, the RSS control uses XSLT to render an RSS feed as HTML. Therefore, the user needs a way to specify which XSLT file to use. Listing 6-4 shows how the `XSLT` property enables this behavior.

Listing 6-4: A property for allowing a user to select an XSLT file

```
[Bindable(true)]
[Category("RSS")]
[DefaultValue("")]
[Description("The XSLT style sheet for transforming the XML.")]
[Editor(typeof(XslTransformFileEditor), typeof(UITypeEditor))]
public string XSLT
{
    get
    {
        EnsureChildControls();
        if (m_xslt == null)
        {
            m_xslt = string.Empty;
        }

        return m_xslt;
    }
    set
    {
        EnsureChildControls();
        m_xslt = value;
        SetTransformSource(value);
    }
}
```

The XSLT property is decorated with an Editor attribute for the XslTransformFileEditor, which provides a comfortable user interface for the user to select an XSLT file. Remember that this editor looks for files in the local directory of the current project, so you need to add the XSLT file to the project to which you added the control. Also, the editor looks for files with a .xsl extension, which means that you'll have to name your XSLT file with the same extension or select the All Files (*.*) option to see *.xslt files. Visual Studio 2005 has a project item template that names XSLT files as *.xslt by default.

If you aren't familiar with XSLT, it is an XML language for performing transformations on XML data files. In our case, we want to take the RSS feed, which is in XML, and transform it into HTML. A good place for free introductory information on XML and XSLT is w3schools.org. Listing 6-5 shows a sample XSLT file you could use.

Listing 6-5: A sample XSLT file

```
<?xml version="1.0" encoding="UTF-8" ?>
<xsl:stylesheet version="1.0"
  xmlns:xsl="http://www.w3.org/1999/XSL/Transform">
<xsl:template match="/">
<table width="100%" cellpadding="5">
  <xsl:for-each select="/rss/channel/item">
    <xsl:if test="not(title = 'Custom List')">
      <xsl:if test="position() &lt; 10">
        <tr>
          <td>
            <xsl:attribute name="bgcolor">
```

(continued)

Listing 6-5 *(continued)*

```
              steelblue
          </xsl:attribute>
          <font color="white">
            <b>
              <xsl:value-of select="title" />
            </b>
          </font>
        </td>
      </tr>
      <tr>
        <td>
          <font size="1">
            <b><xsl:value-of select="pubDate" /></b>
          </font>
        </td>
      </tr>
      <tr>
        <td>
          <font size="2">
            <xsl:value-of select="description"
              disable-output-escaping="yes" />
          </font>
        </td>
      </tr>
    </xsl:if>
  </xsl:if>
  </xsl:for-each>
  </table>
  </xsl:template>
  </xsl:stylesheet>
```

Listing 6-5 shows an XSLT file you could use on your own projects. Most likely, you'll want to make adjustments so it will work better with your site, i.e., configure it to use CSS classes defined for your site.

Quick Custom Type Converters

The default data representation in the Property Grid is text for those properties without a pre-defined type converter. This is okay if the property exposed from your control is type string. However, properties are often of custom object types. You need a way to tell the Property Grid how to convert that string to your type. This is the responsibility of *type converters*. This section discusses how to create a custom type converter.

Creating a Custom Type Converter

When translating property values between string and other types, the Property Grid must know whether it can translate from your type to a string and whether it can translate from a string to your type. Furthermore, you must provide the code that does the actual translation.

Many of the existing .NET types have their own `TypeConverters`. In the `RSSControl` class, the `URL` property is of type `Uri`. When adding the address of an RSS feed into the Property Grid for the `RSSControl`, it is a `string` type. Because `Uri` has a `UriTypeConverter`, this works smoothly, without any work on the developer's part.

Defining the Property and Its Type

When you base a property off a custom type, you are responsible for writing your own type converter. In the case of the `RssControl`, we need a way to give the control a title. One option would be to add a `Name` and `Description` property to the `RssControl`, which would work because they are string types, which convert just fine. However, you could save screen space or make editing the property easier by combining them into a single property. `RssControl` takes the latter approach by combining `Name` and `Description` into an `RssSiteInfo` type and exposing a member property of that type named `SiteInfo`, as shown in Listing 6-6.

Listing 6-6: The RSSControl's SiteInfo property

```
[Bindable(true)]
[Category("RSS")]
[DefaultValue("<Enter Name Here>,<Enter Description Here>")]
[Localizable(true)]
[Description("Provide a Name and Description to describe the RSS feed.")]
[DesignerSerializationVisibility(DesignerSerializationVisibility.Content)]
[PersistenceMode(PersistenceMode.InnerProperty)]
public RssSiteInfo SiteInfo
{
    get
    {
        EnsureChildControls();
        if (m_siteInfo == null)
        {
            m_siteInfo = new RssSiteInfo();
        }

        return m_siteInfo;
    }
    set
    {
        EnsureChildControls();
        m_siteInfo = value;
        title.Text = "<p><b>" + SiteInfo.Name + " - " +
            SiteInfo.Description + "<br></b></p>";
    }
}
```

The `SiteInfo` property in Listing 6-6 is of type `RssSiteInfo`. It is a normal control property with attributes similar to other control properties. The `DesignerSerializationVisibility` attribute set with the `DesignerSerializationVisibility.Content` enum tells the designer to add this type to the HTML page. The `PersistenceMode` attribute set with the `PersistenceMode.InnerProperty` tells the IDE to serialize modified values of this property as a child element of the `RssControl` element in the HTML page. The difference between the two attributes is that the `DesignerSerializationVisibility` attribute tells the designer what to do, whereas the `PersistenceMode` attribute tells the designer how to do it. Listing 6-7 shows the definition of the `RssSiteInfo` class.

Listing 6-7: The RssSiteInfo class

```
[TypeConverter(typeof(RssSiteInfoTypeConverter))]
public class RssSiteInfo
{
    private string m_name = "<Enter Name Here>";

    [NotifyParentProperty(true)]
    public string Name
    {
        get { return m_name; }
        set { m_name = value; }
    }

    private string m_description = "<Enter Description Here>";

    [NotifyParentProperty(true)]
    public string Description
    {
        get { return m_description; }
        set { m_description = value; }
    }
}
```

The RssSiteInfo class in Listing 6-7 is simply a type that holds two properties, Name and Description, of type string. Notice the attributes TypeConverter and NotifyParentProperty. The control needs to represent its properties in the Property Grid as a string. Although the properties are already strings, RssSiteInfo is a type that the Property Grid doesn't recognize. Therefore, we must provide a type converter to convert type RssSiteInfo to and from type string. The next section explains the mechanics of this and why the NotifyParentProperty is necessary, too.

Defining a Custom Type Converter

Lack of a type converter on a custom type would cause errors when the SiteInfo property is edited in the Property Grid. What you need in order to eliminate conversion errors is to be able to define the conversion only one time and associate that piece of logic with the RssSiteInfo class. A type converter can decorate a property, but this is less reusable than if the type converter decorated the property's type.

To help you get started, Listing 6-8 has skeleton code you can use when creating your own custom type editor. The logic is very similar to what is in the Visual Studio 2005 documentation, but I included it here for your information.

Listing 6-8: Skeleton code for a custom type editor

```
class MyTypeConverter : TypeConverter
{
    public override bool CanConvertFrom(
        ITypeDescriptorContext context,
        Type sourceType)
    {
        if (sourceType == typeof(string))
        {
            return true;
```

```
        }
        return base.CanConvertFrom(context, sourceType);
    }

    public override bool CanConvertTo(
        ITypeDescriptorContext context,
        Type destinationType)
    {
        if (destinationType == typeof(string))
        {
        }
        return base.CanConvertTo(context, destinationType);
    }

    public override object ConvertFrom(
        ITypeDescriptorContext context,
        System.Globalization.CultureInfo culture,
        object value)
    {
        string strVal = value as string;

        if (strVal != null)
        {
            // TODO: Add conversion logic
        }
        return base.ConvertFrom(context, culture, value);
    }

    public override object ConvertTo(
        ITypeDescriptorContext context,
        System.Globalization.CultureInfo culture,
        object value, Type destinationType)
    {
        if (destinationType == typeof(string))
        {
            // TODO: Add conversion logic
        }
        return base.ConvertTo(
            context, culture, value, destinationType);
    }
}
```

You can reuse the `TypeConverter` template in Listing 6-8 and in your own programs to get started using type converters. Just change `MyTypeConverter` to a more meaningful name. As a matter of fact, this would make a good snippet. Visual Studio 2005 calls the `CanConvertFrom` and `CanConvertTo` methods to determine whether the conversion is possible. `ConvertFrom` is for converting from a string to your type, and `ConvertTo` is for converting from your type to a string. There is more to `TypeConverters` and I recommend you check out the documentation if you want further information. However, the preceding code is sufficient for demonstrating how to use a custom type converter for the `RssControl` hack.

If you were to use this code snippet, copy it to a class file, open the Task List by selecting View⇨Tasks, or press Ctrl+\, Ctrl+T. Select Comments in the Task List and double-click on each `TODO` comment to add logic for the `ConvertFrom` and `ConvertTo` methods. Regarding the type converter for the `Dimension` class, Listing 6-9 shows how to implement the `ConvertFrom` method.

Listing 6-9: The ConvertFrom method for the DimensionTypeConverter

```
public override object ConvertFrom(ITypeDescriptorContext
    context, CultureInfo culture, object value)
{
    if (value == null)
    {
        return new RssSiteInfo();
    }

    if (value is string)
    {
        string s = (string)value;
        if (s.Length == 0)
        {
            return new RssSiteInfo();
        }

        string[] siteInfo = s.Split(',');

        if (siteInfo.Length < 2)
        {
            throw new ArgumentException(
                "You must include name and description formatted as
\"<name>,<description>\"", "value");
        }

        RssSiteInfo rsi = new RssSiteInfo();
        rsi.Name = siteInfo[0];
        rsi.Description = siteInfo[1];

        return rsi;
    }

    return base.ConvertFrom(context, culture, value);
}
```

A multi-value property is typically represented as a comma-separated list of values. The code in Listing 6-9 uses the string `Split` method to separate those values into an array. Listing 6-10 shows how to convert in the opposite direction, from type `RssSiteInfo` to type `string`.

Listing 6-10: The ConvertTo method for the DimensionTypeConverter

```
public override object ConvertTo(
    ITypeDescriptorContext context,
    CultureInfo culture, object value, Type destinationType)
{
    if (value != null)
    {
        if (!(value is RssSiteInfo))
        {
            throw new ArgumentException(
                "Invalid RSS Site Info", "value");
        }
```

```
        }

        if (destinationType == typeof(string))
        {
            if (value == null)
            {
                return String.Empty;
            }

            RssSiteInfo rsi = (RssSiteInfo)value;

            return rsi.Name + "," + rsi.Description;
        }

        return base.ConvertTo(context, culture, value,
            destinationType);
    }
```

In Listing 6-10, the code simply returns a string of the `Name` and `Description` properties of the `RssSite Info` object, separated by a comma. With a type converter for `RssSiteInfo` that inherits from `Type Converter`, the Property Grid displays a single property entry where you can edit a comma-separated list of values. It could be convenient to edit the `Name` and `Description` values independently in addition to the comma-separated representation. Consider how the `Font` property is edited with a treelike representation where you can click the + symbol and edit the individual parts. You can do that too. Just change the custom type editor so that it inherits `ExpandableObjectConverter`, as shown in Listing 6-11.

Listing 6-11: Exposing properties as a tree in the Property Grid

```
class RssSiteInfoTypeConverter : ExpandableObjectConverter
{
    // content removed for clarity
}
```

Listing 6-11 is a modified version of Listing 6-6. It simply changes the name of the type converter to something more specific and makes it inherit `ExpandableObjectConverter`. An error could occur when changing a type converter to inherit `ExpandableObjectConverter` if you are editing nested property values in the Property Grid. They don't automatically update the parent Property Grid item with the comma-separated list, which also means that the designer UI is not updated. This was the purpose of the `NotifyParentProperty` attribute used in Listing 6-6. The `NotifyParentProperty` attribute should be set to `true` and applied to each property to ensure that all other interested entities in the designer receive notification of the change.

Building Custom Action Lists and Designers

Visual Studio 2005 has a new feature called *action lists*, which is a list of common design-time tasks people will want to perform. When you drag and drop a control on the design surface the control displays an arrow in its top-right corner. Clicking this arrow displays the action list. Action lists contain essential control properties, are not too extensive, and offer a quick way to get to the properties that you need the most. Without action lists you would have to use the Property Grid to set all properties, but the characteristics of the action list can increase productivity.

Developers create action lists via a custom designer. The example in this section creates a designer that inherits from an existing designer and adds specialized support just for action lists. Listing 6-12 shows how to declare a designer.

Listing 6-12: A custom designer

```
class RssControlDesigner : CompositeControlDesigner
{
    public override DesignerActionListCollection ActionLists
    {
        get
        {
            DesignerActionListCollection rssActionLists
            new DesignerActionListCollection();

            // Add a custom list of actions
            rssActionLists.Add(new RssControlActionList(this.Component));

            return rssActionLists;
        }
    }
}
```

RssControlDesigner in Listing 6-12 inherits CompositeControlDesigner because the control it will be used with is a Composite control. The purpose of a designer is to provide design-time support on a control so developers can use that control in the visual design environment. For example, a designer helps manage control appearance, initialization of control state, and the behavior of the control when the user interacts with it. The focus in this chapter is to add design-time support via the new action list feature.

The single property of RssControlDesigner is an override of ActionLists. Its get accessor returns a DesignerActionListCollection that holds a custom action list to be displayed during design time. The RssControlActionList type being added to the DesignerActionListCollection is defined in Listing 6-13.

Listing 6-13: A custom action list: RssControlActionList

```
class RssControlActionList : DesignerActionList
{
    private RssControl rssControl = null;

    public RssControlActionList(IComponent rssControl)
        : base(rssControl)
    {
        // get a reference to control we're designing
        this.rssControl = rssControl as RssControl;
    }

    // make the Action List pop up on start up
    public override bool AutoShow
    {
        get
        {
            return true;
```

```
        }
        set
        {
            base.AutoShow = true;
        }
    }
```

A custom action list inherits `DesignerActionList`, as shown in Listing 6-13. You should initialize it by passing in a reference to the control to which the action list will be applied. Keep a reference to the control because it should be notified when property state changes. I implemented an override of the `AutoShow` property to show off this cool new feature by making the action list pop up as soon as the control is added to the design surface. Another action list method that is called during design time is the `GetSortedActionItems` method. We override this method in the `RssControlActionList`, as shown in Listing 6-14.

Listing 6-14: Overriding the GetSortedActionItems method

```
public override DesignerActionItemCollection GetSortedActionItems()
{
    DesignerActionItemCollection rssActionItems
        = new DesignerActionItemCollection();

    // everything goes in the RSS category

    DesignerActionHeaderItem header =
        new DesignerActionHeaderItem("RSS");
    rssActionItems.Add(header);

    // RSS properties are what a developer
    // will be most interested in.

    DesignerActionPropertyItem siteInfo =
        new DesignerActionPropertyItem(
            "SiteInfo", "Site Info", "RSS",
            "Name and description to display as title. " +
            "Use the format: <Name>,<Description>");
    rssActionItems.Add(siteInfo);

    DesignerActionPropertyItem url =
        new DesignerActionPropertyItem(
            "URL", "URL", "RSS",
            "Web address of RSS feed.");
    rssActionItems.Add(url);

    DesignerActionPropertyItem xslt =
        new DesignerActionPropertyItem(
            "XSLT", "XSLT", "RSS",
            "XSLT file for formatting RSS feed.");
    rssActionItems.Add(xslt);

    return rssActionItems;
}
```

The purpose of `GetSortedActionItems` in Listing 6-14 is to return a `DesignerActionItemCollection` of `DesignerActionItem` derived types. These types allow you to define methods, properties, and text entries that appear in the action list. For the `RssControlActionList`, we're only interested in defining a header and exposing properties, requiring instantiation of a `DesignerActionHeaderItem` and `DesignerActionPropertyItem`, respectively.

A `DesignerActionHeaderItem` simply creates a category with the name, RSS, passed to the constructor. The `RssControlActionList` will have three properties for `SiteInfo`, `URL`, and `XSLT`, which correspond to the same properties in `RssControl`. The `DesignerActionPropertyItem` constructor parameter list sets a code property name, creates a label that shows in the action list, names a category that matches a header, and sets the description that will appear as a ToolTip when the developer's mouse hovers over the property item's label in the designer.

For each of the `DesignerActionPropertyItem` instances added to the `DesignerActionList` `Collection`, the `RssControlDesignerActionList` type needs to implement a like named property. Listing 6-15 shows the three necessary properties.

Listing 6-15: Action list properties

```csharp
public RssSiteInfo SiteInfo
{
    get
    {
        return rssControl.SiteInfo;
    }
    set
    {
        // need to notify designer of changes
        // through the PropertyDescriptor
        PropertyDescriptor propDesc =
            TypeDescriptor.GetProperties(rssControl)["SiteInfo"];

        propDesc.SetValue(rssControl, value);
    }
}

[Editor(typeof(RssTypeEditor), typeof(UITypeEditor))]
public Uri URL
{
    get
    {
        return rssControl.URL;
    }
    set
    {
        // need to notify designer of changes
        // through the PropertyDescriptor
        PropertyDescriptor propDesc =
            TypeDescriptor.GetProperties(rssControl)["URL"];

        propDesc.SetValue(rssControl, value);
    }
```

```
        }

        [Editor(typeof(XslTransformFileEditor), typeof(UITypeEditor))]
        public string XSLT
        {
            get
            {
                return rssControl.XSLT;
            }
            set
            {
                // need to notify designer of changes
                // through the PropertyDescriptor
                PropertyDescriptor propDesc =
                    TypeDescriptor.GetProperties(rssControl)["XSLT"];

                propDesc.SetValue(rssControl, value);
            }
        }
    }
```

Listing 6-15 shows why `RssControlActionList` needs a reference to the control. It uses this reference in each property's `set` accessor to get a property descriptor. By setting the property in the `RssControl` instance through the property descriptor, pertinent entities in the designer receive notification of the change and are then able to make appropriate updates. For example, when the `SiteInfo` property is modified through the action list, the designer receives notification and changes are propagated so that the appearance of the control updates on the design surface where you can see the changes immediately.

Notice the `Editor` attributes on the properties. Though the original control properties contain the same editors, the action list has no way to know this. Therefore, these are necessary to enable the editors in the action list.

Managing Design-Time Support

A control has two audiences: application users and developers. The easiest audience to consider are the application users because they see the visual presentation of the control. The argument could also be made that application users are the most important because their acceptance can make or break the entire application. Another important audience is the developer who uses controls to build applications. A control has the potential to dramatically improve developer productivity. Therefore, you must take care to ensure that the developers' experience with the control is positive.

In the case of getting the RSS feed, `HttpCache` is not available at design time. Therefore, you need to use a local variable, as shown in Listing 6-16.

Listing 6-16: Handling caching at design time and runtime

```
private void LoadRssFeed()
{
    doc = new XPathDocument(URL.ToString());

    if (!DesignMode)
    {
```

(continued)

Listing 6-16 *(continued)*

```
            HttpContext ctx = HttpContext.Current;

            // get RSS feed
            if (ctx.Cache[XPathDoc] == null)
            {
                ctx.Cache.Insert(
                    XPathDoc,                   // key
                    doc,                        // RSS feed
                    null,                       // no dependency
                    DateTime.Now.AddHours(1),   // keep for an hour
                    Cache.NoSlidingExpiration,  // no slide
                    CacheItemPriority.Normal,   // evict normally
                    null);                      // no callback
            }
        }

        // set rss feed
        rssXml.XPathNavigator = doc.CreateNavigator();
    }
```

The `CompositeControl DesignMode` property returns `true` if the control is set in the Visual Studio 2005 designer and returns `false` if the check is made during runtime. The `LoadRssFeed` method in Listing 6-16 checks the `DesignMode` property to decide how to cache information. See the section "Caching for Performance" earlier in this chapter for a description of the benefits of this technique. During design time, it is okay to use a field for holding the `XPathDocument`, but during runtime, using `HttpCache` is the only thing that really makes sense.

Another example of when you should check for `DesignMode` is when setting the `TransformSource` of the XML control. Listing 6-17 describes this method.

Listing 6-17: Locating resources during design time and runtime

```
    private void SetTransformSource(string fileName)
    {
        // in the designer
        if (DesignMode)
        {
            // no need to set TransformSource
            // if there isn't anything to set
            if (fileName != String.Empty)
            {
                // tell XML control where to find XSLT file
                rssXml.TransformSource = GetDesignTimeFilePath(fileName);
            }
        }
        else
        {
            // at runtime
            rssXml.TransformSource =
                HttpContext.Current.Server.MapPath(fileName);
        }
    }
```

Listing 6-17 is similar to Listing 6-16 in that it checks the DesignMode property to help decide how to handle an action. In this case, because Server.MapPath is not available during design time, the code has to perform other actions. These actions, encapsulated in the GetDesignTimeFilePath method, require a hack that uses the Visual Studio 2005 IDE. In the next section, I describe GetDesignTime FilePath as a new hack.

Tapping into the Visual Studio 2005 Automation Object Model

While building the design-time behavior for the RSS control, I thought it would be a simple matter of using one of the several designer interfaces to reference the file entered into the TransformSource property of the XML control. This file is a member of the current project and it seemed like it should be an easy thing to do, but it is far from easy. The reality is that there is no standard interface for accessing project files. This is a serious flaw in the design-time API because accessing project files such as web.config or the XSLT file needed for the RSS control is necessary when building controls.

The workaround for this problem involves a hack that taps into the Visual Studio 2005 Automation Object Model. For your convenience, I wrapped the necessary code into a method and made it as generic as possible so you can copy and paste it. Alternatively, you could add this code to your own library of hacks, reference the library in your project, and then call the method. Listing 6-18 shows the Project File Path Discovery Hack.

Listing 6-18: Tapping into the Visual Studio 2005 IDE to extract a project file path

```
private static string GetDesignTimeFilePath(string fileName)
{
    // get a reference to the IDE.
    EnvDTE80.DTE2 dte;
    dte = (EnvDTE80.DTE2)System.Runtime.InteropServices
        .Marshal.GetActiveObject("VisualStudio.DTE.8.0");

    // the window we're in belongs to the project we will run
    Document doc = dte.ActiveDocument;

    // find the file associated with the active document
    ProjectItem activeFile =
        dte.Solution.FindProjectItem(doc.FullName);

    // get the location of the current project
    string directory = Path.GetDirectoryName(
        activeFile.ContainingProject.FullName);

    // prep for building a fully qualified file name
    string relativeFileName =
        fileName.TrimStart(new char[] { '~', '/' })
        .Replace("/", "\\");

    // build and return the new fully qualified name
    return Path.Combine(directory, relativeFileName);
}
```

In Listing 6-18, DTE2 is at the top of the Visual Studio 2005 Automation Object Model. It is a COM object, so you need to get a reference via its Program ID in the registry. Remember to create a project reference to the EnvDte80 assembly.

The ActiveDocument is the Web form to which the RSS control has been added. You need a reference to the current Web form because it belongs to the project that includes the files you want to reference. Because a solution could have multiple projects, this helps you figure out the right project to look in.

A common pattern in the Visual Studio 2005 Automation Object Model is that in a hierarchy, sub-items often have references to their parent items. We take advantage of this relationship to pull out the fully qualified filename of the ProjectItem's parent project. After trimming extraneous characters from the file prefix, we can build the full path to the file.

For more information about using the Visual Studio 2005 Automation Object Model, check out the Visual Studio 2005 documentation for add-ins. In this case, you wouldn't want to create an add-in because it would be an extra library and you would have to figure out how to interact with the add-in. While harder to initially figure out than an add-in, the code in Listing 6-18 is much simpler to implement and less cumbersome to deploy.

Implementing Custom Type Editors

The .NET Framework includes several type editors for well-known types, including Fonts, Colors, Files, and more. In the RSS control, the XSLT property uses another built-in type editor — UriTypeEditor — to get a reference to an XSLT file. Whenever you have the opportunity to use a built-in type editor, go for it.

Sometimes a built-in type editor isn't available for what you need, or existing type editors don't provide necessary functionality. In those cases, it is better to build a custom type editor. This was the case with the RSS control's URL property. It would have been possible to allow developers to add a string for the URL in the Property Editor. However, it is possible to offer a much better interface and make the control more user-friendly.

The problem with just adding a string for the URL is that the user won't necessarily know whether the URL is returning the right RSS feed. Adding an invalid string would return an error in the control UI that would likely be less than intuitive. Therefore, I created an RssViewerTypeEditor to enhance the user experience. It is an editor dialog box that pops up, enabling the user to enter the URL for the RSS feed, click the GO! button, and visually verify that the URL is correct. The following list outlines the steps necessary to implement a custom type editor, such as the RssViewerTypeEditor:

1. Build the editor interface using Windows Forms technology.
2. Build the type editor.
3. Decorate the target property with an Editor attribute identifying the custom type editor.

Building a Type Editor User Interface

If working with Windows Forms is a bit foreign to you, don't worry. I'm giving you code that you can use "as is" and review after brushing up on Windows Forms programming. If you are going to build your own controls, knowing some Windows Forms programming is a skill you'll certainly want. Reading the Windows Forms Quick Start samples that are part of the Visual Studio 2005 installation should be enough to help you understand this example. If you are already familiar with Windows Forms, this code pulls together a couple of v2.0 controls and concepts you may find interesting.

The first task is to add a Windows Form to the control project. Windows Forms v2.0 uses partial types where editable code is in the `RssViewer.cs` file and IDE-generated code is in the `RssViewer.designer.cs` file. Listing 6-19 shows the IDE-generated code file. The RssViewer provides a simple interface whereby you can enter a URL and see the page it addresses. Rather than discover a typo in the URL at runtime, the RssViewer gives you the design-time convenience of knowing that the URL is correct.

Listing 6-19: Windows Forms user interface generated by Visual Studio 2005

```
namespace Hacks.Controls
{
    partial class RSSViewer
    {
        /// <summary>
        /// Required designer variable.
        /// </summary>
        private System.ComponentModel.IContainer components = null;

        /// <summary>
        /// Clean up any resources being used.
        /// </summary>
        /// <param name="disposing">true if managed resources should be disposed;
otherwise, false.</param>
        protected override void Dispose(bool disposing)
        {
            if (disposing && (components != null))
            {
                components.Dispose();
            }
            base.Dispose(disposing);
        }

        #region Windows Form Designer generated code

        /// <summary>
        /// Required method for Designer support - do not modify
        /// the contents of this method with the code editor.
        /// </summary>
        private void InitializeComponent()
        {
            System.ComponentModel.ComponentResourceManager resources = new
System.ComponentModel.ComponentResourceManager(typeof(RSSViewer));
            this.toolStrip1 = new System.Windows.Forms.ToolStrip();
            this.tstxtAddress = new System.Windows.Forms.ToolStripTextBox();
            this.tsbGo = new System.Windows.Forms.ToolStripButton();
            this.wbRss = new System.Windows.Forms.WebBrowser();
            this.toolStrip1.SuspendLayout();
            this.SuspendLayout();
            //
            // toolStrip1
            //
            this.toolStrip1.Items.AddRange(new System.Windows.Forms.ToolStripItem[]
{
            this.tstxtAddress,
            this.tsbGo});
```

(continued)

Listing 6-19 *(continued)*

```
            this.toolStrip1.Location = new System.Drawing.Point(0, 0);
            this.toolStrip1.Name = "toolStrip1";
            this.toolStrip1.Size = new System.Drawing.Size(292, 25);
            this.toolStrip1.TabIndex = 0;
            this.toolStrip1.Text = "toolStrip1";
            //
            // tstxtAddress
            //
            this.tstxtAddress.Name = "tstxtAddress";
            this.tstxtAddress.Size = new System.Drawing.Size(200, 25);
            //
            // tsbGo
            //
            this.tsbGo.DisplayStyle =
System.Windows.Forms.ToolStripItemDisplayStyle.Image;
            this.tsbGo.Image =
((System.Drawing.Image)(resources.GetObject("tsbGo.Image")));
            this.tsbGo.ImageTransparentColor = System.Drawing.Color.Magenta;
            this.tsbGo.Name = "tsbGo";
            this.tsbGo.Size = new System.Drawing.Size(23, 22);
            this.tsbGo.Text = "GO!";
            this.tsbGo.Click += new System.EventHandler(this.tsbGo_Click);
            //
            // wbRss
            //
            this.wbRss.Dock = System.Windows.Forms.DockStyle.Fill;
            this.wbRss.Location = new System.Drawing.Point(0, 25);
            this.wbRss.Name = "wbRss";
            this.wbRss.Size = new System.Drawing.Size(292, 241);
            this.wbRss.TabIndex = 0;
            //
            // RSSViewer
            //
            this.AutoScaleDimensions = new System.Drawing.SizeF(6F, 13F);
            this.AutoScaleMode = System.Windows.Forms.AutoScaleMode.Font;
            this.ClientSize = new System.Drawing.Size(292, 266);
            this.Controls.Add(this.wbRss);
            this.Controls.Add(this.toolStrip1);
            this.Name = "RSSViewer";
            this.Text = "RSSViewer";
            this.toolStrip1.ResumeLayout(false);
            this.toolStrip1.PerformLayout();
            this.ResumeLayout(false);
            this.PerformLayout();

        }

        #endregion

        private System.Windows.Forms.ToolStrip toolStrip1;
        private System.Windows.Forms.ToolStripTextBox tstxtAddress;
```

```
        private System.Windows.Forms.ToolStripButton tsbGo;
        private System.Windows.Forms.WebBrowser wbRss;
    }
}
```

The `InitializeComponent` method in Listing 6-19 is automatically generated by the IDE when controls are dropped into the visual designer. As indicated in the comments, you should not touch this code. Instead, interact with the visual designer and Property Grid, shown in Figure 6-1, for building the user interface.

Figure 6-1

As shown in Figure 6-1 and coded in Listing 6-19, the `RssViewer` uses a couple of new controls, the ToolStrip and WebBrowser. In v1.x of the .NET Framework, you had to use COM interop to use the IE Web Browser ActiveX control and things didn't always work well. The new WebBrowser control is easy to work with. The ToolStrip control supercedes the v1.x ToolBar control, offers a plethora of new options, and can host many different types of controls, including the TextBox and Button controls shown in Figure 6-1.

Notice the GO! button with the green arrow bitmap. This bitmap should be familiar because it is the same one used for the Internet Explorer GO button. In fact, you can use all the common Windows bitmaps in your applications because Microsoft has included them with Visual Studio 2005. To find them, go to `C:\Program Files\Microsoft Visual Studio 8\Common7\VS2005ImageLibrary`. Unzip `VS2005ImageLibrary.zip` and you'll see a directory structure full of animations, bitmaps, and icons you can use in your own programs.

The `RssViewer.cs` file is for code, such as properties and event handlers, specific to your application. Listing 6-20 shows how the `RssViewer` is implemented.

Listing 6-20: Developer code for the RssViewer Windows Forms interface

```
using System;
using System.Collections.Generic;
using System.ComponentModel;
```

(continued)

Listing 6-20 *(continued)*

```
using System.Data;
using System.Drawing;
using System.Text;
using System.Windows.Forms;

namespace Hacks.Controls
{
    public partial class RSSViewer : Form
    {
        public RSSViewer()
        {
            InitializeComponent();
        }

        public string Address
        {
            get { return tstxtAddress.Text; }
            set { tstxtAddress.Text = value; }
        }

        private void tsbGo_Click(object sender, EventArgs e)
        {
            wbRss.Url = new Uri(tstxtAddress.Text);
        }
    }
}
```

The `Address` property in Listing 6-20 holds the URL of the RSS feed. It encapsulates internal state by using the `TextBox` in the `ToolStrip` control as a backing store. This is necessary because it provides a nice public interface that the `RssViewerTypeEditor`, described in the next section, can access. The `tsbGo_Click` event handler initializes the `WebBrowser` control with the user-entered URL, causing the browser to seek and display the RSS feed. Being able to verify that the URL actually displays the correct RSS feed is the purpose of this form and punctuates its value.

Building the Type Editor Class

A Type Editor class is the glue that enables the Property Grid and User Interface to communicate. The Property Grid invokes the type editor. The type editor gets Property Grid information, passes the information to the user interface, opens the user interface, extracts new information when the user interface is closed, and passes the new information back to the Property Grid. Listing 6-21 shows how to implement the `RssViewerTypeEditor`.

Listing 6-21: Implementing a custom type editor: RssViewerTypeEditor

```
using System;
using System.ComponentModel;
using System.Drawing.Design;
using System.Windows.Forms.Design;

namespace Hacks.Controls
```

```
{
    public class RssViewerTypeEditor : UITypeEditor
    {
        public override UITypeEditorEditStyle GetEditStyle(ITypeDescriptorContext
context)
        {
            // we're going to pop up a dialog
            return UITypeEditorEditStyle.Modal;
        }

        public override object EditValue(ITypeDescriptorContext context,
IServiceProvider provider, object value)
        {
            Uri url = value as Uri;

            if (url == null)
            {
                return value;
            }

            // helps show dialog
            IWindowsFormsEditorService edSvc =
                (IWindowsFormsEditorService)provider.GetService(
                    typeof(IWindowsFormsEditorService));

            // display dialog and get user input
            if (edSvc != null)
            {
                RSSViewer rss = new RSSViewer();
                rss.Address = url.ToString();
                edSvc.ShowDialog(rss);
                value = new Uri(rss.Address);
            }

            return value;
        }
    }
}
```

The RssViewerTypeEditor in Listing 6-21 has two methods, GetEditStyle and EditValue. The GetEditStyle method specifies the type of editor for the type editor. The EditValue method contains the bulk of type editor processing, ensuring that property values are retrieved and set as required.

The two types of editor are specified by members of the UITypeEditorEditStyle enum, returned by the GetEditStyle method. We want the RssViewerTypeEditor to display the RssViewer as a modal dialog box, so GetEditStyle returns the Modal value. This causes an ellipsis button to show in the designer Property Editor. Alternatively, a type editor could display a UI as a drop-down list, which shows in the designer Property Grid as a down arrow button that will display the editor in-place in the Property Grid. The Modal dialog box is the better choice in this case because it enables the user to move the window around and resize it if necessary.

One of the first things you can do in the EditValue method is to validate the data read from the Property Grid, which is passed in the value parameter. In this case, value is converted to type Uri to ensure it is formatted correctly.

The provider parameter enables you to obtain a reference to the IWindowsFormsEditorService, which enables you to interact with the Windows Forms UI. In this case, we simply call ShowDialog. If this were a drop-down UI, the code would have used IWindowsFormsEditorService to drop down and close the UI.

To let the IWindowsFormsEditorService know which UI to display, we must pass an RssViewer reference to the ShowDialog method. Before doing so, set the Address with the URI that was extracted from the Property Grid value. ShowDialog returns when the user closes RssViewer, at which point the code must get the new Address from RssViewer. After converting the Address, which is of type string, to a URI, the RssTypeViewer passes the new URI back to the Property Grid as a return value.

Using a Custom Type Editor

You use custom type editors the same way as the type editors that ship with the .NET Framework class library. Just decorate the target property with the Editor attribute, as shown in Listing 6-22.

Listing 6-22: Using the RssViewerTypeEditor with a property

```
[Bindable(true)]
[Category("RSS")]
[DefaultValue("http://spaces.msn.com/members/jmayo/feed.rss")]
[Description("The Web URL where RSS content is located.")]
[TypeConverter(typeof(UriTypeConverter))]
[Editor(typeof(RssViewerTypeEditor), typeof(UITypeEditor))]
public Uri URL
{
    get
    {
        EnsureChildControls();
        if (m_url == null)
        {
            m_url = new
Uri("http://spaces.msn.com/members/jmayo/feed.rss");
        }
        return m_url;
    }
    set
    {
        EnsureChildControls();
        m_url = value;
        LoadRssFeed();
    }
}
```

Listing 6-22 shows how easy it is to associate a custom type editor with a property. Remember to use the typeof operator because just passing the type name isn't sufficient.

Design-Time Debugging

Once you've created a control, the next logical step is to add it to a Web Form to see what it looks like. If you've written enough controls, and most likely even the first time you write a control, you'll encounter bugs. Often, an error shows up when you drop the control on the Web form, appearing in a gray box with the error message. Because this behavior is occurring at design time, you don't automatically hit a breakpoint.

To debug design-time control behavior, open a second copy of Visual Studio 2005 for the same project as the control. You'll need to attach to the other running copy of Visual Studio 2005 to debug events by selecting Debug⇨Attach to Process, and then selecting the `devenv.exe` process. Once attached, set breakpoints in the attaching copy of Visual Studio 2005 and perform the action with the control in the attached copy of Visual Web Developer. You'll hit the breakpoint in the attaching copy of Visual Studio 2005 and will be able to debug the design-time behavior of the control.

Wrapping Up

This chapter shows control hacks that are new, not well documented, and that solve common problems. When working with data, you should cache it for performance; and this chapter showed how to use a data cache and explained how to handle caching for both design-time and runtime use. Action lists are a new Visual Studio 2005 feature and this chapter showed how to implement them via custom designers. It also showed how to implement custom type converters and custom type editors for a better user experience while using the control. A difficult to figure out, but important, hack in this chapter was the technique required for getting the fully qualified physical path of a project file. Another technique for helping you get through it all is knowing how to debug your control, which is not difficult, but certainly not obvious. Now you have a full-featured RSS control for your own applications. Because the code is included, you can extend and customize it for your own purposes.

GridView Hacks

In this chapter about GridView hacks, you will learn how to extend the GridView in several different ways — for example, how to dynamically expand a row to display a DetailsView control, how to update multiple GridView rows, how to create a custom pager row for the GridView's paging feature, etc. The GridView has several features for helping developers to create powerful web applications for which data should be displayed within a flexible grid. But the GridView control can't have everything that developers want. Every kind of web application can have different ways to use the GridView. Instead of trying to add as much functionality as possible to the GridView control, it was created to make it very easy for developers to extend and add their own functionality to it. Source code for all of the hacks in this chapter can be downloaded from www.wrox.com. All hacks in this chapter can be written by using Visual Studio 2005, which I recommend. Alternatively, you can use Notepad or other editors.

To understand the hacks, you need to have a good understanding of the GridView control, so before you read this chapter I recommend you read about the GridView if you haven't done so before. You can read about it at asp.net/Tutorials/quickstart.aspx or within the MSDN Library that ships with Visual Studio 2005. Most of the code examples in this chapter use the SqlDataSource, so you have to have some basic understanding about how to use this control. You can get information about the control on the following site: http://66.129.71.130/QuickStartv20/aspnet/doc/ctrlref/data/sqldatasource.aspx. The SqlDataSource control is not required for the hacks to work; you can use other DataSource controls as well. I recommend you also take a look at Chapter 8, where you can find tips on SqlDataSource and other DataSource controls.

Dynamic Row Expansion

A GridView control consists of rows of data displayed in columns, where each row often doesn't show much data; for example, in a web application where a list of contacts should be displayed, the GridView control can be used to display customers, one customer on each row, but not all the information about the customer, because it will not fit on the page. In some solutions, a master/detail solution is used whereby users can select a row from a GridView control, and a DetailsView control is used to show more data of the selected row. Another common solution is to navigate to another page when a row is selected, with the new page displaying more information about the selected row. In some cases it could be useful to show more detail for a specific row by expanding the selected row. This solution can be useful if you don't want to navigate to another page, and want to have the detail information close to the selected row, especially to avoid scrolling the page if the GridView displays several rows. This hack is about using the GridView control to expand a row dynamically to show more information about the currently selected row.

Because this hack expands a row dynamically without reloading the page, all data that should be displayed for the rows, including the details, must be retrieved when the page is loaded.

The example for this topic will demonstrate how to expand and collapse a row with client-side script. The example uses the Northwind database to get customers that will be listed within the GridView control. The Northwind database is an example database that is often installed by default when you install Microsoft SQL Server. It will not be shipped with Microsoft SQL Server 2005. You can download the Northwind database sample from `microsoft.com/downloads/details.aspx?FamilyID=06616212-0356-46A0-8DA2-EEBC53A68034&displaylang=en`. It will also work for Microsoft SQL Server 2005. In the example, a TemplateField will be added to the GridView to make it possible to customize the content that should be displayed for each row and column of the GridView control. The GridView in this example will have only one column for which a table is used to show information about a customer. A client-side script is used to hide and display the table that is added to the GridView's TemplateField. An image is added to each row and will be used as the expand and collapse button of a row. The client-side `OpenTable` method that expands and collapses a row is called by the `Image onClick` event. All of this is accomplished in the following code, which is located inside of a client-side `<script>` block:

```
function OpenTable(table, img)
{
    object = document.getElementById(table);

    if (object.style.display=="")
    {
        object.style.display = "none";
        img.src = "open.gif";
    }
    else
    {
        object.style.display = "";
        img.src = "close.gif";
    }
}
```

`OpenTable` uses the `document.getElementById` method to get the object that represents the table to show or hide. To hide and display a HTML element, such as the table that is added to the TemplateField, the table object's style attribute's `display` property can be used. If the value of the `display` attribute is none, the table will be hidden; if the display attribute has no value, the table will be displayed. To know whether to hide or display the table, a unique identifier must be added to each table inside a row. This can be done, for example, by using a server-side method that generates a unique id for each table. The following `server.side` method will generate a unique id for each table:

```
string CreateID(object value)
{
    return "Table_" + value.ToString();
}
```

CreateId has the argument value that will be used to generate the unique identifier for each table. The value passed to the CreateId method can, for example, be a field that will act as a unique identifier for each row inside of the GridView control. CreateId will be used to set the Id attribute of the table that is added to the TemplateField. The following example shows how the CreateID method can be used inside of a TemplateField to set the id attribute of a table to a unique identifier:

```
<asp:GridView ...>
    <Columns>
      <asp:TemplateField ...>
          <ItemTemplate>

            <img
                src="open.gif"
                onclick='OpenTable("<%# CreateID(Eval("CustomerID"))%>", this);'/>

            <table id='<%# CreateID(Eval("CustomerID"))%>'>
                ...
            </table>

          </ItemTemplate>
      </asp:TemplateField>
    </columns>
</asp:GridView>
```

As you can see in the preceding example, the value of the argument that will be passed to the CreateID method will be the value of the field CustomerID that is bond to the GridView control. You can also see that there is an <img> element added to the TemplateField where the OpenTable method will be called when a user clicks on the image. OpenTable will pass the table's generated unique identifier as an argument so it can get the table object that should be displayed or hidden.

Listing 7-1 demonstrates the entire example for this hack. Here, a SqlDataSource is used to get customers from the Northwind database.

Listing 7-1: Using SqlDataSource to retrieve customers form a database

```
<%@ Page Language="C#" %>

<script runat=server>

    string CreateID(object value)
    {
        return "Table_" + value.ToString();
    }

</script>

<html xmlns="http://www.w3.org/1999/xhtml" >
<head id="Head1" runat="server">
    <title>Dynamic row expansion</title>
    <script language="javascript">

        function OpenTable(table, img)
        {
```

(continued)

Listing 7-1 *(continued)*

```
            object = document.getElementById(table);

            if (object.style.display=="")
            {
                object.style.display = "none";
                img.src = "open.gif";
            }
            else
            {
                object.style.display = "";
                img.src = "close.gif";
            }
        }

    </script>

</head>
<body>
    <form id="form1" runat="server">
    <div>
        <asp:GridView
            ID="GridView1"
            Runat="server"
            DataSourceID="SqlDataSource1"
            DataKeyNames="CustomerID"
            AutoGenerateColumns="False">
            <Columns>
                <asp:TemplateField
                    SortExpression="CustomerID"
                    HeaderText="CustomerID">

                    <ItemTemplate>

                        <img
                            src="open.gif"
                            onclick='OpenTable("<%#
CreateID(Eval("CustomerID"))%>", this);'/> 

                        <asp:Label
                            Runat="server"
                            Text='<%# Bind("CustomerID") %>'
                            ID="Label1"/>

                        <br />

                        <table
                            width=100%
                            style="display:none;"
                            id='<%# CreateID(Eval("CustomerID"))%>'>

                            <tr>
                                <td>
```

```
                                    <asp:Label
                                        Runat="server"
                                        Text='<%# Bind("CompanyName") %>'
                                        ID="Label2"/>
                        </td>
                        <td>
                            <asp:Label
                                Runat="server"
                                Text='<%# Bind("ContactName") %>'
                                ID="Label3"/>
                        </td>
                        <td>
                            <asp:Label
                                Runat="server"
                                Text='<%# Bind("ContactTitle") %>'
                                ID="Label4"/>
                        </td>
                        <td>
                            <asp:Label
                                Runat="server"
                                Text='<%# Bind("Address") %>'
                                ID="Label5"/>
                        </td>
                        <td>
                            <asp:Label
                                Runat="server"
                                Text='<%# Bind("City") %>'
                                ID="Label6"/>
                        </td>
                        <td>
                            <asp:Label
                                Runat="server"
                                Text='<%# Bind("Region") %>'
                                ID="Label7"/>
                        </td>
                    </table>
                </ItemTemplate>
            </asp:TemplateField>
        </Columns>
    </asp:GridView>

    <asp:SqlDataSource
        ID="SqlDataSource1"
        Runat="server"
        SelectCommand="SELECT [CustomerID], [CompanyName], [ContactName],
[ContactTitle], [Address], [City], [Region] FROM [Customers]"
        ConnectionString="<%$ ConnectionStrings:NorthwindConnectionString %>">
    </asp:SqlDataSource>

    </div>
    </form>
</body>
</html>
```

You can find the whole example in the file d_expandrow.aspx. If you want more information about the display property used in the preceding example, take a look at the following link: http://msdn.microsoft.com/library/default.asp?url=/workshop/author/dhtml/reference/properties/display.asp.

This section has illustrated a simple example of how you can use client-side script to dynamically expand and collapse a GridView control's row.

Creating a PagerTemplate for the GridView Control

When you retrieve a lot of data from a datasource that will be displayed on the page by using the GridView control, you probably don't want to show every row on a single page, especially not when you have hundreds of rows. Displaying hundreds of rows on a single page will use a lot of resources, both on the server and the client. Every row rendered by the GridView contains a set of rendered HTML elements; those will be sent over the network to the browser. If you have several rows that should be displayed, more data will be sent to the client and more bandwidth is required. To minimize the numbers of rows to be displayed on a page, you can use the GridView's paging feature, which will display rows in pages. You can specify how many rows one page will display, and to switch pages you can click a Next button or the number of the page to switch to. Using paging minimizes the data sent over the network and makes it easier for the user to navigate the data. To enable paging, you set the GridView's AllowPaging property to true. When this is done, an additional row called the *pager row* is automatically displayed in the GridView control. The pager row can be located at the top or the bottom of the GridView control, or both at the top and the bottom of the GridView control. To specify the number of rows that should be displayed on each page, you can use the GridView's PageSize property; by default the value is set to 10, which means that 10 rows will be displayed on each page.

By using the PagerSettings property of the GridView, you can specify how a user switches to another page. You can, for example, specify that you want to use a Preview and Next button, First and Last buttons, and a numeric list, with the number of each page. The user can click the number to move to a specific page. The GridView control only supports a way to specify how the paging row of the GridView should look. You can, for example, use a drop-down list with the number of pages the users can switch to, or use the Previous and Next buttons together with a numeric list. (The GridView doesn't support this currently.) You can create your own pager template to specify exactly how you want the user to switch to another page. To specify your own paging template, you can use the PagerTemplate of the GridView control. The following example uses the PagerTemplate of the GridView to display the selected page and the number of total pages. It also displays Next and Preview buttons for moving between pages:

```
<asp:GridView
    AllowPaging="True"
    Id="GridView1"
    ...>
    <PagerTemplate>
        Selected Index <%= GridView1.PageIndex * GridView1.PageSize %>
        Number of pages <%=GridView1.PageCount %>
        <asp:button
            CommandName="Page"
            CommandArgument="Prev"
```

```
            Text="Preview" ...>
      <asp:button
            CommandName="Page"
            CommandArgument="Next"
            Text="Next" ..>
    </PagerTemplate>
</asp:GridView>
```

The whole code example in which the `PagerTemplate` is used can be found in the file `pager1.aspx` of the examples files for this chapter, which can be downloaded from `www.wrox.com`.

By using a server-side code block within the template, you can create your own pager. If you want to add a First/Last or Next/Prev button, you simply add a Button control and set its `CommandName` to `Page` and the `CommandArgument` to `First`, `Last`, `Next`, or `Prev`. You don't need to add any event to handle the paging; the GridView gets the `CommandArgument` for the buttons you have selected and does the action for you automatically. To add numeric paging, you add Button controls with the `CommandName` set to `Page` and the `CommandArgument` set to the index of the page to navigate to.

You can also programmatically manipulate the top or bottom paging row by using the `TopPagerRow` or `BottomPagerRow` property of the GridView control. As you probably have guessed based on the name, the `TopPagerRow` accesses the pager row located at the top (if you specify rendering the paging control at the top of the GridView) and the `BottomPagerRow` is the paging control located at the bottom of the GridView. The `TopPagerRow` and `BottomPagerRow` are of type `GridViewRow`. The important thing to remember when you decide to manipulate `TopPagerRow` or `BottomPagerRow` is that the manipulation must be performed after the GridView control has been rendered. If you do it before, the changes will be overwritten by the GridView control. A good place to manipulate the pager row is to hook up to the GridView's DataBound event. Listing 7-2 uses the `PagerTemplate` where a DropDownList control is added, and where the DropDownList control's items represent each page to which a user can navigate. `BottomPagerRow` is used to manipulate the pager row.

Listing 7-2: Using PagerTemplate with a DropDownList control

```csharp
<%@ Page language="C#" %>

<script runat="server">

    void PageDropDownList_SelectedIndexChanged(Object sender, EventArgs e)
    {
        // Get the BottomPager row.
        GridViewRow bottomPagerRow = CustomersGridView.BottomPagerRow;

        // Get the PageDropDownList DropDownList from the bottom pager row.
        DropDownList pageList =
bottomPagerRow.Cells[0].FindControl("PageDropDownList") as DropDownList;

        // Set the PageIndex property of the GridView to display that page selected
by the user.
        if (pageList != null)
            CustomersGridView.PageIndex = pageList.SelectedIndex;
    }

    void CustomersGridView_DataBound(Object sender, EventArgs e)
```

(continued)

Listing 7-2 *(continued)*

```
    {
        // Retrieve the pager row.
        GridViewRow pagerRow = CustomersGridView.BottomPagerRow;

        // Retrieve the DropDownList and Label controls from the row.
        DropDownList pageList = pagerRow.Cells[0].FindControl("PageDropDownList")
as DropDownList;
        Label pageLabel = pagerRow.Cells[0].FindControl("SelectedPageLabel") as
Label;

        if(pageList != null)
        {

            //Add the number of pages to the ListBox
            for (int i=0; i<CustomersGridView.PageCount; i++)
            {
                int pageNumber = i + 1;

                //Create a ListItem that represents a page
                ListItem item = new ListItem(pageNumber.ToString());

                //If a page is already selected, make sure the
                //ListBox selects the selected page
                if (i==CustomersGridView.PageIndex)
                    item.Selected = true;

                // Add the ListItem object to the Items collection of the
                // DropDownList.
                pageList.Items.Add(item);
            }
        }

        if(pageLabel != null)
        {
            // Get the current page number.
            int currentPage = CustomersGridView.PageIndex + 1;

            pageLabel.Text = "Page " + currentPage.ToString() +
                            " of " + CustomersGridView.PageCount.ToString();
        }
    }

</script>

<html>
  <body>
    <form id="Form1" runat="server">

      <asp:gridview id="CustomersGridView"
        datasourceid="CustomersSqlDataSource"
        ondatabound="CustomersGridView_DataBound"
        autogeneratecolumns="true"
        allowpaging="true"
```

```
            runat="server"
            pageSize=15>

        <pagerstyle backcolor="LightGray"/>

        <pagertemplate>

          <table width="100%">
            <tr>
              <td>

                  <asp:label
                      id="ViewPageLabel"
                      text="View page:"
                      runat="server"/>

                  <asp:dropdownlist id="PageDropDownList"
                      autopostback="true"
                      onselectedindexchanged="PageDropDownList_SelectedIndexChanged"
                      runat="server"/>

              </td>

              <td align="right">
                  <asp:label id="SelectedPageLabel" runat="server"/>
              </td>

            </tr>
          </table>

        </pagertemplate>

      </asp:gridview>

      <asp:sqldatasource
          id="CustomersSqlDataSource"
          connectionstring="<%$ ConnectionStrings:NorthWindConnectionString%>"
          selectcommand="Select [CustomerID], [CompanyName], [Address], [City],
[PostalCode], [Country] From [Customers]"
          runat="server">
      </asp:sqldatasource>

    </form>
  </body>
</html>
```

The source code to this example can found in the file `pager2.aspx`.

The example here uses the Northwind database to get a list of customers from the Customers table.

Let's split the code into pieces and take a look at it in more detail. The example uses a `pagerTemplate` to specify a custom pager row for the GridView. The `pagerTemplate` has a table with two columns; the first column has a DropDownList control with the id `PageDropDownList`. This is where the number of pages a user can select will be added. The other column represents information about which page a user has selected.

```
<asp:GridView ...>
<pagertemplate>

        <table width="100%">
          <tr>
            <td>

                <asp:label
                    id="ViewPageLabel"
                    text="View page:"
                    runat="server"/>

                <asp:dropdownlist
                    id="PageDropDownList"
                    autopostback="true"
                    onselectedindexchanged="PageDropDownList_SelectedIndexChanged"
                    runat="server"/>

            </td>
            <td align="right">
              <asp:label id="SelectedPageLabel" runat="server"/>
            </td>

          </tr>
        </table>

</pagertemplate>
</asp:GiredView>
```

PagerDropDownList has the AutoPostBack attribute set to true, and when a user selects a page to view, the PageDropDownList_SelectedIndexChanged event is triggered.

```
void PageDropDownList_SelectedIndexChanged(Object sender, EventArgs e)
{
        GridViewRow bottomPagerRow = CustomersGridView.BottomPagerRow;

        DropDownList pageList =
bottomPagerRow.Cells[0].FindControl("PageDropDownList") as DropDownList;

    if (pageList != null)
        CustomersGridView.PageIndex = pageList.SelectedIndex;
}
```

PageDropDownList_SelectedIndexChanged uses the BottomPagerRow property of the GridView (CustomerGridView) control to get the GridViewRow that represents the content of the pagerTemplate. To get the PageDropDownList from pagerTemplate, the FindControl method is used. If the PageDrop DownList is found within the GridViewRow cells, the GridView's PageIndex property will be set to the selected index of the PageDropDownList. The index of the selected items in the DropDownList represents the index of the page to be displayed. The PageIndex property of the GridView is used to specify which page a user will see.

Because the manipulation of the pager row must be done after the GridView is rendered, the GridView's DataBound event is used to manipulate the pager row. If the manipulation takes place before the Grid View is rendered, the GridView will reset the manipulation. The DataBound event is triggered after the data is bound to the DataGrid:

```
<asp:gridview
    id="CustomersGridView"
    ondatabound="CustomersGridView_DataBound"
    ...>
```

The `CustomersGridView_DataBound` method is triggered when the GridView's `DataBound` event is triggered:

```
void CustomersGridView_DataBound(Object sender, EventArgs e)
{
    // Retrieve the pager row.
    GridViewRow pagerRow = CustomersGridView.BottomPagerRow;

    // Retrieve the DropDownList and Label controls from the row.
    DropDownList pageList = pagerRow.Cells[0].FindControl("PageDropDownList")
as DropDownList;

    Label pageLabel = pagerRow.Cells[0].FindControl("SelectedPageLabel") as
Label;
```

The `CustomerGridView_DataBound` method will get the GridViewRow that represents the pager row from the GridView by using the GridView's `BottomPagerRow`. In this method, the pages that a user can select will be added to the `PageDropDownList` inside the GridView's `pagerTemplate`. `FindControl` is used to get the `PageDropDownList` from the `BottomPagerRow`. There is also a Label control—`SelectedPage Label`—added to the pager row which represents the current page that is selected.

To get the number of pages in which the datasource is split, you can use the `PageCount` property of the GridView:

```
if(pageList != null)
{
    //Add the number of pages to the ListBox
    for (int i=0; i<CustomersGridView.PageCount; i++)
    {
        int pageNumber = i + 1;

        //Create a ListItem that represents a page
        ListItem item = new ListItem(pageNumber.ToString());
```

To fill the DropDownList in the pager row with the pages a user can navigate to, a `for` loop is used. The `for` loop starts from zero and goes to the number of pages into which the data is split. Because the text of the items in the DropDownList should start from one and not from zero, 1 is added to the current index of the `for` loop and put into a new variable that represents the text the `ListItem` in the DropDownList will have. A new `ListItem` is created to be added to the `DropDownList` later in the code.

When a user selects a page to view from the drop-down list, the current page item in the drop-down list should be selected. That can be done by getting the current index the GridView is displaying by using the `PageIndex` property of the GridView control:

```
//If a page is already selected, make sure the
//ListBox selects the selected page
if (i==CustomersGridView.PageIndex)
```

```
        item.Selected = true;

    // Add the ListItem object to the Items collection of the
    // DropDownList.
    pageList.Items.Add(item);
```

If the current index of the `for` loop (used to add an item to `DropDownList`) is equal to the GridView's `PageIndex`, the current created item has its `Selected` property set to `true`. The `Selected` property of the `ListItem` is a marker to tell the `DropDownList` which item should be selected by default.

The last thing the code example in this topic does is set the Label control inside the pager row to display which page a user has selected, and the number of total pages from which a user can select:

```
    // Get the current page number.
    int currentPage = CustomersGridView.PageIndex + 1;

    pageLabel.Text = "Page " + currentPage.ToString() +
                     " of " + CustomersGridView.PageCount.ToString();
```

To get the total number of pages into which the data returned from the datasource is split, you use the `PageCount` property of the GridView.

In this section, you learned how to use the `pagerTemplate` of the GridView control to create and define your own template for the GridView's pager feature. You also learned how to use the `BottomPagerRow` to manipulate the pager row dynamically with code, and that the manipulation of the pager row must be done after the GridView is rendered.

Deleting the GridView's Selected Rows

The GridView has support for removing a row but only one single row can be removed at a time. Sometimes it could be useful to give the user the capability to select several rows that can be deleted at the same time — for example, in `hotmail.com`, you can select several e-mail messages and remove them. This section will cover how to add support for the deletion of several rows.

The code example in this hack uses an `ItemTemplate` with an `HtmlInputCheckBox` added to the template. The `ItemTemplate` and the `HtmlInputCheckBox` are used instead of `CheckBoxField`, which represents a data-bound field with `CheckBox`. You do this because `CheckBoxField` doesn't have a `value` property, which is necessary because `Value` represents the value of the datasource id of the row to be deleted. To add an `ItemTemplate` to the GridView, a `TemplateField` must first be added. A `TemplateField` represents a custom field that allows you to specify the content of a column within the GridView. When the `TemplateField` is created, `ItemTemplate` with the content of the column can be added. You add `HtmlInputCheckBox` to the `ItemTemplate` and set the `value` property of `CheckBox` to the current datasource row's primary key. The following code will use an `ItemTemplate` where an `InputCheckBox` is added:

```
<asp:GridView
    AutoGenerateColumns="False"
    DataKeyNames="CustomerID"
    DataSourceID="SqlDataSource1"
    ID="GridView1"
```

```
            runat="server">
            <Columns>

                <asp:TemplateField>
                    <ItemTemplate>
                        <input
                            id="CustomerID"
                            type="checkbox"
                            runat="server"
                            value='<%# Eval("CustomerID") %>' />
                    </ItemTemplate>
                </asp:TemplateField>

                <asp:BoundField
                        DataField="CompanyName"
                        HeaderText="CompanyName"
                        SortExpression="CompanyName"/>

                <asp:BoundField
                        DataField="ContactName"
                        HeaderText="ContactName"
                        SortExpression="ContactName"/>

            </Columns>
        </asp:GridView>
```

In the preceding code, CheckBox is a simple `<input>` element with the type set to checkbox and the element marked `runat="server"`, which is needed so the control can be accessed from the server-side code as an HtmlInputCheckBox control. The value attribute of the `<input>` is bound to the CustomerID field (the primary key of the Northwind's Customers table used in this example). Two BoundFields are added to the GridView, used only to display simple text with the customer's company and contact name.

To fill the GridView with data from the Northwind Customers table, a SqlDataSource is used, as shown in the following code. DeleteCommand specifies the deletion of a single row. The specified delete command is executed when the rows should be removed, which you'll read more about later.

> The Northwind database uses a lot of relationships between its tables, so the Delete command in the code will make the SqlDataSource throw an exception. The code is used for demonstration purposes only; and to make sure it works, you have to remove the relations between the Customers table and the Order table, or create a delete command that will remove all the orders and the order's rows for the specific customer you will delete. I decided to remove the relationship to make it easy to test the code.

```
<asp:SqlDataSource
        ID="SqlDataSource1"
        Runat="server"
        SelectCommand="SELECT [CustomerID], [CompanyName], [ContactName],
[ContactTitle] FROM [Customers]"
        DeleteCommand="DELETE [Customers] WHERE [CustomerID] = @CustomerID"
```

```
                ConnectionString="<%$ ConnectionStrings:NorthwindConnectionString %>">

        <DeleteParameters>
            <asp:Parameter
                    Type="String"
                    Name="CustomerID">
            </asp:Parameter>
        </DeleteParameters>
    </asp:SqlDataSource>
```

To delete the selected rows, you need to add a button for that purpose:

```
<asp:Button
    ID="DeleteSelectedRows"
    OnClick="DeleteSelectedRows _Click"
    runat="server"
    Text="Button" />
```

The following code is the server-side code that will be executed when the Button control is clicked. The code will iterate through the GridView's rows and get the value from the `HtmlInputCheckBox Value` property, but only from the `CheckBoxes` that are selected. The value will be added to the `SqlDataSource` control's `DeleteParameter`. When this is done, the `Delete` method of the `SqlDataSource` control is executed to delete the selected rows:

```
protected void DeleteSelectedRows_Click(object sender, EventArgs e)
{
    //Iterate through all the GridView's Rows
    foreach (GridViewRow row in GridView1.Rows)
    {
        //Get the first column from the row where the HtmlInputCheckBox is located
        TableCell cell = row.Cells[0];

        //Get the HtmlInputCheckBox control from the cells control collection
        HtmlInputCheckBox checkBox = cell.Controls[1] as HtmlInputCheckBox;

        //If the checkbox exists and is checked, execute the Delete command where the
        //value in the HtmlInputCheckBox's Value property is set as the value of the
        //delete command's parameter.

        if (checkBox != null && checkBox.Checked)
        {
            SqlDataSource1.DeleteParameters["CustomerID"].DefaultValue =
checkBox.Value;

            SqlDataSource1.Delete();
        }
    }
}
```

Listing 7-3 shows the entire hack.

Listing 7-3: Deleting multiple rows

```
<%@ Page Language="C#" AutoEventWireup="true" %>
<script runat=server>

 protected void DeleteSelectedRows_Click(object sender, EventArgs e)
 {
        //Iterate through all the GridView's Rows
        foreach (GridViewRow row in GridView1.Rows)
        {
            //Get the first column from the row where the HtmlInputCheckBox is
located
            TableCell cell = row.Cells[0];

            //Get the HtmlInputCheckBox control from the cells control collection
            HtmlInputCheckBox checkBox = cell.Controls[1] as HtmlInputCheckBox;

            //If the checkbox exists and is checked, execute the Delete command
where the
            //value in the HtmlInputCheckBox's Value property is set as the value
of the
            //delete command's parameter.
            if (checkBox != null && checkBox.Checked)
            {
                SqlDataSource1.DeleteParameters["CustomerID"].DefaultValue =
checkBox.Value;
                SqlDataSource1.Delete();
            }
        }
 }

</script>

<!DOCTYPE html PUBLIC "-//W3C//DTD XHTML 1.1//EN"
"http://www.w3.org/TR/xhtml11/DTD/xhtml11.dtd">

<html xmlns="http://www.w3.org/1999/xhtml" >
<head runat="server">
    <title>Deleting the Gridview's Selected Rows</title>
</head>
<body>
    <form id="form1" runat="server">
    <div>

    <asp:GridView
        AutoGenerateColumns="False"
        DataKeyNames="CustomerID"
        DataSourceID="SqlDataSource1"
        ID="GridView1"
        runat="server"
        AllowPaging="True">
    <Columns>
```

(continued)

Listing 7-3 *(continued)*

```
        <asp:TemplateField>

            <ItemTemplate>
              <input
                  id="CustomerID"
                  type="checkbox"
                  runat="server"
                  value='<%# Eval("CustomerID") %>' />
            </ItemTemplate>

        </asp:TemplateField>

        <asp:BoundField
            DataField="CompanyName"
            HeaderText="CompanyName"
            SortExpression="CompanyName"/>

        <asp:BoundField
            DataField="ContactName"
            HeaderText="ContactName"
            SortExpression="ContactName"/>

    </Columns>

    </asp:GridView>

    <asp:SqlDataSource ID="SqlDataSource1" Runat="server"
        SelectCommand="SELECT [CustomerID], [CompanyName], [ContactName],
[ContactTitle] FROM [Customers]"
        DeleteCommand="DELETE [Customers] WHERE [CustomerID] = @CustomerID"
        ConnectionString="<%$ ConnectionStrings:NorthwindConnectionString %>">
        <DeleteParameters>

            <asp:Parameter
                Type="String"
                Name="CustomerID"/>

        </DeleteParameters>
    </asp:SqlDataSource>

    <asp:Button
        ID="DeleteSelectedRows"
        OnClick="DeleteSelectedRows_Click"
        runat="server"
        Text="Delete" />

    </div>
    </form>
</body>
</html>
```

The example code can be found in the file `delete_rows.aspx`.

> This code can be optimized to increase performance by using ADO.NET, creating a batch query instead of using the SqlDataSource control. You can find an example of when a batch query is used in the next section, "Updating All GridView Rows."

This topic demonstrated how to add an ItemTemplate and CheckBox control to make it possible to select several rows and delete them all.

Updating All GridView Rows

The GridView has support for updating a row, but it can't update several rows at once. In some cases you don't want to edit one row at a time; instead, you want to edit several rows, like you do in an Excel sheet. This section describes how to use the GridView to update several rows. Two different examples are provided for this topic, one in which the SqlDataSource control is used to perform a simple UpdateCommand for each row in the GridView, and one example in which a batch query is used to update every row in one single connection, to minimize the access to the datasource.

> If you use a SqlDataSource to update each row, the SqlDataSource will open a new connection and execute the UpdateCommand. This will adversely affect performance, so the solution is to use a batch update instead if you don't need to control each update. With a batch update you only need to have one connection open, enabling you to execute one command instead of several to the database.

Listing 7-4 updates each row with a SqlDataSource control. This example uses an ItemTemplate to add TextBox controls to each column in the GridView. (You can read more about the ItemTemplate in the previous section or in the MSDN Library if you need more information.) The ItemTemplate is used because the Text property of the GridView row's Cell can't be used in this case to get the value of the cells. To get the value from the controls within the cells, the FindControl method is used to locate the control added to the ItemTemplate. All fields added to the GridView are editable controls (TextBoxes). The EditItemTemplate can't be used in this example because the GridView will only show the EditItemTemplate for the row that is marked to be edited — in this example, all fields should be editable from the beginning. A Button control is also added to the page, which will update all the rows when it's clicked. (The example uses the Northwind database.)

Listing 7-4: Using SqlDataSource to update rows

```
<%@ Page Language="C#" %>

<script runat="server">

    void Button1_Click(object sender, EventArgs e)
    {
        for (int i = 0; i < GridView1.Rows.Count; i++)
        {
```

(continued)

161

Listing 7-4 *(continued)*

```
            GridViewRow row = GridView1.Rows[i];

            SqlDataSource1.UpdateParameters[0].DefaultValue =
((TextBox)row.Cells[0].FindControl("TextBox2")).Text;
            SqlDataSource1.UpdateParameters[1].DefaultValue =
((TextBox)row.Cells[1].FindControl("TextBox3")).Text;
            SqlDataSource1.UpdateParameters[2].DefaultValue =
GridView1.DataKeys[i].Value.ToString();

            SqlDataSource1.Update();
        }
    }

</script>

<html xmlns="http://www.w3.org/1999/xhtml" >
<head runat="server">
    <title>Updating All GridView Rows </title>
</head>
<body>
    <form id="form1" runat="server">

    <div>

        <asp:GridView
            ID="GridView1"
            Runat="server"
            DataSourceID="SqlDataSource1"
            DataKeyNames="CustomerID"
            AutoGenerateColumns="False">
            <Columns>

                <asp:TemplateField
                    SortExpression="CustomerID"
                    HeaderText="CustomerID">

                    <ItemTemplate>

                        <asp:TextBox
                            Runat="server"
                            Text='<%# Bind("CustomerID") %>'
                            ID="TextBox1">
                        </asp:TextBox>

                    </ItemTemplate>

                </asp:TemplateField>

                <asp:TemplateField
                    SortExpression="CompanyName"
```

```
                                    HeaderText="CompanyName">

                            <ItemTemplate>

                                    <asp:TextBox
                                            Runat="server"
                                            Text='<%# Bind("CompanyName") %>'
                                            ID="TextBox2">
                                    </asp:TextBox>

                            </ItemTemplate>

                    </asp:TemplateField>

                    <asp:TemplateField
                            SortExpression="ContactName"
                            HeaderText="ContactTitle">

                            <ItemTemplate>

                                    <asp:TextBox
                                            Runat="server"
                                            Text='<%# Bind("ContactTitle") %>'
                                            ID="TextBox3">
                                    </asp:TextBox>

                            </ItemTemplate>

                    </asp:TemplateField>

            </Columns>

    </asp:GridView>

    <asp:SqlDataSource
            ID="SqlDataSource1"
            Runat="server"
            SelectCommand="SELECT [CustomerID], [CompanyName], [ContactName],
[ContactTitle] FROM [Customers]"
            UpdateCommand="UPDATE [Customers] SET [CompanyName] = @CompanyName,
[ContactTitle] = @ContactTitle WHERE [CustomerID] = @CustomerID"
            ConnectionString="<%$ ConnectionStrings: NorthwindConnectionString%>">
            <UpdateParameters>

                    <asp:Parameter
                            Type="String"
                            Name="CompanyName">
                    </asp:Parameter>

                    <asp:Parameter
                            Type="String"
                            Name="ContactTitle">
```

(continued)

Listing 7-4 (continued)

```
              </asp:Parameter>

              <asp:Parameter
                   Type="String"
                   Name="CustomerID">
              </asp:Parameter>

         </UpdateParameters>

     </asp:SqlDataSource>

     <asp:Button
          ID="Button1"
          Runat="server"
          Text="Update"
          OnClick="Button1_Click"/> 
     </div>
     </form>
</body>
</html>
```

The example can be found in the file `update_rows.aspx`.

The important part of the example is the method that will be triggered when the user clicks the button to update all the rows:

```
void Button1_Click(object sender, EventArgs e)
{
    for (int i = 0; i < GridView1.Rows.Count; i++)
    {
        GridViewRow row = GridView1.Rows[i];

        SqlDataSource1.UpdateParameters[0].DefaultValue =
((TextBox)row.Cells[0].FindControl("TextBox2")).Text;
        SqlDataSource1.UpdateParameters[1].DefaultValue =
((TextBox)row.Cells[1].FindControl("TextBox3")).Text;
        SqlDataSource1.UpdateParameters[2].DefaultValue =
GridView1.DataKeys[i].Value.ToString();

        SqlDataSource1.Update();
    }
}
```

To get all values from the rows, the code must iterate through all the GridView's rows. To get the number of GridView rows, you can use the GridView row's `Count` property. The `SqlDataSource`'s Update Parameters will be filled with data from the GridView's cells, and executes the Update command. The previous example will open a new connection against the datasource and execute the specified Update Command for each row. Opening a connection and sending a command to the database for each row is expensive and can affect performance.

Listing 7-5 shows an optimization in which a batch query performs the updates once. The use of ADO.NET saves resources by opening only one connection instead of several for each row, as in the previous example.

Listing 7-5: Performing a batch query

```csharp
<%@ Page Language="C#" %>

<%@ Import Namespace="System.Text" %>
<%@ Import Namespace="System.Data.SqlClient" %>

<script runat="server">

    void Button1_Click(object sender, EventArgs e)
    {
        StringBuilder query = new StringBuilder();

        for (int i = 0; i < GridView1.Rows.Count; i++)
        {

            GridViewRow row = GridView1.Rows[i];

            string value1 =
((TextBox)row.Cells[0].FindControl("TextBox2")).Text.Replace("'","''");

            string value2 =
((TextBox)row.Cells[1].FindControl("TextBox3")).Text.Replace("'","''");

            string value3 = GridView1.DataKeys[i].Value.ToString();

            query.Append("UPDATE [Customers] SET [CompanyName] = '")
                .Append(value1).Append("' , [ContactTitle] = '")
                .Append(value2).Append("' WHERE [CustomerID] = '")
                .Append(value3).Append("';\n");
        }

        SqlConnection con = new SqlConnection(
ConfigurationSettings.ConnectionStrings["AppConnectionString1"].ConnectionString);

        SqlCommand command = new SqlCommand(query.ToString(), con);
        con.Open();

        command.ExecuteNonQuery();

        con.Close();
    }

    void Page_Load(object sender, EventArgs e)
    {
        if (!Page.IsPostBack)
        {
            SqlConnection con = new SqlConnection(
ConfigurationSettings.ConnectionStrings["AppConnectionString1"].ConnectionString);

            SqlCommand command = new SqlCommand(
```

(continued)

Listing 7-5 *(continued)*

```
"SELECT [CustomerID], [CompanyName], [ContactName], [ContactTitle] FROM
[Customers]", con);

            con.Open();

            GridView1.DataSource = command.ExecuteReader();
            GridView1.DataBind();

            con.Close();
        }
    }

</script>

<html xmlns="http://www.w3.org/1999/xhtml" >
<head runat="server">
    <title>Updating All GridView Rows</title>
</head>
<body>
    <form id="form1" runat="server">
    <div>
        <asp:GridView
            ID="GridView1"
            Runat="server"
            DataKeyNames="CustomerID"
            AutoGenerateColumns="False">
        <Columns>

            <asp:TemplateField
                SortExpression="CustomerID"
                HeaderText="CustomerID">

            <ItemTemplate>

                <asp:TextBox
                    Runat="server"
                    Text='<%# Bind("CustomerID") %>'
                    ID="TextBox1">
                </asp:TextBox>

            </ItemTemplate>

            </asp:TemplateField>

            <asp:TemplateField
                SortExpression="CompanyName"
                HeaderText="CompanyName">

            <ItemTemplate>

                <asp:TextBox
                    Runat="server"
```

```
                              Text='<%# Bind("CompanyName") %>'
                              ID="TextBox2">
                      </asp:TextBox>

                  </ItemTemplate>

              </asp:TemplateField>

              <asp:TemplateField
                  SortExpression="ContactName"
                  HeaderText="ContactTitle">

                  <ItemTemplate>

                      <asp:TextBox
                          Runat="server"
                          Text='<%# Bind("ContactTitle") %>'
                          ID="TextBox3">
                      </asp:TextBox>

                  </ItemTemplate>

              </asp:TemplateField>

          </Columns>
      </asp:GridView>

      <asp:Button
          ID="Button1"
          Runat="server"
          Text="Button"
          OnClick="Button1_Click" /> 
    </div>
  </form>
</body>
</html>
```

The difference between this example and the previous one is the implementation of the click event of the Button control that will do the update of the rows. The following code uses ADO.NET's classes to open only one connection and execute only one command, which will do a batch update:

```
void Button1_Click(object sender, EventArgs e)
{
    StringBuilder query = new StringBuilder();

    //Iterate through all rows in the GridView to get data from each
    //row and create an update command for each row.
    for (int i = 0; i < GridView1.Rows.Count; i++)
    {

        GridViewRow row = GridView1.Rows[i];

        //Find the TextBox control that have the updated data
```

167

```
            //Because this example don't use parameters and to avoid
            //SQL-Injection, the "'" will be replaced to "''".
            string value1 =
((TextBox)row.Cells[0].FindControl("TextBox2")).Text.Replace("'","''");

            string value2 =
((TextBox)row.Cells[1].FindControl("TextBox3")).Text.Replace("'","''");

            string value3 = GridView1.DataKeys[i].Value.ToString();

            //Add an Update command for the row to the StringBuilder class.
            query.Append("UPDATE [Customers] SET [CompanyName] = '")
                .Append(value1).Append("' , [ContactTitle] = '")
                .Append(value2).Append("' WHERE [CustomerID] = '")
                .Append(value3).Append("';\n");
        }

    SqlConnection con = new SqlConnection(
ConfigurationSettings.ConnectionStrings["AppConnectionString1"].ConnectionString);

    SqlCommand command = new SqlCommand(query.ToString(), con);
    con.Open();

    command.ExecuteNonQuery();

    con.Close();
    }
```

The example uses a `StringBuilder` to create a batch query. A semicolon separates the `update` commands that should be executed for each row within the GridView. Instead of using the `SqlDataSource` to do the update, ADO.NET's `System.Data.SqlClient` namespace is used. Using ADO.NET instead of the `SqlDataSource` gives the code more control over how the connection should be reused and how to execute the different kind of SQL commands.

In this topic you have learned how to make it possible to update all rows of the GridView control. You have also learned how to do it with the SqlDataSource control and with ADO.NET.

Adding a Selected Row

This hack describes how to add a new row to the GridView programmatically — for example, maybe a DetailsView control should be added beneath the selected row for displaying more information about the row, or other controls such as a new GridView control, etc. In the topic about dynamic row expansion, a client-side script is used to expand and collapse a row to show more information about a row. This hack does something similar as the dynamic row expansion hack, but instead of loading all data for a row, this hack loads only the information displayed, and loads more data after the row is first selected. This hack can be a useful when you don't want to load data that should not be displayed until a row is selected.

To add a new row dynamically to the GridView control, some properties and events can't be used — for example, the Rows property of the GridView is protected from adding new rows, so it can't be used to add a new row programmatically. The RowCreated event will only provide us with the current row that is created by the GridView control; the RowCreated event can't be used to add a new row to the GridView control. It would be possible if the internal table were available from the Parent property of the created row, but the GridView doesn't set the Parent to an object before the RowCreated event is executed. It will be done after the RowCreated event has been executed. But the RowDataBound event will be triggered directly after the row has been added to the internal table. With the RowDataBound event, the table where the row is added can be accessed through the Row's Parent property. The following example will get the table for the current data-bound row:

```
void GridView1_RowDataBound(object sender, GridViewRowEventArgs e)
{
    Table table = e.Row.Parent as Table;
    if (table != null)
        //Add new row to the table
}
```

There is one problem with using the RowDataBound event: Because the RowDataBound executes only the first time the GridView is rendered, the ViewState must be turned off for the GridView control to make it execute the RowDataBound event every time the page is reloaded. The RowDataBound doesn't execute during every postback for performance reasons, because there is almost no need to rebind data during a postback. Therefore, instead of rebinding the data, the information is collected from the ViewState.

> **Turning off the use of** ViewState **can remove some functionality such as paging and sorting, so keep that in mind.**

By using the RowDataBound event to add a new row, each data-bound row has a new row added to the GridView control. Instead of adding a new row for each row, it can be added only when a row is selected. You do this by using the GridView control's PreRender event and the GridView's SelectedRow property to get the row and the row's parent control. The following code uses the PreRender and SelectedRow properties to get the currently selected row of the GridView control:

```
void GridView1_PreRender (object sender, EventArgs e)
{
    if (GridView1.SelectedRow != null)
    {
        Table table = GridView1.SelectedRow.Parent as Table;

        if (table != null)
            CreateRow(table, GridView1.SelectedIndex);
    }
}
```

The preceding code calls the CreateRow method to create the new row. The CreateRow method has two arguments: the table of the selected row and the index of the selected row. The index of the row is passed as an argument to the CreateRow method to ensure that the new row is added to the correct location after the currently selected row. The following code shows how the CreateRow method could look:

```
private void CreateRow(Table table, int index)
{
    GridViewRow row = new GridViewRow(-1, -1, DataControlRowType.DataRow,
DataControlRowState.Normal);

    row.Cells.Add(CreateColumn());

    table.Rows.AddAt(index+2, row);
}
```

The preceding code creates a new GridViewRow and a new column by calling the `CreateColumn` method (the implementation of the method can be found later in this section). The `AddAt` method adds the new row. To ensure that the new row that will be added to the currently selected row will appear under the row, the value of the index argument must be increased by two. If the index is not increased, the row is added above the selected row or on the same position, which will also make the created row appear before the selected row.

The following code shows how a `DetailsView` control can be added to the selected row:

```
private TableCell CreateColumn()
{
    TableCell cell = new TableCell();
    cell.ColumnSpan = GridView1.Columns.Count;
    cell.Width = Unit.Percentage(100);

    DataSourceControl ds = CreateDataSourceControl();

    cell.Controls.Add(ds);
    cell.Controls.Add(CreateDetailsView(ds));

    return cell;
}

private static DetailsView CreateDetailsView(DataSourceControl ds)
{
    DetailsView dv = new DetailsView();
    dv.AutoGenerateRows = true;
    dv.DataSourceID = ds.ID;

    return dv;
}

private DataSourceControl CreateDataSourceControl()
{
    SqlDataSource ds = new SqlDataSource();
    ds.ConnectionString =
WebConfigurationManager.ConnectionStrings["NorthwindConnectionString"].ConnectionSt
ring;
    ds.SelectCommand = "SELECT * FROM [Customers] WHERE [CustomerID] =
@CustomerID";
    ds.ID = "SqlDataSource2";

    Parameter cp = new Parameter("CustomerID", TypeCode.String,
GridView1.SelectedValue.ToString());
    ds.SelectParameters.Add(cp);
```

```
        return ds;
    }
```

The `CreateColumn` method will now call two other methods: one that creates the `DataSourceControl` and one that creates the `DetailsView` control. The `CreateDataSourceControl` method will return the base class of the `SqlDataSourceControl`, which will make it easy to change the code inside the `CreateDataSourceControl` to return another datasource control if that is needed. Creating several methods with a few lines of code makes the code easy to read and maintain.

Listing 7-6 shows the final code for displaying a `DetailsView` control when a row from the GridView is selected.

Listing 7-6: Displaying a DetailsView control when a row is selected

```
<%@ Page Language="C#" %>
<%@ Import Namespace="System.Web.Configuration" %>

<script runat="server">

    void GridView1_PreRender(object sender, EventArgs e)
    {
        if (GridView1.SelectedRow != null)
        {
            Table table = GridView1.SelectedRow.Parent as Table;

            if (table != null)
                CreateRow(table, GridView1.SelectedIndex);
        }
    }

    private void CreateRow(Table table, int index)
    {
        GridViewRow row = new GridViewRow(-1, -1, DataControlRowType.DataRow,
DataControlRowState.Normal);
        row.Cells.Add(CreateColumn());
        table.Rows.AddAt(index + 2, row);
    }

    private TableCell CreateColumn()
    {
        TableCell cell = new TableCell();
        cell.ColumnSpan = GridView1.Columns.Count;
        cell.Width = Unit.Percentage(100);

        DataSourceControl ds = CreateDataSourceControl();

        cell.Controls.Add(ds);
        cell.Controls.Add(CreateDetailsView(ds));

        return cell;
    }

    private static DetailsView CreateDetailsView(DataSourceControl ds)
```

(continued)

Listing 7-6 *(continued)*

```
        {
            DetailsView dv = new DetailsView();
            dv.AutoGenerateRows = true;
            dv.DataSourceID = ds.ID;

            return dv;
        }

        private DataSourceControl CreateDataSourceControl()
        {
            SqlDataSource ds = new SqlDataSource();
            ds.ConnectionString =
WebConfigurationManager.ConnectionStrings["NorthwindConnectionString"].ConnectionSt
ring;
            ds.SelectCommand = "SELECT * FROM [Customers] WHERE [CustomerID] =
@CustomerID";
            ds.ID = "SqlDataSource2";

            Parameter cp = new Parameter("CustomerID", TypeCode.String,
GridView1.SelectedValue.ToString());
            ds.SelectParameters.Add(cp);

            return ds;
        }

</script>

<html xmlns="http://www.w3.org/1999/xhtml">
<head id="Head1" runat="server">
    <title>Adding a Row When a Row Is Selected</title>
</head>
<body>
    <form id="form1" runat="server">
        <div>
            <asp:GridView
                OnPreRender="GridView1_PreRender"
                ID="GridView1"
                runat="server"
                DataSourceID="SqlDataSource1"
                DataKeyNames="CustomerID"
                AutoGenerateColumns="False"
                EnableViewState="False">
                <Columns>
                    <asp:CommandField ShowSelectButton="True"/>

                    <asp:BoundField
                        ReadOnly="True"
                        HeaderText="CustomerID"
                        DataField="CustomerID"
                        SortExpression="CustomerID">
                    </asp:BoundField>

                    <asp:BoundField
```

```
                        HeaderText="ContactName"
                        DataField="ContactName"
                        SortExpression="ContactName">
                    </asp:BoundField>

                </Columns>
            </asp:GridView>

            <asp:SqlDataSource
                ID="SqlDataSource1"
                runat="server"
                SelectCommand="SELECT [CustomerID], [ContactName] FROM [Customers]"
                ConnectionString="<%$ ConnectionStrings:NorthwindConnectionString
%>">
            </asp:SqlDataSource>
        </div>
    </form>
</body>
</html>
```

The code example can be found in the file add_row.aspx.

In this section you learned how easy it is to add a new row to the selected row of the GridView control. You also learned how to dynamically create a DetailsView control and bind it to a dynamically created SqlDataSource control. By using this kind of hack, you can create a more flexible Grid — for example, a hierarchical GridView control.

Using Up and Down Arrows in a Header for Sorting

This hack adds up and down arrows in the header of the GridView control. The GridView control has support for sorting columns, but the problem with the GridView control is that you can't see how the column is sorted. To give users an indication of how a column is sorted — for example, ascending or descending — it could be useful to add arrows to the columns that will indicate how the column is sorted. This hack uses the GridView's RowCreated event to manipulate the header of the GridView control. An image that displays whether the sorting is ASC or DESC is added to the sorted column. Within the RowCreated event, the RowType of the current row determines whether the row that is created is the header row of the GridView control. The following code checks whether the current created row is of type header; if it is, it will iterate through all the cells added to the row:

```
void GridView1_RowCreated(object sender, GridViewRowEventArgs e)
{
    if (e.Row != null && e.Row.RowType == DataControlRowType.Header)
    {
        foreach (TableCell cell in e.Row.Cells)
        {
            //Iterate through all columns added to
            //the header row and manipulate them
        }
    }
}
```

173

Because the `CommandArgument` of the `LinkButton` that is used to sort the column has the name of the column that should be sorted, it's easy to determine the columns to which the image should be added. The value of the `CommandArgument` is the value of the specified `SortExpression` on a `BoundField` column. The GridView's `SortDirection` property determines whether the sort direction is ascending or descending. Based on the direction, different images are added to the sorted column's header. The following code will get the `CommandArgument` from the LinkButton that is added to the header, and add an arrow image that indicates whether the sorting is ascending or descending:

```
LinkButton button = cell.Controls[0] as LinkButton;

if (button != null)
{
    Image image = new Image();
    image.ImageUrl = "default.gif";

    if (GridView1.SortExpression == button.CommandArgument)
    {
        if (GridView1.SortDirection == SortDirection.Ascending)
            image.ImageUrl = "asc.gif";
        else
            image.ImageUrl = "desc.gif";
    }

    //Add the image to the header column
    cell.Controls.Add(image);
}
```

Listing 7-7 is the completed example of the hack.

Listing 7-7: Adding up and down arrows

```
<%@ Page Language="C#" %>

<!DOCTYPE html PUBLIC "-//W3C//DTD XHTML 1.1//EN"
"http://www.w3.org/TR/xhtml11/DTD/xhtml11.dtd">

<html xmlns="http://www.w3.org/1999/xhtml" >

<script runat="server">

    void GridView1_RowCreated(object sender, GridViewRowEventArgs e)
    {
        if (e.Row != null && e.Row.RowType == DataControlRowType.Header)
        {
            foreach (TableCell cell in e.Row.Cells)
            {
                if (cell.HasControls())
                {
                    LinkButton button = cell.Controls[0] as LinkButton;

                    if (button != null)
                    {
                        Image image = new Image();
```

```
                    image.ImageUrl = "default.gif";

                    if (GridView1.SortExpression == button.CommandArgument)
                    {
                        if (GridView1.SortDirection == SortDirection.Ascending)
                            image.ImageUrl = "asc.gif";
                        else
                            image.ImageUrl = "desc.gif";
                    }

                    cell.Controls.Add(image);
                }
            }
        }
    }
}

</script>

<head runat="server">
    <title>Using Up and Down Arrows in a Header for Sorting</title>
</head>

<body>
    <form id="form1" runat="server">
    <div>
        <asp:GridView
            ID="GridView1"
            runat="server"
            DataSourceID="SqlDataSource1"
            AllowSorting="True"
            DataKeyNames="CustomerID"
            AutoGenerateColumns="False"
            OnRowCreated="GridView1_RowCreated">

            <Columns>
                <asp:BoundField
                    DataField="CustomerID"
                    HeaderText="CustomerID"
                    ReadOnly="True"
                    SortExpression="CustomerID" />

                <asp:BoundField
                    DataField="CompanyName"
                    HeaderText="CompanyName"
                    SortExpression="CompanyName" />

                <asp:BoundField
                    DataField="ContactName"
                    HeaderText="ContactName"
                    SortExpression="ContactName" />
            </Columns>
        </asp:GridView>
        <asp:SqlDataSource
```

(continued)

175

Listing 7-7 *(continued)*

```
               ID="SqlDataSource1"
               runat="server"
               SelectCommand="SELECT [CustomerID], [CompanyName], [ContactName]
FROM [Customers]"
               ConnectionString="<%$ ConnectionStrings:NorthwindConnectionString
%>"></asp:SqlDataSource>

    </div>
    </form>
</body>
</html>
```

The code example can be found in the file `sort.aspx`.

In this section you have learned how to manipulate the header row of the GridView control, including how to notice when the header row is created, how to get information about how a column is sorted, and how to add an image to the header column.

Adding Client-Side Script to the GridView Control

When using the GridView you can specify the background color, font, and so on, for a selected row to indicate which row a user has selected. When a user selects a row, the page will do a postback to mark the selected row. The GridView supports only server-side selects; it doesn't support client-side selects.

This hack describes how to add client-side script to the GridView control—for example, to change the background color of a selected row dynamically without doing a postback. It also shows you how to get the current value of the selected row. To add client-side script to a row, use the GridView's `RowCreated` event. The `RowCreated` event argument has a `Row` property to get the current row that is created. The `Row` property returns a `GridViewRow` object that represents the current created row. Because `GridViewRow` inherits `WebControl`, the `Attributes` property that will return an `AttributeCollection` is available. The `Attributes` property can be used to add extra attributes to the HTML element that will represent the `GridViewRow`. To add an attribute, use the `AttributeCollection`'s `Add` method. This method takes two arguments: the name of the attribute and the value of the attribute. To add an event attribute to the `GridViewRow`, such as `onClick`, pass `onClick` as a value of the `name` attribute, which is the first value of the argument of `AttributeCollection`'s `Add` method, and the client-side script—for example, a method—will be passed to the second argument of the method:

```
myWebControl.Attributes.Add("onClick", "alert('Hello World!')");
```

The example in the following code shows how attributes can be added to the `GridViewRow` that is created. Three attributes are added to the current created row, `onMouseOver`, `onMouseOut`, and `onClick`. These attributes will be added to the `<TR>` element created by the GridView control, They represent one row within the GridView:

```
void RowCreated(object sender, GridViewRowEventArgs e)
{
        e.Row.Attributes.Add("onMouseOver", "this.style.background='#ff0000'");
        e.Row.Attributes.Add("onMouseOut", "this.style.background='#ffffff'");
        e.Row.Attributes.Add("onClick", "alert('Selected item index: " +
e.Row.DataItemIndex.ToString() + "')");
}
```

In Listing 7-8 the `onClick`, `onMouseOver`, and `onMouseOut` events are added to each row (the example uses the Northwind database). When the code runs, the row that the mouse pointer is currently over will have its background color set to red. If a row is selected by pressing the left mouse button on a row, then a MessageBox will appear and display the index of the currently selected row.

Listing 7-8: Adding onClick, onMouseOver, and onMouseOut events to each row

```
<%@ Page Language="C#" %>

<script runat="server">

    void RowCreated(object sender, GridViewRowEventArgs e)
    {
        e.Row.Attributes.Add(
                         "onMouseOver",
                         "this.style.background='#ff0000'");

        e.Row.Attributes.Add(
                         "onMouseOut",
                         "this.style.background='#ffffff'");

        e.Row.Attributes.Add(
                         "onClick",
                         "alert('Selected item index: " +
e.Row.DataItemIndex.ToString() + "')");
    }

</script>

<html xmlns="http://www.w3.org/1999/xhtml" >
<head id="Head1" runat="server">
    <title>Adding Client_Side script to the GridView Control</title>
</head>
<body>
    <form id="form1" runat="server">
    <div>
        <asp:GridView
            ID="GridView1"
            Runat="server"
            DataSourceID="SqlDataSource1"
            DataKeyNames="CustomerID"
            AutoGenerateColumns="False"
            OnRowCreated="RowCreated">

            <Columns>

                <asp:CommandField
```

(continued)

Listing 7-8 *(continued)*

```
                      ShowEditButton="True"/>

                  <asp:BoundField
                      ReadOnly="True"
                      HeaderText="CustomerID"
                      DataField="CustomerID"
                      SortExpression="CustomerID"/>

                  <asp:BoundField
                      HeaderText="CompanyName"
                      DataField="CompanyName"
                      SortExpression="CompanyName"/>

                  <asp:BoundField
                      HeaderText="ContactName"
                      DataField="ContactName"
                      SortExpression="ContactName"/>

              </Columns>
          </asp:GridView>

          <asp:SqlDataSource
              ID="SqlDataSource1"
              Runat="server"
              SelectCommand="SELECT [CustomerID], [CompanyName], [ContactName] FROM
[Customers]"
              ConnectionString="<%$ ConnectionStrings:NorthwindConnectionString %>">
          </asp:SqlDataSource>

      </div>
      </form>
</body>
</html>
```

The code example can be found in the file `c_gridview1.aspx` posted on the Wrox.com website.

You can't use `RowCreated` to add a client-side script to the GridView control to get the value from a column located in the selected row because the created row's cells haven't been data-bound when the event is triggered. Instead, use the `RowDataBound` event. The following example gets the value from the second cell of a row when the row is selected by pressing the left mouse button on a row:

```
void GridView1_RowDataBound(object sender, GridViewRowEventArgs e)
{
    if (e.Row.Cells != null && e.Row.Cells.Count > 1)
    {
        e.Row.Attributes.Add("onClick", "alert('Selected value: " +
e.Row.Cells[1].Text + "')");
    }
}
```

In this section you have learned how to add client-side script to a GridView row that will change the background color of the row the mouse is over, and how to get the vale of a specific column when a row is selected.

Extending the GridView with IPostBackEventHandler

The following hack extends the GridView so the user can double-click a row to enter edit mode for the selected row, or select a row and press the Enter key to perform something—for example, to navigate to a new page that will show more details about the selected row. The hack in this section uses the IPostBackEventHandler interface to handle postback.

When the IPostBackEventHandler interface is implemented, the RaisePostBackEvent method must also be implemented. The RaisePostBackEvent method will be automatically called when a postback is performed. When the IPostBackEventHandler is used, the GetPostBackEventReference method of the Page object can be used to create the __doPostBack method that will perform the postback. The RaisePostBackEvent method has one argument of the type string. This argument will have the value of the eventArgument argument of the _doPostBack method.

To implement the IPostBackEventHandler for a page, the Implements directive can be used:

```
<%@ Implements Interface="System.Web.UI.IPostBackEventHandler"%>
```

Instead of adding the _doPostBack by hand, the GetPostBackEventReference method can be used to generate a _doPostBack method:

```
public string GetPostBackEventReference(Control control)
public string GetPostBackEventReference(Control control, string eventArgument)
```

The GetPostBackEventReference method has two overloaded methods. The first overloaded method takes one argument with the control that the postback is made from. The other method takes two arguments: the control and an argument with the event argument. The GetPostBackEventReference will return a generated _doPostBack method in which the _doPostBack's eventTarget argument will have the value of the control's ID passed as an argument to the GetPostBackEventReference. The eventArgument argument will have the value of the GetPostBackEventReference's eventArgument.

The following code uses the GetPostBackEventReference method for generating the _doPostback method, and adds it as a value to the onDblClick attribute of the row when the row is data-bound:

```
void GridView1_RowDataBound(object sender, GridViewRowEventArgs e)
{
e.Row.Attributes.Add("onDblClick", Page.GetPostBackEventReference(this,
e.Row.DataItemIndex.ToString()));
}
```

When the IPostBackEventHandler's RaisePostBackEvent method is implemented, it will be executed when a postback is performed. The following example will take the eventArgument passed to the __Do PostBack method and display it on the page:

```
public void RaisePostBackEvent(string eventArgument)
{
        Response.Write(eventArgument);
}
```

> There can only be one `RaisePostBackEvents` method on the page. If you have used the `GetPostBackEventReference` for other client-side events of the GridView row or for other controls on the page, you have to use the value of the `RaisePostBack Event` method's `eventArgument` to identify what should be done based on which control calls the `__doPostBack` method.

Listing 7-9 uses the `IPostBackEvent` handler and makes a postback when a user double-clicks a row or selects a row and then presses the Enter key on the keyboard.

Listing 7-9: Using the IsPostBackEvent handler to make a postback

```
<%@ Page Language="C#" %>
<%@ Implements Interface="System.Web.UI.IPostBackEventHandler"%>

<script language="javascript">

    var _oldColor;

    function SetNewColor(source)
    {
        _oldColor = source.style.backgroundColor;
        source.style.backgroundColor = '#00ff00';
    }

    function SetOldColor(source)
    {
        source.style.backgroundColor = _oldColor;
    }

</script>

<script runat="server">

    void GridView1_RowDataBound(object sender, GridViewRowEventArgs e)
    {
        e.Row.Attributes.Add(
                "onMouseOver",
                "SetNewColor(this);");

        e.Row.Attributes.Add(
                "onMouseOut",
                "SetOldColor(this);");

        e.Row.Attributes.Add(
                "onDblClick",
                Page.GetPostBackEventReference(this,
e.Row.DataItemIndex.ToString()));

        e.Row.Attributes.Add(
                "onKeyDown",
                "if( event.keyCode == 13 ) " + Page.GetPostBackEventReference(this,
"KEYDOWN" + "$" + e.Row.DataItemIndex.ToString()));
```

```
    }

    // Part of the IPostBackEventHandler interface.
    // you must create this method.
    public void RaisePostBackEvent(string eventArgument)
    {
        GridViewSelectEventArgs e = null;
        int selectedRowIndex = -1;

        if (!string.IsNullOrEmpty(eventArgument))
        {
            string[] args = eventArgument.Split('$');

            if (string.Compare(args[0], "KEYDOWN", false,
System.Globalization.CultureInfo.InvariantCulture) == 0 &&
                        args.Length > 1)
            {
                Int32.TryParse(args[1], out selectedRowIndex);
                e = new GridViewSelectEventArgs(selectedRowIndex);
                OnReturnKeyDown(e);
            }
            else
            {
                Int32.TryParse(args[0], out selectedRowIndex);
                e = new GridViewSelectEventArgs(selectedRowIndex);
                OnDblClick(e);
            }
        }
    }

    protected virtual void OnDblClick(EventArgs e)
    {
        Response.Write("You double clicked on the row with index: " +
((GridViewSelectEventArgs)e).NewSelectedIndex.ToString());

        GridView1.EditIndex = ((GridViewSelectEventArgs)e).NewSelectedIndex;
    }

    protected virtual void OnReturnKeyDown(EventArgs e)
    {
        Response.Write("You pressed enter on the row with index: " +
((GridViewSelectEventArgs)e).NewSelectedIndex.ToString());
}

</script>

<html xmlns="http://www.w3.org/1999/xhtml">
<head id="Head1" runat="server">
    <title>Extending the GridView with IPostBackEventHandler</title>
</head>
<body>
    <form id="form1" runat="server">
        <div>
            <asp:GridView
                ID="GridView1"
```

(continued)

Listing 7-9 *(continued)*

```
                     Runat="server"
                     DataSourceID="SqlDataSource1"
                     DataKeyNames="CustomerID"
                     AutoGenerateColumns="False"
                     OnRowDataBound="GridView1_RowDataBound"
                     AlternatingRowStyle-BackColor="#6699ff"
                     RowStyle-BackColor="#ccccff">

                <Columns>
                    <asp:CommandField
                        ShowEditButton="True"/>

                    <asp:BoundField
                        ReadOnly="True"
                        HeaderText="CustomerID"
                        DataField="CustomerID"
                        SortExpression="CustomerID"/>

                    <asp:BoundField
                        HeaderText="CompanyName"
                        DataField="CompanyName"
                        SortExpression="CompanyName"/>

                    <asp:BoundField
                        HeaderText="ContactName"
                        DataField="ContactName"
                        SortExpression="ContactName"/>

                </Columns>
            </asp:GridView>
            <asp:SqlDataSource
                    ID="SqlDataSource1"
                    Runat="server"
                    SelectCommand="SELECT [CustomerID], [CompanyName], [ContactName]
FROM [Customers]"
                    ConnectionString="<%$ ConnectionStrings:NorthwindConnectionString
%>">
            </asp:SqlDataSource>
        </div>
    </form>
</body>
</html>
```

The example code can be found in the file extendGridView.aspx at www.wrox.com.

In the preceding code, the event argument is used to determine whether a user double-clicked a row or pressed the Enter key. The code checks whether the event argument of the RaisePostBackEvent has the prefix KEYDOWN$. If it doesn't have the KEYDOWN$ prefix, the OnDblClick method will be called. This method will get the index of the double-clicked row from the event argument and use the index to switch the row into edit mode. When the user presses the Enter key after a row has been selected, the OnReturnKey method is called.

Wrapping Up

In this chapter you have learned how to use the `pagerTemplate` of the GridView control to create and define your own template for the GridView's pager feature, such as using a DropDownList instead of using GridView's standard paging, using the Next and Previous links or links with numeric values that represent a page, etc. You also learned how to use the `BottomPagerRow` to manipulate the pager row dynamically with code, and that the manipulation of the pager row must be done after the GridView is rendered. You have also seen a hack in which a new row is added to a selected row of the GridView, and how to dynamically create a `DetailsView` that is added to a selected row. By adding a new row with controls, you can create a more flexible Grid — for example, a hierarchical GridView control. Another hack in this chapter described how you can manipulate the header row of the GridView control to add an image that is displayed to users, indicating how the column is sorted — for example, in descending or ascending order. You have also seen a hack in which a client-side script is added to the GridView, changing the background color of the row the mouse is over, and got the value of a specific column when a row was selected.

8

Extreme Data Binding

In ASP.NET 2.0, extensive enhancements have been made in the data-binding capabilities. These enhancements can be divided into a few distinct areas. Newly introduced is the concept of using DataSource controls, which provide the "glue" between the provider of the data and the visual element, the Web control. Existing controls have been modified as appropriate to support getting data from the DataSource controls. New controls were also introduced to fill needs that were not adequately handled in the existing controls. For example, GridView and DetailsView are examples of a couple of the new controls that will be discussed in more detail in this chapter with regard to how to use data binding more effectively in real applications. You can also read more about the GridView in Chapter 7.

Prior to ASP.NET 2.0, the "glue" portion of data binding required programmatic calling of custom methods to retrieve data from the data repository/provider and setting one or more properties on a control based on the data. The DataSource control concept allows not only binding to data returned from a database query using SQLDataSource, but also extends to XML via the XMLDataSource and objects using the ObjectDataSource. Using the DataSource controls dramatically reduces the need for custom coding to accomplish the retrieval of the data, by allowing controls to request the data that is required.

One thing that is almost always true is that the more features that are added, the more features you want. ASP.NET 2.0 makes great strides toward making data binding not only easy but usable for building "real" applications. Of course, with most products, there's never enough time in the product's development timeline to include every single feature every user would use. Additionally, if every feature were included, nobody would use the product because it would be too complex and heavy to manage.

This chapter picks up where the product leaves off, offering some innovative ways to make using data binding easier to use, and thereby making you more productive. We will discuss inheriting your own DataSource controls so that you can extend the built-in controls with some of your own customizations, which can be reused repeatedly in your applications. Then, adding on to that, we will describe how you might use code generation to build drag-and-drop-ready controls that will help reduce the redundant information on each page. Further adding to the inherited DataSource controls, we will then add support for improving the handling of default values. Turning our attention to the XMLDataSource, we will explore how you can add support similar to how the ObjectDataSource calls your business objects, but make it work with XML. Finally, we will explain how to build custom parameters that will be used with the DataSource controls. Because a discussion on data binding wouldn't be complete without looking at the UI controls, we will also explore ways to also build custom fields.

Inheriting Your Own DataSource Controls

When using the DataSource controls, regardless of whether you are using SQLDataSource, Object Datasource, or another of the typical examples, you drag the control from the Toolbox onto your Web form. Once the control is on your Web form, the next step is to begin to configure it and set the necessary options. If you were going to have only one page on which the DataSource control was going to be used, this would be fine because you would do it only once. Let's take an example of a product list that we will use on 20 different pages. It's not that DataSource controls don't make it easier and require less custom effort, but we always want to look for opportunities to reduce our workload. In this example, one would duplicate the same effort multiple times to set the options on each page. Even worse, when something changes you have to visit all 20 pages to update the controls. This can also cause problems: If you are caching the data and any of the parameters vary, it will result in each of the 20 pages keeping its own copy in cache, instead of sharing one copy of the data. This can be caused by as little as an extra space in the SQL query on a SQLDataSource that is cache enabled.

One possible approach that we will discuss in more detail is creating a custom DataSource control that inherits from the built-in DataSource controls and has the common options for ProductList pre-configured. Using this approach, you will not only reduce the custom work required to configure the control on each page, you will also increase the consistency of your pages. If have to make a change, you would be changing the one custom inherited control instead of finding all 20 pages that use the DataSource to retrieve the product list.

Additionally, you might also find that now or in the future there are common functions or properties that you would like to be on all of your DataSource controls. For example, if you are doing inserts using a DataSource, you might like the capability to set default options without writing code. Later in the chapter we will build on our initial inherited control to add this custom capability, which can be used by all application-specific DataSource controls.

Let's begin by making the concept a little more concrete with an example. For discussion purposes, in this chapter we will work with an ObjectDataSource control, although the same concept and approach can be used with other DataSource controls such as SQLDataSource just as easily. The first thing to do is create a class that inherits from ObjectDataSource. Because this class will be used by many of your application controls, it is best to put it in a common class library. See Chapter 2, "Getting Started," for a more thorough discussion about the reasons and benefits for setting up and using a common class library. In our example we will call the class MVPHacksObjectDataSource. In your application you can name it whatever you prefer, but keeping it as non-application-specific as possible might make the most sense. Here is the code:

```
using System;
using System.Collections.Generic;
using System.Text;
using System.Web.UI.WebControls;

namespace MVPHacks.Common.DataBinding
{
    public class MVPHacksObjectDataSource : ObjectDataSource
    {

    }
}
```

In the preceding example we simply have inherited from ObjectDataSource without adding any additional functionality beyond what is inherited from the built-in ObjectDataSource control. Simply doing just this and using it instead of the built-in ObjectDataSource provides the flexibility to add capabilities in the future without changing all your pages individually.

At this point, if you were to reference the common library and look at the Toolbox while on a Web form, you would see that our inherited control, MVPHacksObjectDataSource, shows up automatically, ready for use on your page (see Figure 8-1). This new control can be used just like the built-in ObjectDataSource — either by dragging it from the Toolbox or by selecting it in the Data Source Configuration Wizard.

Figure 8-1

Working with the DataSource Configuration Wizard

While on the subject of some of the nice things that are carried out automatically by Visual Studio 2005, we should discuss the Data Source Configuration Wizard. This is the wizard that starts up after you drag a GridView or other data-binding-enabled control onto the page. The goal is to enable you to pick the DataSource control you wish to use and bind it to the control. Using our code as created in the preceding section, the MVPHacksObjectDataSource control would show up in the list as an Object DataSource control, which might be confusing (see Figure 8-2).

Duplicate object

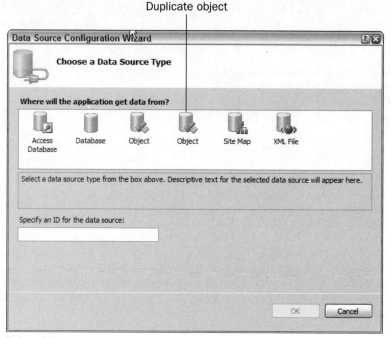

Figure 8-2

To enhance the experience of using our control and eliminate any confusion, we can add the `DisplayName` and `Description` attributes to the class to provide more meaningful information. The following example shows our modified class using those attributes:

```
using System;
using System.Collections.Generic;
using System.Text;
using System.Web.UI.WebControls;
using System.ComponentModel;


namespace MVPHacks.Common.DataBinding
{
    [DisplayName("MVPHacksODS"), Description("MVP Hacks Custom ObjectDataSource")]
    public class MVPHacksObjectDataSource : ObjectDataSource
    {

    }
}
```

If you were to look at the Data Source types displayed in the wizard after adding the attributes, you would be able to clearly see your custom control and its associated description, as shown in Figure 8-3.

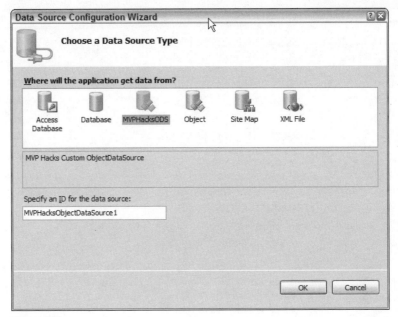

Figure 8-3

Adding the attributes to clearly identify your class becomes even more important as you start looking at building application-specific DataSource controls. Imagine bringing up the wizard and seeing 20 items in the list that all say "Object"!

Now let's build on the control we just created to make an application-specific control. To do that we are going to create a class called `ProductListODS` and inherit from our `MVPHacksObjectDataSource`. While you could inherit from `ObjectDataSource`, that would lose the benefit of future features we might add to our `MVPHacksObjectDataSource` control.

To keep our example simple and focused on the aspects of making application-specific DataSource controls, we will use the following extremely simplified classes as the target of the application-specific DataSource control we are going to build for our product list. The following code listings show examples of a data class that is intended to hold properties and object-centric methods, and then following that you can see a simplified example of a database access class. Remember that the point is not what they are doing, but how they work together conceptually with the ObjectDataSource to perform data binding.

The following is the `Product` data class:

```
using System;
using System.Collections.Generic;
using System.Text;

namespace MVPHacks.Common.Products
{
    public class Product
```

```
{
        private int m_ProductID;

        public int ProductID
        {
            get { return m_ProductID; }
            set { m_ProductID = value; }
        }

        private string m_Name;

        public string Name
        {
            get { return m_Name; }
            set { m_Name = value; }
        }

        private int m_ProductStatus;

        public int ProductStatus
        {
            get { return m_ProductStatus; }
            set { m_ProductStatus = value; }
        }


    }
}
```

The following code shows a class that contains the methods to interact with a database. Keep in mind that we have not implemented the methods, as this is just to illustrate how a class like this interacts with the DataSource control. In practice, these two classes could be separate or combined, depending on your architecture:

```
using System;
using System.Collections.Generic;
using System.Text;

namespace MVPHacks.Common.Products
{
    public class DBProduct
    {
        public int CreateProduct(Product product)
        {
            //real logic to create product goes here

            return -1;
        }

        public Product GetProductByID(int productID)
        {
            return new Product();
        }

        public List<Product> GetProductList()
```

```
        {
            return new List<Product>();
        }

        public void UpdateProduct(Product product)
        {
            //update logic goes here
        }

        public void DeleteProduct(int productID)
        {
            //delete logic goes here
        }
    }
}
```

If you were to use these classes with your MVPHacksObjectDataSource control, looking at the source view of the Web form that used the control in Visual Studio would reveal something like the following:

```
<cc1:MVPHacksObjectDataSource ID="MVPHacksObjectDataSource1" runat="server"
    DataObjectTypeName="MVPHacks.Common.Products.Product"
    DeleteMethod="DeleteProduct" InsertMethod="CreateProduct"
    SelectMethod="GetProductByID"
    TypeName="MVPHacks.Common.Products.DBProduct"
    UpdateMethod="UpdateProduct">
    <DeleteParameters>
        <asp:Parameter Name="productID" Type="Int32" />
    </DeleteParameters>
    <SelectParameters>
        <asp:QueryStringParameter DefaultValue="0" Name="productID"
            QueryStringField="ID"
            Type="Int32" />
    </SelectParameters>
</cc1:MVPHacksObjectDataSource>
```

The preceding markup would be repeated on each page that uses the control. As discussed earlier, if caching is enabled, then those options would be repeated in the markup as well.

The following code sample shows the first attempt at building our application-specific DataSource control. The example shows inheriting from MVPHacksObjectDataSource. The class continues to set up the methods on each of the corresponding properties on the DataSource control. Note that the attributes to provide a description and name for the control in the designer are also designed to be application specific and meaningful for the context in which this control might be used:

```
using System;
using System.Collections.Generic;
using System.Text;
using System.ComponentModel;
using System.Web.UI.WebControls;


using MVPHacks.Common.DataBinding;

namespace MVPHacks.Common.WebControls
```

```
{
    [DisplayName("ProductEditODS"), Description("Edit Product Data Source")]
    public class ProductEditODS :MVPHacksObjectDataSource
    {
        public ProductEditODS()
        {
            SetupDefaultControlInfo();
        }

        private void SetupDefaultControlInfo()
        {
            this.DataObjectTypeName = "MVPHacks.Common.Products.Product";
            this.TypeName = "MVPHacks.Common.Products.DBProduct";
            this.InsertMethod = "CreateProduct";
            this.DeleteMethod = "DeleteProduct";
            this.SelectMethod = "GetProductByID";
            this.UpdateMethod = "UpdateProduct";
        }

    }
}
```

The preceding DataSource control would show up on the Toolbox, enabling you to drag it onto a Web
form. The control will also show up if the Data Source Configuration Wizard is run. If you were to look at
the HTML markup, it would be much simplified from our previous example, as shown in the following
example:

```
<cc2:ProductEditODS ID="ProductEditODS1" runat="server">
</cc2:ProductEditODS>
```

There are two reasons why the markup is significantly less than our prior example. First, the inherited
class takes care of setting the methods and type names for the object as expected. Second, we have not
handled the parameters for Delete and Select to identify the locations from which the DataSource
control will pull those values. To handle the parameters, a few options must be set. If you were to view
the properties of the DataSource control, you could bring up the Parameter Collection Editor by clicking
on the Select or Delete parameter properties. Because none have been defined, the first time the list
will be empty. Another option is to add to the inherited DataSource control, building a default set of
properties based on the most likely scenario. If you do that, even when they need to be adjusted for use
on a specific page, there will be some default values on the Property Collection Editor to start with. The
following method could be called to setup parameters in our inherited DataSource control:

```
private void SetupDefaultControlParameters()
{
    QueryStringParameter qsProductID = new QueryStringParameter();
    qsProductID.Name = "ProductID";
    qsProductID.QueryStringField = "ID";
    qsProductID.Type = "Int32";
    qsProductID.DefaultValue = "0";
    this.SelectParameters.Add(qsProductID);

    ControlParameter cpProductID = new ControlParameter();
    cpProductID.Name = "ProductID";
```

```
        cpProductID.Type = "Int32";
        this.DeleteParameters.Add(cpProductID);

    }
```

Using application-specific controls that inherit from your choice of DataSource can help reduce the amount of customization required each time it is used on a page. The fact that the control starts with a consistent set of options can also help, not only with respect to consistency but to optimize resources by ensuring things like caching share a single copy of the data.

Adding a Control Designer

When you're looking at a DataSource control (including the ones that are built in to ASP.NET) that has been dropped on a Web form, it really doesn't render anything useful other than a gray box with the name (see Figure 8-4).

Figure 8-4

You can specify a Control Designer class that replaces the default design-time rendering of the control. In order to do that you must first reference the System.Design assembly to your project. This contains the base class of System.Web.UI.Design.ControlDesigner, which must be inherited from to build a control designer. A closer look at ObjectDataSource would indicate that it already has a designer: System.Web.UI.Design.WebControls.ObjectDataSourceDesigner. This designer is responsible for the hot link to common tasks but it does not render in a very informative way on the Web form designer view. To ensure we don't lose the features it does well, we will inherit from the existing designer instead of the System.Web.UI.Design.ControlDesigner class.

Now we will add a new class that inherits from ObjectDataSourceDesigner and overrides the GetDesignTimeHtml method. The GetDesignTimeHtml method is called by the Visual Studio designer to obtain the markup that should be rendered for the control during design time. In our example we are going to output the type of control, the ID, and the type names of the objects. This could be customized easily for what you find useful in your project:

```
using System;
using System.Collections.Generic;
using System.Text;

namespace MVPHacks.Common.DataBinding
{

public class MVPHacksObjectDataSourceDesigner :
System.Web.UI.Design.WebControls.ObjectDataSourceDesigner
    {
        /// <summary>
        ///
        /// </summary>
        /// <returns></returns>
        public override string GetDesignTimeHtml()
```

```
        {
            MVPHacksObjectDataSource mvpODS =
                    (MVPHacksObjectDataSource)this.Component;
            StringBuilder htmlSB = new StringBuilder();

            htmlSB.AppendFormat("{0} - {1}<br/>", mvpODS.GetType().Name,
                    mvpODS.ID);

            if (mvpODS.TypeName != null)
                htmlSB.AppendFormat("Type={0}<br/>", mvpODS.TypeName);

            if (mvpODS.DataObjectTypeName != null)
                htmlSB.AppendFormat("DataType={0}<br/>",
                    mvpODS.DataObjectTypeName);

            return htmlSB.ToString();
        }
    }
}
```

In the previous code example using the `this.Component` property, the designer is able to access the instance of our control that is currently being worked on. By casting it to the specific type of control, various properties specific to that control can be accessed. It's important to note that not all environmental properties are available when in Design mode, and you can get errors trying to access those that are not available. A control can use the `IsDesignMode` property to determine the current mode. In this case, because we are designers, it is obvious that we are in that mode or the method would not be invoked!

In order to use a designer on a server control, you must add an attribute to inform Visual Studio what class should be used to provide the Design view rendering. The following shows the `MVPHacksObjectDataSource` with the addition of the `designer` attribute:

```
[DisplayName("MVPHacksODS"), Description("MVP Hacks Custom ObjectDataSource")]
[Designer("MVPHacks.Common.DataBinding.MVPHacksObjectDataSourceDesigner")]
public class MVPHacksObjectDataSource : ObjectDataSource
{

}
```

Whereas Figure 8-4 shows what was rendered by the built-in control, Figure 8-5 shows what is now rendered by our revised control. Notice that not only are the quick tasks still accessible, you can also see some useful information about the DataSource just by looking at the Web form, without having to drill down into the properties of the control.

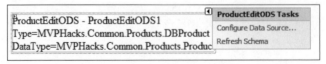

Figure 8-5

Control designers are a good thing to keep in your bag of tricks when you are building server controls. In this example, we showed how you can use the designer to make the control easier to use, and this same technique could be applied to many other controls to provide a richer design-time experience.

Generating Application-Specific DataSource Controls

It's common for code generators of some fashion to be used today to help reduce the manual effort required by developers and to improve the consistency of the code. There's a clear parallel to that in what we have been talking about so far in this chapter. Applying some form of code generation to building the application-specific DataSource controls would further make them easier to use and eliminate a lot of the up-front work that goes into configuring a DataSource control on each page.

Which code generation technique is chosen is not important, and there are a number to choose from. Likewise, choosing the granular level in which you generate the controls, or whether you use ObjectDataSource or SQLDataSource again, is not important for this discussion. What is important is the general concept: Using the chosen tool, you can generate controls like the one used earlier, and they will show up on the Toolbox, where they can be used by developers on your project team to build Web forms. Certainly techniques can be important, but for the purpose of this discussion we will not be addressing that issue.

A more specific example of this concept would be to take an application database that contains 37 tables (yes, 37 is an arbitrary number). In the simplest implementation of this concept using a tool, you would generate 37 DataSource controls (one for each table) that inherit from the MVPHacksObjectDataSource base control or one that you have built to provide similar capabilities. These 37 controls would set up the default values such as the method or SQL query. You might even go as far as generating one that is a List version and one that is a Detail version of the control. By having two versions of each control you would again reduce the number of times you have to "modify" the values that were defaulted when the control was used on a page.

In reality, only a handful of those controls will be used, and a smarter approach would probably be to use a tool that allowed more control over specifying the tables for which controls should be built. At this point, undoubtedly some readers will be saying, "Why generate based on the database table and not from more abstract meta data?" Both points are valid and have merit when you think about how to use the concept of generating controls in your application. The bottom line on this concept is to find a way to reduce the amount of redundant work you are doing to build pages that use DataSource controls.

Extending the DataSource Controls

So far this chapter has discussed how to inherit your own common DataSource control from the built-in controls. You have also explored ways that you can make them application specific. We even explained a concept for automating the creation of the controls to save time. Now with those concepts under your belt, let's discuss some ways that you can further extend the DataSource controls.

This section discusses a few ideas on how the ObjectDataSource and XMLDatasource controls can be enhanced by adding features that would be broadly useful in your applications.

Handling Default Values During Insert

One of the problems that is encountered early on when using either the ObjectDataSource control or the SQLDataSource control is handling default values when the `Insert` operation is performed on the DataSource.

To make this example more specific, suppose you had a Product table that had columns you would expect to find on a Person table: `ProductID`, `ProductName`, and many of the other typical columns. Assume also that on that table was a Product Status column indicating the current status of that Product row. Now suppose that you had a page with a DetailsView control on it, and the sole purpose of the page was to insert new rows into the Product table. This DetailsView control is "glued" to the database using the `DBProduct` and `Product` objects and an ObjectDataSource similar to what we outlined earlier in this chapter. On the DetailsView control we want to allow the user to input the common fields such as `ProductName`. We don't, however, want to have the user specify the initial value for Product Status, and we want to default that value pending review when it's added from this particular page. In this scenario, the built-in support in the DetailsView and ObjectDataSource controls compels you to write code and give up on 100% declarative specification of the data binding. The following example first shows how to do this by writing code each time we need to accomplish providing default values, and then you will see an alternative solution that is handled by extending the ObjectDataSource control.

If you use what you are provided with the built-in ObjectDataSource, one approach to handling the problem of setting default values is to handle the `Inserting` event on the ObjectDataSource control. The following code sample shows the implementation of an `Inserting` event handler that sets the Product Status value prior to returning control. Remember that the `Inserting` event is called after the ObjectDataSource is requested to insert the data, but prior to the actual `InsertMethod` specified on the control being called:

```
protected void ProductEditODS1_Inserting(object sender,
                            ObjectDataSourceMethodEventArgs e)
    {
        Product productInfo =  e.InputParameters[0] as Product;
        productInfo.ProductStatus = (int) enumProductStatus.PendingReview;
    }
```

In the preceding sample code, notice that the second parameter to the handler is an `ObjectdataSourceMethodEventArgs`. The `InputParameters` is an `IOrderedDictionary` of the parameters that are being passed to the `InsertMethod` on the `ObjectDataSource`.

The first problem with this approach is that it requires custom code to set the values. With the built-in controls this cannot be accomplished declaratively. Additionally, similar custom code would have to be added in any of the places you use DataSource controls to perform inserts where you want to default some value. This approach also fails to make it easy to use values that might actually come from other places on the form. For example, what if you wanted to get the default value for the field from a DropDownList control that is located in another place on the form? For that matter, you might want to use any of the ways in which the DataSource parameters allow you to pull data.

Now that we have discussed some of the limitations of the built-in support, let's explore an approach to extend the MVPHacksObjectDataSource started earlier in this chapter to make this easier. Not only do you want to make it easier, you want to make it so that all of the specification can be done declaratively and not require the custom code on each page. Furthermore, the goal is to leverage the `Parameter` objects such as the `QueryStringParameter` and the `ControlParameter` to allow specification of the default values. For example, maybe the default value was passed on the query string by the invoker of the page. Wouldn't it be nice to just use the `QueryStringParameter` to pass in that value?

To accomplish this, you add to the MVPHacksObjectDataSource control a new Parameter collection, `DefaultValueParameters`. This collection will be a property that is available in the Design view like other Parameter collections, such as `InsertParameters`, `SelectParameters`, and others. In fact, the contents of the `DefaultValueParameters` collection will be the same parameters that the other collection supports. From the DataSource wizard experience, the `DefaultValueParamters` collection will also be available to provide a design-time experience without any further custom code. With this capability, no code will be required to set up default values, and the values used will be able to come from anywhere that they can for the other Parameter collections.

The first step in getting this to work is to look at how the existing Parameter collections are implemented and how we might leverage that to implement our `DefaultValueParameter` collection. The existing collections are implemented by exposing `ParameterCollection` properties from the `ObjectDataSource`. Using that knowledge, the first step in adding our default value is to add a `DefaultValueParameters` property based on the `ParameterCollection` type. The following is what it would look like:

```
private ParameterCollection m_DefaultValueParameters;

public ParameterCollection DefaultValueParameters
{
    get
    {
        if (m_DefaultValueParameters == null)
            m_DefaultValueParameters = new ParameterCollection();
        return m_DefaultValueParameters;
    }

}
```

Further exploration of how the other parameter properties are implemented would indicate that some attributes are required to allow the designer wizards to work with our new property and for it to be saved correctly at the end of the wizard. The following example code shows what the property would look like with the appropriate attributes to make it fully behave like one of the other `Parameter` collections:

```
[MergableProperty(false),
        PersistenceMode(PersistenceMode.InnerProperty), DefaultValue((string)null),
        Editor("System.Web.UI.Design.WebControls.ParameterCollectionEditor," +
           " System.Design, Version=2.0.0.0, Culture=neutral," +
           " PublicKeyToken=b03f5f7f11d50a3a", typeof(UITypeEditor))]

public ParameterCollection DefaultValueParameters
{
    get
    {
        if (m_DefaultValueParameters == null)
            m_DefaultValueParameters = new ParameterCollection();
        return m_DefaultValueParameters;
    }

}
```

The `MergableProperty` attribute is used by the property window to determine whether it can combine this property with properties from other objects in the property window. The default value for this attribute is `true`, so in this case we are setting it to `false`, thereby informing the property window to keep our property separate.

The `PersistenceMode` attribute, along with the `DefaultValue` attribute, is used by the `ControlPersister` class. A more complete discussion of this is outside the scope of this book; however, the MSDN documentation provides more detailed information.

The `Editor` attribute is used to specify the `UITypeEditor ParameterCollectionEditor` that is used for all the other parameter collections. It is this designer that makes the wizard shown in Figure 8-6 available for our property, and it is the same design experience for all the built-in Parameter collections.

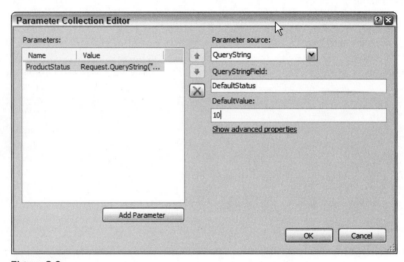

Figure 8-6

After saving the Parameter Collection Editor dialog box, the markup reveals that the default value parameters have been persisted:

```
<DefaultValueParameters>
    <asp:QueryStringParameter DefaultValue="10" Name="ProductStatus"
                              QueryStringField="DefaultStatus" />
</DefaultValueParameters>
```

As you can see from the previous example, we have declaratively specified one or more default value parameters that we want to use. We have also leveraged the existing controls editor to provide a first-class design-time experience for specification of the default values. Furthermore, we are able to specify any of the parameter classes that exist, or possible custom ones that you might build.

The next step is hooking into the `Inserting` event to enable getting the values from our new default value collections and setting them on the object that is passed to the `Inserting` handler. To do this we will again modify and add to our `MVPHacksObjectDataSource` control to register the handler during the constructor. The following code sample takes care of registering our handler. This would be inserted in the constructor in our `MVPHacksObjectDataSource`:

```
public MVPHacksObjectDataSource()
{
    this.Inserting +=
        new ObjectDataSourceMethodEventHandler(MVPHacksObjectDataSource_Inserting);
}
```

Now that the event handler has been registered, we need to implement the handler. The handler will be responsible for getting the values from the `DefaultValueParameters` collection and then applying them to the object that is about to be inserted.

The `ParameterCollection` class provides the `GetValues` method that we will call, and it will force the collection to have its children parameter controls obtain their values, returning them as an `IOrderedDictionary`.

The `IOrderedDictionary` returned from our call to `GetValues` will contain one `DictionaryEntry` object for each parameter that was in our `DefaultValuesParameters` collection. The `Key` property on the `DictionaryEntry` object represents the name of the parameter, and it is what will be used to look up and set the value on the data object about to be inserted.

Because this is utility code and you don't know anything about the type of object that is about to be inserted, reflection will be used to get a reference to the property and set the value. Using the reference you obtain to the `dataObj`, you can call the `GetType` method to get the `Type` object that will identify the type of object we are dealing with. The `Type` object gives us access to a `GetProperty` method. When passed the name of a property such as `ProductStatus`, this method would return a `PropertyInfo` object with information that was obtained from the reflection operation against the `dataObj`. If you are able to get a reference to the `PropertyInfo` object for the class, then you can call the `SetValue` method to set the default value. When you call the `SetValue` method, you are passing the `Value` property on the `DictionaryEntry` that will represent the value that the `DefaultParameterCollection` returned when the call to `GetValues` was done early in the method. The following code sample implements getting the values and setting them on the properties of the data object that is about to be inserted:

```
void MVPHacksObjectDataSource_Inserting(object sender,
                                        ObjectDataSourceMethodEventArgs e)
{
    IOrderedDictionary defaultValues =
            this.DefaultValueParameters.GetValues(HttpContext.Current, this);

    object dataObj = e.InputParameters[0];

    foreach (DictionaryEntry defaultValue in defaultValues)
    {
        PropertyInfo propInfo =
                dataObj.GetType().GetProperty(defaultValue.Key.ToString());

        if (propInfo != null)
        {
            propInfo.SetValue(dataObj, defaultValue.Value, null);
        }

    }

}
```

With your event handler implemented, you have now completed everything necessary to implement a generic way to declaratively handle setup of default values. Unlike the approach that can be used with the built-in control, this approach could be used with any data type without any specific code being required each time the control is utilized.

Extending XMLDataSource to Call Your Object

The XMLDataSource is designed to retrieve and provide XML data to data-bound controls. Unlike ObjectDataSource and SQLDataSource, which inherit from DataSourceControl, the XMLDataSource inherits from HierarchicalDatasourceControl and is designed to work with hierarchical data. To ensure that it can also work with tabular data, it also implements the IDataSource interface.

By implementing the IDataSource interface, the XMLDataSource control provides a GetView and GetViewNames method, which allows it to play in the sandbox and be used like the SQLDataSource and ObjectDataSource controls.

One other difference you might want to keep in mind is that, by default, because XMLDataSource typically deals with read-only data, it turns cache on by default. This can be particularly troublesome when using the enhancements we are going to discuss in this chapter, where it is designed to cause the XMLDataSource to obtain new data based on specific parameters passed.

One of the things that you might want to do is leverage your business objects to retrieve the XML. The built-in XMLDataSource enables you to retrieve data from a file or set it via a property on the object. It does not support the concept of calling an object that would retrieve the data. By extending the built-in XMLDataSource, we are going to add support for combining some of the capabilities of the ObjectDataSource to call a business object with the capability for data-bound controls to still interact with an XMLDataSource.

Another aspect of the enhancement is the capability to provide parameters that are passed to the select method and used to filter the data that is returned. In the implementation proposed here, we will use this to pass to the business object; however, the same concept could be added to support XPath filtering of the XML based on parameter values.

The following example shows MVPHacksXMLObjectDataSource inheriting from XMLDataSource, and implements a combination of an ObjectDataSource and an XMLDataSource:

```
using System;
using System.Reflection;
using System.Drawing.Design;
using System.ComponentModel;
using System.Collections;
using System.Collections.Specialized;
using System.Data;
using System.Configuration;
using System.Web;
using System.Web.Security;
using System.Web.UI;
using System.Web.UI.WebControls;
using System.Web.UI.WebControls.WebParts;
using System.Web.UI.HtmlControls;

namespace MVPHacks.Common.DataBinding
```

```
{
    /// <summary>
    /// Summary description for MVPHacksXmlObjectDataSource
    /// </summary>
    public class MVPHacksXMLObjectDataSource : XmlDataSource
    {

        public override string Data
        {
            get
            {
                return GetData();
            }
            set
            {
                base.Data = value;
            }
        }

        private string GetData()
        {
            IOrderedDictionary defaultValues =
this.SelectParameters.GetValues(HttpContext.Current, this);

            Object[] parms = new object[defaultValues.Count];

            int parmIndex = 0;
            foreach (DictionaryEntry defaultValue in defaultValues)
            {
                parms[parmIndex] = defaultValue.Value;
                parmIndex++;

            }

            Type type = Type.GetType(m_TypeName);
            object objType = Activator.CreateInstance(type);
            MethodInfo method = type.GetMethod(m_SelectMethodName);
            object outputData = method.Invoke(objType, parms);

            return outputData.ToString();

        }

        private string m_TypeName;

        public string TypeName
        {
            get { return m_TypeName; }
            set { m_TypeName = value; }
        }

        private string m_SelectMethodName;

        public string SelectedMethodName
```

```
        {
            get { return m_SelectMethodName; }
            set { m_SelectMethodName = value; }
        }


        private ParameterCollection m_SelectParameters;

        /// <summary>
        ///
        /// </summary>
        [MergableProperty(false),
        PersistenceMode(PersistenceMode.InnerProperty), DefaultValue((string)null),
        Editor("System.Web.UI.Design.WebControls.ParameterCollectionEditor,
    System.Design, Version=2.0.0.0, Culture=neutral, PublicKeyToken=b03f5f7f11d50a3a",
    typeof(UITypeEditor))]

        public ParameterCollection SelectParameters
        {
            get
            {
                if (m_SelectParameters == null)
                    m_SelectParameters = new ParameterCollection();
                return m_SelectParameters;
            }

        }


    }

}
```

By inheriting from XMLDataSource, the control will appear to other controls as if it were bound to as an XMLDataSource. This gives it capabilities such as using an XPath expression against the XML data, caching, and more. To allow control of where the data is retrieved from, the Data property is overridden and GetData is called to facilitate getting the data from the business object.

Parameters for TypeName and SelectMethod are added to allow specification of the business object that should be invoked to obtain the XML. For consistency, these are modeled after the ObjectDataSource.

Following a play from the playbook, we again utilize the ParameterCollection and the related design-time editors to add a SelectParameters collection to the class. This property allows specification of parameters using all the normal built-in DataSource parameters and those we build to collect the parameter values that will be passed to the business object.

Finally, once the values of the SelectParameters are collected, reflection is used to instance the type and call the designated select method.

Using this method we extend the capability to retrieve the XML data that is used by the XMLDataSource from a business object, including the capability to retrieve it from a Web service or other vendor-provided interfaces. By extending the capability using the select parameters, we also allow valuable information either on the page, passed on the query string, or available via custom parameters, to be used to guide the business object invoked regarding what XML data should be retrieved.

In this section of the chapter you have seen examples of how the DataSource controls can be extended and enhanced to make using them easier and to provide ways of reducing the amount of programmatic effort required to do data binding.

The flexible design provided with the DataSource controls provides many opportunities beyond the few documented in this chapter.

Using Custom Parameters

One of the features of the DataSource control concept is the fact that you can use one or more of the built-in parameters to determine where the data comes from for methods such as `Select`, `Delete`, or any of the other DataSource methods. Using parameters, you are able to retrieve information and pass it along to be used in either the query if SQLDataSource is being used, or as a parameter to a method call if an ObjectDataSource is used.

Built in with ASP.NET are a number of parameter controls, described in the following table.

Parameter Type	Description
Parameter	Generic base class that can be used to provide default values that are specified and not retrieved from another source such as the Query String or another control. It's also used as the base class when building a custom parameter, as shown later in the chapter.
ControlParameter	This provides a simple method to get a parameter from a control on a page by specifying the control ID and the property of the control to fetch.
CookieParameter	This allows pulling a value from a cookie that is sent from the client on the request.
SessionParameter	This provides retrieval from the user's session of a parameter value.
ProfileParameter	This allows retrieval of a parameter value from a user's profile.
QueryStringParameter	This allows retrieval from the HTTP query string that was passed with the request.
FormParameter	This allows retrieval from posted form data or other properties on the Request object. For example, this could pull the value from a hidden field.

The preceding list makes it clear how much power can be found in using parameters with the DataSource controls. In this part of the chapter we will explore ways that you can extend these built-in parameters, as well as develop custom parameters that can also be used just like those in the preceding list. Keep in mind that the techniques being discussed can be used anywhere the parameters are used — for example, regardless of whether SQLDataSource or ObjectDataSource is used.

Extending the QueryStringParameter

One of the easiest ways of starting out with custom parameters is to extend or inherit from parameters that are built in to ASP.NET. By inheriting from the built-in parameters, you can start with all the capabilities that already exist and simply add your additional capabilities. In the first example, you extend the QueryStringParameter to add validation. Imagine that you had a DataSource on the page that took ProductID as a parameter to indicate that the results should be filtered on ProductID. For discussion, assume that ProductID is a numeric value. Imagine what might happen if you passed a character value into the page instead of a numeric value.

The following shows an example SQLDataSource control that uses IssueID in the SelectParameters and specifies that it is of type System.Int32:

```
<asp:SqlDataSource ID="SqlDataSource1" runat="server"
        ConnectionString="<%$ ConnectionStrings:MVPHacksConnectionString1 %>"
        ProviderName="<%$ ConnectionStrings:
MVPHacksConnectionString1.ProviderName %>"
        SelectCommand="SELECT [IssueID], [IssueTitle] FROM [Issue] where
issueID=@issueID" >
            <SelectParameters>
                <asp:QueryStringParameter DefaultValue="0" Name="issueID"
QueryStringField="IssueID" />
            </SelectParameters>
        </asp:SqlDataSource>
```

Under the example definition, if the following value were passed to the page on the query string, then an error would occur:

```
Default.aspx? IssueID=AA
```

The following shows the error that occurred because the invalid character data was passed:

```
Exception Details: System.Data.SqlClient.SqlException: Syntax error converting the
nvarchar value 'AA' to a column of data type int.
```

One option to prevent that from happening is simply catching the Selecting event on the SqlDataSource control and canceling the query, as shown in the following example:

```
protected void SqlDataSource1_Selecting(object sender,
SqlDataSourceSelectingEventArgs e)
    {
        try
        {
            int issueID =
int.Parse(e.Command.Parameters["@IssueID"].Value.ToString());
        }
        catch
        {
            e.Cancel = true;
            return;
        }

    }
```

Another option would be to have specified the `Type` attribute on the QueryStringParameter. The following is an example that adds the `Type` attribute:

```
<asp:QueryStringParameter DefaultValue="0" Name="issueID"
QueryStringField="IssueID" Type="int32" />
```

Doing that just allows the error to happen during the `GetValue` call to the `Parameter`, but it still bubbles up as an exception to the page. The following error occurs when this is added:

Exception Details: System.FormatException: Input string was not in a correct format.

Another option might be to create our own `QueryStringParameter`, which, when the data was invalid, simply returned the `DefaultValue`. In Listing 8-1, the class inherits from `QueryStringParameter` and adds a `ValidationExpression` property. This property specifies a regular expression that will run on the data the `QueryStringParameter` collects from the query string, and, if invalid, returns the `DefaultValue`.

Listing 8-1: MVPHacksQueryStringParameter.cs

```csharp
namespace MVPHacks.Common.WebControls
{
    /// <summary>
    /// Summary description for MVPHacksQueryStringParameter
    /// </summary>
    public class MVPHacksQueryStringParameter :
System.Web.UI.WebControls.QueryStringParameter
    {

        protected override object Evaluate(HttpContext context, Control control)
        {

            object dataValue = base.Evaluate(context, control);


            if ((dataValue != null) && (this.ValidationExpression.Length > 0))
                if (!Regex.IsMatch(dataValue.ToString(), m_ValidationExpression))
                    return DefaultValue;

            return dataValue;
        }

        private string m_ValidationExpression = "";

        public string ValidationExpression
        {
            get { return m_ValidationExpression; }
            set { m_ValidationExpression = value; }
        }


    }
}
```

To use this on your page you must first register the control on the page. The following code shows an example of how that is accomplished:

<%@ Register Namespace="MVPHacks.Common.WebControls" TagPrefix="cc1" %>

Next, modify your SqlDataSource to use the `MVPHacksQueryStringParameter` instead of the built-in `QueryStringParameter`. The following shows an example of that as well as specification of the `ValidationExpression` that limits it to all numerics from 0 to 9:

```
<asp:SqlDataSource ID="SqlDataSource1" runat="server"
            ConnectionString="<%$ ConnectionStrings:MVPHacksConnectionString1 %>"
            ProviderName="<%$
ConnectionStrings:MVPHacksConnectionString1.ProviderName %>"
            SelectCommand="SELECT [IssueID], [IssueTitle] FROM [Issue] where
issueID=@issueID" >
            <SelectParameters>
                <cc1:MVPHacksQueryStringParameter DefaultValue="0" Name="issueID"
                    QueryStringField="IssueID" Type="int32"
ValidationExpression="[0-9]" />
            </SelectParameters>
        </asp:SqlDataSource>
```

Now when you run the page and pass invalid data, it simply indicates that no records were found because there is no record on file with your default value. There are several other creative things we could do but this is a good beginning example of how to leverage the built-in parameter controls to inherit and create your own to obtain additional value. Remember also that the parameter controls work with all of the DataSource controls, such as the ObjectDataSource. In this example we chose the SqlDataSource to show that the same example would work with the other controls. In the rest of this section we will continue to explore other creative custom parameters that can be built by inheriting from the base Parameter control.

Building a Custom Parameter to Get Dates

The first custom parameter that you will build is one that deals with getting custom dates. This control might be used in a select type query, for example, where you need to pass in a start date and you want to configure it to pull data from three days prior to the date on which the query is being run.

The first step in building our custom control is creating a class that inherits from `System.Web.UI` `.WebControls.Parameter`. The other thing that will be done is to override the `Evaluate` method and provide our own implementation. In this example the `Evaluate` method will be overridden and will perform the date calculation based on offsetting using a date provided in the `DayOffset`.

```
using System;
using System.Collections.Generic;
using System.Text;
using System.Web.UI;

namespace MVPHacks.Common.DataBinding
{
    public class MVPHacksGetDateParameter: System.Web.UI.WebControls.Parameter
    {
        /// <summary>
```

```
/// calculate the number of days using DaysOffset and return it
/// </summary>
/// <param name="context"></param>
/// <param name="control"></param>
/// <returns></returns>
protected override object Evaluate(System.Web.HttpContext context,
                                    Control control)
{
    return DateTime.Now.AddDays(this.DaysOffset);
}


/// <summary>
/// Number of days to offset
/// </summary>
public double DaysOffset
{
    get
    {
        if (ViewState["DaysOffset"] == null)
            return 0;

        return (double)ViewState["DaysOffset"];
    }
    set
    {
        ViewState["DaysOffset"] = value;
    }
}
}
}
```

As you can see, not a lot of code is required to build a custom parameter. To use this on a page you must declare this control just as you would any other custom control that you build. The following is an example of doing that using the `Register` tag on the page:

```
<%@ Register Assembly="MVPHacks.Common" Namespace="MVPHacks.Common.DataBinding"
TagPrefix="MVPHacksDB" %>
```

ASP.NET 2.0 introduces a new way you can accomplish the same task in the `web.config` file. Using the `web.config` approach is great for controls like the ones we are discussing in this chapter because it allows them to be available to all pages just by placing them in the `web.config`. The following example shows what it would look like in the `web.config` file:

```
<configuration>
  <system.web>
    <pages >
      <controls>
        <add tagPrefix="MVPHacksDB" namespace="MVPHacks.Common.DataBinding"
             assembly="MVPHacks.Common" />
      </controls>
    </pages>
  </system.web>
</configuration>
```

The next example shows the markup that would be added to the Web form to use the custom date parameter with a SQLDataSource:

```
<asp:SqlDataSource ID="SqlDataSource1" runat="server"
    ConnectionString="<%$ ConnectionStrings:NorthWndConnectionString1 %>"
    ProviderName="<%$ ConnectionStrings:NorthWndConnectionString1.ProviderName %>"
    SelectCommand="SELECT [RemoteAddress], [DateAccessed] FROM [AccessHistory]
                where DateAccessed>@MinDate">
    <SelectParameters>
        <MVPHacksDB:MVPHacksGetDateParameter Name="MinDate" DaysOffset="-90" />
    </SelectParameters>
</asp:SqlDataSource>
```

In the preceding markup, MVPHacksGetDateParameter is used, and the DaysOffset is set up to pass -90. When this runs and the DataSource requests the values from the parameter collection, ultimately the Evaluate method will be called and our date will be calculated and returned using the DaysOffset. We tried to keep this example simple, but clearly this control could be expanded to do things like force a time value or provide other meaningful date-related calculations. Additonally, keep in mind that you could put two of these in the parameter collection and use them as a start/end date of a query.

Another example of how this particular control might be used is to fill in date-created and date-modified information on objects or as a parameter to insert/update queries. Specifically, using the enhancement described earlier in the chapter for the ObjectDataSource that allows for a DefaultValuesCollection, you could add these values to that collection to set them on an object prior to creation.

Building a Custom Parameter Using Reflection

The next custom parameter that we will build is designed to use reflection to get the value from an object, possibly a property on the page. It's quite common for a page to perform a calculation based on other data that the page retrieves for other use and that you want to be able to expose as a property or, for that matter, a method that the parameter could use and make available to the DataSource controls.

The following code implements the MVPHacksReflectionParameter:

```
using System;
using System.Reflection;
using System.Data;
using System.Configuration;
using System.Web;
using System.Web.Security;
using System.Web.UI;
using System.Web.UI.WebControls;
using System.Web.UI.WebControls.WebParts;
using System.Web.UI.HtmlControls;


namespace MVPHacks.Common.DataBinding
{
    ///
    /// Custom Parameter for using with DataSource Control that allows
    /// pulling value from a property on the Page via Reflection
    ///
    public class MVPHacksReflectionParameter : System.Web.UI.WebControls.Parameter
```

```
        {
            /// <summary>
            /// evaluate override
            /// </summary>
            /// <param name="context"></param>
            /// <param name="control"></param>
            /// <returns></returns>
            protected override object Evaluate(HttpContext context, Control control)
            {
                //get the type for the page
                Type pageType = control.Page.GetType();

                if (this.UseContainer)
                    pageType = control.Parent.GetType();

                //get the property info for the specified property
                PropertyInfo propInfo = pageType.GetProperty(this.PropertyName,
                                BindingFlags.Public | BindingFlags.NonPublic |
BindingFlags.Instance);

                //if it's not found we are done
                if (propInfo == null)
                    throw new ArgumentException("No Property Found for " +
this.PropertyName);

                if (!this.UseContainer)
                {
                    //return the value from the property
                    return propInfo.GetValue(control.Page, null);
                }
                else
                {
                    return propInfo.GetValue(control.Parent, null);
                }

            }

            private string m_PropertyName;

            /// <summary>
            /// property name to get value from
            /// </summary>
            public string PropertyName
            {
                get { return m_PropertyName; }
                set { m_PropertyName = value; }
            }

            private bool m_UseContainer;

            /// <summary>
            /// use the container not the page to get the value
            /// </summary>
            public bool UseContainer
            {
                get { return m_UseContainer; }
```

```
                    set { m_UseContainer = value; }
            }



        }

    }
```

MVPHacksReflectionParameter is used the same way as your previous custom controls were used. The PropertyName specifies the name of the property that will be exposed. By default, the control is set up to access the properties using the page. It's quite possible that you might want to use this in a different container or in a subcontainer such as a user control. In one common scenario, the page controls and sets certain parameters on one or more user controls. For example, the page could set the ProductID on the user control. In the user control, suppose you wanted to use a details view to retrieve data about that specific Product ID. In that case, you could manually have the user control retrieve the data, or you could use your reflection parameter and set the UseContainer property to true, indicating that you want to use the user control to find the property instead of using the page.

This custom parameter could also be easily enhanced to allow specification of a MethodName and Type string, and provide support for calling a method to retrieve the parameter value. For bonus points it could also allow detection if the method were static (shared in VB.NET) or an instance method requiring instancing of the method. This introduces some interesting possibilities for how parameter values can be retrieved.

Getting Values from Another DataSource

The way the next custom parameter gets its value is a little more creative. Imagine you are passed in a PersonID and have an ObjectDataSource control on the page that will retrieve the information about the person using that ID as a parameter for an ObjectDataSource control pointing to one of your business objects. Somewhere else on the page you want to show the address information for that person. On the Person object that was returned by the first ObjectDataSource control is the property AddressID, which could be used to retrieve that person's address object. The challenge that exists using the built-in capabilities is clear: If a second DataSource control is going to be used to retrieve the address and perhaps bind it to a different FormsView in a different region on the page, how does it get the AddressID to retrieve the correct address? There really is no easy declarative way to do this, so we are going to attempt to leverage the ObjectDataSource that retrieves the Person object to help us get the address back in a separate ObjectDataSource control.

There are many ways this problem could be solved, but because we are talking about custom parameters, let's look at an approach that uses a custom parameter to handle this scenario:

```
using System;
using System.Reflection;
using System.Data;
using System.Configuration;
using System.Web;
using System.Web.Security;
```

```
using System.Web.UI;
using System.Web.UI.WebControls;
using System.Web.UI.WebControls.WebParts;
using System.Web.UI.HtmlControls;
using System.Collections;

namespace MVPHacks.Common.DataBinding
{

    /// <summary>
    ///
    /// </summary>
    public class MVPHacksDataSourceParameter : System.Web.UI.WebControls.Parameter
    {

        /// <summary>
        /// Evaluate and return the value
        /// </summary>
        /// <param name="context"></param>
        /// <param name="control"></param>
        /// <returns></returns>
        protected override object Evaluate(HttpContext context, Control control)
        {
            IDataSource source1 = null;
            if (this.DataSourceID.Length != 0)
            {
                Control control1 =
MVPHacksDataSourceControlHelper.FindControl(control, this.DataSourceID);
                if (control1 == null)
                    return null;

                source1 = control1 as IDataSource;
                if (source1 == null)
                    return null;
            }

            DataSourceView dsView = source1.GetView(this.DataMember);


            ObjectDataSourceView objDSV = dsView as ObjectDataSourceView;
            SqlDataSourceView sqlDSV = dsView as SqlDataSourceView;


            IEnumerable ienumView = null;

            if (sqlDSV != null)
                ienumView = sqlDSV.Select(DataSourceSelectArguments.Empty);

            if (objDSV != null)
                ienumView = objDSV.Select(DataSourceSelectArguments.Empty);

            IEnumerator ien = ienumView.GetEnumerator();
```

```
            ien.MoveNext();

            return DataBinder.GetPropertyValue(ien.Current, this.DataColumn);


    }

    private string m_DataSourceID = "";

    /// <summary>
    /// DataSourceID to use
    /// </summary>
    [IDReferenceProperty(typeof(DataSourceControl))]
    public string DataSourceID
    {
        get
        {
            return m_DataSourceID;
        }
        set
        {
            m_DataSourceID = value;
        }
    }

    private string m_DataMember = "";

    /// <summary>
    /// DataMember to use in target
    /// </summary>
    public string DataMember
    {
        get
        {
            return m_DataMember;
        }
        set
        {
            m_DataMember = value;
        }
    }

    private string m_DataColumn = "";

    /// <summary>
    /// Data column to use
    /// </summary>
    public string DataColumn
    {
        get
        {
            return m_DataColumn;
        }
        set
        {
```

```
                        m_DataColumn = value;
                }
        }

    }
}
```

If you walk through the `Evaluate` function in the previous example, the first thing it does is find the DataSource control that will be the target from which the value is retrieved. The target DataSource is specified using the `DataSourceID` attribute on our custom parameter. Notice that the attribute `[IDReference Property(typeof(DataSourceControl))]` is specified on the `DataSourceID` property. Using this attribute allows the easy determination of which control should be referenced by this property. Using the `DataSourceID`, you now need to find and get a reference to the control on the Web form.

The DataSource control is now referenced using an `IDataSource` interface because you don't care what type of DataSource control you are dealing with. Using that reference you call the `GetView` property to get a `DataSourceView` object for the control and the `DataMember` that is specified. The following example code shows that call:

```
DataSourceView dsView = source1.GetView(this.DataMember);
```

The `DataSourceView` that is returned is specific to the DataSource control being used. For example, an ObjectDataSource would return an `ObjectDataSourceView`. The following code sample shows casting the `dsView` to both SQL and Object views:

```
ObjectDataSourceView objDSV = dsView as ObjectDataSourceView;
SqlDataSourceView sqlDSV = dsView as SqlDataSourceView;
```

Because of the way the cast is done in the preceding sample code, if the type is not matching, then it will set the value to `null`.

The next task is to get an `IEnumerable` interface to the current view. The following sample does that by checking both of the views to determine which one is active, and calls the `select` method on the appropriate object:

```
IEnumerable ienumView = null;

    if (sqlDSV != null)
        ienumView = sqlDSV.Select(DataSourceSelectArguments.Empty);

    if (objDSV != null)
        ienumView = objDSV.Select(DataSourceSelectArguments.Empty);
```

If you use the `IEnumerable` reference, the next thing to do is to advance it to the first item in the set. The following example code takes care of that action:

```
IEnumerator ien = ienumView.GetEnumerator();
ien.MoveNext();
```

Now that the first row is active, it is possible to retrieve the value and return it. The following example code leverages the `DataBinder` to access the property and return it:

```
return DataBinder.GetPropertyValue(ien.Current, this.DataColumn);
```

Clearly, more could be done to handle errors and other situations that might arise in doing this type of operation. Additionally, there may be more efficient methods that you could use to accomplish the same task. The point of this exercise is to demonstrate how you can interact with other DataSource controls on a page and leverage their data.

In this section of the chapter we have explored how easy it is to build custom parameter controls that are then used in conjunction with DataSource controls. These custom parameters can extend, or provide completely new, capabilities that can be used in the various parameter collections on the DataSource controls.

Using Custom Fields

A lot of time in this chapter has been dedicated to getting the data using the DataSource controls. While that is an important part of data binding, so are the controls that actually show the data on the page when it is rendered on the requestor's browser.

In the remaining part of this chapter we are going to explore some techniques that can make working with some of the visual controls easier. Specifically, we are going to focus on the Field controls, which are a key component of both the DetailsView and the GridView controls.

Both the DetailsView and GridView controls are new to the ASP.NET control suite. The GridView steps up to the plate to take over where the DataGrid control left off, offering the developer richer support for common tasks such as sorting, editing, and selecting rows in the grid for further manipulation. The DetailsView was added to fill a gap for a control that would allow for a Label/Value editing experience that is perfect for a lot of the simple administration style edit forms that an application needs.

One of the key common features of both these controls is the fact that they rely on another suite of controls that are all `Field` classes. These classes define the rendering, and the capability to manipulate the data. Using the mode of the control, such as Insert, Edit, or View, they are able to render the output to the browser. For example while in View mode, a label containing the data is rendered and no modifications are allowed. When in Insert or Edit mode, that same `BoundField` would result in a text box being rendered, allowing the user to modify the data.

The following table describes the built-in field types that are supported.

Field Type	Description
BoundField	Displays the text from the field in the data source
ButtonField	Displays as a button, image, or link
CheckBoxField	Used for Boolean type fields and displays a checkbox
CommandField	Used for selecting, editing, and deleting support in the GridView control
HyperLinkField	Displays as a simple hyperlink
ImageField	Used to display an image
TemplateField	Custom layout using an HTML template

These Field controls, `DetailsView`, and `GridView`, combined with the DataSource controls provide for true two-way data binding capability and remove the need for the application developer to implement specific views for the different modes the controls will be in.

As you start using the new UI controls and the associated DataSource controls, some of the shortfalls will quickly become apparent. For example, when using the DetailsView in conjunction with a DataSource control in Insert mode, handling required fields takes extra work. By default, when the DetailsView is added to a page and bound to a DataSource, the configuration wizards will infer columns from the target of the DataSource control. For example, while pointing to the `Product` object created earlier in the chapter, it would create a bound field for each of the public properties, as shown in the following example:

```
    <asp:DetailsView ID="DetailsView1" runat="server" AutoGenerateRows="False"
DataSourceID="ProductEditODS1" Height="50px" Width="125px">
        <Fields>
            <asp:BoundField DataField="ProductID" HeaderText="ProductID"
SortExpression="ProductID" />
            <asp:BoundField DataField="Name" HeaderText="Name"
                    SortExpression="Name" />
            <asp:BoundField DataField="ProductStatus"
                    HeaderText="ProductStatus"
                    SortExpression="ProductStatus" />
        </Fields>
    </asp:DetailsView>
```

If we use the markup in the preceding example, a `DetailsView` would render a text box for each of the bound fields that would allow input of data. If each of the fields were required, there is no built-in support for adding validation to the form. Without any other changes, the user simply clicks the Add button to pass null or empty fields to the DataSource control and ultimately to the associated query or business object. If the target data repository requires those fields to be provided, most likely an error will occur, which will not be handled as a typical validation error, but more like a catastrophic application exception.

By using the built-in support, this can be avoided with the validation controls that are provided with ASP.NET. Specifically, the RequiredFieldValidator control is traditionally used for this task and would not allow submission or postback of the form without some value being input in the control. The most common technique for utilizing the validation controls with the `DetailsView` or `GridView` fields is to convert the field into a `Template` Field. The next example shows what the markup looks like if we convert the `Name` field into a `Template` field. When you have selected one of the fields from the Edit Field Wizard, there is a Convert to Template option. Using that option converts the following line:

```
            <asp:BoundField DataField="Name" HeaderText="Name"
                    SortExpression="Name" />
```

After making it a `Template` field, the markup would look like the following:

```
<asp:TemplateField HeaderText="Name" SortExpression="Name">
            <EditItemTemplate>
                <asp:TextBox ID="TextBox1" runat="server" Text='<%#
Bind("Name") %>'></asp:TextBox>
            </EditItemTemplate>
            <InsertItemTemplate>
                <asp:TextBox ID="TextBox1" runat="server" Text='<%#
Bind("Name") %>'></asp:TextBox>
            </InsertItemTemplate>
```

```
                    <ItemTemplate>
                        <asp:Label ID="Label1" runat="server" Text='<%#
Bind("Name") %>'></asp:Label>
                    </ItemTemplate>
                </asp:TemplateField>
```

By converting it to a `TemplateField` instead of a `BoundField`, you gain complete control over what is rendered to the client in the various modes. That allows you to easily drop a required field validator into the Edit and Insert templates to ensure that a name is always provided. After a few fields, and a few pages of converting and doing all the extra work, it becomes obvious that a more streamlined approach is required for this common problem. The following markup shows what the template looks like after the addition of a `RequiredFieldValidator` control:

```
<InsertItemTemplate>
                        <asp:TextBox ID="TextBox1" runat="server" Text='<%#
Bind("Name") %>'></asp:TextBox>
                        <asp:RequiredFieldValidator ID="RequiredFieldValidator1"
runat="server" ControlToValidate="TextBox1"
                        ErrorMessage="Field is
Required"></asp:RequiredFieldValidator>
                    </InsertItemTemplate>
```

Imagine if you had to do that for every required field. It gets even worse when you consider a more real-istic application validation, because, in addition to the required field, you would most likely have either a range validator or a regular expression validator.

Wouldn't it be easier if you could just click a property on the `BoundField` and mark the field as required? Our next example is going to do just that. By inheriting from `BoundField` we gain all the same capabilities it has, including automatic rendering of labels in view mode and text boxes in insert/edit mode.

The first step in building the `MVPHacksBoundfField` is to inherit from the built-in `BoundField` class:

```
public class MVPHacksBoundField : System.Web.UI.WebControls.BoundField
```

Next, you add a `RequiredField` property; this property will indicate that the field is required and that the control should inject a validator into the rendered output:

```
/// <summary>
        /// Require Validation
        /// </summary>
        public bool RequiredField
        {
            get
            {
                if (ViewState["RequiredField"] == null)
                    return false;

                return (bool)ViewState["RequiredField"];
            }
            set
            {
```

```
                ViewState["RequiredField"] = value;
        }
    }
```

Now you must find the right place to inject the validator into the control collection if the `RequiredField` property is `true`. To override the `InitializeDataCell` method, and when the `RequiredField` property is set, a `RequiredFieldValidator` control is injected into the control collection for the cell, as shown in the following example:

```
protected override void InitializeDataCell(DataControlFieldCell cell,
DataControlRowState rowState)
    {
        base.InitializeDataCell(cell, rowState);

        if (this.RequiredField)
        {
            if (cell.Controls[0] is TextBox)
            {
                TextBox box = cell.Controls[0] as TextBox;
                box.ID = this.DataField;

            }
            RequiredFieldValidator reqField = new RequiredFieldValidator();
            reqField.ControlToValidate = this.DataField;
            reqField.Text = "*";
            reqField.ErrorMessage = this.HeaderText + " is required.";
            reqField.Display = ValidatorDisplay.Dynamic;
            cell.Controls.Add(reqField);


        }

    }
```

Now if you go back and look at the markup for the control using our new MVPHacksBoundField, there is much less markup required, as you can see in the following example:

```
<MVPHacksDB:MVPHacksBoundField DataField="Name" HeaderText="ProductName"
RequiredField="true" SortExpression="Name" />
```

Clearly, much less markup is required to accomplish the same goal of ensuring that good data is input. While you tackled only `RequiredField` in this example, you can see how easy it would be to add a few more properties to enable support for a regular expression or other validation type controls to be rendered in conjunction with the contents of the field as appropriate. If you aren't familiar with regular expressions you could review how the `RegularExpressionValidator` control works and integrate it the same way we did in this example with the `RequiredFieldValidator`.

While we are looking at enhancements that could be made to the field, let's look at a feature that is available in Windows Forms data binding. In Windows Forms applications, if you bind an object to a form and the object has a name like `ProjectStatus`, the data-binding engine will help you out and create a label on the page that says "Project Status." While it is a minor inconvenience, it would be nice if the built-in `HeaderText` property didn't contain a space but that it would then inject a space as appropriate for the contents of the field. The following example code is designed to augment our `MVPHacks` `BoundField` to add similar support that the Windows Forms data binding enjoys:

```
public override string HeaderText
    {
        get
        {
            if (base.HeaderText == null)
                return "";

            string newHeader = string.Empty;

            char[] headerChars = base.HeaderText.ToCharArray();

            foreach (char letter in headerChars)
            {
                if ((letter == char.ToUpper(letter)) && (newHeader.Length > 0))
                    newHeader += " " + letter;
                else
                    newHeader += letter;
            }

            return newHeader;

        }
        set
        {
            base.HeaderText = value;
        }
    }
```

In the preceding example, by simply overriding the `HeaderText` property, we gain control that can be used to return to users a more friendly name.

Using the class inherited from `BoundField`, we demonstrated how easy it is to build a custom field. The `MVPHacksBoundField` reduces the amount of markup required to be configured for real-world usage of the DetailsView and GridView for adding or editing data.

Wrapping Up

This chapter described several methods to extend the built-in data-binding capabilities in ASP.NET 2.0. The built-in capabilities in ASP.NET 2.0 far exceed those of the prior version and provide extensibility points that enable developers to extend and enhance the built-in capabilities to meet the demanding needs of real-world applications.

In this chapter you explored methods in which the DataSource controls can be extended to promote consistency, and the use of common enhancements such as the DefaultValues collection on the ObjectDataSource. During the course of the chapter you built some reusable DataSource controls that you can use in your applications. Use them as a starting point to find additional common functionality that could be added to meet your own application needs. By using the concept of application-specific datasources, you can reduce redundancy across pages and the mundane effort of configuring the same options page after page. Using code-generation techniques described in this chapter combined with other common techniques can further reduce the amount of custom configuration you need to do, in addition to providing further improvements in consistency across your application.

Having parameters that work with the DataSource controls and that enable the passing of values to our queries and methods significantly reduces the custom code required to build realistic applications that don't just simply select all the rows in a table. This chapter demonstrated how, by inheriting from the built-in controls, you can build custom parameters that are appropriate for the application being built. Using the hacks in this chapter as examples, you can build other custom parameters that go beyond those described here.

Using the new UI controls such as DetailsView and GridView and their associated `Field` classes, we explored how we could build robust applications that included capabilities such as validation without sacrificing some of the productivity enhancements that Visual Studio 2005 provides. The fact that you no longer have to make every column a template column to require a field will greatly simplify the complexity of a form, and the required customization.

Finally, using all the techniques in this chapter, it should be clear that you can build more than quick-and-dirty demo applications that were never intended to run in production. The previous version of ASP.NET fell short of this goal and left much of the heavy lifting in the hands of every developer on the team. In ASP.NET 2.0, the bar has been raised for what can be accomplished using the built-in data-binding capabilities. By combining the built-in capabilities with the techniques discussed in this chapter and those that you will create as a result of creative thinking, real applications can now be built that use data binding.

9

ViewState

ViewState was originally intended to provide a way to maintain opaque chunks of state such that ASP.NET controls could experience a true lifecycle and receive events like traditional Windows controls. Controls that stored small bits of state within the Page framework's ViewState could report events such as "this TextBox has changed" that were previously difficult to simulate. For what it does, ViewState does it well. ViewState is fundamental to completing ASP.NET's illusion of an eventing system over HTTP.

However, if you ask developers what part of ASP.NET they hate the most, chances are they will say ViewState. It's bloated, it's obnoxious, it's confusing, it's opaque, and it's a hassle. This chapter won't argue any of these points, but will aim to make a few things clear. ViewState works well for what it does, and the ASP.NET framework is flexible enough that you can often hack a number of ViewState's default behaviors to coax it to meet your needs.

This chapter looks at ways to chop ViewState up, compress it, use its compression for other purposes, move it around the page, and store it outside the page altogether. Each of these hacks should remind you that ASP.NET is a very flexible system; and if you don't like something, you very often have the power to change it. Let's start by digging into the details of how ViewState works.

ViewState: Evil or Clever Like a Fox?

ViewState intends literally to "maintain the state of the view." For example, take a page that includes a single text box and a button. The TextBox is initially rendered with the value foo preloaded in the text box. If the end user typed in bar and submitted the form, an ASP.NET developer would like to see a TextChanged event fired informing them of the change. How could ASP.NET know that the text in the TextBox changed had it not maintained some view state?

Text boxes and most other Web controls implement an interface called `IPostBackDataHandler`, indicating that they are interested in inspecting the data that's sent back via an HTTP POST during a form submit. In its implementation of `IPostBackDataHandler.LoadPostData`, the TextBox compares the data just posted with the data stored in ViewState, updates its `Text` property appropriately, and returns `true`. The page keeps track of all controls that returned `true` during this phase of page initialization and spins through this list of consumers of posted data and raises their `PostData ChangedEvent`, which in turn shows up as a `TextChanged` event to the developer.

The result is that you get an event when a TextBox's text changes between posts, as the TextBox's previous state was saved for you in a "state bag" and carried along for the ride in a hidden form field called `_VIEW-STATE`. Had the ASP.NET framework not included this feature, you would have had to store the previous value elsewhere. ASP.NET uses a not well-known optimized serializer called the LosFormatter to serialize the ViewState state bag into a tight binary format that is then Base64 encoded and rendered in the hidden form field.

You need to be aware of where ViewState fits into the page lifecycle. Note that numerous less significant events are available—even more were added in ASP.NET 2.0—but these are the core events and best represent the major events in a page's life. Figure 9-1 shows the lifecycle during the initial load of a page, and how ViewState is involved during a PostBack.

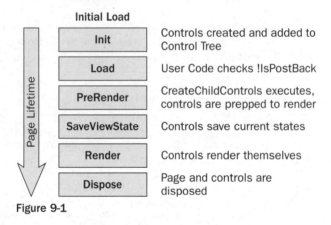

Figure 9-1

Controls on a page take the opportunity to save their data to the ViewState state bag just before they render. Figure 9-2 shows how pages and controls use the ViewState data carried along and returned during a PostBack to synthesize events for the page developer's use.

You may feel this is just background information or plumbing that doesn't concern you. However. if you're interested at all in hacking ASP.NET's ViewState, these little details will come in handy. Now that you know *when* your objects are serialized into ViewState, let's find out *how* your objects are serialized and what kind of hacking can be had.

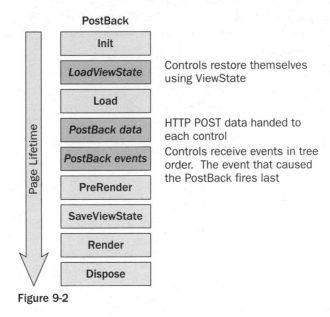

Figure 9-2

LosFormatter: The Missing Serializer

How are objects serialized into an HTML-friendly format that can be output with a hidden form field? You might have used the XmlSerializer or BinaryFormatter to serialize objects within your code, but neither of those really fits the bill. Fortunately there's another lesser known serializer called the LosFormatter that does the work of serializing objects into ViewState. MSDN Online Help has this to say about the mysterious LosFormatter:

> **"The limited object serialization (LOS) formatter is designed for highly compact ASCII format serialization. This class supports serializing any object graph, but is optimized for those containing strings, arrays, and hashtables. It offers second order optimization for many of the .NET primitive types.**
>
> **"This is a private format, and needs to remain consistent only for the lifetime of a Web request. You are not allowed to persist objects serialized with this formatter for any significant length of time."**

The LosFormatter fills in a gap between the verbose XmlSerializer and the terse BinaryFormatter. You can think of the LosFormatter as a BinaryFormatter "light" that is optimized for objects containing very simple types. It's also a nice convenience that LosFormatter creates an ASCII string representation of your object graph.

Many ASP.NET 1.x developers became frustrated with ViewState and started disabling it without considering the consequences. Many controls that required ViewState of some kind stopped working correctly when ViewState was disabled, which frustrated developers even more. ASP.NET 2.0 introduced a new kind of ViewState called ControlState. ControlState can't be turned off and provides a place for controls to put very small bits of state that are absolutely crucial to the operation of their control. However, for ASP.NET 1.x developers who don't have ControlState available, you may want to use the LosFormatter directly and store a bit of state here and there within your own private hidden form field. For example, Listing 9-1 is a small helper function that will take an object and serialize it as a string.

Listing 9-1: Serializing an object with the LosFormatter

C#

```csharp
string LosSerializeObject(object obj)
{
    System.Web.UI.LosFormatter los = new System.Web.UI.LosFormatter();
    StringWriter writer = new StringWriter();
    los.Serialize(writer, obj);
    return writer.ToString();
}

object RetrieveObjectFromViewState( string serializedObject)
{
    System.Web.UI.LosFormatter los = new System.Web.UI.LosFormatter();
    return los.Deserialize(serializedObject);
}
```

VB

```vb
Function LosSerializeObject(ByVal obj As Object) As String
    Dim los As System.Web.UI.LosFormatter = New System.Web.UI.LosFormatter
    Dim writer As StringWriter = New StringWriter
    los.Serialize(writer, obj)
    Return writer.ToString
End Function

Function RetrieveObjectFromViewState(ByVal serializedObject As String) As Object
    Dim los As System.Web.UI.LosFormatter = New System.Web.UI.LosFormatter
    Return los.Deserialize(serializedObject)
End Function
```

The LosFormatter creates an interestingly formatted string just before Base64 encodes it. For example, the code

```
aTw1Pg==
```

looks like this when decoded:

```
i<5>
```

This indicates an integer with the value 5. It's not XML even though it uses angle brackets—it's just an encoding schema. You may think it is odd to use more bytes after Base64 encoding, but remember that the "==" at the end of a Base64-encoded string is a standard suffix. Additionally, the overhead would be less if the value to be encoded were longer. Usually you won't need to use the LosFormatter, but it's good to know it's available in your Toolbox.

Put an integer value in ViewState programmatically as in the following code. You'll be storing this integer within ViewState as the page loads. The ASP.NET subsystem will serialize everything within ViewState as the page renders. That means that the number 5 in this example will be serialized into the_VIEWSTATE hidden form field. We'll then use an inspection utility to examine the contents of the hidden form field and see what it holds.

C#
```
private void Page_Load(object sender, System.EventArgs e)
{
    ViewState["example"] = 5;
}
```

VB
```
private void Page_Load(object sender, System.EventArgs e)
{
    ViewState["example"] = 5;
}
```

Now download Fritz Onion's ViewState Decoder from `pluralsight.com/tools.aspx`. Run your page and, using View Source, copy the ViewState value from the hidden text box and decode it with Fritz's tool. You can also extract it directly by pasting in an URL. Note in Figure 9-3 that Fritz's decoder offers a Tree Display that shows both the name "example" and the value "5." Paul Wilson has also created an online ViewState decoder at `wilsondotnet.com/Demos/ViewState.aspx`.

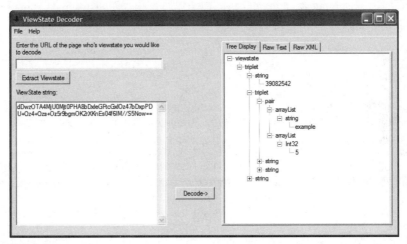

Figure 9-3

The fact that ViewState is so easily decoded underscores the fact that you should avoid storing anything sensitive in it.

Manipulating ViewState

You've seen how ViewState is serialized into a single form field. In this section you'll learn how to split ViewState up into a number of smaller form fields so that you may sneak even your largest ViewState values past unforgiving "smart" firewalls. Although ViewState is stored out in the open in a form field, its manipulation is done entirely by ASP.NET's infrastructure and you don't have to worry about it. However, some inspecting firewalls and proxies are very picky about what they allow through. If your firewall peers within the body of a request or response and enforces strict policies about the maximum size of an HTTP POST or single POST name/value pair, you could see problems. This used to be a problem with AOL but is seen less and less on the open Internet and more often within tight corporate intranets. Often when these systems see what they consider a large value sent via an HTTP POST, they deny it. This, of course, doesn't bode well for your application if it doesn't receive what it's expecting.

Splitting ViewState Using ASP.NET 1.1

The size of ViewState was such a problem that the `MaxPageStateFieldLength` property was added to the `Page` class in ASP.NET 2.0. By default, ASP.NET 2.0 will not split ViewState into multiple chunks, but you can set this value to the maximum number of bytes that a ViewState field should be. However, this feature isn't available on ASP.NET 1.x, so you'll need to hack it!

This clever hack for dealing with ViewState's excessive size was spotted on the Blogosphere when Cliff Harker sent Paul Wilson some code to split ViewState up when sending a response and reassemble it on the way back in from a request, all under ASP.NET 1.1. You can see the original blog post and code at `http://weblogs.asp.net/pwilson/archive/2003/08/21/24867.aspx`.

The ASP.NET `Page` class includes two methods you can override, `LoadPageStateFromPersistence Medium` and `SavePageStateToPersistenceMedium`. This is your chance to jump in and decide what to do with the page's ViewState.

The `SavePageStateToPersistenceMedium` method receives the ViewState object as input and should store it however you like. This example serializes the ViewState object using the LosFormatter discussed earlier, and then chops the now serialized ASCII string into chunks of no more than 1,000 bytes. The `LoadPageStateFromPersistenceMedium` method must load the persisted ViewState from wherever it is stored — in this case, of course, it is stored in the HTTP Request as a series of form fields — and return the resultant object. Listing 9-2 could be added to a BaseUIPage such as the one you created in Chapter 3 so that all your derived pages would have ViewState splitting functionality.

Listing 9-2 shows how you can split the ViewState into as many fields as you need given an arbitrarily small chunk size. This listing includes two method overrides: one for `SavePageStateToPersistence Medium` that creates as many hidden form fields as are necessary and one for `LoadPageStateFrom PersistenceMedium` that reassembles the saved ViewState from however many hidden form fields are returned to the server side after a PostBack.

The `save` method calls `LosFormatter.Serialize` and stores the results in a StringBuilder. A `while` loop spins through the resulting string, chopping it up and storing the segments using the page's own `RegisterHiddenField` method. Notice that the counting variable `cnt` is incremented each time the loop executes and is used to create the name of the hidden field, such as `_VIEWSTATE1`, and so on.

Listing 9-2: Splitting up ViewState within your BaseUIPage

C#

```csharp
protected override void SavePageStateToPersistenceMedium(object viewState)
{
    LosFormatter format = new LosFormatter();
    StringWriter writer = new StringWriter();
    format.Serialize(writer, viewState);
    StringBuilder s = new StringBuilder(writer.ToString());

    int cnt = 1;
    int left = s.Length;

    while( left > 0 )
    {
        //Change to any value other than 1000 as necessary
        int cut = (left > 1000) ? 1000 : left;

        RegisterHiddenField("__VIEWSTATE" + cnt.ToString(),
        s.ToString().Substring(0,cut));

        s = s.Remove(0,cut);
        left -= cut;
        cnt++;
    }
    cnt--;

    RegisterHiddenField("__VIEWSTATE0", cnt.ToString());
    RegisterHiddenField("__VIEWSTATE", "");
}

protected override object LoadPageStateFromPersistenceMedium()
{
    LosFormatter format = new LosFormatter();
    int cnt = Convert.ToInt32(Request["__VIEWSTATE0"].ToString());
    StringBuilder s = new StringBuilder();

    for (int i = 1; i <= cnt; i++)
    {
        s.Append(Request["__VIEWSTATE" + i.ToString()].ToString());
    }
    return format.Deserialize(s.ToString());
}
```

VB

```vb
Protected Overrides Sub SavePageStateToPersistenceMedium(ByVal viewState As Object)
    Dim format As LosFormatter = New LosFormatter
    Dim writer As StringWriter = New StringWriter
    format.Serialize(writer, viewState)
    Dim s As StringBuilder = New StringBuilder(writer.ToString)
    Dim cnt As Integer = 1
    Dim left As Integer = s.Length

    While (left > 0)
```

(continued)

Listing 9-2 *(continued)*

```
            'Change to any value other than 1000 as necessary
            Dim cut As Integer
            If (left > 1000) Then
                cut = 1000
            Else
                cut = left
            End If
            RegisterHiddenField(("__VIEWSTATE" + cnt.ToString), _
                    s.ToString.Substring(0, cut))
            s = s.Remove(0, cut)
            left = (left - cut)
            cnt = (cnt + 1)

        End While
        cnt = (cnt - 1)
        RegisterHiddenField("__VIEWSTATE0", cnt.ToString)
        RegisterHiddenField("__VIEWSTATE", "")
    End Sub

    Protected Overrides Function LoadPageStateFromPersistenceMedium() As Object
        Dim format As LosFormatter = New LosFormatter
        Dim cnt As Integer = Convert.ToInt32(Request("__VIEWSTATE0").ToString)
        Dim s As StringBuilder = New StringBuilder
        Dim i As Integer = 1
        Do While (i <= cnt)
            s.Append(Request(("__VIEWSTATE" + i.ToString)).ToString)
            i = (i + 1)
        Loop
        Return format.Deserialize(s.ToString)
    End Function
```

Note also that while Listing 9-2 uses a monotonically increasing number appended to the word _VIEW-STATE, you could certainly pick another name for the fields.

Compressing ViewState

ViewState is often impugned for its tendency toward large size. Many folks don't realize that ViewState is trying to help them out by completing the illusion of a stateful event model over the stateless protocol that is HTTP. It's good to try to minimize the use of ViewState. Dino Esposito (http://weblogs .asp.net/despos/archive/2005/07/21/420082.aspx) suggests that the ViewState should not exceed more than 30% of a page's total size.

ASP.NET 2.0 introduces a new serialization format in the form of the ObjectStateFormatter, and Nikhil Kothan (nikhilk.net/ViewStateImprovements.aspx) points out a number of other improvements that make ASP.NET 2.0's ViewState nearly 50% smaller than ASP.NET 1.1's. However, using compression to make ViewState smaller in ASP.NET 1.1 is a quick and easy hack.

Vlad Olifier compressed his ViewState using the SharpZipLib library that can be downloaded from icsharpcode.net. Listing 9-3 wraps the ICSharpCode.SharpZipLib library into two shared methods, Compress and Decompress, that we'll use to compress a page's ViewState. Listing 9-4 then applies the helper functions from Listing 9-3 to the ViewState.

Listing 9-3: Compressing ViewState

C#

```csharp
using System.IO;
using Zip = ICSharpCode.SharpZipLib.Zip.Compression;
//Download ICSharpCode.SharpZipLib from
//http://www.icsharpcode.net/OpenSource/SharpZipLib/Download.aspx

public class ViewStateZip
{
    static byte[] Compress(byte[] bytes)
    {
        MemoryStream memory = new MemoryStream();
        object stream = new Zip.Streams.DeflaterOutputStream(memory,
                new Zip.Deflater(Zip.Deflater.BEST_COMPRESSION), 131072);
        stream.Write(bytes, 0, bytes.Length);
        stream.Close();
        return memory.ToArray();
    }

    static byte[] Decompress(byte[] bytes)
    {
        object stream = new Zip.Streams.InflaterInputStream(
                new MemoryStream(bytes));
        MemoryStream memory = new MemoryStream();
        byte[,] writeData;
        int size;
        while (true)
        {
            size = stream.Read(writeData, 0, writeData.Length);
            if ((size > 0))
            {
                memory.Write(writeData, 0, size);
            }
            else {
                break;
            }
        }
        stream.Close();
        return memory.ToArray();
    }
}
```

VB

```vb
Imports System.IO

Imports Zip = ICSharpCode.SharpZipLib.Zip.Compression
'Download ICSharpCode.SharpZipLib from
'http://www.icsharpcode.net/OpenSource/SharpZipLib/Download.aspx

Public Class ViewStateZip
  Shared Function Compress(ByVal bytes() As Byte) As Byte()
    Dim memory As New MemoryStream
    Dim stream = New Zip.Streams.DeflaterOutputStream(memory, _
```

(continued)

Listing 9-3 *(continued)*

```
                   New Zip.Deflater(Zip.Deflater.BEST_COMPRESSION), 131072)
   stream.Write(bytes, 0, bytes.Length)
   stream.Close()
   Return memory.ToArray()
 End Function

 Shared Function Decompress(ByVal bytes() As Byte) As Byte()
   Dim stream = New Zip.Streams.InflaterInputStream(New MemoryStream(bytes))
   Dim memory As New MemoryStream
   Dim writeData(4096) As Byte
   Dim size As Integer
   While True
     size = stream.Read(writeData, 0, writeData.Length)
     If size > 0 Then memory.Write(writeData, 0, size) Else Exit While
   End While
   stream.Close()
   Return memory.ToArray()
 End Function
End Class
```

Using the open-source `ICSharpCode.SharpZipLib` library makes zip compression very easy. While .NET 2.0 includes library support for zip compression, .NET 1.x did not, so this free library fit the bill nicely. The compress and decompress methods are very simple. The first takes a `MemoryStream` and compresses its contents, returning the array of compressed bytes. The latter reads the compressed input data in chunks and writes the decompressed result to a `MemoryStream` that is also returned as an array of bytes.

Now that you have a quick way to zip bytes, Listing 9-4 shows how you can overload `LoadPageStateFromPersistenceMedium` and `SavePageStateToPersistenceMedium` and put the compressed ViewState into a new hidden form field called _VSTATE.

Listing 9-4: Zipping ViewState

C#

```
protected override object LoadPageStateFromPersistenceMedium()
{
    string vState = this.Request.Form("__VSTATE");
    byte[] bytes = System.Convert.FromBase64String(vState);
    bytes = ViewStateZip.Decompress(bytes);
    LosFormatter format = new LosFormatter();
    return format.Deserialize(System.Convert.ToBase64String(bytes));
}

protected override void SavePageStateToPersistenceMedium(object viewState)
{
    LosFormatter format = new LosFormatter();
    StringWriter writer = new StringWriter();
    format.Serialize(writer, viewState);
    string viewStateStr = writer.ToString();
    byte[] bytes = System.Convert.FromBase64String(viewStateStr);
    bytes = ViewStateZip.Compress(bytes);
```

```
        string vStateStr = System.Convert.ToBase64String(bytes);
        RegisterHiddenField("__VSTATE", vStateStr);
    }
```

VB
```
Protected Overrides Function LoadPageStateFromPersistenceMedium() As Object
    Dim vState As String = Me.Request.Form("__VSTATE")
    Dim bytes As Byte() = System.Convert.FromBase64String(vState)
    bytes = ViewStateZip.Decompress(bytes)
    Dim format As New LosFormatter
    Return format.Deserialize(System.Convert.ToBase64String(bytes))
End Function

Protected Overrides Sub SavePageStateToPersistenceMedium(ByVal viewState As Object)
    Dim format As New LosFormatter
    Dim writer As New StringWriter
    format.Serialize(writer, viewState)
    Dim viewStateStr As String = writer.ToString()
    Dim bytes As Byte() = System.Convert.FromBase64String(viewStateStr)
    bytes = ViewStateZip.Compress(bytes)
    Dim vStateStr As String = System.Convert.ToBase64String(bytes)
    RegisterHiddenField("__VSTATE", vStateStr)
End Sub
```

Listing 9-4 overrides the two ViewState management methods from the `Page` object similarly to Listing 9-2. The ViewState's state bag is passed into the `save` method, compressed, and stored as a string in a hidden form field. The load reverses the processes by retrieving the string from the hidden form field, decompressing it, and then deserializing it back into an object.

This hack should be used on a page-by-page basis when all else has failed. Sometimes when you're using a DataGrid and you just can't squeeze any more *out* of the ViewState, you can just squeeze the ViewState itself!

Alternative Storage for ViewState

Storing ViewState within the returned HTML page is convenient, but when ViewState gets to be more than 20K or 30K, it may be time to consider alternative locations for storage. You might want to store ViewState in the ASP.NET `Session` object, on the file system, or in the database to minimize the amount of data shipped back and forth to the user's browser.

The most advanced ViewState hacking product that I've seen is the Flesk ViewStateOptimizer (www.flesk.net), as it enables you to compress ViewState and move it to a file or to the session. When moving ViewState to the `Session` object, you have to take into consideration how ViewState is *supposed* to work. Remember that when ViewState is stored in a page's hidden form field, the ViewState for a page is literally stored along with the page itself. This is an important point, so read it again. When you choose to store ViewState elsewhere — separated from the page — you need a way to correlate the two. Your first reaction might be to think that each user needs a copy of the ViewState for each page they visit. However, it's not as simple as the equation "users * page = number of ViewState instances," as a user can and will visit a page multiple times. Each page instance needs its own copy of ViewState.

There are many ways to squirrel away ViewState. Some folks think that creating unique files on the file system and then collecting them later is a good technique. Personally, I would always rather add more memory than be bound to the always slower disk. No matter where you store ViewState, if you store it outside the page, then you'll need some process to later delete the older bits of state. This could take the form of a scheduled task that deletes files or a SQL Server job that removes rows from a database.

Folks who really want to get their ViewState out of the page have tried many ways to solve this problem. Listing 9-5 shows a hack that stores the ViewState value within the user's ASP.NET Session using a unique key per request. The ViewState string value that is usually sent out in a hidden form field is stored in the Session using the unique key, and then that considerably smaller key is put into a hidden form field instead. Therefore, each page gets its own Guid, as each HTTP request is unique. This Guid is declared as the ViewState "key" and is stored as its own hidden form field. This key is then used to store the ViewState in the Session.

Listing 9-5: Storing ViewState in the ASP.NET Session

C#

```csharp
private string _pageGuid = null;
public string PageGuid
{
    get
    {
        //Do we have it already? Check the Form, this could be a post back
        if (_pageGuid == null)
            _pageGuid = this.Request.Form["__VIEWSTATE_KEY"];
        //No? We'll need one soon.
        if (_pageGuid == null)
            _pageGuid = Guid.NewGuid().ToString();
        return _pageGuid;
    }
    set
    {
        _pageGuid = value;
    }
}

protected override object LoadPageStateFromPersistenceMedium()
{
    return Session[this.PageGuid];
}

protected override void SavePageStateToPersistenceMedium(object viewState)
{
    RegisterHiddenField("__VIEWSTATE_KEY", this.PageGuid);
    Session[this.PageGuid] = viewState;
}
```

VB

```vb
Dim _pageGuid As String = Nothing
Public Property PageGuid As String
    Get
        'Do we have it already? Check the Form, this could be a post back
        If (_pageGuid = Nothing) Then
            _pageGuid = Me.Request.Form("__VIEWSTATE_KEY")
        End If
```

```
            'No? We'll need one soon.
            If (_pageGuid = Nothing) Then
                _pageGuid = Guid.NewGuid.ToString
            End If
            Return _pageGuid
        End Get
        Set
            _pageGuid = value
        End Set
    End Property

    Protected Overrides Function LoadPageStateFromPersistenceMedium() As Object
        Return Session(Me.PageGuid)
    End Function

    Protected Overrides Sub SavePageStateToPersistenceMedium(ByVal viewState As Object)
        RegisterHiddenField("__VIEWSTATE_KEY", Me.PageGuid)
        Session(Me.PageGuid) = viewState
    End Sub
```

The load and save methods are very simple, just storing the PageGuid in the Session object and the ViewState object within the Session. The real magic happens in the new PageGuid page-level property. When the PageGuid is requested the first time, the form is checked for the unique key. If it's not there, a new key is created because it will likely be needed soon after. Remember also that all this code could be stored in a base page as shown in Chapter 3.

Moving ViewState to the Bottom of the Page

If your sites stay in the first few pages of Google's search results, it is said that you have "Google juice." Many developers worry that because ViewState's hidden form field appears very early in the page and almost always before any meaningful content, web bots and spiders such as Google won't bother looking past a giant glob of ViewState. To get around this problem you may want to move ViewState to the bottom of a rendered page. You likely wouldn't want to take the performance hit on every page for this hack, but certainly it's reasonable on occasion. It also gives you a great opportunity to override Render and seriously mess with the resulting HTML to include any other hacks or HTML modifications that you were previously unable to do using standard techniques.

Let's try this technique first. Override your page's Render method and call up to the base class's Render and insist that the page render in its entirety. The downside here, of course, is that by hacking into the render you're bypassing the buffered writing to the response output and dealing with strings. It's almost as if you're saying to the page, "Render yourself . . . stop! Wait. OK, continue, I'm done messing around."

Listing 9-6 uses the standard System.String.IndexOf method to find the first chunk of the ViewState's hidden form field. A little string calculation finds the end of the ViewState value, which you store for use later. After removing the ViewState just found, you look for the end of the form tag and insert the saved ViewState just before </form>.

Listing 9-6: Moving ViewState to the bottom of the page — technique 1

C#

```csharp
protected override void Render(System.Web.UI.HtmlTextWriter writer)
{
    System.IO.StringWriter stringWriter = new System.IO.StringWriter();
    HtmlTextWriter htmlWriter = new HtmlTextWriter(stringWriter);
    base.Render(htmlWriter);
    string html = stringWriter.ToString();
    int StartPoint = html.IndexOf("<input type=\"hidden\" name=\"__viewstate\"");
    if (StartPoint >= 0)
    {
        int EndPoint = html.IndexOf("/>", StartPoint) + 2;
        string viewstateInput = html.Substring(StartPoint, EndPoint - StartPoint);
        html = html.Remove(StartPoint, EndPoint - StartPoint);
        int FormEndStart = html.IndexOf("</form>") - 1;
        if (FormEndStart >= 0)
        {
            html = html.Insert(FormEndStart, viewstateInput);
        }
    }
    writer.Write(html);
}
```

VB

```vb
Protected Overrides Sub Render(ByVal writer As System.Web.UI.HtmlTextWriter)
    Dim stringWriter As System.IO.StringWriter = New System.IO.StringWriter
    Dim htmlWriter As HtmlTextWriter = New HtmlTextWriter(stringWriter)
    MyBase.Render(htmlWriter)
    Dim html As String = stringWriter.ToString
    Dim StartPoint As Integer
    StartPoint = html.IndexOf("<input type=\""hidden\"" name=\""__viewstate\""")
        If (StartPoint >= 0) Then
            Dim EndPoint As Integer = (html.IndexOf("/>", StartPoint) + 2)
            Dim viewstateInput As String
            viewstateInput = html.Substring(StartPoint, (EndPoint - StartPoint))
            html = html.Remove(StartPoint, (EndPoint - StartPoint))
            Dim FormEndStart As Integer = (html.IndexOf("</form>") - 1)
            If (FormEndStart >= 0) Then
                html = html.Insert(FormEndStart, viewstateInput)
            End If
        End If
        writer.Write(html)
End Sub
```

You might think that Listing 9-6 is a little worrisome because of the time it spends searching using IndexOf, a method not known for its speed with larger strings. However, when compared to the similar ViewState-moving method in Listing 9-7 using compiled regular expressions, Listing 9-6 consistently won. However, as with all code, including code in this book, run tests yourself and trust no one. Don't believe the old "measure twice, cut once" adage. I say, "code, measure, code, measure." You can spend all day presuming that some code will do this or that, but why not spend that time proving it? It may be possible that Listing 9-7 gets faster after a certain size threshold is reached by the rendered page. Use ASP.NET's built-in Tracing features to try for yourself!

Listing 9-7: Moving ViewState to the bottom of the page—technique 2

C#

```
static readonly Regex viewStateRegex = new Regex(@"(<input type=""hidden""
name=""__VIEWSTATE"" value=""[a-zA-Z0-9\+=\\/]+""
/>)",RegexOptions.Multiline|RegexOptions.Compiled);

static readonly Regex endFormRegex = new
Regex(@"</form>",RegexOptions.Multiline|RegexOptions.Compiled);

protected override void Render(HtmlTextWriter writer)
{
    //Defensive coding checks removed for speed and simplicity.
    // If these don't work out, you've likely got bigger problems.
    System.IO.StringWriter stringWriter = new System.IO.StringWriter();
    HtmlTextWriter htmlWriter = new HtmlTextWriter(stringWriter);
base.Render(htmlWriter);

    string html = stringWriter.ToString();
    Match viewStateMatch = viewStateRegex.Match(html);
    string viewStateString = viewStateMatch.Captures[0].Value;
    html = html.Remove(viewStateMatch.Index,viewStateMatch.Length);

    Match endFormMatch = endFormRegex.Match(html,viewStateMatch.Index);
    html = html.Insert(endFormMatch.Index,viewStateString);
    writer.Write(html);
}
```

VB

```
Dim viewStateRegex As Regex = New Regex("(<input type=""hidden""
name=""__VIEWSTATE"" value=""[a-zA-Z0-9\+=\\/]+"" />)", (RegexOptions.Multiline Or
RegexOptions.Compiled))

Dim endFormRegex As Regex = New Regex("</form>", (RegexOptions.Multiline Or
RegexOptions.Compiled))

Protected Overrides Sub Render(ByVal writer As HtmlTextWriter)
    'Defensive coding checks removed for speed and simplicity.
    ' If these don't work out, you've likely got bigger problems.
    Dim stringWriter As System.IO.StringWriter = New System.IO.StringWriter
    Dim htmlWriter As HtmlTextWriter = New HtmlTextWriter(stringWriter)
    MyBase.Render(htmlWriter)

    Dim html As String = stringWriter.ToString
    Dim viewStateMatch As Match = viewStateRegex.Match(html)
    Dim viewStateString As String = viewStateMatch.Captures(0).Value
    html = html.Remove(viewStateMatch.Index, viewStateMatch.Length)

    Dim endFormMatch As Match = endFormRegex.Match(html, viewStateMatch.Index)
    html = html.Insert(endFormMatch.Index, viewStateString)
    writer.Write(html)
End Sub
```

Notice that I've included a comment in the code that there aren't any exception blocks to handle things if they go awry. Ideally you would include checks for null object references and a try/catch block within this section. However, it's usually a good idea to catch only those exceptions for which something can be done. In this hack, if moving the ViewState fails, perhaps there's something larger wrong with the page and its rendering process that you'd want to know about. Exceptions are exceptional, and they are there to provide us with information. In this case, it's best to let any exceptions throw and be handled by page- or application-level handlers.

Wrapping Up

ViewState unquestionably serves a useful purpose by layering an eventing subsystem on top of HTML and HTTP, but we can continue to look for ways to minimize its page footprint while still taking advantage of the value it provides. You can inspect it and look for fat to trim, you can move it around, you can chop it up into smaller bits hoping no one will notice, you can compress it in place and pay a CPU cost, or you can hold it on the server side in memory or on the file system.

10

Cache Hacks

This chapter covers two key topics: static caching for object-oriented applications and an example ASP.NET cache viewer. Almost anyone can pick up an introductory book on ASP.NET 2.0, look in the MSDN Library, or even do an Internet search to learn about all the nifty, built-in features for caching that are available in ASP.NET 2.0. Rather than rehash that here, we'll consider an alternative form of caching and a way to look into the built-in cache and even modify it to some degree.

The hacks in this chapter will give you insight into how you can improve the performance of your application in ways that you are not likely to find in the textbooks. In addition, you'll learn how you can view and manage the ASP.NET cache, which gives you more control over your applications that are using the awesome features built into the framework. Even better, you can get this functionality with very little impact on your applications, even ones that are running today.

Static Caching

I'd wager that most Windows developers are familiar with what I'm referring to as *static caching* because what it ultimately boils down to is keeping a reference to an object in memory by using a static (shared in VB.NET) variable. Web developers may not be as familiar with it because they've relied upon the handy caching mechanisms built into the Web server, such as `Application`, `Cache`, and `Session`. But the underlying concept is really as simple as it sounds.

Those same Web developers might be asking why they should consider an alternative way of keeping objects in memory, and that's a perfectly fair question. The answer is that it can be easier to use and it is guaranteed to be there as long as the application domain for the application survives. Unlike the `Cache` object, which reserves the right to clean up cached objects if it feels it needs to, static caching will keep the objects until you specify otherwise, which is desirable for a lot of application-level caching.

In fact, because the static members are shared among all instances in memory, they are by nature more akin to the `Cache` and `Application` objects, so when you are considering the kinds of things you might want to store statically, you should really follow two rules: high read and low write. The main point of keeping the objects in memory is to decrease access time dramatically, but because the objects will be running in a multi-threaded server process, any writes will require exclusive locks to ensure consistency. To minimize locking, we want to only cache things that won't be modified very often. Typically, this would be application configuration, reference objects, and so on. In addition, you normally wouldn't want to cache user-specific objects this way in a Web application because that introduces session management, which has already been taken care of via the Session store. Again, when thinking of the kinds of things to cache statically, think more in terms of application-level objects that, ideally, don't change their state very often. This is where you'll get the biggest bang for the buck with this kind of caching.

Examining the Sample Cache Class

Enough talk—let's look at an example that demonstrates this concept. This section describes the sample Cache class to provide an idea of how static caching works. The following listing shows you the Cache class that is used in this chapter to exemplify static caching. I've trimmed a lot of the details to give you a high-level view of what it looks like:

```
public static class Cache
{
    public static event CacheChangeHandler CacheChanged;

    #region Caches
    private static List<HumanResources.Department> _departments;
    public static List<HumanResources.Department> Departments
    {
        get
        {
            if (_departments == null)
                throw new CacheNotInitializedException(
                    "Departments cache not initialized.");
            return _departments;
        }
    }

    private static List<HumanResources.Employee> _employees;
    public static List<HumanResources.Employee> Employees
    {
        get
        {
            if (_employees == null)
                throw new CacheNotInitializedException(
                    "Employees cache not initialized.");
            return _employees;
        }
    }
    #endregion

    #region RefreshCaches
    private static object _refreshLock = new object();
    public static void RefreshCaches(CacheRefreshOptions options)
    {
    }
```

```
        #endregion

        #region OnCacheChange
        public static void OnCacheChange(CacheRefreshOptions options)
        {
        }
        #endregion

        #region LoadCacheFromDatabase
        public static void LoadCacheFromDatabase<T>(List<T> cache,
            string commandName) where T : DomainBase, new()
        {
        }
        #endregion

        #region GetCachedSubset
        public static List<T> GetCachedSubset<T>(string commandName,
            int parentId, List<T> cache) where T : DomainBase
        {
        }
        #endregion

        #region GetByIdentifier
        public static T GetByIdentifier<T>(List<T> list, int id) where T : DomainBase
        {
        }
        #endregion
    }
```

At a high level, this class is, as I said, rather straightforward. The truly key elements are the caches themselves, which in this sample are static constructed types of the List<T> generic, one for employees and one for departments. At the core, this is what static caching is all about; it gives you a strongly typed direct reference to objects in memory.

The phrases *strongly typed* and *direct reference* are significant because the generic caches that come with ASP.NET provide you with neither of these features. They all give you things of type System.Object from their accessors that you must cast yourself, which with value types can introduce the additional overhead of boxing and unboxing. In addition, the built-in caching devices use dictionaries that introduce the overhead of looking up an item by a key in order to access it. Therefore, not only does static caching provide the added niceties of strong typing, it is also performs better.

Now, I'm not saying that the other caches are worthless — not by any means. They are quite valuable and have great usefulness for certain situations, but when it comes down to a question of objects that need to persist for the life of the application, you should consider static caching for these benefits. In addition, of course, the greater question of whether an application needs this level of engineering also comes into play. If you're not designing a strongly typed model to begin with, this strategy probably won't apply. I suggest using the built-in caching particularly when you want to cache page or page part output or when you want to get the expiration features out of the box. The kind of caching presented here is more useful when you design a strongly typed domain layer containing objects that will live for the duration of the application.

Going back to the previous class example, the next most important thing is the `RefreshCaches` method that is used to refresh (or initially load) the individual caches. The other methods are simply helpers used in the sample application to get at particular objects generically. The `CacheRefreshOptions` enum is listed next:

```
[Flags]
public enum CacheRefreshOptions
{
    None = 0,
    Departments = 1,
    Employees = 2,
    All = CacheRefreshOptions.Departments | CacheRefreshOptions.Employees
}
```

This is a standard flags enumeration that will have one option for each cache that needs to be handled individually. There are also the de facto groups of `None` and `All`; you could, if it made sense in your application, create other named groups, of course. The only other things of particular interest at this level are the `CacheChanged` event and the `OnCacheChange` method. These are used to provide a notification mechanism when the cache is changed. The delegate for the event follows:

```
public delegate void CacheChangeHandler(CacheRefreshOptions options);
```

To be notified of cache changes, you declare a method whose signature matches that of this delegate and then add a new `CacheChangeHandler` to the `CacheChanged` event for that method. Later in this chapter, you look at a possible application of this within a Web farm in order to keep the in-memory cache on servers synchronized.

Sample Solution Detail

For the sample in this chapter, I'm using the AdventureWorks database that comes with SQL Server 2005. I've selected a subset of data, primarily the Departments and Employees tables, to illustrate the concepts of static caching and distributed static cache invalidation. To access this data, I've written a handful of stored procedures: `HumanResources.GetAllDepartments`, `HumanResources.GetAllEmployees`, `HumanResources.GetDepartmentEmployees`, and `HumanResources.SaveDepartment`, all of which are located in the AdventureWorksDb project in the sample solution.

This section looks at the details of the sample solution, providing you with a much firmer understanding of how to implement your own static cache based on the example given here. On the application side of things, there's a simple class hierarchy that looks like this:

```
AdventureWorks.DomainBase
    AdventureWorks.HumanResources.Department
    AdventureWorks.Person
        AdventureWorks.HumanResources.Employee
```

The domain base, as you might imagine, provides common behaviors for the deriving classes to enable some polymorphic programming. It also holds some static configuration data to enable connectivity with the data store.

To centralize the static caching, I've created the `AdventureWorks.Cache` class that you've already looked at. There are also a couple of classes in the `AdventureWorks.Web` namespace that are used as part of the distributed static cache invalidation mechanism and the cache viewer, both of which will be covered later in this chapter.

Finally, there's a sample Web application that provides a listing of departments, employees within a selected department, and the capability to edit a particular department to illustrate that, unlike some forms of caching, static caching does not preclude editing of the data in memory; it also serves to illustrate how you trigger the distributed cache invalidation.

Initializing the Cache

You could initialize the cache in a number of ways. The simplest, and sometimes the best, way is by simply initializing it when the application starts. This, of course, would typically be best for items in the cache that will almost certainly be needed by the application at some point in its life. If there is great uncertainty as to necessity, it is better to use the lazy loading approach, which would involve a little more work and a tiny performance hit (due to the added null checking). In this sample, I took the first approach for simplicity's sake and because, more often than not, this kind of caching is used for the kinds of objects that the application will most likely need.

> While I chose to use employees in this example, it is possible that in a very large organization, it would not be desirable to cache that many objects that may or may not be used. This is another consideration to keep in mind when using static caching: Because it remains in memory for the life of the application, you need to carefully consider the impact that storing a particular class of object in memory will have. Unless you're Google, you probably wouldn't want to keep the entire Internet in memory.

The structure of the `Cache` class is such that you could still selectively initialize particular caches if you want to program that logic into your application—for example, you can call `RefreshCaches` with its individual options, but I think that I would rather build actual lazy loading into the cache accessor properties themselves if I wanted this approach. (In case you are unfamiliar with the term, *lazy loading* means loading when and only when you first access an object.)

Let's look at how to initialize the cache in this sample. In the Web application's `Global.asax` file, I have this method:

```
void InitApp()
{
    if (!initialized)
    {
        try
        {
            AdventureWorks.DomainBase.ConnectionString =
          ConfigurationManager.ConnectionStrings["AdventureWorks"].ConnectionString;
            AdventureWorks.DomainBase.DbFactoryName =
          ConfigurationManager.ConnectionStrings["AdventureWorks"].ProviderName;
```

```
            AdventureWorks.Cache.RefreshCaches(AdventureWorks.CacheRefreshOptions.All);
                AdventureWorks.Cache.CacheChanged +=
                    new AdventureWorks.CacheChangeHandler(RefreshFarm);
                initialized = true;
                this.Context.Cache.Insert("Test", "This is a test of the data cache.");
            }
            catch (Exception e)
            {
                initialized = false;
                throw e;
            }
        }
    }
```

And the application's `BeginRequest` handler looks like this:

```
void Application_BeginRequest(Object sender, EventArgs e)
{
    InitApp();
}
```

You may be asking yourself why I'd call this method in `BeginRequest` as opposed to putting the initialization code in the `Application_Start` method. The reason is because I want to ensure that my cache is initialized properly and that if an error occurs, the application won't run until I've fixed it. When you're dealing with a cache that your application depends upon and you don't bother checking to make sure it is initialized, you will likely get some really unusual red herring exceptions after the first load that can send you down the wrong path when debugging. To avoid this, I use the initialized flag to ensure that at least it thinks it loaded correctly. Similarly, because the `Application_Start` method fires only once on application start, I had to put this in an event handler that would be repeatedly called, like `Application_BeginRequest`.

In any case, whether you choose to follow this pattern or not to prefetch all your objects into the cache, you need to set the data store connection information and then call `Cache.RefreshCaches`, passing in the `All` option of the `CacheRefreshOptions` enumeration. At that point, barring an exception, your cache should be loaded for the duration of the application.

The next thing I did in the `InitApp` method was to wire up a handler for the `CacheChanged` event. This will be used to call other servers in the farm and let them know that the cache was modified. We'll get into the details of that later in this chapter.

Reading the Cache

The more common use of this kind of cache (and indeed the primary reason for using it) is the performance gains in reading. To illustrate how you might use this cache for reading within an ASP.NET application, I created a simple page to list departments and, subsequently, to list the employees in a department when it is selected. You, too, can run this sample assuming that you have ASP.NET 2.0, Visual Studio 2005, and SQL Server 2005 installed and have modified the connection settings for the Web application in the `web.config` file. The output for the department listing is shown in Figure 10-1.

Figure 10-1

Achieving this view was relatively simple. You need only to drag a GridView control onto the form and tell it to use an ObjectDataSource control to get at your cached objects. There is a catch, however: Because you are using the programmatically friendly approach of using static properties on your Cache class, you have to define an intermediary mechanism to present the objects in your cache the way that the ObjectDataSource control expects to see them, which is more aligned with your typical Data Transfer Object (DTO) pattern — static methods to get a data-containing object (or collection of them), to insert, update, and delete them.

Of course, you don't have to use an ObjectDataSource control; you could simply bind your grids like you used to in 1.1, setting the data source to Cache.SomePropertyCache, but that's not the way of 2.0. To avoid having to always write a shim, I would suggest creating a new ObjectDataSource control that can more intelligently interact with your domain layer if you're not using the DTO pattern. Were I writing this application for real, I would have done that to make it easier for ASP.NET to interact with my custom objects, but to stay focused and keep it simple I instead wrote the OdsShim class to provide the ObjectDataSource control with the interface it wants to see. The code for this class follows:

```
public static class OdsShim
{
  public static List<Department> GetDepartments()
  {
    return AdventureWorks.Cache.Departments;
  }

  public static List<Employee> GetDepartmentEmployees(int departmentId)
```

```
    {
        Department dept = AdventureWorks.Cache.GetByIdentifier(
        AdventureWorks.Cache.Departments, departmentId);
        if (dept == null)
            return null;
        return dept.Employees;
    }

    public static Department GetDepartment(int departmentId)
    {
        return AdventureWorks.Cache.GetByIdentifier(
            AdventureWorks.Cache.Departments, departmentId);
    }

    public static void SaveDepartment(string name, string groupName, int
original_departmentId)
    {
        Department dept = AdventureWorks.Cache.GetByIdentifier(
            AdventureWorks.Cache.Departments, original_departmentId);
        if (dept == null)
            dept = new Department();
        dept.Name = name;
        dept.GroupName = groupName;
        dept.SaveToDb();
    }
}
```

The `Select` method for the departments' ObjectDataSource control should be `OdsShim.Get Departments`, which simply returns the value of `AdventureWorks.Cache.Departments`. And that's pretty much it for that list.

If you select a department name, it will then display a list of the employees in that department, as shown in Figure 10-2.

Setting up this list is done more or less the same way as the first was done, except you simply add a control parameter for the ObjectDataSource control to get the selected department identifier from the departments list and pass it into the `OdsShim.GetDepartmentEmployees` method. This method finds the matching department in the department's cache and returns the `Employees` property for that department. If you look at the code for the `Employees` property, this uses the lazy loading pattern mentioned earlier.

Modifying the Cache

Up to this point, you've just looked at how you might want to read from the static cache, but given that there's some chance you may want to modify the data in the cache, I've written a little sample that illustrates the key concepts involved in doing that. This is what the other two methods (`GetDepartment` and `SaveDepartment`) in the `OdsShim` are for. In fact, they illustrate what you'd need to do to modify the cache from anywhere. The same basic steps would apply:

1. Get the object from the cache.

2. Change some state.

3. Save the changes.

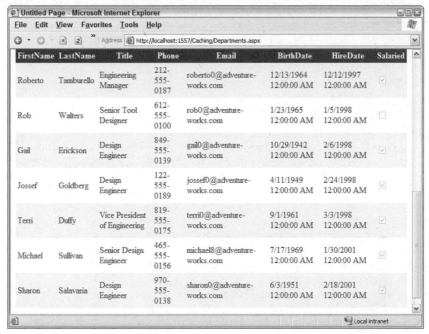

Figure 10-2

The GetDepartment method simply retrieves the department with the matching identifier from the cache. This is used on the following page to get a single instance for the FormView control to work with. Clicking the Edit link for a department takes you to the EditDepartment.aspx page, which has the aforementioned FormView control for editing department data. For this control's ObjectDataSource control, you simply need to set the Select method to the OdsShim.GetDeparment method, and the Insert and Update methods to the OdsShim.SaveDepartment method. I had to mess around with the item templates a bit to show only the department name and group, and I needed to set the DataKeyNames property on the FormView to be the DepartmentId property and tell it to use a QueryString parameter to get the department ID being edited.

After this is set up, you can run the form and edit the selected department. When you click Update, it will call the SaveDepartment method, which, as you can see in the earlier listing, tries to find the department by the original _departmentId using the same GetByIdentifier method. If it doesn't find a matching department, it creates a new one and then sets the properties, calling SaveToDb on the instance to persist the changes to the database.

Ideally, I would suggest writing (into the aforementioned custom ObjectDataSource control) the capability for it to automatically do what the SaveDepartment method does, which is to get the instance from the cache (for edits), set the bound properties on that instance, and then call an instance method on it, such as SaveToDb. At the very least, it would be nice for the standard ObjectDataSource control to accommodate getting a particular instance for an update using the specified Select method. I say this because there is the option for the ObjectDataSource control to pass in an instance with the bound properties set from the FormView, but it always creates a new instance for you, which defeats at least some of the usefulness of the cache itself.

That is the extent of the demo for simply using the cached objects. As you can see, with an approach like this, it is fairly simple to develop user interfaces surrounding the object model. Of course, this ease of use doesn't come for free; it requires a little more coding on the domain model level, but that is inherent to writing a reusable library for your domain solution. Next, you'll look at a way to use this hack in a farm situation to keep the caches on servers synchronized.

Cache Change Notifications

If you're hosting your ASP.NET application on a single Web server, the information presented thus far would be sufficient to get you going using static caching. However, if you are hosting the application on multiple servers in a Web farm, you need a way to let the other servers know when someone has modified this static cache so that they can update themselves to stay in sync.

To address this problem, the `Cache` class exposes the `CacheChanged` event, which you might recall your Web application subscribed to in the `AppInit` method. The code library also exposes the raw materials necessary to set up a Web service to receive cache change notifications, as well as a client class for sending those notifications. These are the `AdventureWorks.Web.Cache` and `AdventureWorks.Web.CacheClient` classes, respectively.

There's not much to either of these classes: The service class exposes one Web method that looks, amazingly enough, just like the `RefreshCaches` method in that is takes the `CacheRefreshOptions` enum to tell it which caches to refresh. And as you might guess, it simply turns around and calls the `RefreshCaches` method in its memory space. The client is just a cleaned-up version of what Visual Studio will generate for you when you add a Web reference to the service.

To implement this in your Web application instances — that is, on each server — you need to add an ASMX file to your Web application. In our sample, there's a `Cache.asmx` file off the application root whose sole content is this line of code:

```
<%@ WebService Language="C#" Class="AdventureWorks.Web.Cache" %>.
```

As you can see, it simply tells ASP.NET to look to the `AdventureWorks.Web.Cache` class for its implementation. Pretty easy, huh?

On the other side of things, you need to have your `CacheChanged` event handler method fire up an instance of the `AdventureWorks.Web.CacheClient` class for each of the servers in your farm, calling the `BeginRefreshCaches` method on each to asynchronously update their caches. This is illustrated in the `RefreshFarm` method in the `Global.asax` file, though it is commented out because the implementation of determining where the other servers are is left to you.

```
internal void RefreshFarm(AdventureWorks.CacheRefreshOptions options)
{
    // loop here through other servers in the farm and call them as follows
    // using (AdventureWorks.Web.CacheClient client =
    //    new AdventureWorks.Web.CacheClient("http://server2/Caching/Cache.asmx"))
    //    client.BeginRefreshCache(options, null, null);
}
```

In one case, I stored a list of the servers in the farm in the database and retrieved that list, looping through it and notifying each of the servers (except the one executing the request, of course) that the cache had changed. You may, alternatively, want to store that information in the `web.config` file if you don't want to bother with setting up and accessing the database. The key is that you are calling this Web service on each of the other servers in the farm to invalidate the caches specified by `CacheRefreshOptions`.

So how does `RefreshFarm` get called? You'll remember that I wired it up to the `CacheChanged` event. This event should be raised (via the `AdventureWorks.Cache.OnCacheChange` method) by any methods in your library that modify the cache. The following example illustrates where you might want to do that:

```
public virtual int SaveToDb()
{
  using (DbConnection conn = DomainBase.DbFactory.CreateConnection())
  {
    conn.ConnectionString = DomainBase.ConnectionString;
    using (DbCommand cmd = DomainBase.DbFactory.CreateCommand())
    {
      cmd.Connection = conn;
      cmd.CommandText = this.PersistenceProcedureName;
      cmd.CommandType = System.Data.CommandType.StoredProcedure;
      cmd.Connection.Open();
      this.AddParametersForSave(cmd);
      DbParameter parm = cmd.CreateParameter();
      parm.ParameterName = this.DatabaseIdentifierParameterName;
      parm.DbType = System.Data.DbType.Int32;
      parm.Value = this.DatabaseIdentifier ?? 0;
      parm.Direction = System.Data.ParameterDirection.InputOutput;
      cmd.Parameters.Add(parm);
      int retVal = cmd.ExecuteNonQuery();
      this.DatabaseIdentifier = (int)parm.Value;
      // If type is cached
      if (this.CacheOption != CacheRefreshOptions.None)
      {
        // add to cache if not there
        this.EnsureInCache();
        // notify cache of change
        AdventureWorks.Cache.OnCacheChange(this.CacheOption);
      }
      return retVal;
    }
  }
}
```

This method is found on the AdventureWorks.DomainBase class. I went to some lengths to make it generic enough to implement it on only the base class (an example of the aforementioned polymorphic behavior). Of course, if I were writing a real domain library, I would most likely use an object-relational mapper to simplify the code I have to write to achieve the same behavior, but I didn't want to introduce such a dependency in this sample.

> You may also note that all of the data access code uses the System.Data.Common factory approach for generic database programming. While obviously not required for this sample, it is nearly as easy as programming against a specific library (for example, SqlClient) and therefore illustrates how you can achieve some level of data store agnostic coding very easily in ADO.NET 2.0. You can find more information on this in Professional ADO.NET 2 by Wallace McClure, et al. (Wrox; ISBN 0-7645-8437-5).

The key thing we're looking at here is the if (this.CacheOption != CacheRefreshOptions.None) block of code in that method. Deriving classes should provide a value for the abstract CacheOption member on DomainBase that indicates the class's related CacheRefreshOption (if one exists). If so, the same class should also implement the EnsureInCache method, which will simply check the particular cache for the instance to make sure it is in it). Then all we need to do is call the OnCacheChange method with the instance's CacheOption to let it know that that particular cache has been modified. The OnCacheChange method looks like so:

```
public static void OnCacheChange(CacheRefreshOptions options)
{
    if (CacheChanged != null)
        CacheChanged(options);
}
```

It is just your standard event raising code; it checks to see whether anyone has subscribed (that it is not null) and then raises the event.

To tie it all back together, some code in your library modifies the cache, and that same code raises the CacheChanged event, as you subscribed to that event in your Web application's initialization, specifying that your RefreshFarm method should be called. The Framework calls your delegate, passing in CacheRefreshOptions, which indicates what in the cache was changed. Your RefreshFarm method then calls the RefreshCaches Web service on each of the other servers in the farm, passing along the information about which caches were changed. Each server, when it receives that request, then calls the RefreshCaches method on its in-memory cache, at which point its cache is refreshed, synchronizing it with the other servers in the farm.

Refreshing the Cache

Before you finish up this section on static caching, you should consider what needs to be done to actually refresh the cache. In order to do that, consider the details of the sample RefreshCaches method:

```
private static object _refreshLock = new object();
public static void RefreshCaches(CacheRefreshOptions options)
{
    lock (_refreshLock)
    {
        // Departments cache
        if ((options & CacheRefreshOptions.Departments) != 0)
        {
            if (_departments == null)
                _departments = new List<HumanResources.Department>();
            lock (_departments)
                LoadCacheFromDatabase(_departments,
                    "HumanResources.GetAllDepartments");
        }

        // Employees cache
        if ((options & CacheRefreshOptions.Employees) != 0)
        {
            if (_employees == null)
                _employees = new List<HumanResources.Employee>();
            lock (_employees)
```

```
                    LoadCacheFromDatabase(_employees,
                    "HumanResources.GetAllEmployees");
        }

    }
}
```

I included the_refreshLock here because it is integral to the method. It is used to ensure that only one thread at a time refreshes the cache. As you might imagine, it's very minimal synchronization, but it should at least prevent unexpected states during the cache refresh cycle.

For each particular cache, you will need to write some code. First, you will need to create a CacheRefresh Option that pertains to that cache (and be sure to add it to the All option). Then you will need to create the static field and property for that cache itself (see examples of this at the beginning of this chapter). Finally, you will need to add a check for the option in the RefreshCaches method and, if it is specified, do whatever's necessary to refresh that cache from its data store.

> **In the implementation in the sample, there is a small chance that another thread could access the cache field before it is fully initialized because it is instantiated and then locked. The worst-case scenario in this situation would be the result of an empty cache (as opposed to the CacheNotInitializedException that is normally thrown). After that, it is locked for the duration of the refresh, and because in this case the initialization should happen only once at the beginning of the application start, it should not be a problem.**

After you've taken these steps, you should be able to start having fun designing user interfaces, services, and so on, that take advantage of this cache and the friendly, strongly typed interface it provides. You will also likely notice your application running faster because of the caching itself and the increased performance that direct references give you over lookups.

Viewing the ASP.NET Cache

As I mentioned in the introduction, I'm not going to cover the details of the built-in caching in ASP.NET. That's not what this book is about. Rather, this book is about nifty ways of doing things, tricks of the trade that you can use to more fully round out your knowledge. With that in mind, the next thing we'll look at is an HTTP handler that you can plug into your application to see the items in the ASP.NET cache. In addition, excepting system cache entries, you can also use this utility to force items out of the cache. For more on HTTP handlers, see Chapter 17.

For simplicity's sake, the sample solution has the cache viewer built into the AdventureWorks library in the Web namespace; however, possibly the most valuable aspect of HTTP handlers is that you can plug them into your applications without having to build them into your applications' code. All you need to do is drop the assembly into your bin directory and add an entry in web.config to notify ASP.NET that you want it to plug in that handler. Although I chose to build it into the AdventureWorks library to reduce the number of projects in the solution, you could just as easily rip that class out and put it in its own assembly to be plugged into whatever applications you would like to use the cache viewer with.

Just what do you need to do to start using this great little utility? Because it is already built into a library that the Web application references, its assembly will already be copied to your Web application's `bin` directory; therefore, the only thing you need to do is add the following to `web.config`:

```
<httpHandlers>
  <add verb="*"
       path="CacheViewer.aspx"
       type="AdventureWorks.Web.CacheViewer, AdventureWorks"/>
</httpHandlers>
```

That's it! Now you're good to go; you can just browse to the mythical `CacheViewer.aspx` page off the application root and start looking at your application's use of the ASP.NET cache. I say "mythical" because you need to keep in mind that the path you specify for the HTTP handler is not a path to an actual file on the file system. It is just a moniker that ASP.NET uses to recognize that you want it to run requests for this path through the handler that you are registering.

Before you get into what makes it possible, let's look at just what this puppy can do. If you navigate to the path — that is, with no query string — it will display items that you have placed in the cache. In the sample application, it looks similar to Figure 10-3.

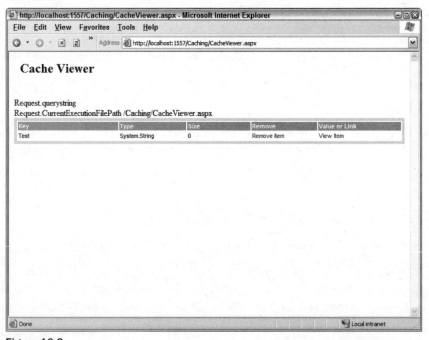

Figure 10-3

The only thing in there is a simple `Test` string that, if you'll recall from the previous section, was added in the `AppInit` method. This isn't very exciting, but I don't have to tell you that if you use the cache much in your applications and have wondered what's going on with it, then this could be a very valuable tool. It doesn't take much to imagine, and for a bit more detail, you can click the View Item link to bring up a page that provides additional detail, including the item's value, as shown in Figure 10-4.

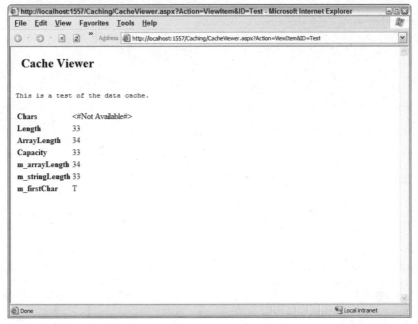

Figure 10-4

For the standard object, the viewer iterates through its fields and properties and attempts to display their values. For a data table, it has special handling to display it as an HTML table, and there is some special handling for a few other types such as `ArrayList`, `ListDictionary`, and `DataSet`.

Naturally, because you have the code and the know-how, you can write your own special handlers for types that you are storing in the cache. You can simply check the type (as is already being done for the others) in the `ProcessViewItem` method to add special handling for any type you like.

Similarly, for non-system items, you have the capability to remove them from the cache. This uses basically the same mechanics as viewing the item details in that it simply uses the key to remove the selected item from the cache. No rocket science there.

But that is not the genius of this hack. The genius, or rather the key contribution that this hack brings you, is how to get at and list the items in the cache because this is anything but intuitive. It is, in fact, not supposed to happen, so it is a hack in the more popular sense of the word as well. To do this, you have to use a little bit of reflection to get at the non-public members of the `Cache` object. This happens in the `GetCache` method that follows:

```
private Hashtable GetCache(HttpContext currentContext)
{
  FieldInfo fieldCacheInt =
   currentContext.Cache.GetType().GetField("_cacheInternal",
    BindingFlags.NonPublic | BindingFlags.Instance | BindingFlags.GetField);

  object cacheInt = fieldCacheInt.GetValue(currentContext.Cache);

  FieldInfo fieldEntries = cacheInt.GetType().GetField("_entries",
```

```
            BindingFlags.NonPublic | BindingFlags.Instance);

    Hashtable hashEntries = fieldEntries.GetValue(cacheInt) as Hashtable;
    Hashtable hashCopy = new Hashtable(hashEntries.Count);

    lock (hashEntries)
    {
      foreach (DictionaryEntry entry in hashEntries)
      {
        hashCopy.Add(entry.Key, entry.Value);
      }

    }

    return hashCopy;

}
```

The first thing this method does is get the `_cacheInternal` field on the `Cache` type and retrieve the current context's instance value for that field. On that instance, you need the `_entries` field to get a hashtable that contains all the items in the cache, including system items that were placed there by the ASP.NET runtime. The final step before returning is to make a shallow copy of that hashtable so that the rest of the process can hack away at that table without worrying about it being modified by other threads and, consequently, throwing an exception.

Now that we've got this list of entries, you'd think we could just render out the key-value pairs in that table, but the types of the entries are not so friendly; they're actually instances of the `System.Web` `.Caching.CacheEntry` type, so there is still a little more magic to work to display the actual information that you are after. That magic happens in the `ProcessDefaultView` method, of which an excerpt is shown next:

```
foreach (DictionaryEntry objItem in m_CacheCopy)
{
  object cacheEntry = objItem.Value;
  FieldInfo fieldCacheEntry = objItem.Key.GetType().GetField("_key",
    BindingFlags.NonPublic | BindingFlags.Instance | BindingFlags.GetField);

  strName = (string)fieldCacheEntry.GetValue(objItem.Key);

  FieldInfo fieldCacheEntryValue = cacheEntry.GetType().GetField("_value",
    BindingFlags.NonPublic | BindingFlags.Instance | BindingFlags.GetField);

  object itemObject = fieldCacheEntryValue.GetValue(cacheEntry);


  PropertyInfo propPublic = cacheEntry.GetType().GetProperty("IsPublic",
    BindingFlags.NonPublic | BindingFlags.Public | BindingFlags.Instance
        | BindingFlags.GetProperty);


  bool publicEntry = (bool)propPublic.GetValue(cacheEntry,null);

  if (strName != null)
  {
```

```
    bAltRow = BuildCacheItem(currentContext, tbl, strName,
        bAltRow,itemObject,publicEntry);
    }
}
```

This little beauty loops through each entry in our copy of the Cache's _entries hashtable and, again using reflection, gets the _key field on the key instance and the _value field on the value instance to get the actual key-value pair that we are looking for. Because we know the key will be a string, we can cast to it directly. For the value, of course, we have to stick with System.Object because it could be anything.

The last thing this does is get the value of the IsPublic property on the cache entry to determine whether this was something added by user code or system code. That information comes in handy when rendering because in the BuildCacheItem method, it is used to determine first whether the item should even be displayed and second whether it can be removed by the viewer.

Whether it is displayed is determined by a query string option that you can specify. If you add ShowSystem=true to the query string, it displays the system items as shown in Figure 10-5. Note how the only item you can remove is the one you added in your application start.

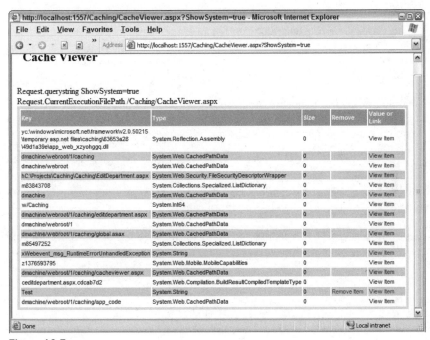

Figure 10-5

Those are the really key contributions that this hack makes. Everything beyond that is candy to make displaying the things in the cache more meaningful, and I encourage you to take the code and run with it, modifying it to suit you or to handle your own special types. Or, of course, you might be able to just use the basic utility provided here and drop it into your applications today. Either way, I'm sure it can add value to your tool repertoire.

Wrapping Up

This chapter covered two hacks. The first is a combination showing how ASP.NET developers can use object-oriented design to their advantage via statically caching their strongly typed domain objects and how they can keep those caches in sync in a Web farm scenario. The second hack is a drag-and-drop utility that can enable you to start viewing items in your ASP.NET caches today.

If you are building or want to build reusable domain class libraries and want to make them easier and faster to use for building user interfaces like ASP.NET applications, you can use the concepts outlined in the first section of this chapter. The key things to remember are that you want to consider caching objects that are high use, high read, and, preferably, low write. They don't need to be read-only, but if you are going to modify them, you need to be concerned with thread synchronization (because ASP.NET is multi-threaded), which introduces the need for locking, and locking can introduce performance bottle-necks, especially if it is not done correctly. That's why storing only low-write objects is best.

In addition, you need to concern yourself with the use of the objects in question. If they are user-specific, you will be better off using a user-specific store such as ASP.NET's Session store, which is very flexible when it comes to storage location. While you could fairly easily store per-user objects in a static cache, you would also have to think about how to clean them out as sessions die.

The last caveat to consider with static caching is memory usage. The ASP.NET `Cache` object has a lot of built-in memory management to help alleviate potential memory problems. Be especially mindful of the size of the things that you are statically caching on a server. Some things may be low-write but also involve an unacceptable need for storage space in memory, in which case you're better off sticking with the built-in `Cache` object.

Caching can dramatically improve your application performance, but you need to be aware of the potential issues and plan accordingly. If you are in doubt about caching a particular thing, test it. Testing is the best way to find out in a concrete way how caching will affect your application.

However, if you do run into problems, it is great to have a utility that you can plug into your application to help you find and diagnose potential caching problems in your application. The second hack in this chapter is just that tool, and even provides you with a possible resolution for some scenarios by allowing you to manually remove items cached by your application.

All of the code and concepts in this chapter are yours for the taking. The ball's in your court, and, if I may quote Brian Foote, "go ye forth and hack!"

11

Moving to ASP.NET 2.0 from 1.x

ASP.NET v2.0 offers a plethora of new functionality for being more productive in building Web applications. Its features are so compelling that you will want to move to it as quickly as possible. However, before dumping that clunky old ASP.NET v1.1 application, consider how much time you've put into building it. Your time has value for yourself, your employer, or the customer for whom you are providing services. There could be cost involved in reworking a project, and throwing it away may not be the most economical solution. It is often sensible to preserve your investment in existing code.

One smart strategy that preserves investment is to migrate an existing ASP.NET v1.x application to ASP.NET v2.0. To help with this process, Visual Studio 2005 has an automated wizard to convert your legacy ASP.NET 1.x applications to ASP.NET 2.0. This gives you the best of all worlds: preserving investment while taking advantage of new features as you add new functionality.

For the simplest scenarios, this works great. However, you need to know several things to keep out of trouble. ASP.NET 2.0 has specially named directories, files are moved, and other transformations occur during the process, all of which I discuss in relevant portions of this chapter. This chapter identifies several challenges with the migration process and offers strategies for helping you make the transition smoother.

The approach we take is to build a sample ASP.NET v1.1 application. It contains features that expose some of the problems you'll encounter during migration. We'll then perform the migration and identify those problems and show how to work around them. Because each site is different, this chapter can't begin to describe every conceivable scenario, but it is hoped that it will give you a strategy for performing a migration with much greater success than if you went through the process alone.

Creating the Demo v1.*x* Application

You perform a conversion from an existing application to a new one so that you can save time up front by moving to ASP.NET v2.0 and then beginning to use new features gradually, when time is available. Upgrading an existing code base can preserve investment and save money, while enabling you to take advantage of new features to enhance an application.

This section shows how to create a small application that is built using ASP.NET v1.1. It encompasses many of the features that you'll have to pay attention to when doing an upgrade. Therefore, you can use this application yourself and practice working around the problems you'll encounter when upgrading your own Web applications. The sample application does not represent a specific site that you can find on the Web, nor is it a complete application. Its purpose is simply to show you conditions that exist in ASP.NET v1.1 and demonstrate the conversion to ASP.NET v2.0. This section simply describes the application; the "Understanding Migration" section, which follows, demonstrates the conversion that occurs when you run this sample application through the ASP.NET v2.0 Migration Wizard.

User Controls

The sample site has two user controls: Header.ascx and Menu.ascx.

Header.ascx

The Header control appears at the top of each page and simply provides a title for the site. Listing 11-1 shows the HTML from this control. Because the Header control doesn't have a code implementation, the code-behind is not shown.

Listing 11-1: The Header control

```
<%@ Control
  Language="c#"
  AutoEventWireup="false"
  Codebehind="Header.ascx.cs"
  Inherits="MvpHacks.Header"
  TargetSchema="http://schemas.microsoft.com/intellisense/ie5"%>
<H1 align="center">
  <FONT style="BACKGROUND-COLOR: red" color="white">
       Professional ASP.NET 2.0 MVP Hacks
  </FONT>
</H1>
```

During conversion in the section "Understanding User Control Reference Changes," you'll see how the Conversion Wizard modifies the code in Listing 11-1.

Menu.ascx

The Menu control provides navigation among the pages in the MVPHacks site. Listing 11-2 shows the HTML for this control. It doesn't have a code implementation, so the code-behind is not shown.

Listing 11-2: The Menu control

```
<%@ Control
 Language="c#"
 AutoEventWireup="false"
 Codebehind="Menu.ascx.cs"
 Inherits="MvpHacks.Menu"
 TargetSchema="http://schemas.microsoft.com/intellisense/ie5"%>
<TABLE id="Table1" style="WIDTH: 96px; HEIGHT: 63px" cellSpacing="0"
cellPadding="10" width="96"
    bgColor="red" border="0">
    <TR>
        <TD>
            <P>
                <asp:HyperLink
                    id="hlnkHome"
                    runat="server"
                    ForeColor="White"
                    Font-Bold="True"
                    NavigateUrl="Default.aspx">
                        Home
                </asp:HyperLink><BR>
                <asp:HyperLink
                    id="hlnkHacks"
                    runat="server"
                    ForeColor="White"
                    Font-Bold="True"
                    NavigateUrl="Hacks.aspx">
                        Hacks
                </asp:HyperLink>
                <asp:HyperLink
                    id="hlnkLogin"
                    runat="server"
                    ForeColor="White"
                    Font-Bold="True"
                    NavigateUrl="Login.aspx">
                        Login
                </asp:HyperLink></P>
        </TD>
    </TR>
</TABLE>
```

Classes

The Default.aspx page has a single class named TypeViewer. Listing 11-3 shows the code for this class. One significant thing to pay attention to is that this class is defined in the code-behind file of the Default.aspx page. This is bad form, but it is defined this way to show the problems it will cause during conversion. In the next section, you'll see what problems this causes and how to fix them.

Listing 11-3: The TypeViewer class

```
internal class TypeViewer
{
    public string GetTypeInfo(Type type)
    {
        StringBuilder typeInfo =
            new StringBuilder("<p>Type Info:</p>");

        MemberInfo[] members = type.GetMembers();

        foreach (MemberInfo member in members)
        {
            typeInfo.AppendFormat("{0} {1}<br>",
                member.MemberType,
                member.Name);
        }

        return typeInfo.ToString();
    }
}
```

The code in Listing 11-3 is part of the `Default.aspx` code-behind page. During conversion, the Conversion Wizard will extract this class and move it to the `App_Code` directory.

Pages

The sample website has three Web form pages: `Default.aspx`, `Hacks.aspx`, and `Login.aspx`. These pages demonstrate conversions that occur during the migration process. The `Default.aspx` and `Hacks.aspx` pages, not shown, are simply added to the sample website to demonstrate that changes made to all of the pages are consistent. If you are interested in the contents of all these pages, you can see them in the code associated with this book.

The `Login.aspx` page offers forms-based authentication for the sample website. It is included to show that your existing ASP.NET v1.1 forms-based authentication code is not changed during the conversion. Listing 11-4 shows the HTML for this page.

Listing 11-4: The Login.aspx page

```
<%@ Page
    language="c#"
    Codebehind="Login.aspx.cs"
    AutoEventWireup="false"
    Inherits="MvpHacks.Login" %>
<%@ Register TagPrefix="uc1" TagName="Menu" Src="Menu.ascx" %>
<%@ Register TagPrefix="uc1" TagName="Header" Src="Header.ascx" %>
<!DOCTYPE HTML PUBLIC "-//W3C//DTD HTML 4.0 Transitional//EN" >
<HTML>
    <HEAD>
        <title>MVP Hacks</title>
    </HEAD>
    <body>
        <form id="Form1" method="post" runat="server">
```

```
<uc1:Header id="Header1" runat="server"></uc1:Header>
<TABLE
    id="Table1"
    cellSpacing="1"
    cellPadding="1"
    width="100%"
    border="0">
    <TR>
        <TD style="WIDTH: 110px" vAlign="top" align="left">
            <uc1:Menu id="Menu1" runat="server"></uc1:Menu>
        </TD>
        <TD vAlign="top" align="left">
            <P align="center"><BR>
                <asp:Label
                    id="lblError"
                    runat="server"
                    ForeColor="Red"></asp:Label><BR><BR>
            </P>
            <P>
                <TABLE
                    id="Table2"
                    cellSpacing="1"
                    cellPadding="1"
                    width="300"
                    align="center"
                    border="0">
                    <TR>
                        <TD>
                            <asp:Label
                                id="lblUserID"
                                runat="server">
                                    User ID:
                            </asp:Label>
                        </TD>
                        <TD>
                            <asp:TextBox
                                id="txtUserID"
                                runat="server"
                                Width="175px"></asp:TextBox>
                        </TD>
                    </TR>
                    <TR>
                        <TD>
                            <asp:Label
                                id="lblPassword"
                                runat="server">
                                    Password:
                            </asp:Label>
                        </TD>
                        <TD>
                            <asp:TextBox
                                id="txtPassword"
                                runat="server"
                                TextMode="Password"
```

(continued)

259

Listing 11-4 *(continued)*

```
                                        Width="175px"></asp:TextBox>
                        </TD>
                    </TR>
                    <TR>
                        <TD colSpan="2">
                            <asp:CheckBox
                                id="chkRememberMe"
                                runat="server"
                                Text="Remember Me"></asp:CheckBox>
                        </TD>
                    </TR>
                </TABLE>
            </P>
            <P align="center">
                <asp:Button
                    id="btnLogin"
                    runat="server"
                    Text="Log In"></asp:Button>
            </P>
            <P>
                <asp:Label
                    id="lblTypeInfo"
                    runat="server"></asp:Label>
            </P>
        </TD>
    </TR>
</TABLE>
    </form>
</body>
</HTML>
```

> Your days spent writing login pages are numbered. With the upcoming release of
> ASP.NET v2.0, you won't need to do all this manual work because it includes an entire
> suite of security controls, including the Login control, that make all of this so easy.

The Conversion Wizard will convert the `Login.aspx` page, shown in Listing 11-4 with no problem. This demonstrates that you will be able to migrate existing sites based on ASP.NET v1.1 Forms Authentication to ASP.NET v2.0.

The new Login control will also allow you to avoid writing any code for implementing forms-based authentication. Of course, the current application is ASP.NET v1.1, so you must write code to authenticate the user. Listing 11-5 shows the code-behind for `Login.aspx.cs`.

Listing 11-5: Code for Login.aspx.cs

```
using System;
using System.Collections;
using System.ComponentModel;
```

```
using System.Data;
using System.Drawing;
using System.Web;
using System.Web.Security;
using System.Web.SessionState;
using System.Web.UI;
using System.Web.UI.WebControls;
using System.Web.UI.HtmlControls;

namespace MvpHacks
{
    public class Login : System.Web.UI.Page
    {
        protected System.Web.UI.WebControls.TextBox txtUserID;
        protected System.Web.UI.WebControls.TextBox txtPassword;
        protected System.Web.UI.WebControls.Button btnLogin;
        protected System.Web.UI.WebControls.Label lblError;
        protected System.Web.UI.WebControls.Label lblUserID;
        protected System.Web.UI.WebControls.Label lblPassword;
        protected System.Web.UI.WebControls.CheckBox chkRememberMe;
        protected System.Web.UI.WebControls.Label lblTypeInfo;

        private void Page_Load(object sender, System.EventArgs e)
        {
            TypeViewer typeView = new TypeViewer();

            // display type information on page
            lblTypeInfo.Text = typeView.GetTypeInfo(this);
        }

    // OnInit and InitializeComponent elided for clarity

        private void btnLogin_Click(object sender, System.EventArgs e)
        {
            // verify login credentials
            if (FormsAuthentication.Authenticate(
                txtUserID.Text, txtPassword.Text))
            {
                // issue authentication ticket (cookie) and
                // send them to their original destination
                FormsAuthentication.RedirectFromLoginPage(
                    txtUserID.Text, chkRememberMe.Checked);
            }
            else
            {
                lblError.Text = "Invalid Credentials!";
            }
        }
    }
}
```

You don't have to use the new security controls. Migrating an existing site is a valid reason not to use them. Otherwise, I would choose to be more productive, especially when building a new ASP.NET v2.0 site, and use the new security controls.

Understanding Migration

The easy part of performing a migration is using the Conversion Wizard. Most of the time the migration occurs without error. If there are errors during conversion, you will be able to see them in a report that the Migration Wizard creates for you. The more challenging parts of migration are understanding where files went to, the internal changes to the files, and problems that could occur during deployment. The following sections look at each of these issues and provide ideas that can help in your own migrations.

Performing the Migration

Given an existing website, starting a migration is simple. You can take the following actions to perform the conversion:

1. Open Visual Studio 2005 and then open the existing website. The Open Web Site dialog box has numerous options, including File System, Local IIS, FTP Site, Remote Site, and Source Control, so you can specify the type of website to open. Select Local IIS, select the site that appears in the tree on the right, and then click Open. The site is the sample site that I introduced in the previous section. For the purposes of this discussion, you can assume that the site is in a virtual directory named MvpHacks. If you are using the code that comes with this book, create an IIS virtual directory named MvpHacks that refers to the physical directory where you decide to put the code.

2. Visual Web Developer recognizes when an ASP.NET 1.1 site is being opened and launches the Visual Studio Conversion Wizard. Click the Next button when you see the Welcome screen.

3. On the Choose Whether to Create a Backup screen, choose Yes to create a backup before converting. If you don't want the default location, click the Browse button to change it. Click the Next button.

4. The Ready to Convert screen summarizes your choices. Click the Finish button, allowing Visual Web Developer to perform the conversion.

5. When done, the wizard displays a Conversion Complete screen. Leave Show the Conversion Log When the Wizard Is closed checked. Click the Close button.

After you run the Conversion Wizard, the project opens in your work environment with several changes. One of the first things you might notice is that there is no longer a project file. The project node in Solution Explorer refers to the virtual directory for the website. Structurally, there is a new ConversionReport.txt file, and AssemblyInfo.cs, Global.asax.cs, and other class files have been moved into a new App_Code directory:

```
C:\Documents and Settings\%user%\My Documents\Visual Studio 2005\Projects\
MvpHacks\UpgradeLog.XML
```

Figure 11-1 shows the project after the Conversion Wizard runs.

The log files don't overwrite each other. Instead, a new one is added with a higher number. For example, a second conversion would produce a file named UpgradeLog2.XML in the same directory.

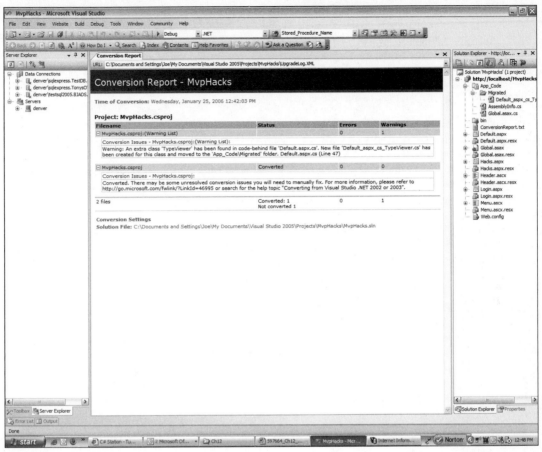

Figure 11-1

Where Did My Old Website Go?

While running the Conversion Wizard, if you selected "Yes" to create a backup before converting, then your ASP.NET v1.1 files will be copied to the location you specified. By default, the conversion wizard copies them to `C:\Documents and Settings\%user%\My Documents\Visual Studio 2005\ Projects\MvpHacks\Backup`.

To prevent overwriting an old backup, subsequent backups are copied to a new directory. The directory name is incremented by 1. For example, the default second backup of the MvpHacks website would be `C:\Documents and Settings\%user%\My Documents\Visual Studio 2005\Projects\ MvpHacks\Backup1`.

Backing up is a smart thing to do because you could have problems with the conversion and want to revert to the original version to start over. You'll also be safe if you're using source control and have ensured that everything has been checked in before the conversion. In some cases, you'll want to revert back to the original website to make corrections and then redo the conversion. Having the backup available for a quick copy and paste is convenient.

When you need to restore, consider backing up the current conversion copy. That way, if your second shot at conversion doesn't yield the desired results or you decide that modifying the converted site would be easier, you can restore the conversion.

To avoid Windows file-locking problems, ensure that Visual Web Developer is closed before restoring the site. Then copy the ASP.NET v1.x backup files from the backup directory to the physical directory, referred to by the virtual directory. You must also change the IIS ASP.NET version back to 1.x by opening IIS, navigating to and right-clicking the virtual directory, selecting Properties, clicking the ASP.NET tab, and selecting the proper version from the drop-down list, shown in Figure 11-2.

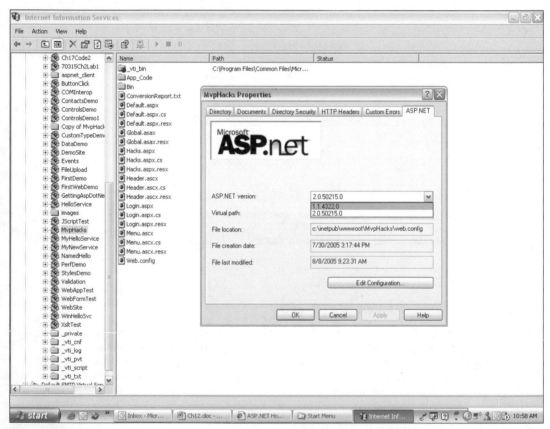

Figure 11-2

You'll see the error message shown in Figure 11-3 if you don't change the ASP.NET version number. The message "Unable to start debugging on the web server" likely won't make sense to many people. It is more a symptom of the true problem, rather than a descriptive root cause.

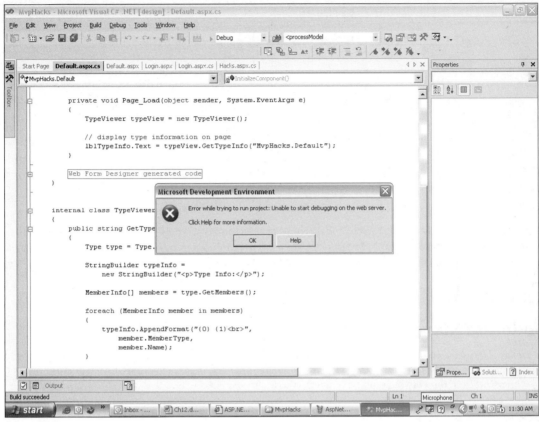

Figure 11-3

Significant File Changes

This section discusses the file changes that occur in the sample website. The following code snippet shows the Page directive from Default.aspx after the conversion:

```
<%@ Page Language="c#" Inherits="MvpHacks.Default" CodeFile="Default.aspx.cs" %>
```

This differs from Listing 11-4 in that the CodeBehind attribute is replaced with CodeFile. You no longer have AutoEventWireup. Also, the Inherits attribute is a little misleading. Because the CodeFile and the HTML page are partial types of the same type, they both inherit the Page class. If I were designing ASP.NET v2.0, I would have renamed Inherits to TypeName or something more meaningful.

What was once called a code-behind file is now referred to as a CodeFile in the Page directive of the HTML page. There are a few significant changes that you should be aware of. Listing 11-6 shows these changes.

Listing 11-6: A converted code file

```
public partial class Default : System.Web.UI.Page
{

    protected void Page_Load(object sender, System.EventArgs e)
    {
        TypeViewer typeView = new TypeViewer();

        // display type information on page
        lblTypeInfo.Text = typeView.GetTypeInfo(this);
    }

     // OnInit and InitializeComponent elided for clarity
}
```

Listing 11-6 shows what happens to code-behind classes after conversion. All control declarations are removed. This is because the Default class has a partial modifier, meaning that it is part of the same class as the HTML page. When code is generated for the HTML page, it will contain declarations for all the types on the page. The variable names used for controls in the CodeFile must match control ids in the HTML. The Conversion Wizard doesn't change any ids.

Understanding User Control Reference Changes

In ASP.NET v1.1 you needed a reference to all controls in your code-behind file. This developed from the natural hierarchy whereby the ASP.NET HTML page inherited the code behind. Because the controls were protected, the HTML could be converted to a derived class where the code could properly reference the control.

This changes in ASP.NET v2.0 because both the HTML and code file (formerly code-behind) are part of the same partial class. Therefore, both are compiled together. Because they are the same type, an explicit declaration of controls is not required in the code file because it is already declared in the HTML file. All you need to do is reference the control with a variable name that is the same as the id attribute of its corresponding HTML element.

Conversion Problems

While the conversion itself appears to run fine, a couple of things may not work quite right afterwards. You may not see them by running the new ASP.NET v2.0 project in the development environment, but they could appear during deployment.

Here's a typical example: Referring to the sample application for this chapter, the TypeViewer class (refer to Listing 11-3) resides inside the code-behind file of the Default class. In the development environment, code runs and executes as a single assembly. In this case, the Conversion Wizard is smart enough to avoid a problem by moving the class into the Migrated folder under App_Code (refer to Figure 11-1). (I mention this behavior because it could surprise you if you aren't expecting it.) The Conversion Report, also shown in Figure 11-1, provides a warning, and you should take the time to review the new class file to ensure that your code will work properly.

Again, in the spirit of hacks, we add value only to existing features, rather than duplicate documentation. For more information on specific issues, check out the article by Michael Bundschuh titled "Common ASP.NET 2.0 Conversion Issues and Solutions" at `http://msdn.microsoft.com/asp.net/default.aspx?pull=/library/en-us/dnaspp/html/upgradingaspnet.asp`, which offers additional guidance on conversion problems.

> MSDN is notorious for breaking links, so you may have to do a search for Michael Bundschuh's article sometime in the future.

Wrapping Up

This chapter introduced a sample application you can use to experiment with the conversion process. It included a few features to demonstrate what still works and what will break. For example, forms-based authentication still works but classes inside a code-behind file will break the application.

Visual Web Developer detects an ASP.NET 1.x application and automatically launches a wizard to help you step through the process. The wizard is easy to use, but files are changed and moved and you need to understand these changes. You also need to know how to step back out of a conversion, in case the conversion doesn't produce the results you want or changes would be easier to make before converting, rather than after.

12

Deployment Hacks

Congratulations. If you have made it this far then you have successfully built an ASP.NET application that you want to deploy. Deployment can take many forms, so this chapter does not cover all possible options. In fact, the approach I take here is to build on the other excellent resources that are out there to try to provide additional information that is not as easily found.

By now I think it is common knowledge that deployment of an ASP.NET application could be as simple as using the xcopy command or Windows Explorer to copy the files to the target server followed by setting up the virtual directory or website on IIS to point to the copied files. Production deployment is much more than that and ties in with a much broader configuration management of your application. It also entails making choices and trade-offs with regard to the amount of information and customization that takes place and the impact on the overall application lifecycle.

Like testing, how you will deploy an application is as important a task to think about early in your application development process as the development itself. One of the most critical concepts that is decided is who will do the "production build" of the application. Ideally, the application in question is stored in a source control system — for example, Visual Source Safe or Team System. When it comes time for deployment, a copy of that version is pulled, built, and deployed.

In this chapter we will explore the built-in capabilities of Visual Studio 2005 to handle deployment of Web applications. We will also be exploring the Web Deployment Tool, which the ASP.NET team later released as an add-in, to make deployments even easier.

Copy Web Site Wizard

New to Visual Studio 2005 is the capability it offers from the Website menu to select the Copy Web Site option (Website➪Copy Web Site). This new option opens up the user interface shown in Figure 12-1, which shows the files on the left side that make up the website. The right side is intended to show the files from the target server. Using this tool you would select between one of the following supported protocols (as shown in Figure 12-1): File System, Local IIS, FTP Site, and Remote Site. By far, the best addition for those who host their site with a hosting company is the support for FTP.

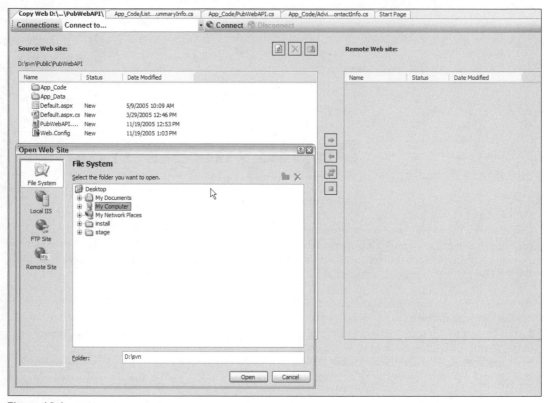

Figure 12-1

Not only does this tool give you the capability to move files, it attempts to make sure you know the status of the files on the target server. Care should be taken to ensure that if you use the option to copy files from the host that you don't overwrite your project files. If you are going to copy files from the host, creating a backup of your local files would be a good idea.

It's important to note that using this option does not pre-compile your website and therefore it is necessary to deploy to the target site the source files that are part of the website. If you reference any other components they will also be copied. Having source for your application on the server is not always the best option, as it leaves it open for prying eyes to discover your coding secrets. Later in this chapter you will look at how to use the pre-compile option, which can pare the website down to assemblies that need to be deployed.

In ASP.NET 1.1 you were able to minimize this problem and not copy the code-behind (or *code separation files* in ASP.NET 2.0 lingo) to the server. The reason you could do this was because they had already been compiled into the website assembly. In ASP.NET 2.0, unless you are using the pre-compiled option discussed later in this chapter, the assembly for the website is not created until the website is used, and then only a temporary one is created.

This feature of Visual Studio 2005 is best used for smaller projects that don't involve multiple developers. Because user intervention is required to operate the wizard, it is not suited for use on a build server. Furthermore, if you have multiple developers, it opens up the possibility that each time you deploy your files, a different set of referenced files will be deployed. For example, assume that the website references an additional component library. Developer A deploys to the test or production site and has a version of that file from the same day. Later in the day another deployment happens and Developer B does the deploy. Developer B is not as good at getting the latest source code so the component that is referenced on his computer is three days old. When he does the publish, the three-day-old component is referenced and put on the server. That creates inconsistent results, and could crash your website in an obvious way if you're lucky, or just simply create problems that are hard to track down and waste your team's time. Versioning issues created during the build process can be some of the hardest-to-detect problems and can consume an unpredictable amount of the team's time to resolve.

Ultimately, Copy Website is a good additional feature but one best used on your own projects or in a very controlled environment with multiple developers.

Publish Web Site Wizard

When using Visual Studio 2005 as a developer, another simple option of deploying is to use the Publish Web Site menu option (Build⇨Publish Web Site), which can be found under the Build menu in Visual Studio 2005. Figure 12-2 shows the dialog box that appears, which will prompt you for options prior to creating a directory that is a copy of the relevant files for deployment.

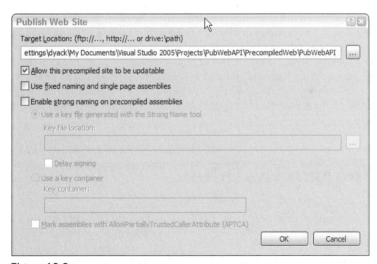

Figure 12-2

The Publish Web Site process is started by user intervention but it takes care of running the pre-compile on a site and building a folder with the appropriate output files. The biggest difference between this wizard and the Copy Web Site Wizard to start with is that assemblies are actually built for the site contents and placed in the bin folder. When using the Publish Web Site process, the code-behind or code separation files are not needed at deploy time so they are not copied.

An important choice you make in this dialog is whether or not you check the "Allow this precompiled site to be updatable" option. When this option is disabled (unchecked), the markup for the pages is deployed with the following text in the file:

```
This is a marker file generated by the precompilation tool, and should not be
deleted!
```

That's what you would see if you were to open default.aspx in the output folder after running the pre-compilation.

As a general rule of thumb, turning off this option is best suited for vendor applications or applications that you deploy on servers that you do not control. Prior to ASP.NET 2.0, you could use code obfuscators to hide the code in an assembly but you couldn't get around having to give someone the markup on the page. Most people would agree that the markup is not as easy to hack compared to having the code to the application as well, but it still leaves a lot of room for creative thinking to be done.

If your application is deployed only to your own servers, the benefit of this option is less useful; and in fact because it would preclude doing any of those quick tweaks to text on a page without an assembly deployment, it might make more sense to allow it to be updatable.

The output from this Publish Web Site option is a folder containing the set of files that you can deploy to the target site. Care must be taken when deploying this with respect to two types of files. First, if you have a customized web.config on the target server, you will overwrite those changes because the Publish Web Site option also places a copy of the project's web.config into the folder. For example, if you had modified connection strings to point to test or production data and the web.config in your project folder points to the development server, then after the copy you will overwrite those changes. Another more important and obvious problem is the copying of files from the app_data folder. If you use the default settings to create a project and enable membership, roles, or other ASP.NET services that require a database, one will be created for you in SQL Express if it is installed. That database will be stored in the app_data folder. During Publish Web Site process, the app_data folder is put in the output folder. If you were to simply xcopy or copy the files from the publish folder to the production server without first removing the development copy of the database, you risk overwriting the production database.

Using Windows Installer

Another option that is available is using the Web Setup Project option that is included as a Visual Studio Template project. The output produced by the Web Setup Project is a Windows Installer set of files that can be run on a target server to set up the website. This type of deployment enables users to see the installed package on the Add/Remove program list on the target server after the install is complete. From the Add/Remove program list, the user can easily remove the component to uninstall the website from the target server.

You can add one of these to your solution by choosing Add New Project from the File Menu and looking under the Other Project Types category. In that category, select the Setup and Deployment subcategory and then select the Web Setup Project from the list of templates. The Web Setup Project will result in the creation of files that will run via the Windows Installer. This option is a popular one among independent software vendors (ISVs) that need a more professional packaged application. *Wrox Pro ASP.NET 2.0* covered this type of project in a great amount of detail so we are not going to expand on it here.

A Hack from the Product Team

As you can see from what we have discussed so far there are numerous ways you can deploy or prepare to deploy websites. The addition of pre-compilation has been well received, but like many new features it created several more issues that needed to be addressed. For example, it would be nice to have more control over the pre-compile to determine the number and naming of the assemblies. Additionally, if you want to truly automate the deployment preparation process you need a tool that supports running on a build server without human intervention to tell a wizard what to do.

The cry for help from the community was heard by the ASP.NET team. Unfortunately, it came too late to affect the initial release of ASP.NET 2.0 and Visual Studio 2005. That didn't stop them, though; they have created the concept of Web Deployment Projects, which will be handled as an add-in package to Visual Studio 2005. At the time of this writing, Web Deployment Projects were still in the beta stage of availability.

In its simplest form, the Web Deployment Project is an `MSBuild` project file for a website. The goal of the project is to help automate the deployment preparation steps such as pre-compilation. Because it is a project file, it could be integrated into your automated build process using Team Build, Cruise Control, Draco, or another build control process.

Additionally, more control over the options used is provided. For example, you can now control whether you want a single assembly for the entire website, one assembly per folder, one assembly for all UI components, or simply one for each compiled file. This is especially important in large sites where the number of assemblies generated could cause potential problems.

Installing the Add-in

Because this is an add-in, you will need to download it using the following link: `http://msdn .microsoft.com/asp.net/reference/infrastructure/wdp/default.aspx`. (If the link doesn't work, check the errata for this book because at the time of publication this was still a beta version of the tool and it is possible it has since moved.)

After installation, to add a Web Deployment Project to your solution you will need to look on the Build menu, shown in Figure 12-3. You might be wondering why this doesn't just show up in the Add Project list. The reason is because this is an add-in, so it isn't handled as a project template.

Figure 12-3

If you are using a build server with your solution you can, and will need to, install the add-in on the server. It is not necessary to install Visual Studio on the server in order to install the add-in. You simply run the install.

Adding to Your Solution

When you select Add Web Deployment Project from the Build menu, you will see the dialog shown in Figure 12-4, prompting for the name and location for the project. It is typically best to locate the project inside the same folder as other projects in your solution. See Chapter 2, "Getting Started," for more recommendations on how to set up a solution with multiple projects. Something to keep in mind as you are selecting the name for your project is that it is possible to have more than one deploy project for each website; and it is possible to have more than one Web project inside your overall solution. You will want to pick a name that does not cause conflict as your project grows. A simple `web_deploy` project name might back you into a corner in the future.

Figure 12-4

After It's Added

After adding the project you will see it in the solution tree in Solution Explorer with the name you input, but otherwise you will not see any other visual changes to the solution. If you were to run a build, you would see something similar to the following in your output window, indicating that the Web deploy project is in fact doing something:

```
C:\WINDOWS\Microsoft.NET\Framework\v2.0.50727\aspnet_compiler.exe -v /web -p
D:\dyackweb\web -u -f -d D:\dyackweb\dyackweb_deploy\Debug\
Running aspnet_merge.exe ...
C:\Program Files\MSBuild\Microsoft\WebDeployment\v8.0\aspnet_merge.exe
D:\dyackweb\dyackweb_deploy\Debug -o dyackweb_deploy -debug -copyattrs
Successfully merged 'D:\dyackweb\dyackweb_deploy\Debug'.
```

At this point, assuming you are in debug configuration for your build, you would have just populated the debug folder inside your deployment project. The contents of this folder would be very similar to what you would get if you used the Publish Web Site Wizard discussed previously.

Changing the Default Options

Unlike other projects in your solution, the Web Deployment Project will not have any files show up in the tree in Solution Explorer. The only way to really interact with the project and modify settings (without actually just editing the MSBuild Script directly) is to right-click the project in Solution Explorer and select the Property Pages menu item. The dialog shown in Figure 12-5 appears and allows you to customize the settings of the project. These settings are specific to that project. We will explore these options in more detail later in this chapter.

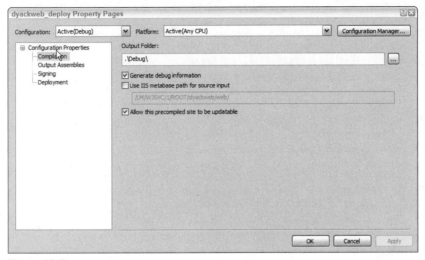

Figure 12-5

Speeding Up Your Developer Build

If you don't do any other customizations to the Web Deployment Project, you need to make sure that it stops running when you build the solution in the Debug configuration. By default, your solution will have two configurations: Debug and Release. Typically, most developers spend their time with this set to Debug. When we added the Web Deployment Project to the solution, it also enabled it for the Debug configuration. What that means is that every time you build, it will try to run the deployment project and take additional cycles to attempt to build a pre-compiled version of your site.

Turning this off is simple and just requires a quick visit to the Configuration Manager, which has a button on the Properties Page, making it easy to access (refer to Figure 12-5). Figure 12-6 shows the Configuration Manager dialog that will pop up and allow you to select or deselect what should be included in the build.

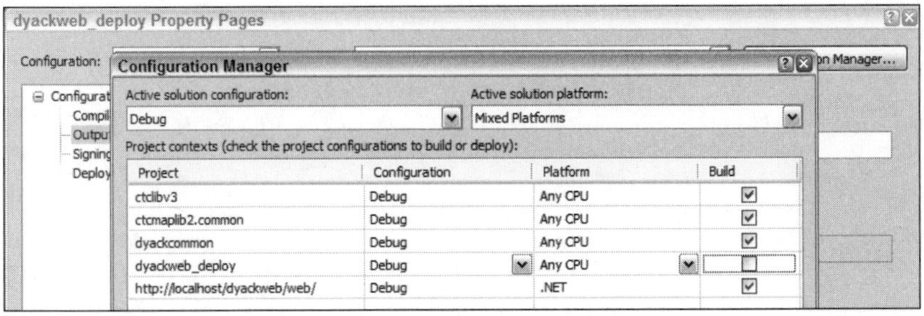

Figure 12-6

Notice that in Figure 12-6 I have unchecked the build option for the deploy project. Now, if we were to rerun the build for the solution, we should see a message similar to the following, indicating that the deploy project was skipped because it wasn't included in this configuration:

```
------ Skipped Build: Project: dyackweb_deploy, Configuration: Debug Any CPU ------
Project not selected to build for this solution configuration
```

BuildServer Special Configuration

While we are on the topic of configurations, let's touch on the concept of using this with a build server. A *build server* is simply a server or machine that is used to build software so it is not done on the developer's system. Using build servers can promote stability in the build environment by ensuring that the output produced is not subject to other work-in-progress items that the developer might have if built on their own system.

One thing you might want to consider is creating a special configuration that is used only by the build server. When MSBuild invokes the solution to build, it is possible for you to indicate via arguments to the MSBuild invocation that you want to run a specific configuration.

For our purposes here, we will create a new configuration called `BuildServer`. In your application you could call it whatever you like, and in fact you could create multiple configurations if you had built different build server configurations. For example, sometimes companies will build a debug and a release version on their build server, so they might create a `BuildServerDebug` and a `BuildServerRelease` configuration.

Creating a new configuration is easy. While in the Configuration Manager dialog box shown in Figure 12-6, select the New item from the Active Solution Configuration drop-down list, as shown in Figure 12-7.

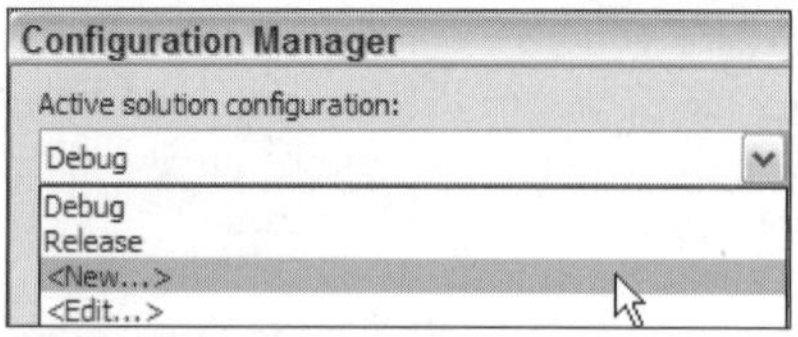

Figure 12-7

Once selected, the New Solution Configuration dialog shown in Figure 12-8 will appear, prompting you to name the configuration. The important thing here is you probably want to copy settings from your release version. This will give you a starting point on the configuration.

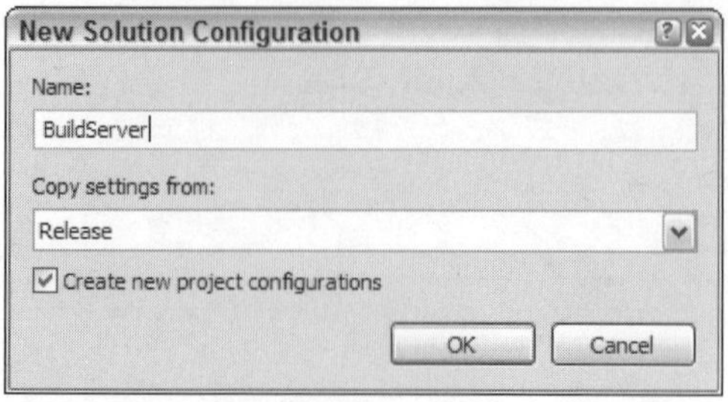

Figure 12-8

After saving the new configuration, you should be returned to the Web Deployment Project property page. Make sure that the `BuildServer` project highlighted in the drop-down is the one that you are setting options for now.

Invoking this configuration on your build server might vary depending on the package you are using to facilitate your build server automation. The following example shows a command-line invocation of `Msbuild` with this special configuration:

```
Msbuild mvphacks.sln /t:rebuild /p:configuration=BuildServerRelease
```

Setting Compilation Options

As shown earlier in Figure 12-5, the first Property Page is the Compilation page. If you are building for production you will want the "Generate debug information" and "Use IIS metabase path for source input" options left unchecked. As we discussed earlier in the "Publish Web Site Wizard" section, the "Allow this precompiled site to be updatable" option is typically okay for internal sites, but it could be beneficial to turn it off on sites deployed outside your organization. The "Use IIS metabase" option comes into play when you have subwebs. For a more formal discussion on that, see the white papers that have been released with the Deployment tool add-in.

Output Assemblies Options

This panel (shown in Figure 12-9) controls how assemblies are output and what level of merging occurs. If you are looking for output to be created closer to Visual Studio 2003, you will want to enable the "Merge all outputs to a single assembly" option. Like VS 2003, this will create one assembly that contains all the code. This is the simplest option and will work for most sites.

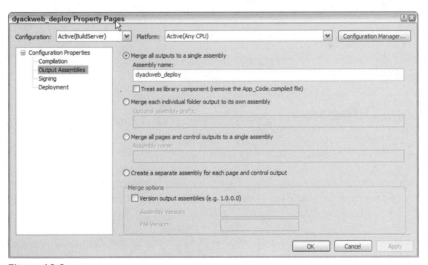

Figure 12-9

The "Merge each individual folder output to its own assembly" option is useful if you think you will be doing partial deployments of assemblies. Because each folder will be represented by an assembly, it would be possible to deploy just that folder to the production site if needed. You can provide an assembly prefix when you select this option, which is recommended to avoid confusion. You could use your company name or the production/application name as appropriate for your organization.

If you really want granular control, the "Create a separate assembly for each page and control output" option offers that. Keep in mind that in a very large site this could result in a large number of assemblies to be managed and loaded into memory on the Web server.

Sharing App_Code with Other Projects

One option we haven't mentioned on this page is "Treat as library component." There are a few cases where this option can come in handy. First, by combining and treating output as a library component, it is possible to attempt to use this to share master pages, user controls, or other common items with another website.

Another case where this is helpful is handling a conversion issue of 1.1 sites. In 1.1 it was possible to build another Web project, or, for that matter, any type of project that references an assembly from a 1.1 Web project. When that 1.1 application is converted to 2.0, by default there is no single assembly to be referenced. Using the "Treat as library component" option would cause all the items to be combined into an assembly for that website, which could be referenced.

While this works, it is at best a good short-term workaround to allow you to convert to ASP.NET 2.0 quicker without having to move your code from app_Code. A better practice, if all you are sharing is code and not the web-specific elements, and a longer term fix is to create a class library that is common to the various projects and move this code into that library.

Signing Options

There's not a lot to say about the Signing options panel. It basically enables you to specify a key that would be used to sign the assemblies.

Deployment Options

The final panel, Deployment (shown in Figure 12-10), allows final customization of what will be output and enables you to exclude certain items such as the data directory.

The first option on this page, "Enable Web.config file section replacement," reflects the fact that you might want to have different settings in your web.config based on the target. For example, you might have test-specific URLs, as well as a different set that is specific to production. In the example in Figure 12-10, the appSettings section will be replaced by the contents of the appSettings.config file. Keep in mind that this is a full replacement and the appSettings.config file should contain only that section.

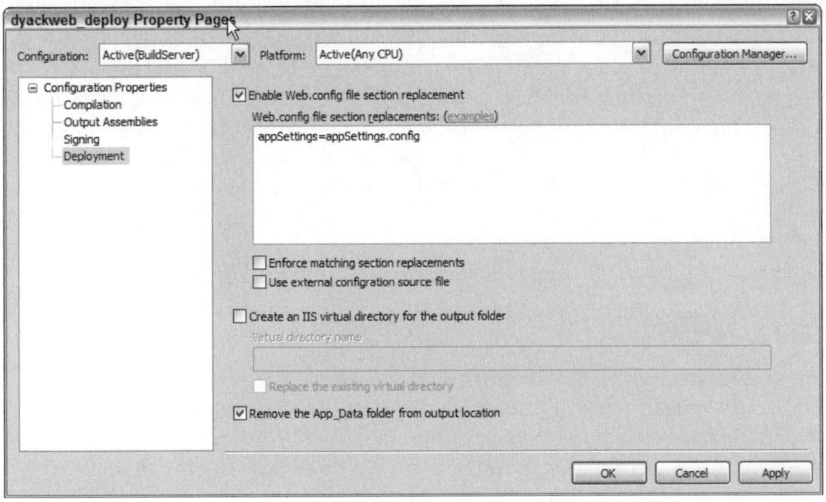

Figure 12-10

The next option on this panel is the capability to create an IIS virtual directory for the output folder. Keep in mind that, although in ASP.NET 1.1 it was common to already have a virtual IIS directory with the new concept of a file system website and the development Web server, this is no longer required. This option is best used when you want to have a virtual setup on your machine so you can test your deployment output prior to shipping it off to the final server. For example, a company could have a policy that the developer runs under the development Web server until check-in of code. At that point, the developer could be required to do a final check on a release build using IIS to make sure the application is working as desired. This option would allow that process to be automated as part of the release build. The replace option is almost mandatory because an error will be generated if it attempts to create the virtual directory and it already exists. This option is also only applicable to the local IIS; don't get confused thinking it could help you create the virtual directory on the ultimate production target IIS.

Save Your Database from Destruction!

It is hoped that this title got your attention and that your ears are perked wondering what the heck we are talking about. As discussed earlier in the chapter, by default the pre-compile and Web Deployment Projects will place a copy of your app_data folder in output that is created. This makes sense the first time you deploy; but after that, unless the database is read-only on production, if you deploy again you will destroy and replace your production copy. This is not a lesson you want to learn the hard way. This option also sets up so that you could replace SQLExpress in development with a full SQL Server database located on another server in production. In those scenarios, there is no reason to deploy the app_data folder to production.

Further Customizing the Deployment Project

Once nice thing about the Web Deployment Project is that at the heart it really is just an MSBuild file. Therefore, when you are making changes via the property pages we have just discussed, they are being saved to the build file as MSBuild properties or items. Using typical MSBuild constructs, you can, if needed, further customize the process. Keep in mind that the more you customize, the more you risk making a change that might conflict with the deployment tool in the future.

More info on MS Build can be found on msdn.com. You can also find additional community tasks that you can use with your project at http://msbuildtasks.tigris.org/.

Excluding Web.config

A good example of a customization that you might want to consider is excluding web.config from being put in the deployment folder. Earlier in the chapter, you saw how you can modify the contents of the web.config file and cause things such as links and other environment-sensitive information to be customized. While that is powerful, it doesn't enable you to build a deployment folder that could simply be copied to QA, and then also to Production without modification of the web.config file. To take that example a little further, the output from the deploy step could be zipped up for archiving and to allow copying to the various servers during actual deployment.

To accomplish excluding web.config, or, for that matter, any file, you can modify the MSBuild file that is used by the deploy step. To access the MSBuild file, right-click on the Web Deployment Project from the Solution Explorer and select the Open Project File menu option. This will open the MSBuild file for the deployment project in Visual Studio for editing. Inside the <Project> element, you will add the following to cause web.config to be excluded from the output:

```
<ItemGroup>
    <ExcludeFromBuild Include="$(SourceWebPhysicalPath)\web.config" />
</ItemGroup>
```

The ExcludeFromBuild element could be used to exclude other files that you might not want to build and deploy, simply by specifying their names in additional ExcludeFromBuild elements. As written, the preceding exclusion will only exclude the web.config file from the root of the site. If you intended to exclude it from all subfolders as well, you would use the following:

```
<ItemGroup>
    <ExcludeFromBuild Include="$(SourceWebPhysicalPath)\**\web.config" />
</ItemGroup>
```

Inserting the **\ into the path causes it to apply that exclusion to the subfolders. This also applies it to the root of the site.

Using the ExcludeFromBuild might not always work for what you are doing, especially with the web .config file. This approach might not work, for example, if you depend on specification of your control references in web.config. By using the ExcludeFromBuild, web.config will not be available during page compilation and will result in build errors.

First, in case you aren't familiar with the new option to include controls in web.config, let's look at a quick example. New to ASP.NET 2.0 is the capability to include references to controls in the web.config file's `<Pages>` element. By specification in the `web.config`, any Web form can use the control without having to have a `<%@Register` declaration for each control on each page. This is a great way to save time when the same controls are used on a significant number of pages in your site. The following example demonstrates how to configure that in the `web.config` file:

```
<pages >
   <controls>
      <add assembly="MVPHacksCommon" namespace="MVPHacksCommon.WebControls.Grid"
           tagPrefix="MVPHGRID"/>
      <add assembly="MVPHacksCommon"
namespace="MVPHacksCommon.WebControls.DataBinding"
           tagPrefix="MVPHDB"/>
   </controls>
</pages>
```

The controls named in the preceding example are for illustrative purposes, of course. You would substitute the names of your own libraries.

If you are using control references or other build support in the `web.config` for your site that are custom configured in the site's `web.config`, you need an alternative approach to accomplishing the exclusion The following section describes how you could override one of the build targets to accomplish this.

Web Deploy Project Extension Points

The example in the preceding section was a modification to the items specified in the Deployment Project build file. Another option for customization is to use some of the MSBuild targets that were put in place to allow you *extension points*. (These extension points are intentional targets called during the build script to allow you to customize the build process.)

If you want to explore more about how the Web Deployment Projects work, the first place to start exploring is the `targets` file that comes with the installation. You can find that in the installation directory, which is typically under `c:\Program Files\MSBuild\Microsoft\WebDeployment\v8.0\Microsoft.WebDeployment.targets`.

In there you will see several defined targets that can be redefined in your project's deployment file to cause your own MSBuild tasks to be invoked at each of the extension points.

Some of the extension points that exist are as follows:

Target	Description
BeforeBuild	Allows control just before the build starts; most targets other than _prepareBuild have not yet completed
AfterBuild	Allows control after all build-related targets have completed
BeforeMerge	Allows control before the merge targets are invoked
AfterMerge	Allows control after the merge targets have completed

To continue our previous exercise of trying to remove `web.config` from the output directory, we will redefine the `AfterBuild` event and use the MSBuild `Delete` task to accomplish the removal. Because `AfterBuild` is invoked after the compilation occurs, we should be well past the errors we would have had with the other approach. The following is an example of the extra lines we would add to our project file instead of the `ExcludeFromBuild`:

```
<Target Name="AfterBuild">
  <Delete Files="$(WDTargetDir)\web.config" />
  <Message Text="delete task ran for $(WDTargetDir)\web.config" />
</Target>
```

It is important to add this after the import of the `WebDeployment.targets` file; otherwise, your redefined target will never be invoked because it will be redefined by the blank one in the `WebDeployment.targets` file.

Creating a Zip Archive

Another example of how you might leverage the `AfterBuild` extension point is to add a task that would zip up a copy of the site that was just built. `MSBuild` itself does not come with a Zip task, but a community effort has created a number of additional tasks that you can install as part of the MSBuild Community Project, which you can download from `http://msbuildtasks.tigris.org/`.

For this example we are going to use two of the MSBuild tasks from the community project. We will use `Zip` to create the Zip archive, and we will use `Version` to get a version number for naming the archive file. In order to use those in an MSBuild file, we must identify where the assembly that has the custom task is located. To accomplish this, we add `UsingTask` statements to our build file, as shown in the following example:

```
<UsingTask AssemblyFile="C:\Program
Files\MSBuild\MSBuildCommunityTasks\MSBuild.Community.Tasks.dll"
          TaskName="MSBuild.Community.Tasks.Version"/>
  <UsingTask AssemblyFile="C:\Program
Files\MSBuild\MSBuildCommunityTasks\MSBuild.Community.Tasks.dll"
          TaskName="MSBuild.Community.Tasks.Zip"/>
```

The next example shows our `AfterBuild` target, which creates a directory, gets a version number for the build, and then zips up all the files into a zip archive:

```
<Target Name="AfterBuild">
    <MakeDir Directories="$(Configuration)Zip"/>
    <Version VersionFile="build.number" RevisionType="Increment">
      <Output TaskParameter="Major" PropertyName="Major" />
      <Output TaskParameter="Minor" PropertyName="Minor" />
      <Output TaskParameter="Build" PropertyName="Build" />
      <Output TaskParameter="Revision" PropertyName="Revision" />
    </Version>
    <Message Text="Version: $(Major).$(Minor).$(Build).$(Revision)"/>
    <CreateItem Include="$(Configuration)\**\*.*" >
      <Output ItemName="DeployZipFiles" TaskParameter="Include" />
    </CreateItem>
    <Zip Files="@(DeployZipFiles)"  WorkingDirectory="$(Configuration)"
```

```
        ZipFileName="$(Configuration)Zip\$(MSBuildProjectName)-
$(Major).$(Minor).$(Build).$(Revision).zip" />

    </Target>
```

In the preceding example, we use the `MakeDir` built-in task to create a directory to store our zip archives. Using a predefined property, `$Configuration`, we will create a directory that is either `DebugZip` or `ReleaseZip`, depending on the build that is running.

The MSBuild Community Project has a Version task that we are using to get a traditional version number consisting of `Major.Minor.Build.Revision`. This task will store the last build number in the `build.number` file that we specified using the `VersionFile` attribute on the Version task.

> The first time you run this, you may note that in the build output the `build.number` file wasn't found. The file should be created for you at that point.

Next, we use the built-in Message task to output the build number to the build output. If nothing else, the Message task is handy for noting an event in the build output log. Depending on your settings for build verbosity, it is possible you won't see the message in the build log. For information on how to alter your build verbosity, see the section later in this chapter titled "Turning on MSBuild Debug."

Prior to calling the Zip task, we use `CreateItem` to help us gather a list of files to be included in the zip. `CreateItem` is a built-in task that enables you to create an item collection. In the `WebDeployment.targets` file, a similar collection is created called `PrecompiledOutput`. You could use that, but if you had added or removed any items from the output directory then it would not be included in the `PrecompiledOutput` item collection.

Finally, using the Zip task from the MSBuild Community Project, we create our zip archive. You might notice that we specify the `WorkingDirectory` attribute on the task that allows the zip archive to start with the contents of the site. By doing that, our zip archive can be unzipped directly into a deployment directory on a host without regard to the parent folder hierarchy.

This example might not fit all scenarios, but it offers another look at the power of using the extension points in Web Deployment Projects.

Turning on MSBuild Debug

In working with the ASP.NET team to understand how to further customize using the deployment projects, they enlightened me about an option that you can turn on to get more details from MSBuild. To access this capability, select Tools⇨Options⇨Projects and Solutions⇨Build and Run. Located on this panel is a drop-down menu (MSBuild project build output verbosity) from which you can select the amount of detail that you want to see from MSBuild. The diagnostic level causes a bunch of useful information to be retrieved if you are working through MSBuild-related issues. This option is not specific to any particular deployment option we have discussed, and in fact can be used on your typical projects to see what is happening behind the scenes.

Preparing Your Server

A complete discussion on the preparations necessary for your production servers is beyond the scope of this book. However, because this seems to be one of the most common questions when you start talking about deployment, we wanted to touch on what is necessary to deploy an ASP.Net 2.0 application to a production server.

The first key component that is required is the .NET 2.0 Framework. You can download that from the Microsoft download site. You do not need to install Visual Studio 2005 or even the .NET 2.0 SDK on your production server; only the framework is required.

Another common question is whether the capability exists to run the 2.0 .NET runtime with an older version. The short answer to that is absolutely; they can co-exist. In fact, a lot more work went into support for this in the 2.0 release than in prior versions. If you click Properties in IIS on either the website or the virtual directory that is hosting the application, you will see a new ASP.NET tab after you install the 2.0 Framework. As shown in Figure 12-11, using this tab you can select the version of the runtime that will be used for the application.

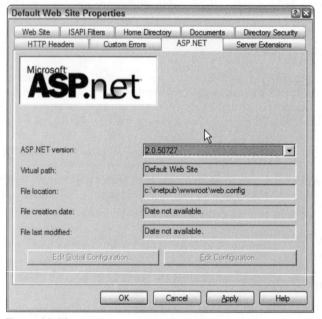

Figure 12-11

It's important to note that if you are using IIS 6 and your 2.0 application will co-exist alongside it with an application that is using different versions of the .NET runtime, then you must isolate these applications in at least one IIS application pool for each .NET version. Simply put, you cannot run more than one .NET runtime version in the same IIS application pool.

Wrapping Up

Visual Studio 2005 and ASP.NET provide significant improvement in support for deploying applications, regardless of your deployment target or the size of your project. In this chapter we have reviewed the majority of techniques that are available, as well as discussed some of the pro and cons of each approach.

The capability to have pre-compiled websites that go as far as including compilation of the markup so you don't have to have the page source vulnerable to prying eyes is a huge advancement. Using the new compilation model and the capability to have your assemblies as granular as one per file or control also gives you a lot of power, so much so that the ASP.NET team jumped in with their own hack, which will save the day for those of you who want even more control over the building of the deployment folder.

Deployment doesn't have to be hard, but it should be repeatable. If you take nothing else away from reading this chapter, understand that all real Web projects should address deployment. Don't depend on your developers, or yourself for that matter, to put in place a consistent process for deploying without using some of the capabilities discussed in this chapter.

The Web Deployment Project concept is easy; and using the guidance in this chapter, setting it up on a new Web project should only take minutes. Do keep in mind that as of this writing, it is still in beta, so you should check for any changes at www.wrox.com.

Other Deployment Resources

Visit www.wrox.com for any errata.

Download for Web Deployment Projects (Beta V2 Preview): http://msdn.microsoft.com/asp.net/reference/infrastructure/wdp/default.aspx.

MSBuild Task List Reference on MSDN: http://msdn2.microsoft.com/7z253716.aspx.

MSBuild Community Tasks Project: http://msbuildtasks.tigris.org/.

13

Leveraging Visual Studio

Visual Studio 2005 offers many features to make you more productive during development. In fact, it has several new extensibility features, helping you to create your own hacks, including snippets, custom page templates, and various settings to customize your development environment.

This chapter looks at Visual Studio 2005's snippet capability, including how to use the Code Snippets Manager, how to create custom snippets, and how to create snippets that use built-in functions.

Part of this chapter discusses settings that can help you be more productive with Visual Studio 2005. You'll learn how to make a Web form appear in Design view, rather than the default HTML view, and you'll learn how to set up the Cassini Web server. If you're working on a team, this chapter shows you how to import and export all of the Visual Studio 2005 settings so everyone on your team can import the settings to make their development environments work similarly.

Besides additional tips on getting the most from the Visual Studio 2005 environment, we'll look at templates, which are pre-made code for project items or entire projects. Every time you create a new project or add a new item to a project, you are using templates. For example, the Windows Application, Web Site, and Console Application Project Wizards are templates that ship with Visual Studio 2005. You'll learn how to create custom item templates and how to create entire project templates. Along the way, we'll inject undocumented tips into the discussion to help you be more productive while using tools such as snippets and templates.

ASP.NET Code Snippets

A *snippet* is a piece of code that you can reuse in many different applications. Visual Studio 2005 has built-in support for snippets, including a snippet library, a snippet management console, and editor shortcuts for including snippets.

Using Snippets

You can use snippets in Web applications, whether the language is C# or VB.NET. VB.NET has about 500 snippets to choose from, organized into several categories. There are fewer C# snippets, but they are just as useful. Clearly, this is an opportunity for the C# community to pitch in and add more snippets. One point is evident, though: The numerous snippets available in VB.NET proves that there is great potential for reuse (and new hacks) in the area of snippets. Visual Studio 2005 also supports XML snippets in the XML editor.

> **The XML editor also supports XML snippets.**

Regardless of the language you're using, there are a few different ways to insert existing snippets into code. Notice that I used the word "existing," implying that more can be added. The section titled "Creating Custom Snippets," later in this chapter, will show you how to create your own custom snippets. As you'll see, you can add snippets by selecting an option from the context menu, typing a question mark (?), and pressing Tab (VB.NET only), or those who know the snippet shortcut name can type the shortcut name and press Tab.

Using Pre-Made Snippets

Many snippets have parameters for you to fill in. For example, a C# property snippet has parameters for type, backing store name, and property name. To try this out, open a C# class file and click in the editor inside of a class declaration. Type **prop** (IntelliSense will appear before you finish), press Tab to accept the IntelliSense recommendation, and press Tab again to make the snippet template appear. When you fill in the type, it changes the property type too. After specifying the type, press Tab to change the variable name, which also changes the accessor code working with that variable. Press Tab again after entering the variable name, to give the property a name. You can continue pressing Tab to cycle through parameters and change your previous entries, and then press Enter to stop editing the snippet.

Creating Custom Snippets

Although there are several pre-made snippets to choose from, many developers are likely to want to create their own snippets for reuse. Additionally, if you have created a hack of your own, one way to publish the hack could be through a snippet you could share with others. This section offers a few tips on how to create your own snippets.

The Snippet Template format is documented in the Visual Studio 2005 help system, which you can copy and paste into a file before changing the pertinent information to create your own snippet. However, a technique that is a little bit quicker leverages the fact that there is support for snippets in XML. Here are the steps:

1. Create an XML file and name it `<snippetName>.snippet`, where `<snippetName>` is a meaningful name for the snippet you want to create.

2. Right-click in the new file and select Insert Snippet.

3. In the IntelliSense breadcrumb trail, type **Snippet** and press Enter.

4. Fill in each field and press Tab to traverse to the next field.

5. Change the Language attribute of the Code element to the appropriate language for which the snippet is being built.

6. Press Enter when done.

Listing 13-1 shows a ViewState property snippet you could use in your custom controls.

Listing 13-1: A snippet for building a property that uses ViewState as a backing store

```xml
<?xml version="1.0" encoding="utf-8" ?>
<CodeSnippet Format="1.0.0"
xmlns="http://schemas.microsoft.com/VisualStudio/2005/CodeSnippet">
 <Header>
   <Title>propViewState</Title>
   <Author>John Smith</Author>
   <Shortcut>propViewState</Shortcut>
   <Description>Property with ViewState backing store</Description>
   <SnippetTypes>
     <SnippetType>Expansion</SnippetType>
   </SnippetTypes>
 </Header>
 <Snippet>
   <Declarations>
       <Literal>
       <ID>type</ID>
       <ToolTip>Property type</ToolTip>
       <Default>int</Default>
     </Literal>
     <Literal>
       <ID>property</ID>
       <ToolTip>Property name</ToolTip>
       <Default>MyProperty</Default>
     </Literal>
     <Literal>
       <ID>comment</ID>
       <ToolTip>Property Comment</ToolTip>
       <Default></Default>
     </Literal>
     <Literal>
       <ID>defaultValue</ID>
       <ToolTip>Property default value</ToolTip>
       <Default>"Default Value"</Default>
     </Literal>
   </Declarations>
 <Code Language="csharp">
   <![CDATA[
/// <summary>
/// $comment$
/// </summary>
public $type$ $property$
{
   get
```

(continued)

Listing 13-1 *(continued)*

```
    {
        if (ViewState["$property$"] == null)
        return $defaultValue$;

        return ($type$) ViewState["$property$"];
    }
    set
    {
        ViewState["$property$"] = value;
    }
}
$end$
    ]]>
</Code>
</Snippet>
</CodeSnippet>
```

When building snippets, be sure to fill in `Description` and `ToolTip` elements with meaningful information. This will help other developers trying to determine what the snippet does, and make each parameter more understandable while using the snippet. If only part of a snippet appears when adding it to code, double-check the IDs in the `Code` element to ensure that each parameter is surrounded by $ symbols.

Managing Snippets

Once a snippet is created, you'll want to load it into the IDE. Visual Studio 2005 includes a Code Snippets Manager that can be opened by selecting Tools⇨Code Snippets Manager. Alternatively, you can type Ctrl+K, Ctrl+B. This opens the Code Snippets Manager dialog box shown in Figure 13-1.

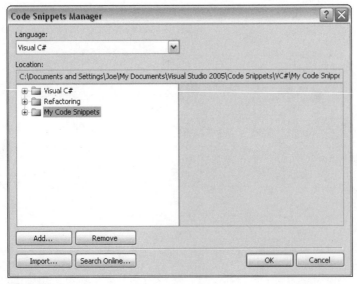

Figure 13-1

When using the Code Snippets Manager, be sure to select the proper language (Visual Basic, Visual C#, Visual J#, or XML) in the Language drop-down list. The Add button opens a dialog box from which you can select a folder, which is added to the list. Any snippets in that folder will appear when that folder is opened. It includes subfolders also. This is only for folders and not individual files.

If you want to add an individual snippet file, like the one in Listing 13-1, click the Import button. It will open a dialog box that enables you to navigate to and select a snippet file. Once you select a file, the Import Code Snippet dialog shown in Figure 13-2 appears, asking which folders you want to add the snippet to. Check the folders you want the snippet to be added to and click the Finish button. You could potentially add a snippet to multiple folders. For example, suppose you wanted to keep properties listed in a language folder and, because there are so many ways to write properties, keep them in a properties folder. Back at the Code Snippets Manager dialog, opening each of the checked folders will reveal the new snippet. Though an individual snippet can be added to multiple folders, IntelliSense is smart enough to show it only one time when adding it to code.

> The default value of the Language element for the XML snippet is XML. If you forget to change it to the language you are using, the Import Code Snippet dialog will show only folders for XML snippets. Once you change the Language attribute of the Code element appropriately, the proper language folders will appear in the Import Code Snippet dialog.

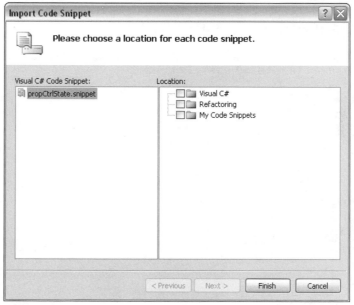

Figure 13-2

If you change a snippet and need to replace the old copy, perform the import operation again. When you click Finish, you'll be informed that the snippet already exists and asked whether you would like to overwrite or rename the existing snippet. Press the Overwrite button to replace the old snippet or press the Rename snippet to rename the old snippet and insert the new one.

Similar to the Add functionality, the Remove button operates only on folders. It will remove a selected folder from the list. Be careful, though: It does not ask "Are you sure?" Therefore, caution is advised when clicking around on this dialog to see what happens. If you do something you're not sure of, click the Cancel button and reopen the Code Snippets Manager to start over.

Although the Code Snippets Manager lets you remove entire folders, it doesn't allow removing individual snippets. You must physically delete the file from each folder to which it has been added. The Location section of the Code Snippets Manager dialog shows where a snippet resides on the file system for the currently selected folder. Just go to that location and delete the file. If the Code Snippets Manager dialog is open when you delete the snippet, you'll need to close and reopen it to confirm that the snippet no longer appears.

The Search Online button opens the help system, which has links to external references where you can find additional snippets.

Using Snippet Functions

Functions are another feature of snippets that dynamically inject context-sensitive code when the snippet is executed. For example, the GenerateSwitchCases function will inject case statements into a switch statement with an enum parameter for each value of the enumeration. To test it, create a variable of an enum type, type **switch**, press Tab, and use the enum variable in the switch_on parameter.

Because the GenerateSwitchOn function is so specialized, it isn't very reusable. However, the other functions, such as ClassName, SimpleTypeName, and CallBase (all documented), could be reused in other snippets. For example, Listing 13-2 shows a snippet implementing the Dispose pattern using the ClassName function.

Listing 13-2: A snippet that uses a function

```xml
<?xml version="1.0" encoding="utf-8" ?>
<CodeSnippet Format="1.0.0"
xmlns="http://schemas.microsoft.com/VisualStudio/2005/CodeSnippet">
  <Header>
    <Title>dispose</Title>
    <Author>John Smith</Author>
    <Shortcut>dispose</Shortcut>
    <Description>Implements the Dispose pattern</Description>
    <SnippetTypes>
      <SnippetType>SurroundsWith</SnippetType>
      <SnippetType>Expansion</SnippetType>
    </SnippetTypes>
  </Header>
  <Snippet>
    <Declarations>
      <Literal>
        <ID>type</ID>
        <ToolTip>Destructor</ToolTip>
        <Function>ClassName()</Function>
      </Literal>
    </Declarations>
    <Code Language="csharp">
```

```
        <![CDATA[
        // TODO:  Make type implement IDisposable

        // has Dispose been called yet
        private bool disposed;

        /// <summary>
        /// TODO: Dispose may or may not have been overridden
        /// depending on whether this is a stand alone class,
        /// base class or a derived class.
        /// Implement virtual Dispose method for base class
        /// and implement override methods for derived
        /// classes, as appropriate.
        /// </summary>
        public override void Dispose()
        {
            Dispose(true);
            GC.SuppressFinalize(this);

            // TODO: call base.Dispose() if override
        }

        public void Dispose(bool calledFromUser)
        {
            // only the first time
            if (!disposed)
            {
                // called from Dispose() - not destructor
                if (calledFromUser)
                {
                    // release managed resources
                }

                // release unmanaged resources

                disposed = true;

                // TODO: call base.Dispose(calledFromUser) if override
            }
        }

        ~$type$()
        {
            Dispose(false);
        }        $end$
        ]]>
      </Code>
    </Snippet>
</CodeSnippet>
```

The code in Listing 13-2 uses the ClassName function, which returns the name of the containing class. Notice the Literal element with the <Function>ClassName()</Function> element. A default element is not required and would be redundant. When the snippet is run, each parameter with the ID matching the function is replaced with the results of that function.

Settings That Make Your Life Better

Visual Studio 2005 offers a plethora of options to help maximize your productivity. This section describes a few options that are particularly helpful in building Web applications.

Source View versus Design View

The default view in Visual Studio 2005 is HTML, which changed from Visual Studio 2003 in which a Web form displayed in Design view. To change this, select Tools⇨Options⇨HTML Designer⇨General, and click the Design View option. From now on, Web forms will display in Design view.

Using a Different Web Server

With Visual Studio 2005, you no longer have a dependency on an external Web server, as there is one built into the IDE. However, there may be times when you want to target another Web server because part of your user base could be using other Web servers. In particular, some users may have the open-source Cassini Web server deployed on their system. You'll want to test your application with Cassini to ensure that it runs properly.

One might wonder why someone would want to use Cassini, as Visual Studio 2005 already includes a built-in Web server. However, consider the fact that Cassini is open source and someone may have created a custom implementation with services they want to continue supporting. For example, one possible modification is to allow external machines to connect to Cassini, which is something the built-in Visual Studio 2005 Web server doesn't allow.

You can find the Cassini Web server at the ASP.NET Community Web Site at www.asp.net. Look in the Downloads section. Follow the instructions to compile the code but be sure to do it through a .NET v2.0 command prompt. If you try to launch a version of Cassini that was compiled with a version of the C# compiler earlier than v2.0, it will not work with your Visual Studio 2005 website. When running Cassini, set the physical path to the location of your website and set the virtual directory to /. Remember to set a port number that doesn't conflict with existing ports in use on your machine. Most of the time, 8080 will be okay and won't cause a problem unless some other application is using that port.

To configure Visual Studio 2005, right-click on your project in Solution Explorer, select Property Pages⇨Start Options; in the Server area, click Use Custom Server; and type **http://localhost:8080** in the Base URL text box, as shown in Figure 13-3. Remember to replace 8080 in the Base URL text box with the actual number of the port on which Cassini was launched.

After you have configured Cassini as your Web server, press Ctrl+F5 in Visual Studio 2005 to launch your application without debugging. If you want to debug your application, change the server option back to Use Default Web Server.

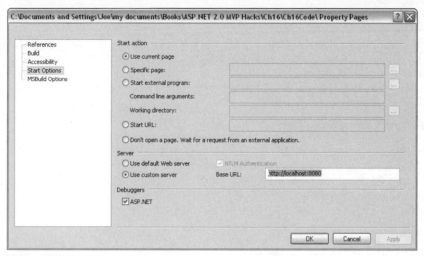

Figure 13-3

Importing and Exporting Team Settings

Visual Studio 2005 allows you to export and import your system settings for practically every configurable IDE setting. Here are a few reasons why you would want to use this:

❑ To recover from system crashes, you can export the most recent version of settings and back them up. When you rebuild, you can import these settings from the back-up copy and have your environment work the same way as before.

❑ When you need to transfer settings to another computer, perhaps a laptop, you can export settings. Then import those settings on the other computer and work with Visual Studio 2005 the same way.

❑ In a team environment, developers often help each other with projects. By exporting common settings from one machine and importing them on all developer machines, each environment can be similar. This saves time when you help someone with a problem. In pair programming scenarios, having a common environment makes it easier for programmers to work in each other's environment, without having to adjust every time they sit down at another computer. Consistency can help productivity.

To work with the settings tool, select Tools⇨Import and Export Settings. The rest is a wizard that is simple to use. If you want to revert to standard system settings, run the Import and Export Settings tool and select the Reset All Settings option.

Another way to import settings is to select Tools⇨Options⇨Environment\Import and Export Settings, check Use team settings file, and browse and select the settings file. When you click OK, Visual Studio 2005 applies the new settings.

Templates

Templates are pre-made items and projects that help you get started with a task. Typical project templates include those for a new website or a new setup project. Common item templates are those for Web Form, Class File, or User Control. This section shows how to create custom item and project templates and describes workarounds for limitations in the tools so you can more easily accomplish your job.

Custom Item Templates

Visual Studio includes many reusable templates for adding items to projects, such as New Web Form and Class File. These are the most common tasks that people need in their day-to-day work. However, it would be nice if we could create our own custom items. For example, what if you wanted to create a Snippet template or a Disposable Class template? In this section, you'll learn how to create a new Snippet template that you can use to get a quick start on your own snippets.

In a previous section of this chapter, "Creating Custom Snippets," you learned how to create a snippet by adding an XML template to your project and modifying it. In this section, you'll learn how to take that a step further by creating your own item template, which makes creating a snippet even easier. The first thing to do is create a file you want to use as the template. Listing 13-3 has a suggested Snippet template.

Listing 13-3: A snippet template

```xml
<?xml version="1.0" encoding="utf-8" ?>
<!--
  To get started:
      1. Right-click below and select Insert Snippet
      2. Type Snippet
      3. Press Enter
      4. Follow template to create snippet
  -->
```

Save the file as **SnippetFile.snippet**. Optionally, you can also create an icon file to associate with this snippet when it appears in the New Item dialog box. To load this snippet into Visual Studio 2005, select File⇨Export Template, choose Item template, select the project and template type, and click the Next button.

In the Select Item to Export screen, select `SnippetFile.snippet`, or whatever you named the file for which you want to create a template, and click the Next button. The Select Item References page is for checking which assemblies your project should reference when this snippet is added. For example, if your snippet used ADO.NET types, you would want to check the box for the `System.Data` assembly.

In the Select Item to Export window, choose an icon if you created a new one. Otherwise, you can use the default. Enter **SnippetFile.snippet** as the name. It is important to include the file extension (.snippet) so it will appear in the user's wizard when they add the item to their project. If you want the template to appear in Visual Studio 2005's New Item dialog box, you must check "Automatically import template into Visual Studio." Click the Finish button to create the new Snippet template.

You can now use this snippet by right-clicking the project name and selecting Add New Item. The Snippet template appears under the My Templates section of the Templates list. You can rename the file by changing the Name field and clicking the OK button to add the Snippet template to your project.

One annoyance of the Export Template Wizard is that it doesn't offer the capability to separately specify the name and file extension. This results in the Snippet template appearing in the Templates list as Snippet.snippet. It would make more sense if it were Snippet File instead. If you set the name in the Export Template Wizard to Snippet, then the filename in the Add New Item dialog box would be missing the file extension. The solution is to manually change the file.

The snippet template is physically located in `C:\Documents and Settings\%user%\My Documents\Visual Studio 2005\My Exported Templates` in a zip file. To modify the contents of the template, extract the files from the zip file. Open the file named `MyTemplate.vstemplate` and change the `Name` element to **Snippet File**. Then select each file and add it to a new zip file named `SnippetFile.snippet.zip`. Replace the original `SnippetFile.Snippet.zip` with the new modified one. To be tidy, delete the intermediate files so you don't have unused residue sitting around your file system. Now copy the new template over to `C:\Documents and Settings\%user%\My Documents\Visual Studio 2005\Templates\ItemTemplates\Visual Studio 2005\CSharp` and replace the `SnippetFile.snippet.zip` file there. This process replaces the Snippet template everywhere it was added by the Export Template Wizard. If you are working with another language, be sure to change the path for the location of templates in that language. When selecting Add New Item, you will now see Snippet File in the Templates list and the filename will still have the .snippet extension.

Custom Project Templates

In addition to individual item templates, you can also create custom project templates. You would want to create a Custom Project template if you can find a better way to set a start-up project. For the purposes of this section, the example project is based on recommendations from Chapter 2. Of the many things you will do at startup to get your project configured properly, using a good project template can save you time and effort.

The first thing you should do when making a project template is to create a new project. Add the folders and files you want all projects of this type to have. The sample code for this chapter created a project template that includes an `App_Code` folder containing base classes for both Master and Page code-behind classes, an `App_Themes` folder with a Basic theme, and a Default Web Form that uses a Master Page.

The purpose of the project will guide what you add. For example, if you wanted a project that everyone can use, you would make it more generic. However, if you needed something that would only be used in your company or department, you could make specific customizations to the Master Page, create a DataBase project for a specific database, or do anything else related to what the intended audience of the project would need.

To create the project template, select File⇨Export Template, choose Project Template, and click the Next button. In the Select Template Options window, add a new template name and template description, verify that "Automatically import the template into Visual Studio" is checked, and optionally uncheck "Display an explorer window on the output files folder." Unlike the Item template, you don't have to worry about including a file extension in the name because this is the name of the project and doesn't have anything to do with an individual file. Clicking the Finish button creates a new Web project.

To use this Web project, select File⇨New⇨Web Site, and select the new project template under My Templates. Note that this will only show up as a Web Site project and not under other projects.

Alternatively, you can create a project template from an existing project. This is an option if you have a small project that already includes everything you want in other projects. The trade-off is that you'll need to modify the project template after it has been created. You just need to use the Export Template Wizard described in the preceding paragraphs.

When creating project templates from existing projects, you are likely to have files included in the project that you don't want to be there. The wizard doesn't give you the option to select what you want to include. The workaround for this problem is to modify the generated template files.

To modify the project template, expand the zip file, located at `C:\Documents and Settings\%user%\My Documents\Visual Studio 2005\My Exported Templates`. Open the `*.vstemplate` file and observe that there are multiple `ProjectItem` elements. Delete the `ProjectItem` elements with `TargetFileName` attributes corresponding to the name of the files you need to exclude from the project. The rest of the `*.vstemplate` file format is documented, so you should refer to the documentation to understand what the rest of the file means and if there is anything you want to change. For the purposes of this discussion, removing unwanted `ProjectItem` elements is sufficient.

For each `ProjectItem` element removed, delete its corresponding file in the file system. The files are extracted from the zip file and forced into MS-DOS 8.3 notation, so the names won't always match exactly. When in doubt, open the file and look at its contents to make sure.

After modifications, zip the files back into a compressed file with the same name as the project template. Then replace the zip file at both `C:\Documents and Settings\%user%\My Documents\Visual Studio 2005\My Exported Templates` and `C:\Documents and Settings\%user%\My Documents\Visual Studio 2005\Templates\ProjectTemplates\Visual Studio 2005\CSharp`.

Wrapping Up

Snippets are a convenient way to package and distribute your own hacks. Visual Studio 2005 supports pre-made snippets and custom snippets. You can use the Code Snippets Manager to add, organize, and remove snippets.

Visual Studio 2005 has many features to improve the user experience. You can import and export settings, customize the development experience for either Design or Source view, and even set up the environment to run with other Web servers such as Cassini.

Another way to customize your environment and potentially distribute hacks is via templates. You can create individual item templates or custom project templates.

14

Security Hacks

When most people launch a new website, they are optimistic and look forward to successfully meeting the goals they originally envisioned. Unfortunately, in today's world the hopes of individuals and companies can be instantly dashed by someone with malicious intent. The reality is that part of building a website is considering security. The question to be asked is not "if" but "when" your site will be attacked. Everyone must include security as an integral part of Web application requirements if they are to achieve success.

This chapter includes some techniques to use to harden your system a little better. A couple of the hacks address a particularly insidious attack called the *SQL injection attack*—including the first hack in the following section, "Avoiding SQL Injection." This chapter includes a related hack that enables you to parameterize a SQL IN expression, which is another way to avoid SQL injection. You'll also find a couple of hacks dealing with *canonicalization attacks*—those involving URIs that try to bypass normal address and filename checking. For those of you who have OS resources, such as files on a system guarded by Windows authentication, this chapter includes an impersonation hack you can use. Last, but not least, there is a hack for extending the ASP.NET Login control to validate a strong password. Certainly, there is much more to cover in the world of security, but it is hoped that the hacks in this chapter give you some important reusable code and techniques and stimulate your own thinking about how to make your applications more secure.

Avoiding SQL Injection

One of the more serious threats you'll encounter when exposing a Web application on the Internet is the SQL injection attack. A hacker launches this type of attack by adding extra information to an input field. Your code then interprets this extra input as part of the SQL that it sends to the database.

For example, Figure 14-1 shows an input form in which a hacker is attempting an attack by inserting the following string:

```
', ''); drop table MyTable;--
```

The hacker is hoping that the code does something insecure, such as concatenate the input with the SQL statement to build the SQL string on the fly. In many situations, this is exactly what is happening in the code, and this section provides some advice about how to avoid it.

> With SQL injection, it isn't too hard for attackers to quickly extract data and then figure out your entire database schema. To see how they do it, visit your favorite search engine, starting with the keywords "SQL injection."

Figure 14-1

In Figure 14-1, the example has two buttons, Bad Add Shipper and Good Add Shipper. The hacker hopes the code like that shown in Listing 14-1 executes when he or she submits the page. The Bad Add Shipper button will run the code in Listing 14-1.

Listing 14-1: The wrong way to build an ad hoc SQL query

```
protected void btnBadAddShipper_Click(object sender, EventArgs e)
{
    string connStr = "Server=(local);Database=Northwind;Integrated
Security=SSPI";

    // this is *bad* because the user can
    // enter anything they want
    string cmdStr =
        "insert into Shippers (CompanyName, Phone) values ('" +
        txtCompanyName.Text + "', '" + txtPhone.Text + "')";

    using (SqlConnection conn = new SqlConnection(connStr))
    using (SqlCommand cmd = new SqlCommand(cmdStr, conn))
    {
        conn.Open();
        cmd.ExecuteNonQuery();
    }
}
```

The code in Listing 14-1 is bad is because it concatenates the input with the rest of the SQL statement. This causes the resulting SQL command to be sent to the database as follows:

```
insert into Shippers (CompanyName, Phone) values ('', ''); drop table MyTable;--',
'')
```

The first part of this statement adds a new row with blank values to the Shippers table. The second part, after the first semicolon (;), removes the MyTable table from the database. The rest of the statement, after the second semicolon, is commented out to prevent errors.

As you can see, attackers can do a lot of damage to your system or view information they aren't supposed to see. Even worse, although it may not be totally obvious by this example, through SQL injection an attacker could potentially take over your entire system.

To fix this problem, you need to use parameters, as shown in Listing 14-2. When the user clicks the Good Add Shipper button, shown in Figure 14-1, it runs the `btnGoodAddShipper` method, shown in Listing 14-2.

Listing 14-2: The proper way to build an ad hoc SQL query

```
protected void btnGoodAddShipper_Click(object sender, EventArgs e)
{
    string connStr = "Server=(local);Database=Northwind;Integrated
Security=SSPI";

    // this is good because all input becomes a
    // parameter and not part of the SQL statement
    string cmdStr =
        "insert into Shippers (CompanyName, Phone) values (" +
        "@CompanyName, @Phone)";

    using (SqlConnection conn = new SqlConnection(connStr))
    using (SqlCommand cmd = new SqlCommand(cmdStr, conn))
    {
        // add parameters
        cmd.Parameters.AddWithValue("@CompanyName", txtCompanyName.Text);
        cmd.Parameters.AddWithValue("@Phone", txtPhone.Text);

        conn.Open();
        cmd.ExecuteNonQuery();
    }
}
```

The code in Listing 14-2 is more secure because all input is treated as a parameter, rather than part of the SQL statement. Refer to the documentation on `SqlParameter`, or the corresponding type for whatever data provider you're using, for information on how to use parameters. An even more secure example would have instantiated a `SqlParameter` and explicitly set type, size, and other arguments to constrain the input.

ASP.NET v2.0 includes new datasource controls that enable you to add a bindable object to your Web form for populating data controls, such as GridView. These datasource controls accept parameters, meaning that they are also a safe way to get input from the user. For more information, see Chapter 8, "Extreme Data Binding."

> In addition to increasing performance, stored procedures are more secure because they require passing input as parameters.

To re-create this scenario, add a test table to your database, such as the one shown in Listing 14-3, and add input as shown in Figure 14-1. Clicking the Bad Add Shipper button deletes the table. However, clicking the Good Add Shipper button processes the input properly.

Listing 14-3: Example table for demonstrating a SQL injection attack

```
create table MyTable
(
TempColumn      char(5)
)
```

Figure 14-2 shows the output in SQL Query Analyzer after running a couple of queries. Row 4 shows the results of running the insecure code from Listing 14-1 (clicking the Bad Add Shipper button). Row 5 shows the results of running the more secure code from Listing 14-2 (clicking the Good Add Shipper button). As you can see by looking at Row 5, processing input via parameters prevents interpretation of the input as part of the SQL statement and saves that input as column data.

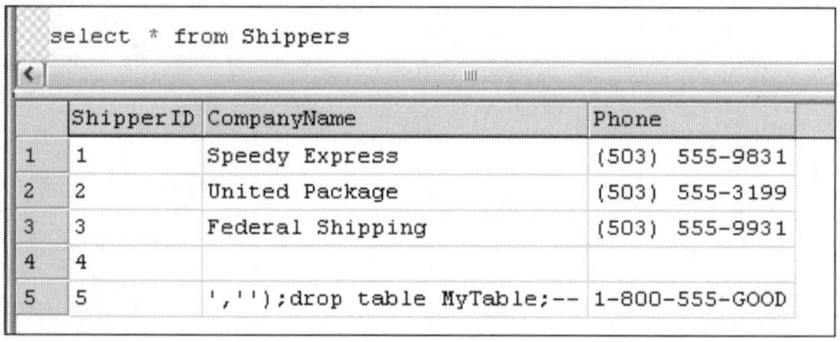

```
select * from Shippers
```

	ShipperID	CompanyName	Phone
1	1	Speedy Express	(503) 555-9831
2	2	United Package	(503) 555-3199
3	3	Federal Shipping	(503) 555-9931
4	4		
5	5	','');drop table MyTable;--	1-800-555-GOOD

Figure 14-2

If you are coding ad hoc SQL statements, using parameters is one of the best techniques you can use to increase the security of your entire application.

Parameterizing an IN Expression

The last section discussed using parameters to secure your code with ad hoc queries. That works fine when you are doing a comparison in a `where` clause. However, it doesn't work at all if you want to pass a parameter to an `IN` expression. For example, the following does not work:

```
select EmployeeID, LastName from Employees
where EmployeeID in (@list)
```

One way to get around this limitation is to use a SQL function. An `IN` will accept a table. Therefore, you can call a function that parses each element in a comma-separated list, passed in the parameter, and build a table. The function's return value would be the table, which works fine with the `IN`. Listing 14-4 shows a function that accomplishes this.

Listing 14-4: A function that accepts a parameter and returns a table

```
SET QUOTED_IDENTIFIER OFF
GO
SET ANSI_NULLS OFF
GO
ALTER  FUNCTION dbo.ufStringToIntTable (@list varchar(8000))
    RETURNS @tbl TABLE (val int,seqnum int) AS
  BEGIN
    DECLARE @ix  int,
            @pos int,
            @seq int,
            @str varchar(8000),
            @num int

    SET @pos = 1
    SET @ix = 1
    SET @seq = 1

    WHILE @ix > 0
    BEGIN
      -- extract next parameter
      SET @ix = charindex(',', @list, @pos)
      IF @ix > 0
         SET @str = substring(@list, @pos, @ix - @pos)
      ELSE
         SET @str = substring(@list, @pos, len(@list))
      SET @str = ltrim(rtrim(@str))

      -- ensure valid number
      IF @str LIKE '%[0-9]%' AND
         (@str NOT LIKE '%[^0-9]%' OR
          @str LIKE '[-+]%' AND
            substring(@str, 2, len(@str)) NOT LIKE '[-+]%[^0-9]%')
      BEGIN
        -- convert and add number to table
        SET @num = convert(int, @str)
        INSERT @tbl (val,seqnum) VALUES(@num, @seq)
      END

      -- prepare for next parameter
      SET @pos = @ix + 1
      SET @seq = @Seq + 1
    END

    -- return table with all parameters
    RETURN
  END

GO
SET QUOTED_IDENTIFIER OFF
GO
SET ANSI_NULLS ON
GO
```

The function in Listing 14-4 accepts a parameter and returns a table. The content of the input parameter is a comma-separated list of numbers. The function parses the values, converts each value to an integer, and adds each integer as a row into the table. This dynamically created table is then returned to the caller. Because an IN expression accepts a table, this works out well. Listing 14-5 shows how this function can be used to accept a parameter for an IN expression.

Listing 14-5: Using a function for an IN Expression

```
<%@ Page Language="C#" AutoEventWireup="true" CodeFile="InParameter.aspx.cs"
Inherits="InParameter" %>

<!DOCTYPE html PUBLIC "-//W3C//DTD XHTML 1.1//EN"
"http://www.w3.org/TR/xhtml11/DTD/xhtml11.dtd">

<html xmlns="http://www.w3.org/1999/xhtml" >
<head runat="server">
    <title>IN Parameter</title>
</head>
<body>
    <form id="form1" runat="server">
    <div>
        <h1>View Employees</h1>
        <asp:Label ID="Label1" runat="server" Text="Employee IDs (comma separated):
"></asp:Label><br />
        <br />
        <asp:TextBox
            ID="txtEmployeeIDs" runat="server" Width="227px"></asp:TextBox><br />
        <br />
        <asp:Button ID="Button1" runat="server" Text="Update" /><br />
        <br />
        <asp:GridView ID="GridView1" runat="server" AutoGenerateColumns="False"
DataKeyNames="EmployeeID"
            DataSourceID="SqlDataSource1">
            <Columns>
                <asp:BoundField DataField="EmployeeID" HeaderText="EmployeeID"
InsertVisible="False"
                    ReadOnly="True" SortExpression="EmployeeID" />
                <asp:BoundField DataField="LastName" HeaderText="LastName"
SortExpression="LastName" />
                <asp:BoundField DataField="FirstName" HeaderText="FirstName"
SortExpression="FirstName" />
            </Columns>
        </asp:GridView>
        <asp:SqlDataSource ID="SqlDataSource1" runat="server"
            ConnectionString="<%$ ConnectionStrings:NorthwindConnectionString %>"
            SelectCommand="SELECT [EmployeeID], [LastName], [FirstName], [Photo]
FROM [Employees] WHERE ([EmployeeID] IN (select val from
ufStringToIntTable(@EmployeeID)))">
            <SelectParameters>
                <asp:ControlParameter ControlID="txtEmployeeIDs" DefaultValue="1"
Name="EmployeeID"
                    PropertyName="Text" Type="string" />
            </SelectParameters>
        </asp:SqlDataSource>
```

```
        </div>
      </form>
  </body>
  </html>
```

Listing 14-5 uses a SqlDataSource control to populate a GridView control. Notice the IN expression in the SelectCommand attribute. It contains ...WHERE ([EmployeeID] IN (select val from ufString ToIntTable(@EmployeeID))).ufStringToIntTable is the function from Listing 14-4. As shown in the SelectParameters element, the @EmployeeID parameter is populated from the txtEmployeeIDs TextBox control. You can test this by running the Web form in Listing 14-5 and adding a comma-separated string of numbers. The Northwind Employees table contains nine records, so you can select some, none, or all of them. Pressing the Update button causes a postback that repopulates the GridView control.

Protecting against Canonicalization Attacks

A canonicalization attack occurs when someone enters a filename requesting a file they aren't allowed to have or overwrites a file they shouldn't. Returning files that a user shouldn't have opens security holes because the file can contain sensitive information you don't want to expose. Allowing users to overwrite files causes a couple of problems. Perhaps they delete important information necessary for the operation of the site or the business. Another problem occurs when someone overwrites a file that is executable with a malicious file that can launch a virus.

The operating system tries to be user friendly and can resolve a filename, regardless of how you specify it. For example, the following four lines are equivalent:

```
type c:\log.txt

type \log.txt

type \..\log.txt

type c:\log.txt;;;
```

It is difficult to test for every case. Figure 14-3 shows a fictitious example of input that renames a file. Notice that the New Name field is set to C:\\SomeData.xml, which should never be allowed. Sure enough, it is possible to write code that is not secure enough to prevent this. Listing 14-6 shows what happens when you click the Bad Rename button.

Figure 14-3

Listing 14-6: The wrong way to handle filename input

```
protected void btnBadRename_Click(object sender, EventArgs e)
{
    // bad file handling - open to attack
    string appPath = Request.PhysicalApplicationPath;

    string oldPath = Path.Combine(appPath, txtOldName.Text);
    string newPath = Path.Combine(appPath, txtNewName.Text);

    File.Move(oldPath, newPath);
}
```

The problem with Listing 14-6 is that it grabs the input filename with no processing at all. The `File` class has no knowledge that it is an ASP.NET environment and you get no protection at all. Therefore, it does exactly as told and you'll have to hope that other security mechanisms, such as ACLs, help you out.

To work with filenames, most people use the `Request.MapPath` or `Server.MapPath` calls. Besides being a convenient way to get a full path to a file, the `MapPath` methods also help protect against canonicalization attacks. Listing 14-7 shows the secure way to work with filename input.

Listing 14-7: The proper way to handle filename input

```
protected void btnGoodRename_Click(object sender, EventArgs e)
{
    // good file handling - Server.MapPath
    // keeps files in application directory
    string oldPath = Server.MapPath(txtOldName.Text);
    string newPath = Server.MapPath(txtNewName.Text);

    File.Move(oldPath, newPath);
}
```

I know that most people use the `MapPath` methods all the time. However, some people just like to be different. Also, if you are calling a reusable library that handles files, it may not have security in mind. You should test the library with bad input to determine whether it is secure. If not, you can write your own routine or wrap the call in your own type that does proper validation on the input. Using `Request` `.MapPath` and `Server.MapPath` makes your ASP.NET application more resistant to canonicalization attacks.

> If you're wrapping a third-party library to validate input with your own class, you won't have direct access to the `Server` property. However, you can still get to the `MapPath` method by calling `HttpContext.Current.Server.MapPath();`.

Using the New File Upload Control

ASP.NET 2.0 includes a new File Upload Web Server control. It works like the HTML File Upload control does except it is object-oriented with Web control properties and you no longer have to manually set the `enctype` attribute on the form element. What is more significant in terms of security is that you now have a `FileName` property on the ASP.NET File Upload control. The ASP.NET File Upload control still has the `PostedFile` property, but you don't need to use it for obtaining the filename anymore. Because the `FileName` property returns only the filename, and not the full path, there is less opportunity for mishandling the file and opening any security holes:

```
// the only way to get a file name from an HTML control
string htmlFilePath = fupHtmlUpload.PostedFile.FileName;

// still supported in ASP.NET Web control
string aspNetFilePath = fupAspNetUpload.PostedFile.FileName;

// new FileName property in ASP.NET Web control
string filePath = fupAspNetUpload.FileName;

// use it like this
string fileName = Path.Combine(Server.MapPath("."), filePath);
fupAspNetUpload.SaveAs(fileName);
```

This discussion assumes that you have weighed the benefits of allowing file uploads and have determined that it is a requirement. Remember that allowing file uploads is another vector that attackers can use to cause Denial-of-Service attacks on your site. You still need to be careful about file permissions you give the ASP .NET user. For example, if you are saving to a directory with a configuration file, the user could upload a file named `web.config` and overwrite yours. To stop this, put a deny write on the `web.config` ACL for the ASP.NET user (or the NETWORK SECURITY user on Windows Server 2003). For a more thorough security review, examine the identity that a user is operating to ensure secure settings.

Using Dynamic Impersonation Safely

Impersonation refers to the capability of code to run with the identity of a specific user. Typically, this is the logged on user, but it can also be a designated user (see the `userName` and `password` attributes of the `identity` element in `web.config`). You would use impersonation so that a user can access a

Windows operating system resource with specific permissions. This could be a file on the file system. This is one way to access that resource that would be impossible to access otherwise. Alternatively, you could expand the permissions on the resource, but that may not be good for security.

The `identity` element in `web.config` enables you to perform impersonation. When it is turned on, the application runs with the credentials of the currently logged on user. This setting applies to all files in the same directory as the `web.config` file. Because you don't want every logged on user to have access to protected resources, it is common to put the page that accesses the resource in a separate directory and add a `web.config` to that directory with impersonation turned on. Then configure security so only a certain user or role can access anything in that directory. After accessing a page in the subdirectory where impersonation is enabled, the user will run with impersonation and be able to access the resource.

When setting the identity element in `web.config`, a security hazard could exist whereby we can turn on impersonation for all files within the scope of that `web.config` file. This is convenient, as are many other things in ASP.NET. However, if you are following the security principle of least privilege, it may not be the most secure solution. In fact, it may open a security hole either now or in the future when more pages are added or when maintaining the site. Because the logged on user is impersonating during the entire time they have access to any pages in the same directory, they also have access to everything else to which the impersonated user has access. The most secure solution is to allow access to a resource for only the briefest amount of time possible and only when necessary.

I'm not advocating that you not use impersonation through `web.config` because if you need it you should use it. Conversely, if you want to restrict access to resources to only those who need it and only when they need it, then *dynamic impersonation* could be a good choice for you. Listing 14-8 shows how to do this.

Listing 14-8: Dynamic impersonation in code

```csharp
protected void btnViewGrades_Click(object sender, EventArgs e)
{

    Response.Write(WindowsIdentity.GetCurrent().Name + "<br>");

    // impersonate current user
    WindowsImpersonationContext ctx =
        ((WindowsIdentity)User.Identity).Impersonate();

    Response.Write(WindowsIdentity.GetCurrent().Name + "<br>");

    try
    {
        DataSet ds = new DataSet();

        // throws exception when user doesn't have permission
        ds.ReadXml(Server.MapPath("Grades.xml"));

        GridView1.DataSource = ds.Tables[0];
        GridView1.DataBind();
    }
    catch (UnauthorizedAccessException)
    {
        lblResult.Text = "Not Authorized!";
```

```
        }

        // turn impersonation off
        ctx.Undo();

        Response.Write(WindowsIdentity.GetCurrent().Name + "<br>");
    }
```

Calling the `Impersonate` method of the current user's `WindowsIdentity` makes the program run with the permissions of the current user. The impersonation context is closed when calling `Undo` on the `WindowsImpersonationContext` object that was returned by the call to `Impersonate`. Therefore, all code between the call to `Impersonate` and the call to `Undo` in Listing 14-8 runs with the permissions of the caller. All code outside these bounds runs as the NETWORK SERVICE account (on Windows Server 2003) or the ASPNET account (all other OSs).

Listing 14-8 puts access to a file named `Grades.xml` within the block of code where we are impersonating. To demonstrate how this works, set ACLs to deny access to this file to everyone but a single person. Then log on with an account that doesn't have access to demonstrate that an `UnauthorizedAccess Exception` will be raised when you run the program. You can also prove that it works by logging on as the person who does have access and then running the program. Dynamic impersonation allows you to follow the principle of least privilege by limiting impersonation to a single block of code, only when necessary.

Validating a Strong Password in Login Controls

When using both the Create User Wizard and the Change Password controls, users are allowed to enter any password they want. This opens new security holes because too many users enter passwords that are common words. These passwords are easy for the user to remember, but they are also easy for a hacker to figure out. Because the Login controls don't check for weak password vulnerabilities, your site is at risk.

The hack in this section adds validation capabilities to passwords. We're simply going to add a `RegularExpressionValidator` control. To get started, perform the following actions:

1. Add a Create User Wizard to a Web form.

2. Drag a Regular Expression Validator to the right side of the same table cell as the Password TextBox.

3. Change the `RegularExpressionValidator` `ErrorMessage` property to `"Must have at least 1 number, 1 special character, and more than 6 characters."`

4. Change the `RegularExpressionValidator` `Text` property to `*`.

5. Change the `RegularExpressionValidator` `ControlToValidate` property to `Password`.

6. Change the `RegularExpressionValidator` `ValidationExpression` property to `"(?=^.{6,}$)(?=.*\d)(?=.*\W+)(?![.\n]).*$"`.

As its name suggests, a RegularExpressionValidator control uses what is called a *regular expression* to perform its validation. Regular expressions are a pattern matching language, which at first glance look cryptic and terse. However, once you know how to use them, you are very likely to find them fast and powerful. A good regular expressions site on the Web is `regexlib.com`.

The HTML for the cell where the `Password` is located should now look like this:

```
<td>
    <asp:TextBox ID="Password" runat="server"
        TextMode="Password"></asp:TextBox>
    <asp:RequiredFieldValidator ID="PasswordRequired" runat="server"
        ControlToValidate="Password"
        ErrorMessage="Password is required."
        ToolTip="Password is required."
        ValidationGroup="CreateUserWizard1">*</asp:RequiredFieldValidator>
    <asp:RegularExpressionValidator ID="RegularExpressionValidator1" runat="server"
        ControlToValidate="Password"
        ErrorMessage="Must have at least 1 number, 1 special character, and more
than 6 characters."
        ValidationExpression=
"(?=^.{6,}$)(?=.*\d)(?=.*\W+)(?![.\n]).*$">*</asp:RegularExpressionValidator>
</td>
```

You can cut and paste the highlighted `RegularExpressionValidator` element from the preceding HTML into the Password cell of your own templated Create User Wizard. While you're at it, you can add a RegularExpressionValidator control to the Create User Wizard e-mail address, too. The RegularExpressionValidator `ValidationExpression` property already has a pop-up dialog in which a regular expression for e-mail is available for selection from a list of other regular expressions.

The same technique works for the Change Password control. After adding the Change Password control to your page, select Create Template, and use the same RegularExpressionValidator described above. The only difference will be that you should set the `ControlToValidate` property to `NewPassword`.

Wrapping Up

One of the best ways to protect a site against malicious users is to guard your code against SQL injection attacks. The technique is to simply parameterize your code. Using a SQL function allows you to pass a parameter to an `IN` expression.

Most code is safe from canonicalization attacks if you are using `Server.MapPath` or `Request.MapPath` API calls. It is when you use some of the file manipulation commands that you open potential security holes. The new File Upload Web control contains a `FileName` property that returns the name of the file without its full path. This could be made more secure by reducing the chance that the path could somehow be handled improperly, potentially opening a security hole.

The dynamic impersonation technique highlights the principle of least privilege by showing you how to limit resource exposure only in specific places in your code and only when it is needed. The alternative is using the `identity` attribute of the `web.config` file, which opens security holes by allowing everyone who has access to any page in a directory to have the same permissions associated with the user they are impersonating. The new ASP.NET Login controls make it easy to work with security, but they can be enhanced for even better security. You can add a `RequiredFieldValidator` component to their templates to further refine the validation you need to apply. For example, you can define a regular expression to ensure that users enter strong passwords in the Create User Wizard and Change Password controls.

15

Building Your Own Hacks

Progress in our profession comes from the need to constantly improve. Many people have seen this progress in software development starting from binary switches, moving to assembly language, on to high-level languages, continuing through object-oriented programming, and adopting component-oriented programming. In the future, service-oriented programming and model-driven application development will be the norm. Each step of the way has fostered the betterment of your condition as software professionals and has enabled you to contribute to society via ever greater means.

This need for continuous improvement is the essence of a hack. Hacks are all about breaking away from today's status quo and improving on what is there. It involves taking a given technology and extending it in such a way that you come up with something that provides additional value.

To put the importance of this into greater perspective, consider a salient example of what is happening today with ASP.NET during the current transition from v1.1 to v2.0. In ASP.NET 1.x there was no tool-supported visual inheritance, so developers came up with hacks that enabled them to accomplish what they needed. Because these inheritance hacks were so prevalent, it sent a clear signal to Microsoft that this type of functionality was necessary. They responded with Master Pages in v2.0.

The hacks drove the technology. Similar circumstances existed in the way of data access, security, UI controls, and more. Because people come up with their own hacks and share them, everyone benefits because, in many ways, tools are getting better in the specific areas you need.

As we look into the future, there is a good example of a current hack that promises to deliver huge benefits. Regardless of who originated the technology, Microsoft added XmlHttp, JScript, and Dynamic Hypertext Markup Language (DHTML) to Internet Explorer. Individually, these are cool technologies. However, some great mind threw them all into the same pot and cooked them up together to form Asynchronous JavaScript and XML (AJAX). Because of its popularity, AJAX has inspired Microsoft to develop similar tools for us in a project code-named Atlas. Hacks help us all.

To illustrate the concept, this chapter looks at a hack that improves security. Security is critical, and if we can help others work with it in more effective ways, we've done more for our profession. In Chapter 14, you looked at a hack to prevent SQL injection attacks. Here, you extend that protection with a related hack for massaging input data to prevent other malicious behavior. The rest of this chapter focuses on this hack called *Input Filter Protection*.

Determining When You Have a Hack

It isn't that hard to create your own hack. Most developers do it every day when they write code that builds upon the basic capabilities of existing tools. They create their own libraries that include hacks and share them with other people. To know whether you have your own hack, consider questions such as the following:

❑   Is it documented?

❑   Have you found new uses for an existing capability?

❑   Can it be reused?

❑   Can you share it?

Does Your Hack Go Beyond the Technical Documentation?

If it is already part of the Visual Studio or .NET Framework SDK technical documentation, then it isn't a hack. However, if you've figured out how to do something that is made up of different parts of what already exists, then it is a potential candidate for a hack. You've gone beyond what is documented in front of you and have created something new.

Reading the documentation, it is obvious that the `string.Replace` method is well documented, which means that it doesn't even approach the qualifications for being a hack. However, what you can do with that method is translate the wildcards of a SQL statement so they are delimited, preventing malicious input. This is something that combines what exists (`Replace`) with a necessary application (`Security`). It could be a hack. Here's an example of how this potential hack would look:

```
str = str.Replace("%", "[%]");
```

> The examples in this chapter use the following lines of code to examine different approaches to creating a hack. It would be better for you to get the point about creating hacks, rather than get bogged down with what the code does. Nevertheless, some of you will want to know more, so I'll provide additional info here:
>
> ```
> str = str.Replace("[", "[[]");
>
> str = str.Replace("%", "[%]");
>
> str = str.Replace("_", "[_]");
> ```
>
> If a malicious user were to prefix the parameter of a `LIKE` operator with any of the aforementioned pattern characters, they could slow down your system because it can't be covered by an index. This could lead to a denial-of-service attack. The `replace` operation ensures that the percent sign is interpreted as a literal, rather than a wildcard.

Did You Find a New Use for an Existing Capability?

Another possible hack is when you take something that was written for one purpose and figure out how to apply it in another useful way. For example, consider the `Request.MapPath` statement. Sure, it is commonly used for obtaining the full path to the current application directory, but how many people consider it as security protection against canonicalization attacks (see the following box)? If you've taken something and used it in a way that requires thinking outside the box, you may have a hack.

> Canonicalization attacks can occur when a malicious user attempts to access a file by altering the filename — for example, try typing notepad `Default.aspx.cs.` in the command line (including the trailing dot). It works just fine because the operating system is trying to be user friendly. However, if you had a protection mechanism that prevented people from accessing any files with the `*.cs` extension, your security could be compromised.

If you subscribe to the reasonable assumption that the `string.Replace` method would typically be used in text processing, it isn't difficult to believe that this is the way most people see and use it. Furthermore, with a mindset that a feature is for a specific purpose, you must step out of the box to envision it used in a different way. In this case, the `string.Replace` method is used in the context of enhancing security. Security is not an application foremost in every developer's mind and thus represents a new use for an existing capability. In fact, you should enhance the concept to protect more strings in a SQL statement as follows:

```
str = str.Replace("[", "[[]");
str = str.Replace("%", "[%]");
str = str.Replace("_", "[_]");
```

Is It Relatively Unknown?

There are many capabilities in the .NET Framework that a lot of people don't know about. You could classify many of these things as hidden gems. These types of hacks are harder to recognize because it is difficult to know how many people are really aware of them. One way to get a better idea is by talking to people about the hack. You could also do an online search to see whether people have discussed the subject much. By exposing your hidden gem as a hack, you may be helping many others. For example, techniques and tools exist to enhance the security of your applications, but many developers don't know how to use them to secure their applications.

Security is something that is not in the forefront of every developer's mind. When writing ASP.NET applications, the attack surface has wider exposure. Instead of a single attacker physically sitting in front of a computer using a desktop application, many people can access a Web application across a network. If the network is the Internet, the number of potential attackers is even greater. While more developers are being educated in security every day, there is still a gap in knowledge between the few who understand the risks and best practices and the many who lack sufficient appreciation and skills. Security is an area ripe for new hacks to make it easier for developers to harden their applications.

The reason to use the `string.Replace` method to modify input is to protect against malicious users. For example, suppose a malicious user entered the following information that you intended to use as a filter in your query:

```
%Denial of Service
```

By implementing the `string.Replace`, your application neutralizes any harmful effects of the malicious input. Given the select statement

```
Select * from customers where ContactName like @ContactName
```

the previous malicious input would be run through a `string.Replace` statement, producing the following output:

```
Select * from customers where ContactName like [%]Denial of Service
```

Given that prefixing the criteria of a SQL `LIKE` clause with a wildcard prevents an index lookup, query performance suffers. Therefore, this technique forces certain characters to be interpreted literally, rather than as wildcards. Because you are able to use existing capabilities to fill a useful need in an unknown area, this could be classified as a hack.

Is It Reusable?

There are plenty of situations in which you can put together code to build upon what's in the .NET Framework or find a new way to use an existing tool, but can it be used in other places? In other words, does the code apply only to the situation for which you wrote it? To qualify as a hack, your code should be something you can reuse in other parts of your application or with other applications. If it isn't just a one-off solution, you could have a hack.

Because using databases is a common task, it is likely that you will be able to use the Input Filter Protection hack in other applications. In this case, you could use it on every page in all your applications that accept input that will be used as a filter.

Can You Share It with Others?

This question builds upon the last question in that a hack should be something you can share. Are other people interested in the code you wrote? Maybe it is reusable but applies primarily to a single domain. While a hack doesn't have to be universally applicable, it should be of interest to others. It should be something you can share with other programmers working in other domains.

Accepting input to use as a data filter is a common programming task. As such, it is reasonable to assume that other people would be interested in using the same technique to secure their Web pages.

You Could Have a Hack

If your code or idea results in an answer of "yes" to any of the questions presented in the previous sections, you could very well have a hack. If you think you have a hack and desire to share it, polish it and let others know so you can make your own contribution to the community.

Polishing Your Hack to Publish It

If you see the importance of hacks and understand some of the elements that make a hack, chances are good that you're currently thinking about hacks you've already created. If you have a desire to share a hack, it's time to polish it and publish it. This section offers guidelines for helping to make your hack more effective.

Comment Your Code

It helps to put yourself in someone else's shoes when commenting code. If you've ever done maintenance on someone else's code, you know how important it is to understand what the original programmer was trying to do. Assume the other developer knows the technology and can figure out the syntax of any given statement. The real value you have to instill is the "intent" of a certain piece of code. Let them know what you are trying to accomplish.

This Input Filter Protection hack may not be intuitively obvious to people first looking at the code. The `string.Replace` method is understandable enough, but maybe the code wouldn't be as understandable if it were a regular expression. You should comment it because in the face of modification, someone still needs to understand the purpose of important steps. Here's an example of how the Input Filter Protection code could be commented:

```
// stop attackers from manipulating the wild-card.
// i.e. if they input "%DenialOfService" they could cause
// performance degradation because filter is changed to
// "[%]DenialOfService" the attack in neutralized.
str = str.Replace("[", "[[]");
str = str.Replace("%", "[%]");
 str = str.Replace("_", "[_]");
```

As you can see, there is a lot of meaning to a single statement. Instead of the inane "`// replace the '%' character with '[%]'`" comment, another person can understand why the code is there. Furthermore, if it were later optimized or changed, the person changing the code would be more likely to adhere to the intent of the code.

Make Code Self-Documenting

This builds upon the last tip in trying to make the task of another developer easier. Give identifiers meaningful names that help other developers figure out their purpose. Through a combination of good comments and easy-to-read code, your hack will be better understood.

Using an identifier with the name of `"s"` or `"str"` is practically meaningless in the Input Filter Protection hack. The whole purpose of the code is to keep attackers from entering malicious input to a SQL statement. With this in mind, you could reasonably assume that a meaningful name for this identifier would be `filter` and should be coded as follows:

```
filter = filter.Replace("[", "[[]");
filter = filter.Replace("%", "[%]");
 filter = filter.Replace("_", "[_]");
```

This is something that should be done if someone else will be reading the code. The easier you make it, the better the chances are that someone can trust and reuse your hack.

Use Common Coding Conventions

The .NET Framework Software Development Kit (SDK) has common coding guidelines for writing .NET code. Some people use it, while others prefer their own standards. However, by using common conventions, you increase the chances of other developers being able to understand the code.

For example, if `myFilter` is a local variable, you wouldn't Pascal case it as `MyFilter` or use an underscore as in `My_Filter`. The common coding convention for local variables and parameters is camel casing, so `myFilter` would be correct and could be considered more approachable by other developers.

> It is abundantly clear that common coding conventions are a matter of opinion and the subject of much debate. As with everything, you will have to evaluate whether this is something to be applied to your situation. The example in this section is just a single instance of one coding convention. However, it is created in the spirit of making it as easy as possible for other developers to read your code, and therefore worthy of consideration.

Write Generic Routines

Sometimes you create example code and leave literals and constants hard-coded into statements. Such code often breaks when other programmers try to reuse what you've written. It means that they will have to manually change the hard-coded content themselves and probably go through the steps of making the code more generic.

For example, if a piece of code operated on a file, you wouldn't want the example to hard-code the filename. Instead you would create a string parameter that was passed into a method that performed the routine. Along these lines, if your routine were written in the `Main` method for simplicity, you could consider moving it to a method because that is what others will do anyway. In the case of the Input Filter Protection hack, the code would be more useful if transformed into this:

```
public static void GetSecureText(string filter)
{
    filter = filter.Replace("[", "[[]");
    filter = filter.Replace("%", "[%]");
    filter = filter.Replace("_", "[_]");

    lblSearchResult.Text = "Search Term: " + filter;
}
```

The `GetSecureText` method could be called like this:

```
lblSearchResult.Text =
    SecurityUtilities.GetSecureText(txtSearch.Text);
```

If your code operates on different types, consider building an interface that cooperating types could implement to work with your code. Another option is to allow `System.Object` parameters if you don't know the type of the object to be passed in. For example, the Input Filter Protection hack could be implemented as an object, as shown in Listing 15-1.

Listing 15-1: An object for implementing a hack: IProtectSqlStatements.cs and InputFilterProtector.cs

```csharp
public interface IProtectSqlStatements
{
    string SecureText
    {
        get;
    }
}

public class InputFilterProtector : IProtectSqlStatements
{
    object m_inputControl;

    public InputFilterProtector(object inputControl)
    {
      m_inputControl = inputControl;
    }

    public string SecureText
    {
        get
        {
            ITextControl textControl = m_inputControl as ITextControl;

            string filter = "No Text";

            if (textControl != null)
            {
                filter = textControl.Text;

                // stop attackers from manipulating the wild-card.
                // i.e. if they input "%DenialOfService" they could cause
                // performance degradation because filter is changed to
                // "[%]DenialOfService" the attack in neutralized.
                filter = filter.Replace("[", "[[]");
                filter = filter.Replace("%", "[%]");
                filter = filter.Replace("_", "[_]");
            }

            return filter;
        }
    }
}
```

You can call the code in Listing 15-1 like this (`Default.aspx.cs`):

```csharp
IProtectSqlStatements objectFilterProtector;

protected void Page_Load(object sender, EventArgs e)
{
    // wrap the textbox with a secure object
```

```
            objectFilterProtector = new InputFilterProtector(txtSearch);
    }
    protected void btnObjectSearch_Click(object sender, EventArgs e)
    {
        lblSearchResult.Text = objectFilterProtector.SecureText;
    }
```

Because `IProtectSqlStatements` is implemented, the user has the flexibility to access the object via interface or class. Notice that the code is passing a reference to the `TextBox` control when instantiating `filterProtector` in `Page_Load`. This way, you can use `filterProtector` multiple times during page processing. As you can see, a single call to the `SecureText` property is all the user needs to do.

Version 2.0 of both C# and VB.NET support the use of *generics,* which are also referred to as *parameterized types.* Generics enable you to build types that in many cases perform better and are more type safe. You can also use generic constraints to better specify the types and semantics of parameters. For example, Listing 15-1 would be rewritten as the generic type shown in Listing 15-2.

Listing 15-2: A hack written as a generic type — GenericInputFilterProtector.cs

```
public class GenericInputFilterProtector<ControlWithText> : InputFilterProtector
    where ControlWithText : Control, ITextControl
{
    ControlWithText m_inputControl;

    public GenericInputFilterProtector(ControlWithText inputControl)
    {
        m_inputControl = inputControl;
    }

    public string SecureText
    {
        get
        {
            filter = m_inputControl.Text;

            // stop attackers from manipulating the wild-card.
            // i.e. if they input "%DenialOfService" they could cause
            // performance degradation because filter is changed to
            // "[%]DenialOfService" the attack in neutralized.
            filter = filter.Replace("[", "[[]");
            filter = filter.Replace("%", "[%]");
            filter = filter.Replace("_", "[_]");

            return filter;
        }
    }
}
```

You can call the code like this (`Default.aspx.cs`):

```
    IProtectSqlStatements genericFilterProtector;

    protected void Page_Load(object sender, EventArgs e)
```

```
    {
        // wrap the textbox with a secure object
        genericFilterProtector = new
GenericInputFilterProtector<TextBox>(txtSearch);
    }

    protected void btnGenericSearch_Click(object sender, EventArgs e)
    {
        lblSearchResult.Text = genericFilterProtector.SecureText;
    }
```

In Listing 15-2 you could have implemented the `InputFilterProtector` class without generics and operated only on type `ITextControl`. However, implementing the class as a generic with an `ITextControl` constraint makes it possible to add other constraints for more flexibility. For example, if you needed to access the control properties of the object being passed in and guarantee that it was indeed a control, you would specify the base class constraint for the `System.Web.UI.Control` class in addition to the `ITextControl` constraint. By setting the constraint as `ITextControl`, you leave open the possibility for third-party text-box-like controls that implement `ITextControl`, to be used with the `InputFilterProtector` class. The `ITextControl` constraint also guarantees that the control passed in will have a `Text` property.

> If you need help understanding how generics work, see the .NET Framework documentation. However, you can get more terse information from the language specifications or find one of the many books available for learning language syntax. This explanation itself is in the spirit of hacks in that the description of a hack doesn't include things that are already well documented elsewhere.

Consider Implementing Your Hack as a Component or Control

In case you haven't noticed, let me point out that we've covered several useful techniques for implementing components and controls in earlier chapters. To understand why this was necessary, consider that a desirable attribute of a good hack is to be reusable. Along these lines, the entire purpose of components and controls is to provide units of reuse. Therefore, it makes a lot of sense to implement a hack as a component or control, if the situation fits.

You don't always have to start a component or control from scratch. If there is an existing control that has most of the required functionality and you just need to add a little more to it, remember that you can use the object-oriented principle of inheritance to reuse an existing control. This is what we've done in Listing 15-3.

Listing 15-3: Hack implemented as a derived class of an existing control— SecureTextBox.cs

```
[ToolboxBitmap(typeof(TextBox))]
public class SecureTextBox : TextBox
{
```

(continued)

Listing 15-3 *(continued)*

```
        public string SecureText
        {
            get
            {
                string filter = Text;

                filter = filter.Replace("[", "[[]");
                filter = filter.Replace("%", "[%]");
                filter = filter.Replace("_", "[_]");

                return filter;
            }
        }
    }
```

All that was necessary for this control was a `SecureText` property. Now the `SecureTextBox` control can be used anywhere a `TextBox` control is used. The difference is that you would call the `SecureText` property to get a secure SQL statement string, as shown here (Default.aspx.cs):

```
        protected void btnSecureSearch_Click(object sender, EventArgs e)
        {
            lblSecureResult.Text = "Result: " +
                txtSecureSearch.SecureText;
        }
```

Wrapping your hack in a component or a control can require more work than just writing a method. However, as shown here, it makes it a whole lot easier to use.

Write Documentation

One of the friendliest things you can do is to write documentation for your hack. If the hack involves code, documentation will be a great help in assisting other programmers in understanding and using your hack. While much of this discussion focuses on code hacks, there are procedural hacks that need to be described also. Some hacks must be documented.

If you don't feel very comfortable writing, do a rough draft and ask a friend to help you make it better. It isn't about having to be a good writer as much as it is just telling another programmer how to use your hack.

Using the Community to Test Your Hack and Provide Feedback

If you have a hack you want to share and you've polished it, the next step is to get it out to the rest of the world where it can do some good. Fortunately, the .NET community is alive and vibrant, offering countless opportunities to share your hack. Consider newsgroups, websites, blogs, and any other venue for sharing the hack.

These days, newsgroups are avenues for posting reusable code and examples, many hacks in their own right. Because Google keeps an archive of all newsgroup postings, people can always search for it and provide a link for others to find it. Be sure to post some keywords in the body of the message that you think people will be searching for.

If you have a website, post it. There are also numerous other community websites that will host your hack. Some that come to mind immediately are `GotDotNet.com` and `CodeProject.com`. They also provide comment pages where people can discuss what you've published.

A fast-growing new medium for communication on the internet is the *weblog*, commonly referred to as a *blog*. A blog enables you to have a two-way conversation with people about any subject you want. You can post your hack to your blog and people will be able to link to it and communicate with you about it, and you'll also have the opportunity to reply and do updates.

Wrapping Up

Hacks are important because they help move the developer's profession forward by building upon what exists to influence future technological offerings. You should ask yourself the following questions to determine whether the code you have is a hack: Is it already documented? Have you found a new use for an existing capability? Is it relatively unknown? Is it reusable? Can you share it?

If you feel you have a hack and want to share it, there are certain things you can do to prepare it for distribution to others. Make sure it is commented and readable, use common coding conventions, rewrite it in a generic way, and consider packaging it as a component or control for maximum reuse.

16

Master Pages

Providing a consistent look and feel across a website has been a challenge that developers have been trying to solve since the introduction of the Internet. While most websites have a header, footer, and menu structure, they all handle the placement of those items differently. Over the years, several different techniques for addressing this challenge have emerged, such as server-side includes, Cascading Style Sheets (CSS), custom template files, XML and XSLT, and, more recently, ASP.NET user controls. While each of these technologies has its own set of pros and cons, no single technology provides "the" solution for providing consistency across a website.

User controls (combined with CSS) arguably provide the best option for maintaining a consistent website layout in ASP.NET 1.1 because they're object-oriented and make it trivial to define a common header, footer, and menu within one or more pages. However, most developers reference user controls in each page using the `Reference` directive with the associated `TagPrefix` and `TagName` attributes, resulting in duplication of code (albeit minimal). To get around these duplication issues, some developers have tried embedding user controls within other user controls. While this technique certainly works, it results in a nested object model that is fairly difficult to work with when controls need to be accessed programmatically during load or postback operations.

To alleviate this problem, several different template frameworks targeted at ASP.NET 1.1 have been developed to minimize the amount of work required for Web developers to change the layout of headers, footers, menus, and other common parts of a website. Initial .NET template frameworks relied upon custom classes that extended the `System.Web.UI.Page` class. These custom classes often hard-coded the common HTML elements of a site (the header and footer, for example) into the class, making maintenance and deployment difficult. Other solutions extended the `PageBase` class but defined the website's common layout components in an external template file. An example of this type of template framework can be found at `xmlforasp.net/codeSection .aspx?csID=102`. While custom template frameworks get the job done, they provide little to no design-time support in Visual Studio.NET and don't provide a standard way for .NET developers around the world to define a website's overall structure.

With the release of ASP.NET 2.0, a powerful new way of providing websites with a consistent layout and structure is available for Web developers of varying skill levels to use. Instead of resorting to nested user controls or custom classes and templates, ASP.NET 2.0 *Master Pages* can be used to define a website's overall layout with a minimal amount of time and effort. They can be defined in one place and shared across an entire website without hard-coding header, footer, and menu user controls into each and every page. This chapter provides an introduction to Master Pages and demonstrates various tips and tricks you can use in your ASP.NET 2.0 websites. The first two sections provide an overview of creating and consuming Master Pages, and the sections that follow provide more in-depth insight into using Master Pages.

Master Pages Fundamentals

Master Pages provide a simple and efficient template framework that allows common components of a website such as menus, headers, and footers to be defined in a single template file. This makes changing a website's overall look, feel, and layout quick and easy because changes made to a Master Page template are automatically applied throughout the entire website. While many websites may need only a single Master Page, multiple Master Pages can be created as needed — one for the home page and one for subpages, for example. Master Pages can also be loaded dynamically based upon a user's profile or other conditions. This makes it easy to provide printable versions of pages without having to change the page content.

All Master Pages have a .master extension that is mapped to a handler named System.Web.Http ForbiddenHandler. This mapping is defined in the Web server's default web.config file and it prevents Master Pages from being viewed directly in the browser, just as files with .ascx and .config extensions can't be viewed using a browser. Attempts to view a file with a .master extension in the browser will result in a "This type of page is not served" error.

Master Pages rely on existing classes in the .NET Framework to perform their magic. They derive directly from the UserControl class:

```
public class MasterPage : System.Web.UI.UserControl
```

As a result of deriving from UserControl, Master Pages expose a standard set of properties such as Page, Session, Request, and Response that can be accessed programmatically. Master Pages cannot be shared across Internet Information Services (IIS) applications (like user controls) and will generate an error in situations where sharing occurs. Later in this chapter you'll learn a way to remedy this problem, enabling a Master Page to be shared across multiple IIS applications on a server.

Creating Master Pages

You can create a Master Page in Visual Studio .NET 2005 by using the Add New Item menu or you can create one by hand by opening a new file in your favorite text editor and adding the Master directive to the top of the file. An example of a simple Master Page is shown in Listing 16-1.

Listing 16-1: A simple Master Page

```
<%@ Master Language="C#" AutoEventWireup="true"
    CodeFile="WebsiteMasterPage.master.cs" Inherits="WebSiteMasterPage" %>
<html>
```

```
<head runat="server">
    <title>Master Page Demo</title>
</head>
<body>
    <form id="form1" runat="server">
        <table width="100%">
            <tr>
                <td colspan="2">
                    <!-- Header -->
                    <img src="/GolfClubShack/Images/header_image.gif" />
                </td>
            </tr>
            <tr>
                <td width="25%">
                    Menu
                </td>
                <td width="75%">
                    <asp:ContentPlaceHolder ID="cphMain" runat="server">
                    </asp:ContentPlaceHolder>
                </td>
            </tr>
            <tr>
                <td colspan="2">
                    Footer
                </td>
            </tr>
        </table>
    </form>
</body>
</html>
```

The code in Listing 16-1 defines where the standard header, menu, and footer should be positioned in the overall structure of a page. It also defines where the page content should go within the Master Page by using the ContentPlaceHolder server control. ContentPlaceHolder derives from Control and doesn't actually add any properties, methods, or events of its own. Its entire purpose is to mark where page content should go within the Master Page template. Although the Master Page shown here has only one ContentPlaceHolder control in it, multiple controls can be added in cases where content from a page should be placed in different areas (left and right columns, for instance). When adding multiple controls, you'll need to ensure that each one has a unique ID.

It's important to note that paths to images and other resources defined within a Master Page are relative to the actual page that is rendered using the Master Page. Paths are not relative to the location of the Master Page itself. For example, if a page sits at the root of a website and an Images subfolder exists, then defining an image in the Master Page using Images/ImageName.gif will work great because the Images subfolder sits one level below the page. For pages that aren't located at the root of the website, however, that path won't work and will ultimately lead to a broken image when rendered in the browser.

You should always define Master Page paths to images, style sheets, JavaScript files, and so forth from the root of the website in which you're working. The Master Page shown in Listing 16-1 contains an img tag with a src attribute that starts with /GolfClubShack so that the image path is defined starting from the root of the website. This type of path will work with pages nested at any level. For ASP.NET server controls such as the Image control, the tilde (~) character can be used to start the image path at the root of the website:

```
<asp:Image id="imgHeader" runat="Server" ImageUrl="~/Images/header_image.gif" />
```

Master Pages can have code files associated with them to keep a clean separation between HTML code and programming code, just as ASP.NET Web forms and user controls can. The Master Page example in the preceding listing is associated with a C# class named `WebsiteMasterPage` located in a file named `WebsiteMasterPage.master.cs`. Standard event handlers such as `Page_Load`, `Page_PreRender`, and so forth can be included to dynamically change Master Page content at runtime.

Creating Content Pages

Now that you've seen some of the fundamentals of Master Pages, it's time to switch gears and talk about how Master Pages can be used by ASP.NET pages. Pages that reference a Master Page are referred to as *content pages*. Content pages differ from regular ASP.NET pages in several ways. First, regular ASP.NET pages represent a complete page, including HTML and body and form tags, whereas content pages do not have these tags because they're normally defined in the Master Page (content pages may or may not have a form tag). Second, content pages must contain a server control named Content, whereas regular ASP.NET pages do not contain this control. Finally, regular ASP.NET pages do not use Master Pages, whereas content pages rely upon a Master Page to control the page's overall structure and layout. Even though they're quite different, both types of pages use the .aspx file extension.

Referencing a Master Page from within a content page can be accomplished using the `MasterPageFile` attribute of the `Page` directive. The path defined in the `MasterPageFile` attribute should start from the root of the Web application so that if the page is moved to a different level in the website's folder hierarchy it will still have the correct path to the Master Page. The tilde (~) character can be used to ensure that the path starts from the root of the website:

```
<%@ Page Language="C#" MasterPageFile="~/WebsiteMasterPage.master"
    Title="Master Demo" %>
```

In addition to referencing the Master Page file location, a content page also needs to contain a server control named Content that contains the actual content of the page. The Content control inherits from the `Control` class and extends it by adding a `ContentPlaceHolderID` property. `ContentPlaceHolderID` is used to identify the `ContentPlaceHolder` control in the Master Page where the page's content should be placed. An example of a simple content page that uses the `MasterPageFile` attribute and Content server control is shown in Listing 16-2.

Listing 16-2: A simple content page that uses the MasterPageFile attribute and Content server control

```
<%@ Page Language="C#" MasterPageFile="~/WebsiteMasterPage.master"
    AutoEventWireup="true" CodeFile="Default.aspx.cs" Inherits="Default"
    Title="Master Demo" %>
<asp:Content ID="Content1" ContentPlaceHolderID="cphMain" Runat="Server">
    Page Content
</asp:Content>
```

Notice that the content page does not contain any HTML or body tags because these tags are defined in the Master Page file (named `WebsiteMasterPage.master`). In this case, the form tag is also defined within the Master Page. The page's content is placed within a Content server control that has a `ContentPlaceHolderID` value that corresponds to the Master Page's `ContentPlaceHolder` ID value. Failure to match the Content control's `ContentPlaceHolderID` value with the Master Page's `ContentPlaceHolder` control's ID value will result in an error because the ASP.NET runtime will not know where to put the page content within the Master Page's controls collection.

Because all content within a content page must be placed within one or more Content server controls, you won't typically see a `Title` tag defined, as there is no head tag to put it in. Instead, the `Page` directive contains a `Title` attribute that can be used to set the title of the content page. The title can also be programmatically changed, as you'll see in the next section.

```
<%@ Page Language="C#" MasterPageFile="~/WebsiteMasterPage.master"
    Title="Master Demo" %>
```

Figure 16-1 shows how a content page looks within Visual Studio .NET 2005 at design time. Notice that the content page is automatically merged with the Master Page, providing a nice design-time view of the overall page. The content page is shown in the middle, white area of the figure and is editable directly in design view The Master Page is grayed out and not editable.

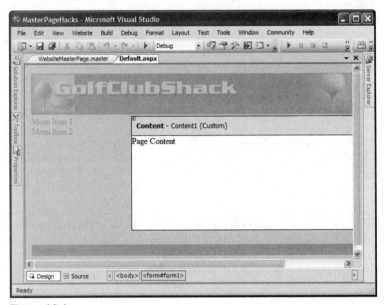

Figure 16-1

While you can certainly create content pages by hand, Visual Studio .NET allows you to more easily create them by adding a new item into your website and then checking the Select Master Page checkbox. Figure 16-2 shows the first step in creating a content page using Visual Studio .NET 2005. After adding the item you can then choose the Master Page that should be referenced. Going this route automatically creates a content page with the `MasterPageFile` attribute and one or more Content server controls (depending upon how many ContentPlaceHolder controls are defined in the Master Page).

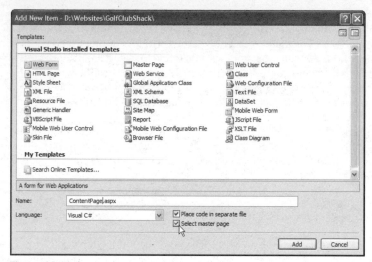

Figure 16-2

Content pages can also be created by right-clicking the desired Master Page in the Solution Explorer and selecting Add Content Page from the menu. The content page will be placed at the same location as the Master Page and will be given a name of `Default.aspx` unless a file with that name already exists.

Programmatically Modifying Master Pages

Creating Master Pages and content pages is quite straightforward but there's much more that you can leverage to create dynamic websites. Master Pages can be programmatically manipulated from within a content page using a property of the `Page` class available in ASP.NET version 2 called `Master`. The `Master` property gives you programmatic access to the Master Page referenced by the content page and allows you to do things such as change the title, add additional metadata attributes, add a style sheet reference, change the controls collection, plus more.

Modifying the Head Section of a Master Page

For example, to access the head section of a Master Page, you can make a call to `Master.Page.Header` from within a content page. Once the header is accessed, you can change the title and even add new metadata content as shown here:

```
//Content Page
protected void Page_Load(object sender, EventArgs e) {
    HtmlHead head = this.Master.Page.Header;
    head.Title = "Working with the head section of a Master Page";
    HtmlMeta meta = new HtmlMeta();
    meta.Name = "Keywords";
    meta.Content = "Master Pages,ASP.NET";
    head.Controls.Add(meta);
}
```

The preceding code accesses the content page's `Master` property and uses it to get to the `Header` property. It then changes the title and adds a new `HtmlMeta` control into the header's `Controls` collection, which specifies keywords associated with the content page. The `head` tag defined in the Master Page must have the `runat="server"` attribute added to it in order for the `Header` property to return an `HtmlHead` object instance:

```
<head runat="server">
    <title>Master Page Demo</title>
</head>
```

If the head tag does not have the `runat="server"` attribute, then the code will return an error because the `HtmlHead` object is null.

Finding Controls in a Master Page

Making calls to the `Master` property from within a content page can also be useful when you need to show or hide controls defined in the Master Page or add new controls programmatically. Finding controls can be done using the standard `FindControl()` method. To demonstrate using `FindControl()`, first examine the following code snippet from a Master Page:

```
<asp:Panel ID="pnlLogin" runat="Server">
    <td align="center" valign="middle" nowrap="true">
        <asp:LoginStatus ID="ctlLoginStatus" runat="server"
          OnLoggingOut="ctlLoginStatus_Logout" CssClass="whiteText" />
    </td>
    <td class="divider" style="width: 18px">
         | 
    </td>
    <td align="center" valign="middle" nowrap="true">
        <a href="/GolfClubShack/OrderList.aspx" class="whiteText">My Orders</a>
    </td>
    <td class="divider">
         | </td>
    <td align="center" valign="middle" nowrap="true">
        <a href="/GolfClubShack/Personalize.aspx" class="whiteText">Personalize
        </a>
    </td>
    <td class="divider">
         | </td>
</asp:Panel>
```

Assume that the My Orders and Personalize links should be shown to all users so that they know what the site offers. However, if users click one of the links, they are redirected to a login page to be authenticated. While on the login page, you would like to hide the links so users don't try to click one of them, causing a redirect to the login page again. This fairly trivial task can be done by setting the `pnlLogin's` `Visible` property to `false`. The trick is knowing how to access controls within the Master Page from the content page. To get to `pnlLogin`, you can use the `Master` property along with the `FindControl()` method, as shown here:

```
//Access pnlLogin in the Master Page from the content page
protected void Page_Load(object sender, EventArgs e) {
    Panel pnl = this.Master.Page.Form.FindControl("pnlLogin") as Panel;
```

```
    if (pnl != null) {
        pnl.Visible = false;
    }
}
```

Defining Master Page Properties

Although the `FindControl()` technique works, casting is required because it returns an object of type `Control`. While it can be argued that the overhead of doing the cast is minimal, there is an easier way to access `pnlLogin` within the Master Page. Rather than use `FindControl()`, a public property can be defined within the Master Page that returns `pnlLogin` directly as a `Panel` type:

```
public partial class GolfClubShackMaster : System.Web.UI.MasterPage {

    public Panel PnlLogin {
        get {
            return this.pnlLogin;
        }
    }

    protected void Page_Load(object sender, EventArgs e) {

    }

}
```

The `PnlLogin` property shown here does nothing more than define a `get` block that returns a direct reference to the `pnlLogin` Panel control within the Master Page. However, accessing the property still requires casting. An attempt to call `Master.PnlLogin` from a content page will fail because `PnlLogin` isn't a valid property of the `MasterPage` object returned from calling the `Master` property. To get to the `PnlLogin` property you have to cast the `MasterPage` object to the appropriate Master Page type, as shown here:

```
GolfClubShackMaster master = (GolfClubShackMaster)this.Master;
master.PnlLogin.Visible = false;
```

This is much cleaner and more efficient than using `FindControl()` because the Master Page's `Controls` collection doesn't have to be iterated through to locate `pnlLogin`, but it still requires casting to get the job done. It also assumes that the Master Page is always of type `GolfClubShackMaster`, which may or may not be the case depending upon how dynamic the site is.

Using the MasterType Directive

In order to call the Master Page's `PnlLogin` property without any casting at all, you need to utilize the `MasterType` directive in the content page. The `MasterType` directive is placed at the top of the content page and provides strongly typed access to the Master Page, making it easy to call custom properties or methods. It allows you to specify either the virtual path to the Master Page using the `VirtualPath` attribute or the name of the Master Page class using the `TypeName` attribute. Keep in mind that you can use `VirtualPath` or `TypeName` but not both at the same time. If `TypeName` is used, then the Master Page class must be available in a linked assembly such as the assembly created from code located in the `App_Code` folder.

An example of using the `MasterType` directive with the `VirtualPath` attribute is shown next:

```
<%@ Page Language="C#" MasterPageFile="~/Templates/GolfClubShack.master"
    Title="GolfClubShack" %>
<%@ MasterType VirtualPath="~/Templates/GolfClubShack.master" %>
<asp:Content id="Content1" ContentPlaceHolderID="cphMain" runat="server">
    Content goes here
</asp:Content>
```

When the `Master` property is called from within a content page that uses the `MasterType` directive, the appropriate Master Page type will automatically be made accessible, with all of its associated properties and methods. The `PnlLogin` property defined in the Master Page can now be accessed directly without any casting:

```
protected void Page_Load(object sender, EventArgs e) {
    //Preferred way to get to pnlLogin...uses the MasterType directive
    this.Master.PnlLogin.Visible = false;
}
```

Using the `MasterType` directive provides the best possible situation because the Master Page's `Controls` collection does not have to be iterated through using `FindControl()` to get to `pnlLogin`, no casting is required to the appropriate Master Page type that defines the `PnlLogin` property, and a minimal amount of code has to be written, leading to fewer bugs and greater productivity.

Nesting Master Pages

Many businesses have multiple departments that publish to their website. Each department is often free to create its own layout and content, which can present a challenge when trying to keep the company website's overall structure and layout consistent as end users navigate from department to department. Fortunately, Master Pages can help out in this situation by leveraging nested Master Pages capabilities.

Creating Nested Master Pages

A default Master Page defining the standard company header, footer, and menu can be created, which each departmental site must use. Each departmental site can in turn create its own Master Page that represents the layout of its individual business site Web pages. This departmental Master Page can then be nested inside of the standard website Master Page. Doing this benefits end users because they always see the standard header, footer, and menu no matter what department site they visit, but it gives the departmental website publishers some control because they can create their own nested Master Page.

To understand how to nest Master Pages, let's first look at a company's standard Master Page, shown in Listing 16-3.

Listing 16-3: A typical website Master Page

```
<%@ Master Language="C#" AutoEventWireup="true"
    CodeFile="WebsiteMasterPage.master.cs" Inherits="WebsiteMasterPage" %>
<html>
<head runat="server" id="head">
```

(continued)

Listing 16-3 *(continued)*

```
        <title>Master Page Demo</title>
    </head>
    <body>
        <form id="form1" runat="server">
            <table width="100%">
                <tr>
                    <td bgcolor="#006633" colspan="2">
                        <table border="0" cellpadding="0" cellspacing="0" width="100%">
                            <tr>
                                <td align="left">
                                    <a href="/MasterPageHacks/Default.aspx">
                                        <img alt="Home Page" border="0"
                                         src="/MasterPageHacks/images/logo.gif" />
                                    </a>
                                </td>
                                <td align="right">
                                    <img src="/MasterPageHacks/images/header_image.gif"/>
                                </td>
                            </tr>
                        </table>
                    </td>
                </tr>
                <tr>
                    <td width="25%">
                        Menu Item 1
                        <br />
                        Menu Item 2
                        <br />
                    </td>
                    <td width="75%">
                        <asp:ContentPlaceHolder ID="cphMain" runat="server">
                        </asp:ContentPlaceHolder>
                    </td>
                </tr>
                <tr>
                    <td colspan="2"> </td>
                </tr>
                <tr>
                    <td bgcolor="#006633" colspan="2">
                        Footer
                    </td>
                </tr>
            </table>
        </form>
    </body>
</html>
```

This Master Page defines the location of the company's header, footer, and menu. It also defines where the page content should go using the ContentPlaceHolder control.

Each department can leverage the standard company Master Page to create its own, which is specific to that department. The department Master Page is somewhat unique, though, because it needs to reference the standard company Master Page. This can be done by adding the `MasterPageFile` attribute to the `Master` directive. An example of a departmental Master page is shown in Listing 16-4.

Listing 16-4: A departmental Master Page

```
<%@ Master MasterPageFile="~/Templates/WebsiteMasterPage.master" Language="C#"
    AutoEventWireup="true" CodeFile="NestedMasterPage.master.cs"
    Inherits="NestedMasterPage" %>
  <asp:Content ID="Content1" ContentPlaceHolderID="cphMain" runat="server">
    <table width="100%">
      <tr>
        <td style="background-color: Navy; font-weight: bold; coloar: white">
          Departmental Master Page Horizontal Menu
        </td>
      </tr>
      <tr>
        <td>
          <asp:ContentPlaceHolder ID="cphNestedMain" runat="server" />
        </td>
      </tr>
    </table>
  </asp:Content>
```

Looking through the departmental master page you'll notice that it references a standard company website Master Page named `WebsiteMasterPage.master`. It also defines a Content server control that references the ContentPlaceHolder ID defined in the standard Master Page (`cphMain` in this case). The Content control must be added because this Master Page is nested inside of the standard company Master Page. In addition to the Content server control, the departmental Master Page also defines a ContentPlaceHolder control that specifies where the content from each of the department's content pages should be placed in the overall Master Page hierarchy.

Now that the departmental Master Page has been properly nested within the standard company Master Page, content pages can reference the nested Master Page and automatically inherit the standard company header, footer, and menu. This maintains the overall consistency that the company's website manager would like to see, and gives each department freedom within its own area of the website. An example of the two Master Pages in action is shown in Figure 16-3.

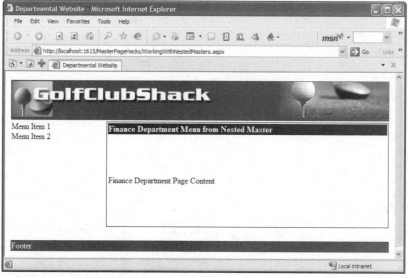

Figure 16-3

335

Working with Nested Master Pages in Visual Studio .NET 2005

Let's assume that you're running a particular department and you've created your nested Master Page, referenced it from several content pages, and would like to edit the content page in Design view within Visual Studio .NET 2005. As you switch to Design view, you'll receive the error shown in Figure 16-4.

Figure 16-4

Unfortunately, Visual Studio .NET 2005 does not allow content pages that reference nested Master Pages to be edited in Design view. If you enjoy working strictly with code this probably won't bother you at all, but if you prefer to use the smart tag functionality and other great visual features available in Design view, you'll probably be quite disappointed. Before giving up all hope, there are a few tricks you can employ to continue using nested Master Pages while getting some of the design-time functionality back for your content pages.

The easiest way to work around the nested Master Page Design view problem is to simply go into the content page and change the `MasterPageFile` attribute on the Page directive to empty strings, as shown in the following code. This will allow you to switch to Design view and drag-and-drop controls onto the design surface, use smart tags, plus more.

```
<%@ Page Language="C#" MasterPageFile="" Title="Departmental Website" %>
```

While in Design view, you won't be able to see how the page content looks within the overall nested Master Pages framework, but you will be able to work with the content controls to add and remove controls, use smart tags, and perform other actions. The downside of this approach is that you'll need to remember to put the path to the nested Master page back into the `MasterPageFile` attribute once you're done editing the content page and are ready to move the page to production.

If you don't want to remember to update the `MasterPageFile` attribute path each time you move a file to production, yet you want to leverage Visual Studio .NET's Design view functionality, you can do so with a little additional work. To trick Visual Studio .NET into showing a Design view representation of your content page, you can create a new class that derives from `System.Web.UI.Page`. This new class (named `BasePage` in the code that follows) should define a property named `RuntimeMasterPageFile` (the property can actually be named anything you like). The following code shows how to derive from `Page` and create the `RuntimeMasterPageFile` property:

```csharp
public class BasePage : System.Web.UI.Page {
    private string _RuntimeMasterPageFile;

    public string RuntimeMasterPageFile {
        get {
            return _RuntimeMasterPageFile;
        }
```

```
        set {
            _RuntimeMasterPageFile = value;
        }
    }

    protected override void OnPreInit(EventArgs e) {
        if (_RuntimeMasterPageFile != null) {
            this.MasterPageFile = _RuntimeMasterPageFile;
        }
        base.OnPreInit(e);
    }
}
```

In addition to exposing the `RuntimeMasterPageFile` property, `BasePage` also overrides `OnPreInit()` so that it can dynamically assign the `MasterPageFile` path to the content page before the page is loaded.

Now that the `BasePage` class is available, you can derive each content page from it instead of `System .Web.UI.Page`:

```
public partial class WorkingWithNestedMasterAndBasePage : BasePage {

    //Page members

}
```

In the `.aspx` file, change the `MasterPageFile` value to empty strings, add the `RuntimeMaster PageFile` attribute to the `Page` directive, and set its value to the nested Master Page path. Then set the `CodeFileBaseClass` attribute to a value of `BasePage` on the `Page` directive. All of these steps are shown in the following code:

```
<%@ Page Language="C#"
    MasterPageFile=""
    RuntimeMasterPageFile="~/Templates/NestedMasterPage.master"
    CodeFileBaseClass="BasePage"
    Inherits="WorkingWithNestedMasterAndBasePage" AutoEventWireup="true"
    CodeFile="WorkingWithNestedMasterAndBasePage.aspx.cs" Title="Untitled Page" %>

<asp:Content ID="ContentNested" runat="server"
    ContentPlaceHolderID="cphNestedMain">
    <p>
         </p>
    <p>
         </p>
    Finance Department Page Content
    <p>
         </p>
    <p>
         </p>
</asp:Content>
```

At runtime, the `BasePage` object will be instantiated and the `MasterPageFile` property of the content page will dynamically be set to the value assigned to the `RuntimeMasterPageFile` property. At design time, the Design view functionality of Visual Studio .NET 2005 will be available because the

`MasterPageFile` value is an empty string. While this requires a small amount of initial work, it's quite easy to put into practice as new content pages are created. Microsoft has stated that future versions of Visual Studio .NET will enable developers to work with content pages that reference nested Master Pages more easily.

Sharing Master Pages Across IIS Applications

When ASP.NET user controls were first introduced in version 1.0 of the .NET Framework, developers immediately latched onto them because they provided a great way to reuse content in multiple pages in an object-oriented manner. However, developers quickly discovered that user controls could not be shared across IIS applications. This meant that if a standard menu user control used throughout a website was defined in one IIS application, then it could not be used in another, such as a subdepartment within a company website. To get around this issue, developers converted the user controls into server controls and installed them into the Global Assembly Cache (GAC) or created virtual directories within each IIS application that referenced the folder that contained the user controls that needed to be shared.

With ASP.NET version 2, user controls still cannot be shared between IIS applications, and because Master Pages derive from `UserControl`, they cannot be shared either. However, with a little work it is possible to share user controls and Master Pages between IIS applications using Visual Studio .NET 2005's Website publishing functionality as well as a new Web deployment tool.

You might be wondering why you'd ever need to share a Master Page across multiple IIS applications. That's certainly a valid question. To answer it, consider a company that has its core pages stored at the root of the Web server (the home page, the sitewide search page, the sitemap, etc.), but has each department within subfolders that are marked as applications in IIS. Each department folder is marked as an IIS application so that the department can have its own complete `web.config` file, specify its own security, and perform other tasks that require an IIS application. An example of how this might look for the Finance department in IIS is shown in Figure 16-5. Notice that the FinanceDepartment application exists under the MasterPageHacks application.

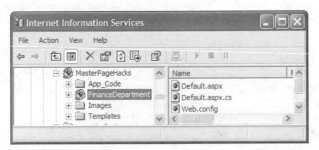

Figure 16-5

The company would like the header, footer, and menu defined in the website's root Master Page to be used by all departments (think back to the nested Master Page discussion earlier in this chapter). Because each departmental subfolder is marked as an application in IIS this isn't possible. In fact, the error shown in Figure 16-6 will occur if departments try to use the company's Master Page located at the root of their site. The error makes it clear that you can't map to a virtual path in another IIS application.

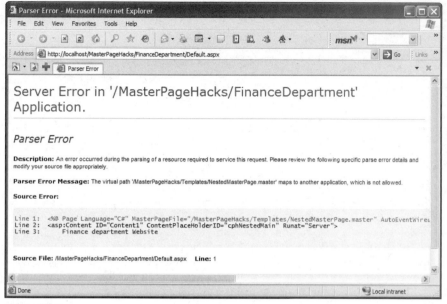

Figure 16-6

There's no way to get around this error without either creating a virtual directory within every departmental IIS application that points to the folder where the root Master Page is stored or converting the header, footer, and menu into server controls that can be stored within the Global Assembly Cache (GAC), which could prove fairly time-consuming. Fortunately, another solution exists that is quick and easy to implement.

Publishing Master Pages as an Assembly

Visual Studio .NET 2005 provides functionality to publish precompiled websites to production servers through its Publish Website menu entry (located directly off the Build menu). This publishing capability can be used to convert a Master Page into an assembly that can be given a strong name and installed into the GAC. Once in the GAC, the Master Page can be shared across multiple IIS applications on the Web server. There are a few steps that you need to go through to implement this solution, so the explanation that follows provides step-by-step instructions:

1. To start this process, create an empty website in VS.NET 2005. Delete everything in it, including `App_Data` and `Default.aspx`.

2. Add a Master Page to the empty website and add to it the content that you would like to share across applications. The following master page is named `MasterPageBase.master`:

```
<%@ Master Language="C#" %>
<html>
<head runat="server">
```

```
    <title>Sharing Master Pages Across IIS Applications</title>
</head>
<body>
    <form id="form1" runat="server">
    <div>
        Header
        <br />
        <asp:contentplaceholder id="ContentPlaceHolder1" runat="server">
        </asp:contentplaceholder>
        <br />
        Footer
    </div>
    </form>
</body>
</html>
```

3. Select Build⇨Publish Website from the Visual Studio .NET 2005 menu.

4. From the Publish Web Site dialog box that appears, select a target site where the output will be published, and check all of the checkboxes except for the top one that allows for dynamic updates (see Figure 16-7). Notice that a strong name key file named `keyfile.snk` is referenced. (A strong name key file contains public/private cryptographic key pairs that can be used to digitally sign an assembly.) You'll need a key file in order to sign the assembly and install it into the GAC. To create a key file, use the `sn.exe` command-line tool that ships with .NET. At the Visual Studio .NET 2005 command prompt, type the following to generate the file: **sn.exe -k keyfile.snk**.

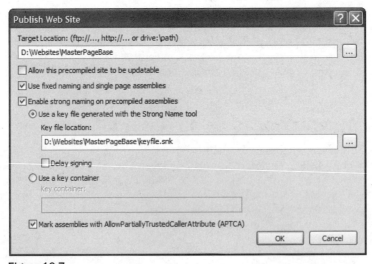

Figure 16-7

5. After the publish operation completes, open the new website that was created in VS.NET 2005 (named `MasterPageBase` in the previous example). You should see a new assembly with a fairly strange name in the `Bin` folder. This assembly is your master page in compiled form.

6. Install the assembly into the GAC using `gacutil.exe` or drag-and-drop it into `c:\Windows\Assembly` using Windows Explorer. Once you've done this, delete the original assembly as well as the newly created XML files from the MasterPageBase website.

7. Add a `web.config` file into your website project and add the following within the `<system.web>` begin and end tags:

```
<compilation debug="false">
    <assemblies>
        <add assembly="App_Web_masterpagebase.master.cdcab7d2, Version=0.0.0.0,
            Culture=neutral, PublicKeyToken=cceb8435cfc68486" />
    </assemblies>
</compilation>
```

You'll need to change the name of the assembly to the name that is generated for your project (the one you added into the GAC) and change the `PublicKeyToken` to the one you see in the GAC. Note that the `assembly` attribute value shouldn't wrap at all. Although a version wasn't assigned to the original Master Page before it was published, one can be added by applying the `assembly` attribute in the code file for the Master Page:

```
[assembly: AssemblyVersion("1.0.0.0")]
```

8. Add a master page into the website but don't create a code file for it (you can, but it's not needed in this case).

9. Remove all code within the new Master Page and add the following at the top. This should be the only code in the Master Page. If you named your original master page (the one created in step 2) differently, then you'll need to change the `Inherits` value appropriately. Use the object browser to see the name of the class within the `.dll` generated in step 4. It should be within an ASP namespace:

```
<%@ Master Language="C#" Inherits="ASP.masterpagebase_master" %>
```

10. Create a content page that references the Master Page you created in the previous step. The default `ContentPlaceHolderID` is `ContentPlaceHolder1`, so use that in the `<asp:Content>` tag unless you gave the ID a different value in step 2.

11. Test the content page.

While testing more complex Master Pages, you may receive a "could not find string resource" error when running the content page. Using a tool such as Reflector (`aisto.com/roeder/dotnet/`) to analyze the assembly, you'll see one or more calls to a method named `CreateResourceBasedLiteralControl()` where you would expect the HTML from the Master Page to be embedded. The Publish Web Site option automatically attempts to convert long strings with carriage returns into a literal resource, rather than embed the HTML string into the assembly. To eliminate the call to `CreateResourceBasedLiteralControl()` and the error it causes, you'll need to adjust the HTML code that wraps across multiple lines onto a single line. For example, the following code spans multiple lines for the HtmlOutput server control:

```
<td align="left" valign="top" height="45">
    <www:HtmlOutput ID="egovHeader" runat="Server"
        XmlSource="/XML/SiteLinks.xml"
```

```
        XsltSource="/XSLT/Header.xslt"
        LanguageCookieName="EgovCookie/Language" />
    </td>
```

To eliminate the "could not find string resource" error, the content can be moved onto a single line (some wrapping occurs below due to page constraints):

```
<td align="left" valign="top" height="45"><www:HtmlOutput ID="egovHeader"
runat="Server" XmlSource="/XML/SiteLinks.xml" XsltSource="/XSLT/Header.xslt"
LanguageCookieName="EgovCookie/Language" /></td>
```

After making any necessary adjustments, publish the Master Page again, install it into the GAC, and test the content page. Continue the process until the "could not find string resource" error goes away.

These steps may seem like a lot of work, but once they're completed, multiple IIS applications can share a single Master Page. However, there are a few disadvantages to this approach. First, you have to recompile the base Master Page and put it back into the GAC each time you need to make a change. That can be a hassle if you have a site that changes its overall look and feel frequently. For many sites this probably won't present a problem. Second, the assembly name created during the publish process isn't a very friendly name and can make it hard to determine which assembly is responsible for the output of which Master Page in cases where multiple Master Pages are installed into the GAC. Finally, a blank Master Page must be placed into each website that needs to reference the Master Page installed into the GAC. While having an empty Master Page in each website isn't much of a problem, it does result in the loss of design-time functionality in Visual Studio .NET. A few workarounds for the problem associated with nested Master Pages in Visual Studio .NET were provided earlier in this chapter.

Using the Web Deployment Projects Add-in

While there's not much that can be done about re-installing an assembly into the GAC each time a Master Page being shared across IIS applications is changed, the name of the assembly can be fixed up and made more user friendly. Microsoft released a Visual Studio .NET 2005 add-in called Web Deployment Projects that can be used to pre-compile a website and perform several other build and deployment tasks. While a complete discussion of this tool is outside the scope of this chapter, Microsoft summarizes its features in the following way:

"Visual Studio 2005 Web Deployment Projects provide additional functionality for building and deploying Web site applications that you create in ASP.NET 2.0 and Visual Studio 2005. This add-in includes a new tool that enables you to merge the assemblies created during ASP.NET 2.0 precompilation, and it provides a comprehensive UI within Visual Studio 2005 for managing build configurations, merging, and pre-build and post-build tasks using MSBuild."

In addition to using Visual Studio .NET's Publish Web Site functionality to convert a Master Page into an assembly, the Web Deployment Projects tool can also be used. One of the main differences between the two tools is that Web Deployment Projects enables you to control the name of the assembly that is generated, rather than being forced into using an unfriendly assembly name such as `App_Web_masterpage base.master.cdcab7d2`.

After installing the Web Deployment Projects tool (it can be downloaded from `http://msdn`
`.microsoft.com` or `www.asp.net`), you can right-click on the MasterPageBase project mentioned in the
steps shown earlier and select Add Web Deployment Project from the menu. On the screen that appears,
you can name your deployment project. The default project name will be `MasterPageBase_deploy` in
this case. After selecting the deployment project name, a new file will show up in your Visual Studio
.NET 2005 website, as shown in Figure 16-8.

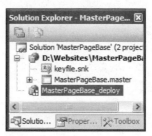

Figure 16-8

Right-click the `MasterPageBase_deploy` file and select Property Pages from the menu to access the different deployment project options. Several different screens are available, including Compilation,
Output Assemblies, Signing, and Deployment (note that these screens may change, as the tool was in
beta at the time this was written). On the Compilation screen (see Figure 16-9) change the Configuration
drop-down to Release. This will cause the output folder to be changed to `.\Release\`. Ensure that the
"Allow this precompiled site to be updatable" checkbox is unchecked. This will cause the HTML found
in the Master Page to be embedded into the assembly.

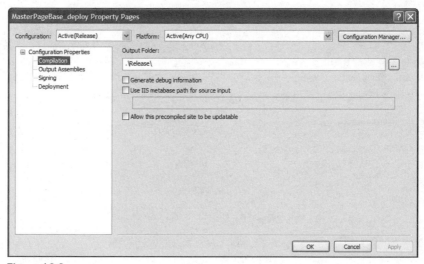

Figure 16-9

On the Output Assembly menu, change the name to `MasterPageBase` and check the "Treat as library component (remove App_Code.compiled file)" checkbox. Also check the "Version output assemblies" checkbox and provide a version such as 1.0.0.0 for both the assembly and the file. Figure 16-10 shows what this screen should look like.

On the Signing screen, check the "Enable strong naming" checkbox and select a strong name key file (a file created using `sn.exe`). Once you've made these various changes, click the Apply button.

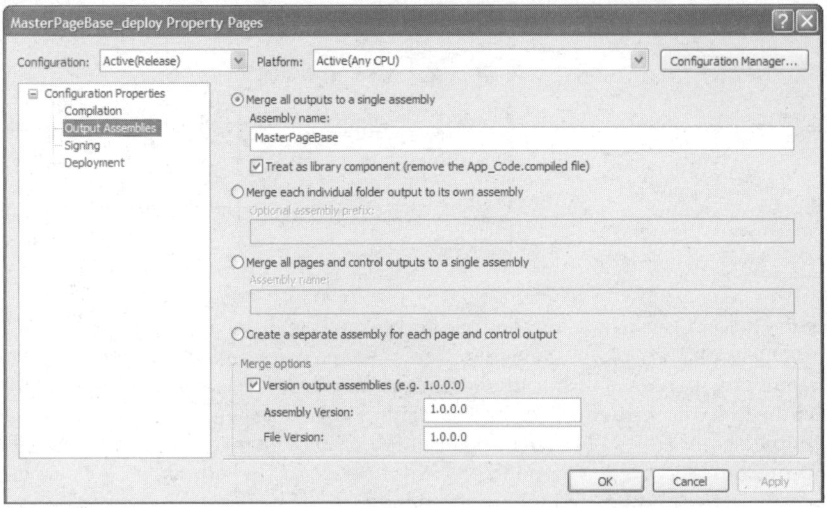

Figure 16-10

Before generating the `MasterPageBase` assembly, switch your ASP.NET website to Release mode. Right-click on the deployment project file and select Build from the menu. A new assembly named `MasterPage Base.dll` will appear in the `MasterPageBase_deploy` folder (it'll be within the `release\bin` folder). This assembly can now be installed into the GAC and added to `web.config` (ensure that the assembly attribute does not wrap):

```
<compilation debug="false">
   <assemblies>
      <add assembly="MasterPageBase, Version=1.0.0.0,
         Culture=neutral, PublicKeyToken=cceb8435cfc68486" />
   </assemblies>
</compilation>
```

Refer to steps 6 through 11 in the previous section for a review of the process.

Using the Web Deployment Projects tool generates the same assembly content as the Publish Web Site tool does, but it provides direct control over the name and version. If you view the assemblies created by the two tools in Reflector (`aisto.com/roeder/dotnet/`), you'll see that they both contain embedded HTML from the Master Page (see Figure 16-11). Once in the GAC, the Master Page can be shared across multiple IIS applications.

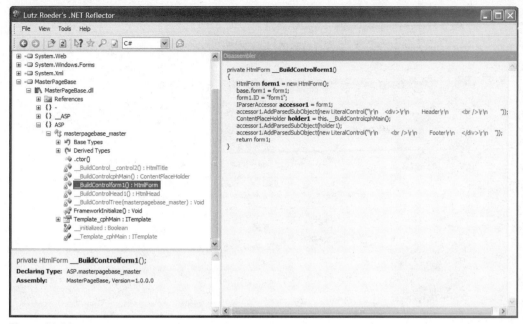

Figure 16-11

Dynamically Changing Master Pages in a Content Page

Content pages typically reference a Master Page using the `MasterPageFile` attribute of the `Page` directive. For many websites, the path to the Master Page is fixed and doesn't need to change. Other websites may allow users to personalize a page or provide printable versions of a page, which may require the path to the Master Page to be changed dynamically. Fortunately, changing between two or more Master Pages on-the-fly is straightforward and can be done with a minimal amount of code in ASP.NET version 2.0. To see dynamic Master Pages in action, consider the following scenario involving a fictitious website called GolfClubShack.

GolfClubShack sells a variety of golf products, including drivers, putters, irons, wedges, and an assortment of golf balls. Users can search the GolfClubShack website and get more details about any product that is carried. The GolfClubShack website uses a standard Master Page across the entire site in order to provide a consistent interface for end users. This Master Page defines a standard header and menu. An example of a product details page that uses the Master Page is shown in Figure 16-12.

Figure 16-12

GolfClubShack wants to allow users to be able to print a more concise version of the product details page that doesn't have unnecessary information in it such as menus and links. In order to accomplish this goal, they need to dynamically change the Master Page as the user clicks the print icon (located to the right of the product title in Figure 16-12).

A GolfClubShack developer can leverage the `Page_PreInit` event handler available in the content page to change Master Pages. Because Master Pages are ultimately merged into the content page as a control, changing the Master Page dynamically requires interacting with the `Page` object early in its lifecycle. The `PreInit` event makes this possible.

In order for GolfClubshack to make a printable version of the product details page, they'll need to create a Master Page that strips out unwanted content, as shown next:

```
<%@ Master Language="C#" %>
<html>
<head runat="server">
    <title>GolfClubShack</title>
    <link type="text/css" rel="Stylesheet" href="/GolfClubShack/Style/Style.css" />
</head>
<body leftmargin="0" topmargin="0"
    rightmargin="0" bottommargin="0" marginheight="0" marginwidth="0">
    <form id="frmMain" runat="server">
        <table width="640" cellpadding="0" cellspacing="0">
            <tr>
                <td valign="top">
                    <table cellspacing="0" cellpadding="0" width="100%" border="0">
```

```
                          <tr>
                              <td align="left">
                                  <a href="/GolfClubShack/default.aspx">
                                      <img border="0"
                      src="/GolfClubShack/images/logo.gif" alt="Home Page" />
                                  </a>
                              </td>
                              <td align="right">
                                  <img src="/GolfClubShack/images/header_image.gif"
                                  />
                              </td>
                          </tr>
                      </table>
                  </td>
              </tr>
              <tr>
                  <td>
                      <asp:ContentPlaceHolder ID="cphMain" runat="server">
                      </asp:ContentPlaceHolder>
                  </td>
              </tr>
          </table>
      </form>
  </body>
  </html>
```

This simple Master Page adds a basic header but omits menu, search functionality, and links available in the standard Master Page. Once the printable Master Page is created, GolfClubShack needs to change from the standard Master Page to the printable Master Page when a user clicks the print icon. The print icon shown earlier in Figure 16-12 links back to the product details page using an ASP.NET Hyperlink control that has a QueryString parameter named Print added to the end of the URL. The Print parameter is added dynamically in Page_Load:

```
public partial class ProductDetails : System.Web.UI.Page {

    bool _ShowPrintImage = true;
    protected void Page_Load(object sender, System.EventArgs e) {
        if (this._ShowPrintImage) {
            this.hlPrint.NavigateUrl = Request.Url.ToString() + "&Print=true";
        } else {
            this.hlPrint.Visible = false;
        }
    }
}
```

The Page_PreInit event handler of the product details page checks the QueryString for the Print parameter and changes the Master Page when it's found. This is done by calling the MasterPageFile property of the Page class:

```
public partial class ProductDetails : System.Web.UI.Page {

    bool _ShowPrintImage = true;

    protected void Page_PreInit(Object sender, EventArgs e) {
```

```
            if (Request.QueryString["Print"] != null) {
                this.MasterPageFile = "~/Templates/GolfClubShackPrint.master";
                this._ShowPrintImage = false;
            }
        }
    }
}
```

Figure 16-13 shows what the page looks like after the printable Master Page has been dynamically assigned to the content page.

Figure 16-13

This same technique can be used in a variety of situations where a Master Page needs to be loaded dynamically.

Wrapping Up

Master Pages are one of the most exciting new features in ASP.NET 2.0. They eliminate the need to use nested user controls or custom ASP.NET 1.1 template frameworks. By using Master Pages you can define a website's layout and structure in a single file and make sitewide changes with a minimal amount of time and effort.

In this chapter you've learned how to create and consume Master Pages as well as how to modify controls and change properties. You've also seen how Master Pages can be shared across IIS applications by compiling and installing them into the Global Assembly Cache. Finally, you've learned how Master Pages can be dynamically changed within a content page using the `MasterPageFile` property of the `Page` class.

Handlers and Modules

ASP.NET is so much more than just pages. Pages are, in fact, HttpHandlers, as is any class within ASP.NET that handles a request via HTTP. Whereas an HttpHandler handles a request for a particular URL or type of file, an HttpModule listens into all requests and acts on them appropriately. Both of these constructs are ripe for hacking new functionality into your application.

This chapter drops one level below pages to discuss HttpModules and HttpHandlers, the unsung workhorses of ASP.NET. HttpModules get a first look at all HTTP traffic routed to ASP.NET, so first you'll create an HttpModule to block blacklisted IP addresses from seeing your content. Then, you'll learn how to add a URL rewriting HttpModule to an existing application, making "vanity" URLs easily.

Then, turning away from handling all traffic to handling specific HTTP requests, you'll generate images dynamically using an HttpHandler. Finally, we'll bring together the two concepts of specific handlers and non-specific modules into an error-handling application you can use to instrument your applications.

HttpModules

HttpModules are fantastically powerful, as they see all and can control all. HttpModules can listen in on every request your ASP.NET application receives. Much of ASP.NET's most powerful functionality — such as output caching, session management, authentication, and authorization — is implemented via HttpModules. Modules can make sweeping and fundamental changes to the way your application works. The following sections contain a few hacks using modules that should give you some ideas.

An IP Blacklisting HttpModule

I do not have direct access to the IIS administrative console at my ISP, so when I wanted to block some troublesome IP addresses that were spamming my blog, I needed a software solution that would run in ASP.NET. An `HttpModule` was the easiest solution to write — it is easily configurable and easily added to my ASP.NET application without recompiling. This module will listen on the `BeginRequest` event that fires for every `HttpRequest` that comes into the configured application. Because modules like this listen on every request, you'll want to be especially diligent about the work you do and get out of the module as soon as possible.

This module, shown in Listing 17-1, reads in a list of IP addresses and sends an HTTP 404 File Not Found message to any blocked IP. Additionally, while this module was being written, a nasty worm called PHPBB/WGET was attacking many blogs. I took the opportunity to add a check for this worm and blocked it as well.

Listing 17-1: An IP Blacklisting HttpModule

C#

```csharp
using System;
using System.Text.RegularExpressions;
using System.IO;
using System.Web;
using System.Web.Caching;
using System.Collections.Specialized;

namespace MVPHacks
{
    public class IPBlackList : IHttpModule
    {
        public IPBlackList(){}

        void IHttpModule.Dispose(){}

        void IHttpModule.Init(HttpApplication context)
        {
            context.BeginRequest += new EventHandler(this.HandleBeginRequest);
        }

        const string FILE = "~/blockedips.config";
        const string CACHEKEY = "blockedips";

        public static StringDictionary GetBlockedIPs(HttpContext context)
        {
            StringDictionary ips = (StringDictionary)context.Cache[CACHEKEY];
            if (ips == null)
            {
                ips = GetBlockedIPs(GetBlockedIPsFile(context));
                context.Cache.Insert(CACHEKEY, ips,
                    new CacheDependency(GetBlockedIPsFile(context)));
            }
            return ips;
        }

        private static string BlockedIPFileName = null;
```

```
private static object blockedIPFileNameObject = new object();
public static string GetBlockedIPsFile(HttpContext context)
{
    if (BlockedIPFileName != null) return BlockedIPFileName;
    lock(blockedIPFileNameObject)
    {
        if (BlockedIPFileName == null)
        {
            BlockedIPFileName = context.Server.MapPath(FILE);
        }
    }
    return BlockedIPFileName;
}

public static StringDictionary GetBlockedIPs(string configPath)
{
    StringDictionary retval = new StringDictionary();
    using (StreamReader sr = new StreamReader(configPath))
    {
        String line;
        while ((line = sr.ReadLine()) != null)
        {
            line = line.Trim();
            if (line.Length != 0)
            {
                if (retval.ContainsKey(line) == false)
                {
                    retval.Add(line, null);
                }
            }
        }
    }
    return retval;
}

private void HandleBeginRequest( object sender, EventArgs evargs )
{
    HttpApplication app = sender as HttpApplication;
    if ( app !- null )
    {
        string IPAddr = app.Context.Request.ServerVariables["REMOTE_ADDR"];
        if (IPAddr == null || IPAddr.Length == 0)
        {
            return;
        }

        //Block the PHPBB worm and other WGET-based worms
        if (app.Context.Request.QueryString["rush"] != null
            ||
            app.Context.Request.RawUrl.IndexOf("wget") != -1)
        {
            app.Context.Response.StatusCode = 404;
            app.Context.Response.SuppressContent = true;
            app.Context.Response.End();
```

(continued)

Listing 17-1 *(continued)*

```
                return;
            }

            StringDictionary badIPs = GetBlockedIPs(app.Context);
            if (badIPs != null && badIPs.ContainsKey(IPAddr))
            {
                app.Context.Response.StatusCode = 404;
                app.Context.Response.SuppressContent = true;
                app.Context.Response.End();
                return;
            }
        }
    }
}
}
```

VB

```
Imports System
Imports System.Text.RegularExpressions
Imports System.IO
Imports System.Web
Imports System.Web.Caching
Imports System.Collections.Specialized

Namespace MVPHacks


    Public Class IPBlackList
        Implements IHttpModule

        Private Const FILE As String = "~/blockedips.config"
        Private Const CACHEKEY As String = "blockedips"
        Private Shared BlockedIPFileName As String = Nothing
        Private Shared blockedIPFileNameObject As Object = New Object

        Public Sub New()
            MyBase.New
        End Sub

        Sub IHttpModule_Dispose() Implements IHttpModule.Dispose
        End Sub

        Sub IHttpModule_Init(ByVal context As HttpApplication)
                Implements IHttpModule.Init
            AddHandler context.BeginRequest, AddressOf Me.HandleBeginRequest
        End Sub

        Public Overloads Shared Function GetBlockedIPs
          (ByVal context As HttpContext) As StringDictionary
            Dim ips As StringDictionary =
                    CType(context.Cache(CACHEKEY),StringDictionary)
            If (ips is Nothing) Then
                ips = GetBlockedIPs(GetBlockedIPsFile(context))
```

```
            context.Cache.Insert(CACHEKEY, ips, New
                CacheDependency(GetBlockedIPsFile(context)))
        End If
        Return ips
    End Function

    Public Shared Function GetBlockedIPsFile(ByVal context As HttpContext)
            As String
        If (Not (BlockedIPFileName) Is Nothing) Then
            Return BlockedIPFileName
        End If
        SyncLock blockedIPFileNameObject
            If (BlockedIPFileName = Nothing) Then
                BlockedIPFileName = context.Server.MapPath(FILE)
            End If
        End SyncLock
        Return BlockedIPFileName
    End Function

    Public Overloads Shared Function GetBlockedIPs(ByVal configPath As String)
            As StringDictionary
        Dim retval As StringDictionary = New StringDictionary
        Dim sr As StreamReader = New StreamReader(configPath)
        Dim line As String
        line = sr.ReadLine()
        While (line IsNot Nothing)
            line = line.Trim
            If (line.Length <> 0) Then
                If (retval.ContainsKey(line) = False) Then
                    retval.Add(line, Nothing)
                End If
            End If
            line = sr.ReadLine()
        End While
        Return retval
    End Function

    Private Sub HandleBeginRequest(ByVal sender As Object,
            ByVal evargs As EventArgs)
        Dim app As HttpApplication = CType(sender,HttpApplication)
        If (Not (app) Is Nothing) Then
            Dim IPAddr As String =
                app.Context.Request.ServerVariables("REMOTE_ADDR")
            If ((IPAddr = Nothing) _
                    OrElse (IPAddr.Length = 0)) Then
                Return
            End If

            'Block the PHPBB worm and other WGET-based worms
            If ((Not (app.Context.Request.QueryString("rush")) Is Nothing) _
              OrElse (app.Context.Request.RawUrl.IndexOf("wget") <> -1)) Then
                app.Context.Response.StatusCode = 404
                app.Context.Response.SuppressContent = true
                app.Context.Response.End
                Return
```

(continued)

Listing 17-1 *(continued)*

```
                End If

        Dim badIPs As StringDictionary = GetBlockedIPs(app.Context)
        If ((Not (badIPs) Is Nothing)  _
                AndAlso badIPs.ContainsKey(IPAddr)) Then
            app.Context.Response.StatusCode = 404
            app.Context.Response.SuppressContent = true
            app.Context.Response.End
            Return
        End If
            End If
        End Sub
    End Class
End Namespace
```

With this HttpModule, now I can upload a text file called `blockedips.txt` with one IP address per line to my site and the changes are recognized immediately. The IP addresses are stored in ASP.NET's cache as a StringDictionary and the cached object is invalidated if the underlying file is updated.

Notice that this module returns a 404 when an IP address is blocked. I wanted to discourage the spammers as much as possible so I decided to fool them into thinking my website had no content at all:

```
<system.web>
    <httpModules>
        <add type="MVPHacks.IPBlackList, MVPHacks" name="IPBlackList" />
    </httpModules>
</system.web>
```

The assembly's qualified name (QN) for this or any `HttpModule` is added to the `httpModules` section of the application's `web.config`. A QN consists of the full namespace and class name, a comma, and then the actual assembly filename without the .dll extension.

Rewriting or Redirecting URLs with an HttpModule

Fritz Onion (`http://pluralsight.com/blogs/fritz/archive/2004/07/21/1651.aspx`) has a great URL redirecting engine, very similar to the URL rewriting module written for DasBlog (`www.sf.net/projects/dasblogce`). There is often confusion between URL redirecting and the URL rewriting.

Redirecting is the server's way of informing the client that something has moved. For example, a browser requests `http://www.computerzen.com` and the server responses with an HTTP 302 Status Code and points the browser to `http://www.hanselman.com/blog`. The browser then has to request `http://www.hanselman.com/blog` itself, and receives an HTTP 200 Status Code indicating success. During this redirection, the URL in the browser's address bar will be updated. The final successful URL will ultimately appear in the address bar.

Rewriting, on the other hand, occurs entirely on the server side; the browser only requests a page once and the address bar's displayed URL doesn't change. For example, if you type `http://www.hanselman.com/blog/zenzoquincy.aspx` into your browser's address bar, you'll get a page showing off my infant son. However, the file `zenzoquincy.aspx` doesn't actually exist anywhere on the disk. The only page that does exist is `permalink.aspx`, the page that my blog engine uses to show all blog posts. The real page is `permalink.aspx?guid=cee8aa6e-de46-43ad-8d27-e1c764df30f5`. However, that unique post ID isn't very memorable and certainly not any fun. When the blog engine I run, DasBlog, sees `ZenzoQuincy.aspx` requested, it looks in its data store to see whether the words "ZenzoQuincy" are associated with a unique blog post ID and then *rewrites* the requested URL on-the-fly, on the server side, and ASP.NET continues dispatching the request.

URL redirecting and URL rewriting are together the most powerful techniques you have available to control the URL presented to the user, as well as to maintain your site's permalinks. It is very important to most website content owners that their links remain permanent, hence "permalink." Netiquette — Internet etiquette — dictates that if the URL does change, then you at least provide a redirect to inform the browser automatically that the resource has moved. As a protocol, HTTP provides two ways to alert the browser: the first is a temporary redirect, or 302, and the second is a permanent redirect, or 301.

To extend the example, my website uses a temporary redirect to send visitors from `http://www.computerzen.com` to `http://www.hanselman.com/blog`. It's temporary because I might change the location of my blog at some point, pointing my top-level domain somewhere else. I use a permanent redirect for my blog's RSS (Rich Site Summary) feed to inform aggregators and syndicators that I would prefer they always use a specific URL. When aggregators receive a 301, or permanent redirect, they know to update their own data and never visit the original URL again.

Fritz's HttpModule uses a configuration section like this, which includes regular expressions to match target URLs to destination URLs via a redirect. Note that Fritz's, and most, rewriting modules use regular expressions to express their intent. Regular expressions give a concise description of intent. For example, `^/(fritz|aaron|keith|mike)/rss\.xml` matches both the strings /fritz/rss.xml and /mike/rss.xml. Regular expressions are used in both the target and destination URL. The destination URL uses an expression like `/blogs/$1/rss.aspx`, where $1 is the first match in parentheses, in this case `"fritz"` or `"mike"`.

```
<redirections type="Pluralsight.Website.redirections, redirectmodule">
    <add targetUrl="^/(fritz|aaron|keith|mike)/rss\.xml"
        destinationUrl="/blogs/$1/rss.aspx" permanent="true" />
    <add targetUrl="/foo.aspx" destinationUrl="/bar.aspx" permanent="true" />
    <add targetUrl="/quux.aspx" destinationUrl="/bar.aspx" />
</redirections>
```

A simple hard-coded 301 redirect looks like this within ASP.NET:

```
response.StatusCode = 301;
response.Status = "301 Moved Permanently";
response.RedirectLocation = "http://www.hanselman.com/blog";
response.End();
```

Here's an example of how DasBlog uses URL rewriting to service HTTP requests for files that don't exist on the file system. Within my blog's `web.config` file is a custom configuration section that includes regular expressions that are matched against the requested file. For example, the file `http://www.hanselman.com/blog/rss.ashx` doesn't exist. There's no handler for it, and the file doesn't exist on disk. However, I'd like people to think of it as my main URL for the RSS XML content on my site. I'd like to easily change which service handles it internally with just a configuration change. I add this exception to my `web.config` custom section:

```
<newtelligence.DasBlog.UrlMapper>
     <add matchExpression="(?&lt;basedir&gt;.*?)/rss\.ashx"
          mapTo="{basedir}/SyndicationService.asmx/GetRss?" />
</newtelligence.DasBlog.UrlMapper>
```

Note that it is mapped to
"http://www.hanselman.com/blog/SyndicationService.asmx/GetRss" with the {basedir}
having expanded. That URL isn't nearly as friendly as rss.ashx, is it? Remember that the name
rss.ashx isn't special, it's just unique. I picked it because the extension was already mapped within
ASP.NET. It could have been something else like foo.bar, as long as the .bar extension was mapped to
ASP.NET within the IIS configuration.

Listing 17-2 is a slightly simplified view of the source code that makes the rewriting happen. The configuration section is read into a NameValueCollection. Each of the regular expressions is run, in order,
until one matches the requested URL. If a match, or more than one match, occurs for a specific expression, the source matches are copied into the destination match. In the example expression, basedir is
anything that appears before rss.ashx.

Listing 17-2: DasBlog's regular expression–based URL rewriter

C#

```csharp
private void HandleBeginRequest( object sender, EventArgs evargs )
{
    HttpApplication app = sender as HttpApplication;
    string requestUrl = app.Context.Request.Url.PathAndQuery;
    NameValueCollection urlMaps =
(NameValueCollection)ConfigurationSettings.GetConfig("newtelligence.DasBlog.UrlMapp
er");
    for ( int loop=0;loop<urlMaps.Count;loop++)
    {
        string matchExpression = urlMaps.GetKey(loop);
        Regex regExpression = new Regex(matchExpression,RegexOptions.IgnoreCase|
                    RegexOptions.Singleline|RegexOptions.CultureInvariant|
                    RegexOptions.Compiled);
        Match matchUrl = regExpression.Match(requestUrl);
        if ( matchUrl != null && matchUrl.Success )
        {
            string mapTo = urlMaps[matchExpression];
            Regex regMap = new Regex("\\{(?<expr>\\w+)\\}");
            foreach( Match matchExpr in regMap.Matches(mapTo) )
            {
                Group urlExpr;
                string expr = matchExpr.Groups["expr"].Value;
                urlExpr = matchUrl.Groups[expr];
                if ( urlExpr != null )
                {
                    mapTo = mapTo.Replace("{"+expr+"}", urlExpr.Value);
                }
            }
            app.Context.RewritePath(mapTo);
        }
    }
}
```

VB

```vb
Private Sub HandleBeginRequest(ByVal sender As Object, ByVal evargs As EventArgs)
    Dim app As HttpApplication = CType(sender,HttpApplication)
    Dim requestUrl As String = app.Context.Request.Url.PathAndQuery
    Dim urlMaps As NameValueCollection =
        CType(ConfigurationSettings.GetConfig("newtelligence.DasBlog.UrlMapper"), _
        NameValueCollection)
    Dim loop As Integer = 0
    Do While (loop < urlMaps.Count)
        Dim matchExpression As String = urlMaps.GetKey(loop)
        Dim regExpression As Regex = New Regex(matchExpression,
                (RegexOptions.IgnoreCase _
                    Or (RegexOptions.Singleline _
                    Or (RegexOptions.CultureInvariant Or
                        RegexOptions.Compiled))))
        Dim matchUrl As Match = regExpression.Match(requestUrl)
        If ((Not (matchUrl) Is Nothing) _
                AndAlso matchUrl.Success) Then
            Dim mapTo As String = urlMaps(matchExpression)
            Dim regMap As Regex = New Regex("\\{(?<expr>\\w+)\\}")
            For Each matchExpr As Match In regMap.Matches(mapTo)
                Dim urlExpr As Group
                Dim expr As String = matchExpr.Groups("expr").Value
                urlExpr = matchUrl.Groups(expr)
                If (Not (urlExpr) Is Nothing) Then
                    mapTo = mapTo.Replace(("{" + (expr + "}")), urlExpr.Value)
                End If
            Next
            app.Context.RewritePath(mapTo)
        End If
        loop = (loop + 1)
    Loop
End Sub
```

Listing 17-2 starts by getting the `NameValueCollection` of URLs from the `web.config` file. The regular expression for each potential match is run against the request URL, which is pulled from `HttpContext.Current.Request.Url.PathAndQuery`. If an expression is found to match, each match in the requested URL is mapped to its spot in the destination URL. For example, note in the following code how the `{postid}` is extracted from the request URL and reused in the destination. Any good URL rewriting engine has support for this in some fashion, whether by `{token}` or by numeric position such as $1.

```xml
<!-- Translates
    FROM: /blog/archive/2004/07/27/194.aspx
    TO: /blog/permalink.aspx?guid=194
  -->
<newtelligence.DasBlog.UrlMapper>
  <add matchExpression="(?&lt;basedir&gt;.*?)/archive/
            (?&lt;year&gt;\d{4})/(?&lt;month&gt;\d{2})/(?&lt;day&gt;\d{2})/
            (?&lt;postid&gt;\d+)\.aspx"
      mapTo="{basedir}/permalink.aspx?guid={postid}" />
</newtelligence.DasBlog.UrlMapper>
```

Check out the source code for DasBlog, or one of the other redirecting/rewriting modules I've mentioned, for more details and ideas on how you can create more "hackable" URLs for your application. Christopher Pietschmann has a nice VB version for ASP.NET 2.0 at `http://pietschsoft.com/blog/post.aspx?postid=762`.

HttpHandlers

Every HttpRequest that comes into ASP.NET is handled by an HttpHandler. It seems like a silly thing to say, but it's true. The IHttpHandler interface is the magic that makes it all happen. Every page you write is indirectly an HttpHandler. Every file that is requested is mapped to an HttpHandler. Therefore, if you want to handle a request yourself, perhaps to generate a dynamic file download or graphic, then this is where you'll want to get started.

Boilerplate HttpHandler

Phil Haack (http://haacked.com/) took a boilerplate HttpHandler that I liked to use via copy/paste reuse and created a cleaner abstract base class, shown in Listing 17-3. This class is a creative way to start writing any new HttpHandler. You can certainly just implement IHttpHandler yourself, but you'll find yourself writing and rewriting the same chunks repeatedly. Inheriting from this class expands your derived HttpHandler to include virtual methods — that you can override — that more accurately correspond to the kinds of things an HttpHandler needs to worry about: Are the parameters correct? Does the handler require authentication? What is the caching policy? Simply derive your class, and override as appropriate.

Listing 17-3: An abstract base class for creating an HttpHandler

C#

```csharp
public abstract class BaseHttpHandler : IHttpHandler
{
    public BaseHttpHandler() {}

    public void ProcessRequest(HttpContext context)
    {
        SetResponseCachePolicy(context.Response.Cache);
        if(!ValidateParameters(context))
        {
            RespondInternalError(context);
            return;
        }

        if(RequiresAuthentication && !context.User.Identity.IsAuthenticated)
        {
            RespondForbidden(context);
            return;
        }

        context.Response.ContentType = ContentMimeType;
        HandleRequest(context);
    }

    public bool IsReusable { get { return true; } }

    /// <summary>
    /// Handles the request.  This is where you put your business logic.
    /// </summary>
```

```csharp
    public abstract void HandleRequest(HttpContext context);

    public abstract bool ValidateParameters(HttpContext context);

    public abstract bool RequiresAuthentication {get;}

    public abstract string ContentMimeType {get;}

    public virtual void SetResponseCachePolicy(HttpCachePolicy cache)
    {
        cache.SetCacheability(HttpCacheability.NoCache);
        cache.SetNoStore();
        cache.SetExpires(DateTime.MinValue);
    }

    protected void RespondFileNotFound(HttpContext context)
    {
        context.Response.StatusCode = (int)HttpStatusCode.NotFound;
        context.Response.End();
    }

    protected void RespondInternalError(HttpContext context)
    {
        context.Response.StatusCode =
            (int)HttpStatusCode.InternalServerError;
        context.Response.End();
    }

    protected void RespondForbidden(HttpContext context)
    {
        context.Response.StatusCode = (int)HttpStatusCode.Forbidden;
        context.Response.End();
    }
}
```

VB

```vb
Public MustInherit Class BaseHttpHandler
    Inherits IHttpHandler

    Public Sub New()
        MyBase.New

    End Sub

    Public ReadOnly Property IsReusable As Boolean
        Get
            Return true
        End Get
    End Property

    Public MustOverride Property RequiresAuthentication As Boolean
    End Property

    Public MustOverride Property ContentMimeType As String
```

(continued)

Listing 17-3 *(continued)*

```vb
    End Property

    Public Sub ProcessRequest(ByVal context As HttpContext)
        SetResponseCachePolicy(context.Response.Cache)
        If Not ValidateParameters(context) Then
            RespondInternalError(context)
            Return
        End If
        If (RequiresAuthentication _
                AndAlso Not context.User.Identity.IsAuthenticated) Then
            RespondForbidden(context)
            Return
        End If
        context.Response.ContentType = ContentMimeType
        HandleRequest(context)
    End Sub

    ' <summary>
    ' Handles the request.  This is where you put your business logic.
    ' </summary>
    Public MustOverride Sub HandleRequest(ByVal context As HttpContext)

    Public MustOverride Function ValidateParameters(ByVal context As HttpContext) _
        As Boolean

    Public Overridable Sub SetResponseCachePolicy(ByVal cache As HttpCachePolicy)
        cache.SetCacheability(HttpCacheability.NoCache)
        cache.SetNoStore
        cache.SetExpires(DateTime.MinValue)
    End Sub

    Protected Sub RespondFileNotFound(ByVal context As HttpContext)
        context.Response.StatusCode = CType(HttpStatusCode.NotFound,Integer)
        context.Response.End
    End Sub

    Protected Sub RespondInternalError(ByVal context As HttpContext)
        context.Response.StatusCode = _
            CType(HttpStatusCode.InternalServerError,Integer)
        context.Response.End
    End Sub

    Protected Sub RespondForbidden(ByVal context As HttpContext)
        context.Response.StatusCode = CType(HttpStatusCode.Forbidden,Integer)
        context.Response.End
    End Sub
End Class
```

Phil has taken the `ProcessRequest` method and created a number of new methods that can be overridden in your base class to handle parameter validation and response caching policy as well as to provide standard responses for errors.

This is a good place to get started writing handlers. However, I don't want to thrust my worldview on you, so the rest of this chapter will write handlers the classic way.

Discouraging Leeching Using an Image-Specific HttpHandler

Bandwidth leeching happens when you have an image hosted on your site and another site links directly to your image using an `<img>` tag. The page serves from the other site, but the image is served from yours. Browsers typically include the name of the host that obtained the request. Images that are requested from your web server by a page hosted elsewhere will have a referrer header that doesn't match your site's URL.

> Interestingly, the HTTP Referrer header field is actually misspelled in the spec, and has always been that way, as "referer" with a single "r." See `http://www.w3.org/Protocols/rfc2616/rfc2616-sec14.html`.

The static file handler in Listing 17-4 will check the current host with the referrer field of the current request. If they don't match, a "backoff.gif" file is returned no matter what file was originally requested! That means if you link to "scott.jpg" from your site, effectively leaching from me, you'll end up getting "backoff.gif" informing you and your readers that you were too lazy to just copy the file locally. It's a coarse technique, true, but these are crazy times on the open Internet and sometimes bandwidth leeches need a little reminder of the rules. The nice thing is that because it is a handler, it can be easily removed without recompiling the application by editing your `web.config`, so the functionality can be put up for a limited time.

The code is simple. Once ASP.NET and IIS are configured to handle image files, this handler will fire for every request image. First, the HTTP Referrer is checked to ensure that the site they are on is the same site requesting the image. If not, they receive the warning image. Otherwise, `Response.WriteFile` writes the image out to the client and no one notices the difference.

Listing 17-4: A leech-preventing HttpHandler for images

```C#
using System.IO;
using System.Web;
using System.Globalization;

namespace MVPHacks
{
    public class NoLeechImageHandler : IHttpHandler
    {
        public void ProcessRequest(System.Web.HttpContext ctx)
        {
            HttpRequest req = ctx.Request;
            string path = req.PhysicalPath;
            string extension = null;

            if (req.UrlReferrer != null && req.UrlReferrer.Host.Length > 0)
```

(continued)

Listing 17-4 *(continued)*

```csharp
                {
                    if (CultureInfo.InvariantCulture.CompareInfo.Compare(req.Url.Host,
                            req.UrlReferrer.Host, CompareOptions.IgnoreCase) != 0)
                    {
                        path = ctx.Server.MapPath("~/images/backoff.gif");
                    }
                }

                string contentType = null;
                extension = Path.GetExtension(path).ToLower();
                switch (extension)
                {
                    case ".gif":
                        contentType = "image/gif";
                        break;
                    case ".jpg":
                        contentType = "image/jpeg";
                        break;
                    case ".png":
                        contentType = "image/png";
                        break;
                    default:
                        throw new NotSupportedException("Unrecognized image type.");
                }

                if (!File.Exists (path))
                {
                    ctx.Response.Status = "Image not found";
                    ctx.Response.StatusCode = 404;
                }
                else
                {
                    ctx.Response.StatusCode = 200;
                    ctx.Response.ContentType = contentType;
                    ctx.Response.WriteFile (path);
                }
            }

        public bool IsReusable { get {return true; } }
    }
}
```

VB

```vbnet
Namespace MVPHacks
    Imports System.IO
    Imports System.Web
    Imports System.Globalization

    Public Class NoLeechImageHandler
        Inherits IHttpHandler

        Public ReadOnly Property IsReusable As Boolean
```

```
                Get
                        Return true
                End Get
            End Property

            Public Sub ProcessRequest(ByVal ctx As System.Web.HttpContext)
                Dim req As HttpRequest = ctx.Request
                Dim path As String = req.PhysicalPath
                Dim extension As String = Nothing
                If ((Not (req.UrlReferrer) Is Nothing) _
                            AndAlso (req.UrlReferrer.Host.Length > 0)) Then
                    If (CultureInfo.InvariantCulture.CompareInfo.Compare( _
                            req.Url.Host, req.UrlReferrer.Host, _
                            CompareOptions.IgnoreCase) <> 0) Then
                        path = ctx.Server.MapPath("~/images/backoff.gif")
                    End If
                End If
                Dim contentType As String = Nothing
                extension = Path.GetExtension(path).ToLower
                Select Case (extension)
                    Case ".gif"
                        contentType = "image/gif"
                    Case ".jpg"
                        contentType = "image/jpeg"
                    Case ".png"
                        contentType = "image/png"
                    Case Else
                        Throw New NotSupportedException("Unrecognized image type.")
                End Select
                If Not File.Exists(path) Then
                    ctx.Response.Status = "Image not found"
                    ctx.Response.StatusCode = 404
                Else
                    ctx.Response.StatusCode = 200
                    ctx.Response.ContentType = contentType
                    ctx.Response.WriteFile(path)
                End If
            End Sub
        End Class
    End Namespace
```

Associating a file extension with a particular HttpHandler is a two-step process. First, IIS needs to know which extensions are routed to ASP.NET's worker process by associating the extension with aspnet_ isapi.dll within IIS's administration tool. Then, within your application's web.config, each extension is associated with an assembly's qualified name (QN) to a specific HttpHandler:

```
<configuration>
    <system.web>
        <httpHandlers>
            <add verb="*" path="*.jpg"
                type="MVPHacks.NoLeechImageHandler, MVPHacks "/>
            <add verb="*" path="*.gif"
                type="MVPHacks.NoLeechImageHandler, MVPHacks "/>
            <add verb="*" path="*.png"
```

```
                    type="MVPHacks.NoLeechImageHandler, MVPHacks "/>
          </httpHandlers>
      </system.web>
  </configuration>
```

The configuration of the web.config matches the switch statement within the code, so unless you associate an extension that isn't handled in the switch, you'll never throw the exception within Listing 17-5. This handler could be extended to handle other kinds of illicit leaching, including PDF or any other file that you feel is being stolen from your website.

Compositing Images with an HttpHandler

Recently, I had a back-end black-box system that was sending me two images that were Base64 encoded — that is, binary data encoded as a string, within an XML response. The images were of the front and back of a check. However, the requirement from the client was to show a *single* composite check image in the user's browser with the front image stacked on top of the back image with a single HTTP GET request. Of course, it has to be secure because this is a check we're talking about, so no writing to temp files!

Here's my solution, implemented as an HttpHandler, so the HTML would include something like the following:

```
<img src="checkimage.ashx?whatever=4&something=6">
```

The checkimage.ashx endpoint could be configured in the application's web.config HttpHandlers section, or presented as a small text file like this:

```
<% @ webhandler language="C#" class="MVPHacks.ExampleCompositingImageHandler" %>
```

The point is to make sure that ASP.NET knows how to map a request to that request's handler. The simple one-line ashx file exists for one purpose and one purpose only — to be an endpoint, and in existing, to provide a mapping. Most folks prefer to do their mapping within the web.config because everything is centralized and easily changed. Others find this frustrating because their first instinct is to assume that every file that appears in the browser's address bar corresponds to a file on disk. Neither way is better than the other but I prefer the flexibility of the web.config method.

Listing 17-5 has a few details snipped out that are specific to the request I made to the back-end mainframe system. I've replaced that with the simple request/response model to imply an XML Web Services method. The check images are in the res.ImageFront and res.ImageBack properties as byte arrays.

Listing 17-5: An image compositing HttpHandler

```csharp
C#
public class ExampleCompositingImageHandler : IHttpHandler
{
    public SomeCheckImageHandler(){}

    public void ProcessRequest(HttpContext context)
    {
        context.Response.ContentType = "image/jpeg";
        //some stuff snipped
        GetCheckImageRequest req = new GetCheckImageRequest();
        //some stuff snipped, get the params from the QueryString
```

```csharp
        GetCheckImageResponse res = banking.GetCheckImage(req);
        //some stuff snipped
        if (res.ImageBack != null)
        {
            //merge them into one image
            using(MemoryStream m = new MemoryStream(res.BackImageBytes))
            using(Image backImage = System.Drawing.Image.FromStream(m))
            using(MemoryStream m2 = new MemoryStream(res.BrontImageBytes))
            using(Image frontImage = System.Drawing.Image.FromStream(m2))
            using(Bitmap compositeImage = new
                Bitmap(frontImage.Width,frontImage.Height+backImage.Height))
            using(Graphics compositeGraphics = Graphics.FromImage(compositeImage))
            {
                compositeGraphics.CompositingMode = CompositingMode.SourceCopy;
                compositeGraphics.DrawImageUnscaled(frontImage,0,0);
                compositeGraphics.DrawImageUnscaled(backImage,0,frontImage.Height);
                compositeImage.Save(context.Response.OutputStream,
                    ImageFormat.Jpeg);
            }
        }
        else //just show the front, we've got no back
        {
            using(MemoryStream m = new MemoryStream(frontImageBytes))
            using(Image image = System.Drawing.Image.FromStream(m))
            {
                image.Save(context.Response.OutputStream, ImageFormat.Jpeg);
            }
        }
    }
}
```

VB

```vb
Public Class ExampleCompositingImageHandler
    Inherits IHttpHandler

    Public Sub ProcessRequest(ByVal context As HttpContext)
        context.Response.ContentType = "image/jpeg"
        'some stuff snipped
        Dim req As GetCheckImageRequest = New GetCheckImageRequest
        'some stuff snipped, get the params from the QueryString
        Dim res As GetCheckImageResponse = banking.GetCheckImage(req)
        'some stuff snipped
        If (Not (res.ImageBack) Is Nothing) Then
            'merge them into one image
            Using m As MemoryStream = New MemoryStream(res.BackImageBytes)
                Using backImage As Image = System.Drawing.Image.FromStream(m)
                    Using m2 As MemoryStream = New MemoryStream(res.BrontImageBytes)
                        Using frontImage As Image = System.Drawing.Image.FromStream(m2)
                            Using compositeImage As Bitmap = New Bitmap(frontImage.Width,
(frontImage.Height + backImage.Height))
                                Using compositeGraphics As Graphics =
                                    Graphics.FromImage(compositeImage)
            compositeGraphics.CompositingMode = CompositingMode.SourceCopy
            compositeGraphics.DrawImageUnscaled(frontImage, 0, 0)
```

(continued)

Listing 17-5 *(continued)*

```
            compositeGraphics.DrawImageUnscaled(backImage, 0, frontImage.Height)
            compositeImage.Save(context.Response.OutputStream, ImageFormat.Jpeg)
                End Using
              End Using
            End Using
          End Using
        End Using
      End Using
    Else
        Dim m As MemoryStream = New MemoryStream(frontImageBytes)
        Dim image As Image = System.Drawing.Image.FromStream(m)
        image.Save(context.Response.OutputStream, ImageFormat.Jpeg)
    End If
  End Sub
End Class
```

Note a few interesting things about this example. First, the manipulation of streams enables you to save the contents of the stream directly to the response object, as in this line:

```
image.Save(context.Response.OutputStream, ImageFormat.Jpeg)
```

Another thing of note is my potentially excessive use of the using statement. Many classes within the .NET Base Class Library are disposable. That is, they are thin wrappers around physical resources that really should be released as soon as you are done with them. Many of the classes within GDI+, the Graphics Device Interface, hold on to unmanaged resources. Rather than wait for the garbage collector to clean up after me, I prefer to be very explicit and dispose of these resources directly. The using statement provides determinism, and while it doesn't release the object reference itself, it does promise to clean up the resources that object manages. After an object is disposed, you mustn't use it. Some may call this stylistic and may disagree, but I feel that is deterministic and a best practice.

The last interesting thing to note is that in the interest of robustness this handler draws the front check image by itself if the back is not returned. This allows more flexibility and renders the hack reusable.

> Note that the Using statement was added in VB in .NET 2.0. You'll need to remove it to use this code under VB.NET 1.1. The Using statement in VB is equivalent to a try/finally block in which the finally block calls Dispose() on the variable referenced.

HttpHandlers are fantastic for generating or manipulating images in memory. Let's take a look at an even more interesting example.

Generating Sparklines with an HttpHandler

Edward Tufte, in an 18-page chapter for his book *Beautiful Evidence* (http://tinyurl.com/2mfko), describes the concept of *sparklines*. Sparklines are "intense, simple, word-sized graphics." Tufte argues that writing a sentence like "My blood sugar was between 120 and 150 all week" isn't as effective as a sentence that includes a sparkline: "My blood sugar was between 120 and 150 all week."

Joe Gregorio (`http://bitworking.org/projects/sparklines`) later wrote a Python implementation of sparklines that took parameters directly from the URL and dynamically generated graphics. Eric W. Bachtal expanded on Joe's idea and ported it to an ASP.NET `HttpHandler`, adding bar charting and a host of other features along the way (`http://ewbi.blogs.com/develops/2005/07/sparklines.html`).

For example, the querystring that generated the sparkline in the previous paragraph looked like this:

```
type=smooth&d=86,66,82,44,64,66,88,96,26,14,0,0,26,8,6,24,52,36,6,10,30&height=30&min-color=red&max-color=blue&last-color=green&step=2&last-m=true&max-m=true&min-m=true
```

Eric's sparkline implementation offers very rich functionality considering that its only method of input is the URL query string. It's also worth noting that his entire implementation is less than 400 lines of C# code. He would likely be much more modest in describing his accomplishment, but both Joe and Eric have created a powerful Web Service with a convenient hackable API. This sparkline HttpHandler supports bar charting, discrete line charts, and smooth line charts. Listing 17-6 shows a few choice snippets from Eric's implementation, along with a VB translation. While I cannot agree with his positioning of curly braces, I can't disagree with the results.

Listing 17-6: An HttpHandler for generating Tufte's sparklines

C#

```csharp
MemoryStream PlotSparklineSmooth(int[] results) {
try {
  int step = int.Parse(GetArg("step", "2"));
  int height = int.Parse(GetArg("height", "20"));
  Color minColor = GetColor(GetArg("min-color", "#0000FF"));
  Color maxColor = GetColor(GetArg("max-color", "#00FF00"));
  Color lastColor = GetColor(GetArg("last-color", "#FF0000"));
  Color rangeColor = GetColor(GetArg("range-color", "#CCCCCC"));
  bool hasMin = bool.Parse(GetArg("min-m", "false"));
  bool hasMax = bool.Parse(GetArg("max-m", "false"));
  bool hasLast = bool.Parse(GetArg("last-m", "false"));
  int rangeLower = int.Parse(GetArg("range-lower", "0"));
  int rangeUpper = int.Parse(GetArg("range-upper", "0"));
  bool scale = bool.Parse(GetArg("scale", "false"));

  ResultsInfo resultsInfo = EvaluateResults(results, scale);

  if ((rangeLower < 0) || (rangeLower > 100)) return PlotError();
  if ((rangeUpper < 0) || (rangeUpper > 100)) return PlotError();

using (Bitmap bitmap =
    new Bitmap((results.Length-1)*step+4, height, PixelFormat.Format32bppArgb)) {
    using (Graphics g = Graphics.FromImage(bitmap)) {
      using (SolidBrush br = new SolidBrush(Color.White)) {
        g.FillRectangle(br, 0, 0, bitmap.Width, height);
      }

      if ((!((0 == rangeLower) && (0 == rangeUpper))) &&
          (rangeLower <= rangeUpper)) {
        using (SolidBrush br = new SolidBrush(rangeColor)) {
```

(continued)

Listing 17-6 *(continued)*

```
            int y = height - 3 - (int) Math.Ceiling(rangeUpper/(101F/(height-4)));
            int h = (height - 3 - (int) Math.Ceiling(rangeLower/(101F/(height-4))))
                - y + 1;
            g.FillRectangle(br, 1, y, bitmap.Width-2, h);
        }
    }

    Point[] coords = new Point[results.Length];
    for (int x = 0; x < results.Length; x++) {
      int r = results[x];
      int y = height - 3 - (int) Math.Ceiling(r/(101F/(height-4)));
      coords[x] = new Point(x*step+1, y);
    }
    using (Pen p = new Pen(GetColor("#999999"))) {
      g.DrawLines(p, coords);
    }

    if (hasMin) { DrawTick(g, minColor, coords[resultsInfo.MinIndex]); }
    if (hasMax) { DrawTick(g, maxColor, coords[resultsInfo.MaxIndex]); }
    if (hasLast) { DrawTick(g, lastColor, coords[results.Length-1]); }

    MemoryStream m = new MemoryStream();
    bitmap.Save(m, ImageFormat.Gif);
    return m;
    }
  }
} catch {
  return PlotError();
}
}
}
```

VB

```
Private Function PlotSparklineSmooth(ByVal results() As Integer) As MemoryStream
    Try
        Dim step As Integer = Integer.Parse(GetArg("step", "2"))
        Dim height As Integer = Integer.Parse(GetArg("height", "20"))
        Dim minColor As Color = GetColor(GetArg("min-color", "#0000FF"))
        Dim maxColor As Color = GetColor(GetArg("max-color", "#00FF00"))
        Dim lastColor As Color = GetColor(GetArg("last-color", "#FF0000"))
        Dim rangeColor As Color = GetColor(GetArg("range-color", "#CCCCCC"))
        Dim hasMin As Boolean = Boolean.Parse(GetArg("min-m", "false"))
        Dim hasMax As Boolean = Boolean.Parse(GetArg("max-m", "false"))
        Dim hasLast As Boolean = Boolean.Parse(GetArg("last-m", "false"))
        Dim rangeLower As Integer = Integer.Parse(GetArg("range-lower", "0"))
        Dim rangeUpper As Integer = Integer.Parse(GetArg("range-upper", "0"))
        Dim scale As Boolean = Boolean.Parse(GetArg("scale", "false"))
        Dim resultsInfo As ResultsInfo = EvaluateResults(results, scale)

        If ((rangeLower < 0) _
                    OrElse (rangeLower > 100)) Then
            Return PlotError
        End If
```

```
                If ((rangeUpper < 0) _
                        OrElse (rangeUpper > 100)) Then
                    Return PlotError
                End If
                Dim bitmap As Bitmap = New Bitmap((((results.Length - 1) _
                            * step) _
                            + 4), height, PixelFormat.Format32bppArgb)
                Dim g As Graphics = Graphics.FromImage(bitmap)
                Dim br As SolidBrush = New SolidBrush(Color.White)
                g.FillRectangle(br, 0, 0, bitmap.Width, height)
                If (Not ((0 = rangeLower) AndAlso (0 = rangeUpper)) _
                        AndAlso (rangeLower <= rangeUpper)) Then
                    Dim br As SolidBrush = New SolidBrush(rangeColor)
                    Dim y As Integer = _
                            (height - (3 - CType(Math.Ceiling((rangeUpper / (101! _
                            / (height - 4)))),Integer)))
                    Dim h As Integer = _
                            (((height - (3 - CType(Math.Ceiling((rangeLower / (101! _
                            / (height - 4)))),Integer))) _
                            - y) _
                            + 1)
                    g.FillRectangle(br, 1, y, (bitmap.Width - 2), h)
                End If
                Dim coords() As Point
                results.Length
                Dim x As Integer = 0
                Do While (x < results.Length)
                    Dim r As Integer = results(x)
                    Dim y As Integer = (height - (3 - CType(Math.Ceiling((r / (101! _
                                / (height - 4)))),Integer)))
                    coords(x) = New Point(((x * step) _
                                + 1), y)
                    x = (x + 1)
                Loop
                Dim p As Pen = New Pen(GetColor("#999999"))
                g.DrawLines(p, coords)
                If hasMin Then
                    DrawTick(g, minColor, coords(resultsInfo.MinIndex))
                End If
                If hasMax Then
                    DrawTick(g, maxColor, coords(resultsInfo.MaxIndex))
                End If
                If hasLast Then
                    DrawTick(g, lastColor, coords((results.Length - 1)))
                End If
                Dim m As MemoryStream = New MemoryStream
                bitmap.Save(m, ImageFormat.Gif)
                Return m
        Catch  As System.Exception
                Return PlotError
        End Try
    End Function
```

Reading source code like this may be daunting at first. It helps to mentally chop up the responsibilities of this handler. The first job is to retrieve all of the parameters for the query string, including reasonable defaults when a parameter is missing or invalid. The next step is to parse the comma-delimited list of points to be plotted and throw an error if anything is wrong. Then, he creates a bitmap in memory of the specified size, and spins through the array of results, drawing lines in tic marks as appropriate. The final bitmap is entirely generated in memory, is saved as a GIF to a memory stream, and is then saved out to the response stream, as shown in the previous HttpHandler example.

The System.Drawing namespace makes dynamic creation and manipulation of images very easy. Combining these techniques with HttpHandlers adds a whole new level of dynamic content creation to your ASP.NET applications. Be sure to visit Eric's site for updates to this implementation of sparklines, including support for transparent GIFs. My excitement level about sparklines is

Handlers and Modules Working Together

Really amazing things happen when an HttpModule and HttpHandler are used together to create highly componentized code that can add functionality to ASP.NET application without recompilation.

The prototypical example of a highly powerful customization to any ASP.NET site is Atif Aziz and Scott Mitchell's ELMAH — Error Logging Modules and Handlers. This amazing free utility is a series of modules and handlers that provide applicationwide error logging that is totally customizable and pluggable. ELMAH code can be downloaded, including source, from its GotDotNet.com workspace at http://tinyurl.com/b77pf.

ELMAH uses an HttpModule to capture all errors via the HttpApplication's Error event. This event is raised anytime an uncaught exception occurs within your application. Additionally, ELMAH includes a series of HttpHandlers that enable viewing and transformation of the error log. The storage for these unhandled errors is completely pluggable. The errors can be stored in memory until the next application recycle, in a file or in SQL Server. These errors can be presented via a Web interface or as RSS, the syndication XML format, so an administrator can receive this information within a standard RSS aggregator.

The ELMAH HttpModule is added via the web.config as usual:

```
<httpModules>
  <add name="ErrorLog" type="GotDotNet.Elmah.ErrorLogModule,
    GotDotNet.Elmah, Version=1.0.5527.0, Culture=neutral,
    PublicKeyToken=978d5e1bd64b33e5" />
</httpModules>
<httpHandlers>
    <add
        verb="POST,GET,HEAD"
        path="elmah/default.aspx"
        type="GotDotNet.Elmah.ErrorLogPageFactory,
          GotDotNet.Elmah, Version=1.0.5527.0, Culture=neutral,
          PublicKeyToken=978d5e1bd64b33e5" />
</httpHandlers>
```

Error handling and reporting can be added in this manner to an application in minutes without recompilation of the application. In fact, the monitor application doesn't even realize it is being monitored! Be sure to visit Atif Aziz's site at www.raboof.com and Scott Mitchell's at www.scottonwriting.net.

Wrapping Up

In this chapter, we looked at some creative ways to use `HttpModules` and `HttpHandlers`. Both can be configured into an application without requiring code change. Typically, that type of flexibility alone is powerful. However, using `HttpModules`, you can take that to the next level and eavesdrop on each of the requests at specific points of the lifecycle of the ASP.NET request. The blacklist example showed how an `HttpModule` could plug in, eavesdrop on the request and make it seem like the page wasn't even on the server. The `BaseHttpHandler` example shows how you can make these even easier to build by having a pattern you follow.

At first, you might think they are complex, but once you have created a few they are only as complex as the logic that is being attempted. Use the examples in this chapter to get started, and modify them as needed to work in your application.

Index

D

G

W